Advance Praise for *Radical Son*

"David Horowitz has written a vivid and compelling memoir in which it's the life as it was really lived that matters, not just the politics. *Radical Son* may be a 'generational odyssey,' but it's also a work of literature."

—JAMES ATLAS, Author of *The Book Wars: What It Takes to Be Educated in America*

"*Radical Son* is one of the best political memoirs I've ever read. Though it is really a love story—one man becomes passionately enamored with freedom, responsibility, and reason. Or maybe it's a book about faith healing, a true account of how belief in human dignity and individual rights cures blindness, folly, and hatred. Anyway, everyone who was ever involved with or influenced by the New Left should read David Horowitz's words, and then eat their own. I think the last political book that affected me this strongly was Hayek's *Road to Serfdom*."

—P. J. O'ROURKE, Author of *Age and Guile Beat Youth, Innocence, and a Bad Haircut*

"David Horowitz's political pilgrimage from a Sixties radical to a Reagan conservative—and the friends and enemies he has made along the way—makes for a very interesting, very compelling story. Speaking as a conservative: it's much better to have David Horowitz with you than against you. *Radical Son* demonstrates why."

—WILLIAM J. BENNETT, Author of *The Moral Compass*

"Watch out all of you statist shills and racialist hucksters out there who think you have gotten away with murder and mayhem over the last five decades, with alibis and applause from the media and the academy; David Horowitz has got your number and your jugular. In the first great American autobiography of his generation, this ardent writer on the ramparts remorselessly tracks them all down, going deep into the lairs of the professional liars of the left—the guilty and the gulled, the sadistic and the philanderous, the vain and the vicious—and strips away their tawdry veneer of glamour and idealism to reveal the vile truth—about the Black Panthers and the rest of the revolutionary felons and felines, and finally, in gut-wrenching candor, himself."

—GEORGE GILDER

"David Horowitz's powerful autobiography details a long journey from a boyhood in the ambit of American Stalinism through young adulthood at the vanguard of the New Left to a mid-life recognition that his various gods had failed. Horowitz's gift for irony and eye for detail haven't deserted him. His book is hard to put down."

—ERIC BREINDEL, Editorial Page Editor of *The New York Post*

Radical Son

A Generational Odyssey

30th Anniversary Edition
with a New Preface by the Author

David HOROWITZ

BOMBARDIER
BOOKS

A BOMBARDIER BOOKS BOOK
An Imprint of Post Hill Press

Radical Son:
A Generational Odyssey
© 2020 by David Horowitz
All Rights Reserved

ISBN: 978-1-64293-400-7

Cover Design by Jomel Cequina
Interior design and composition by Greg Johnson, Textbook Perfect

Post Hill Press
New York • Nashville
posthillpress.com

Published in the United States of America

This book is for

My children—Jon, Sarah, Ben, and Anne—
Who lived this story with me;
My grandchildren—Julia, Mariah, and Sophia—
Who will one day read it;

And for

April—Who has already made the next chapter
a happy one.

CONTENTS

PART 6: PRIVATE INVESTIGATIONS (1975–1980)

PART 7: COMING HOME (1980–1992)

EPILOGUE: THE BEAUTY OF RECOGNITION

ACKNOWLEDGMENTS

A N AUTOBIOGRAPHY IS NOT THE COMPLETE RECORD OF A LIFE, BUT an effort to make sense of one. Accordingly, I have left out of this account some people who were close to me and some who were important. I want to take this opportunity to apologize to any of them who might feel slighted by not being included in this book. I ask them to think of others who may not have wanted to be included but who appear because they are integral to the narrative I have written. My apologies to them as well and particularly to my family who, having had to put up with being part of my public life, now find *themselves* characters in my public story.

My family read this book in manuscript and was helpful in their comments and, even more, in their support. Others who read it in whole or in part and commented usefully on the text are Ron Radosh, Sol Stern, Bob Kaldenbach, Constance Miller, and Peter Collier. My daughter Sarah helped me to set the tone and to correct a number of mistakes.

I am grateful for all the affection and encouragement my children and friends gave me in the writing of this book and in the life it seeks to represent. I am especially grateful to Elissa, who never wanted to be part of any public document and for whom some of this narrative is a memory of unwanted pain.

I am also grateful to Mary Collier, not only for her own friendship but for the support she has given to her husband's friendship with me, the most important bond, beyond family, of my life.

I want to thank Adam Bellow for inviting me to write my autobiography and for taking time as an editor, rare these days, to make line edits in my text. I am grateful to my production editor, Loretta

Denner, and my copy editor, George A. Rowland, for making the text as good as it could be. I also want to thank Georges Borchardt, my agent, for all the help he has given me throughout my writing career.

My only regret comes from thinking of all those young radicals just entering the arena who, if they were to consider this story, would benefit most from its lessons, but who unfortunately will not read it at all.

Note to the Paperback Edition: Only a few changes have been made to the hardcover text to correct typographical errors and some minor errors of fact that were pointed out by readers (e.g., B-29s were only used in the Pacific theater of the war, and therefore the planes I saw in 1944 must have been B-17s or B-24s). One emendation, however, requires an explanation. The anecdote about Ann Colloms that appears on page 76 has been altered in light of new information from the recently published "Venona transcripts," the deciphered communications between American agents and their Soviet controllers. The information was brought to my attention by Professor Harvey Klehr, coauthor of The Secret World of American Communism. Thirty years ago, Ann Colloms told me her story in the veiled manner of progressives that I have described in this book, referring only to the fact that she was "involved in the Trotsky assassination." Since Ann Colloms has been deceased for more than twenty years, and there was no one else that I could question about this incident, I had to reconstruct it for my text. As a result, I mistakenly attributed to Ann a role in the actual assassination. Now Professor Klehr has kindly corrected this mistake and I have revised my account accordingly. However, the point of the anecdote, namely the availability of American communists for Soviet agendas, remains the same.

PREFACE

O F ALL THE BOOKS I HAVE WRITTEN—AND THERE HAVE BEEN many—*Radical Son* is the one that has touched the most people, and touched them the most deeply. I think the reason for this is that it describes a personal odyssey through the political labyrinths of our times. Its narrative addresses the psychological and religious dimensions of what it means to be a radical and to harbor utopian dreams of re-creating the world and making it just. Secular radicals have variously called these dreams of a heaven on earth, "socialism," "communism," or "social justice." These fantasies are consolations for the flawed world in which we actually find ourselves, and cannot escape. Their seductive power is so great as to have lured legions of intelligent and otherwise compassionate individuals into supporting movements and regimes that are among the cruelest and most oppressive in all human history. *Radical Son* is an account of my journey into the heart of this radical evil, and of my release from the illusions that led me there.

There is no other account by members of my radical generation, of which I am aware, that pursues the gut-wrenching interrogations that writing a witness like this required. Others had second thoughts, and wrote political repudiations of the movement they had served. But none examined the human consequences of those political beliefs and their rejection, or the internal struggles they provoked.

There was a severe injunction against an honest confrontation with the past. To leave the Left as I did was to turn against human hope and promise, and to join instead the forces of darkness—so my ex-comrades believed. When I was thirty-six years old and publicly announced my departure in an article called "Goodbye to All That," which I wrote with my friend and political fellow traveler Peter Collier, I lost every friend I had acquired in my life until then, and countless platforms for my work. It was why Whittaker Chambers famously said in *Witness* that he had left the winning side for the losing side. The "winning" side was the side with the ideas—however delusional and destructive—that people were willing to die for. The promise of an earthly redemption was a hard hope to beat. Armed with such ideas, the radical generation of the Sixties was able to engineer a turning point in America's political life whose ramifications are still shaking the nation's political foundations sixty years later.

I wrote *Radical Son* in the years 1993–1995, following the fall of Soviet Communism and the exposure of its crimes, which included the impoverishment of whole continents under the yoke of socialist policies that did not and could not work. In the prologue to the original edition, I wrote triumphantly: "The collapse of Communism and the progressive future reveals how the moral language of politics has been hijacked by radicals. The fallen angels of the progressive Left— Marxist and socialist—have been exposed as the reactionary ghosts of an oppressive past. It is the ideological adversaries of the Left who float on the wave of a future that is free."

I was wrong. The Left did not die or reform itself in the face of the human catastrophes it had helped to create. I was wrong in assuming that leftists would take this lesson to heart as I had myself. I was wrong that the nation would finally free itself from those destructive delusions. I had underestimated the power of a crypto-religion.

It is twenty-three years now since the publication of this autobiography, and the messianic Left is stronger and more influential than ever before. In 2016, Senator Bernie Sanders, a lifelong supporter of Communist dictators and causes, was poised to win the Democratic Party's presidential nomination until he was stopped by the Clinton machine. By the time the Democratic Party nominees had assembled themselves for the 2020 presidential election, their principal themes were the Marxist formulas that had failed on such an epic scale, and that Sanders had successfully introduced into the political mainstream.

The thoughtless radicalism of the Sixties had not died with the tyrannies it promoted. Well before the Communist collapse, the Left had already begun what its leaders referred to as, "the long march through the institutions," itself an *homage* to the mass murderer Mao whose "Long March" had concluded with his conquest of state power. The New Left's long march had begun in Chicago with the riot Tom Hayden staged in 1968 at the Democratic National Convention. Its purpose was to destroy the electoral chances of Hubert Humphrey because he was an *anti*-Communist liberal. This debacle was followed by the infiltration of the Democratic Party by the same street radicals who had sabotaged its electoral chances. They proceeded to create "radical caucuses" as platforms for their goal, which was the eventual takeover and transformation of the Party. This goal was accomplished forty years later with the election of a lifelong veteran of their ranks, Barack Obama.

Of even greater long-term consequence was a parallel offensive, which eventually transformed America's liberal arts colleges into one-party Marxist states. This led to the subversion of America's cultural and media institutions and their transformation into partisan advocates for the radical Left. During these years, I wrote six books analyzing and chronicling this phenomenon: *Uncivil Wars: The Controversy Over Reparations for Slavery*, (2001); *The Professors*, (2004), *Indoctrination U.* (2007), *One-Party Classroom*, (2009), *Reforming Our Universities*, (2010) and *The Left in the University*, (2017), which was published as Volume 7 in a series of 9 I have written about these developments, called *The Black Book of the American Left*.

To sum up these developments: while Communism had been vanquished, outside the lands of the Iron Curtain—and particularly in America—there was no triumphant dancing on Communism's grave, and no *mea culpa* by its progressive allies. In America and Western Europe, a renascent Left explained away the atrocities and catastrophes it had supported by saying that what took place in Russia wasn't "real socialism." Real socialism hadn't been tried, and therefore hadn't failed. Nothing could capture the invincible arrogance of leftists so clearly as this pathetic sophistry to cover up their crimes.

Liberalism had given way to a cultural Marxism, which denied the very idea of the individual and revived Marx's class war as a war against racial and gender oppression. This "identity politics" was itself racist, and obliterated the fundamental principles of America's democracy which is based on individual equality, individual freedom, and individual accountability. Races and genders are not mentioned in the Constitution for good reason. Because the Founders intended to create a society composed of equals. The Left's long march through the institutions had created an infrastructure of support for these anti-American currents, which were dedicated to the destruction of the very foundations of America's constitutional order.

At the center of *Radical Son* is the story of my engagement with a murderous street gang, the Black Panther Party, whom the Left had raised to national prominence and anointed as "the vanguard of the revolution" and "America's Vietcong." I had become involved with the Panthers out of a kind of radical innocence, which caused me to judge them according to their synchronicity with the radical ideas I had embraced. Like other progressives, I ignored—or was simply blind to—the warning signs and actions that kept others at a distance, including the black community itself. Without understanding whom I had become involved with, I recruited a forty-two-year-old woman who worked for me, named Betty Van Patter, to help their cause, not realizing that one day they would kill her, and alter my life forever.

Although I survived my own encounters with Betty's killers, I paid a terrible price for my blindness, whose consequences were painful for me to describe in print. I was willing to embarrass myself and bare my wounds because the truth they revealed could serve as a warning to others. Few episodes better illuminated how "idealistic" radicals like myself could become involved with criminal actors and events. Few stories were so revealing of how corrupted our educational and cultural institutions had become through their openness to radicals and their hatreds, and also their support for the criminal activities and agendas associated with them.

Readers of the original edition of *Radical Son* will be familiar with the terrible events that changed my life, and also with the investigations I conducted on my own to learn the true nature of a cause I had so foolishly served. In the course of these inquiries, I discovered a very different reality from the political mythologies that the Panthers used to cover their tracks. Underneath the pretense that they were a party of the people defending the oppressed against the powerful, they were in fact a criminal gang that preyed on poor communities and murdered more than a dozen people, all but one of them black. I collected this information from news stories and reporters I knew, and checked it with what I knew from my Panther contacts.

Long after I had put my experiences with the Party behind me, a memoir appeared, whose insider account of the Party's activities made it a perfect measure of what had happened to the country, and to the Left I had turned my back on. The memoir was called *Will You Die With Me?* and was written by Flores Forbes, who had been the head of the Panther's team of internal enforcers, which my informants had referred to as "The Squad." Flores Forbes was also the individual the Oakland District Attorney's office believe murdered Betty Van Patter. Because police were unable to get other members of The Squad to talk, however, no one was ever charged in the case.

Forbes's book corroborated the investigations I had conducted by myself and reported in *Radical Son*. Although Forbes's memoir remains loyal to the mythology of the Black Panther Party and to its leader, "my prince, Huey Newton," virtually every page of his book testifies to the fact that the Panthers were a black mafia, and that their ethical code was that of common thugs and killers, masked by their political aura.

The case that eventually sent Forbes to prison was an attempt to assassinate Crystal Gray, a black prostitute who had witnessed Newton's murder of another prostitute named Kathleen Smith, who was eighteen years old and also black. She had made the mistake of calling Newton "baby," which enraged him, prompting him to pull a small pistol from his shirt and kill her. Newton was charged with the crime, and a trial date had been set.

In an aside that sheds a rare light on the thought processes by which gangsters like Forbes bend their "revolutionary" principles to the service of criminal ends, he recalls a passage from Frantz Fanon's revolutionary classic, *Wretched of the Earth*. "[Fanon] states that it is the oppressed people's right to believe that they should kill their oppressor in order to obtain their freedom," writes Forbes. "We just modified it to mean anyone who's in our way."

The assassination of Crystal Gray was planned for the day before the trial hearings were scheduled to begin. Forbes and his partner showed up in the early morning hours at the humble apartment complex in Richmond, California, where Gray lived. But they made a fatal mistake and broke in the door of a forty-eight-year-old black bookkeeper who reached for her weapon and began firing. In the ensuing melee, Forbes was wounded, and inadvertently shot and killed his partner. After fleeing the scene, he recruited the Panthers' ambulance driver, Nelson Malloy, to help him as he fled to Las Vegas.

Although Forbes pretends the assassination attempt was entirely his idea, this makes no sense. It was not how the party functioned, or how Forbes related to his leader. Forbes's fiction is transparently designed to protect Newton who was behind the whole plot. When Forbes and Malloy reached Vegas, Newton sent two other members of The Squad to catch up with them and kill Malloy. Nelson Malloy was not a gangster, but one of many idealistic young people who joined the Panthers in response to their political appeals. Newton feared that Malloy would talk and link him to the crime. The Panthers shot Malloy twice in the back and buried him in a shallow grave by the side of the road, thinking he was dead. However, passing tourists heard his moans and dug him up. He survived but was permanently paralyzed from the neck down.

Forbes was on the run for three years, housed, hidden, and cared for by radical lawyers and activists who inhabited the same revolutionary fantasy and regarded him as a "political fugitive." After three years of flight, Forbes grew tired of being unable to contact friends and family. Calculating that he was only facing a few years in jail for killing his friend, he turned himself in and was convicted of "felony murder," for which he was made to serve five years in Vacaville and Soledad prisons. Following his release, he was able, with the help of his radical networks and his status as a revolutionary hero, to obtain a college degree from San Francisco State University, and then a full scholarship to NYU, where he became an urban planner and was welcomed into the Democratic power structure in New York.

One incident in Forbes's upward climb throws a particularly clear light on the political attitudes of the time. Through contacts he was able get a job in the office of the Manhattan Borough President, a Democrat. Four months into the job he received a call from the New York City Department of Investigation, who informed him that they had just received the results of his FBI inquiry. The following conversation then took place:

"I see you have had about eight major felony arrests, two felony convictions that involve use of a firearm, with one resulting in a felony murder conviction and one prison term. Well, what were you doing to compile such a record?"

"I was a member of the Black Panther Party in California for ten years."

"Oh, okay. That answers that. Now let's move on to your taxes."

Seven years after the publication of *Will You Die With Me?*, Forbes attempted an autobiographical sequel. It's title, *Invisible Men: A Modern Slave Narrative in an Era of Mass Incarceration*, was an implausible attempt to portray his post-prison success as part of the saga of black oppression. The book came with an introductory preface by Communist Party historian and UCLA professor Robin D.G. Kelley, attacking prisons as a modern form of slavery, a common trope of the anti-American Left.

In his narrative, Forbes makes clear that he regards the inconveniences he suffered as a result of his crimes as an injustice to him. He exhibits no remorse for his victims and no appreciation for the short jail time he spent for plotting the assassination of Crystal Gray or killing his friend, or for the cold-blooded, botched execution attempt which ruined the life of the ambulance driver, Nelson Malloy, who tried to help him. The fantasy of the "revolution" he served by committing violent crimes, mainly against vulnerable black people who were not political, remains for Forbes a source of inordinate pride. Equally revealing is his continuing adoration for the criminal who recruited him to the Panthers when he was sixteen, made him a gangster, murdered an eighteen-year-old black woman, and ordered him to assassinate another.

Flores Forbes's story is emblematic of what America's political culture has become. His title today is Associate Vice President of Strategic Planning and Program Implementation at Columbia University, where he is a pillar of the academic community. Meanwhile, those of us who worked to bring the criminal reality of the "revolutionary" charade to light are *persona non-grata* among administrators and faculty at Columbia, which happens to be my own *alma mater*.

And this travesty is not confined to one Ivy League school. There are academic tributes and shrines to Panther gangsters at UCLA, Stanford, UC Santa Cruz, UC Berkeley, the Smithsonian, and numerous similar institutions across the country. This is a pretty fair measure of the Left's institutional ascendance in America in the wake of the mayhem its radical activists have created and the atrocities they have committed.

Radical Son was written as a witness to the dark undercurrents of American politics and to their enduring power in the nation's life. It has definitely had an impact. Whether the revelations contained in its narrative can seriously affect the course of this history is unlikely. But as long as the book has open-minded readers, the possibility exists that new generations will be able to put together these lessons with others, and perhaps affect the outcome. Or maybe just one individual will have been affected by this book in such a way as to avoid experiences as painful as I had to endure. That would be sufficient reward for the ordeals of writing it.

PROLOGUE

IN THE AUTUMN AFTER MY MOTHER DIED, I VISITED THE CEMETERY where I had buried her alongside my father in the Long Island earth. The soil on her grave was grown with grass and had begun to be almost indistinguishable from his, joining them again, a couple in death as they were in life. Picking some pebbles from the path beneath me, I placed them on their headstones, tokens of remembrance, according to the Jewish custom. My mother's bore the inscription "Always," a song which had become her favorite in her last years in California, and which symbolized to me the steadfastness with which she had stood behind her family and especially myself. My father's, which I had put up five years earlier, was already beginning to weather. I had directed the mason to inscribe it with the words "Life Is Struggle," a favorite quote from his mentor, Karl Marx. It was a struggle he had lost long before we finally laid him to rest.

This return to origins, if only symbolic, was a way of measuring the distance I had come. It often seemed as far as the poles themselves. By the time I was a parent myself, my own parents were already strangers, so remote in experience that I hardly looked to them for counsel. And yet, at times, it had not seemed that far at all. There was not a moment in my adult life—not even now that they had been returned to their primordial dust—that they failed to assume in my imagination the aspect of fifty years before, when I felt they could see through me as though I were glass and provide all the comfort I needed. It seemed to me a metaphor for life itself, which sets us free only to bring us relentlessly back to earth.

Feeling my parents' presence again, I tried to imagine myself as I had appeared to them when they were alive. But, try as I might, I could not put myself in their place. I could not imagine how they saw me, how they felt the personal agonies I endured, or how they understood the metamorphosis I underwent: the murder that had changed my life in midcourse; the breakup of the family I had loved so intensely and worked so hard to create; the pilgrimage I had made from the snug progressive ghettos they inhabited all their lives to an America they barely knew and ultimately rejected.

I thought about the way I had become a stranger to them politically, joining the other side in a cold war against a faith they had embraced as humanity's best hope. I was like Whittaker Chambers in their generation—a young man inspired by the high-minded passions of the Left who had broken through to the dark underside of the radical cause. Like Chambers, I had encounters with totalitarian forces that involved betrayal and death, and even a Soviet spy. Like him, I had been demonized for my second thoughts by a culture sympathetic to the Left and hostile to its adversaries. I, too, had to face the savage personal attacks by my former comrades that were designed to warn others to remain within the fold.

Like Chambers, I had become the most hated ex-radical of my generation. And like him, I had discovered that the enemies against whom I once battled so furiously were more fantastic than real. I also discovered that I was not alone. Second thoughts turned out to be a natural process that others, less publicly visible than myself, had also pursued. Eccentric as my life seemed—at times even to me—it was not isolated, but more like a piece of the epoch itself.

As a result of my experience, I have often thought of how different a life looks from the outside in. Of the name that identifies me but describes someone else; the external details that convey little of who I am, yet represent me. The problem is not unique to myself, but the serpentines of my life have made its progress unusually difficult for others to follow. Even allies who applaud the present acts of my public self often reserve suspicions of the private man whose experience they do not share and whose intentions they do not fully trust. As for the comrades I have left behind, who are still at odds with what I have become, it is as though I have ceased to exist. To them I can never be someone who felt what they felt, dreamed what they dreamed, suffered, and learned through pain. Seeing me as one of them would pose questions too humbling to face: What second thoughts might they have had too? What illusions would they have to give up now? Instead, they prefer the easier path of denial, and revile me as a symbol of one who left them. Worse still, of someone they fear to become.

I am now as prominent on the conservative side of the ideological divide as I once was in the ranks of the Left. But the conservatives I have joined are unlike the enemies I once imagined. The name itself does not begin to identify who they are. Or who I am. The collapse of Communism and the progressive future reveals how the moral language of politics has been hijacked by radicals. The fallen angels of the progressive left—Marxist and socialist—have been exposed as the reactionary ghosts of an oppressive past. It is the ideological adversaries of the Left who float on the wave of a future that is free.

Among my new comrades-in-arms, many began with second thoughts, having started out as Sixties radicals like myself. Indeed, in the last few years, the nation as a whole has begun to draw back from the radical decade and its destructive agendas. What I had learned, one way or another in the course of my journey, other Americans seem to have learned as well. Irving Kristol, who had second thoughts before me, has observed that every generation faces a barbarian threat in its own children, who need to be civilized. This is the perennial challenge: to teach our young the conditions of being human, of managing life's tasks in a world that is (and must remain) forever imperfect. The refusal to come to terms with this reality is the heart of the radical impulse and accounts for its destructiveness, and thus for much of the bloody history of our age. My own life, which has often been painful and many times off course, is ultimately not discrete—a story to itself—but part of the narrative we all share.

PART 1

BLACK HOLES

(1904–1939)

He had no home in a dat rock
Don't you see...

—Negro Spiritual

FIVEL

WHAT MY FATHER LEFT ME, REALLY, WAS A FEW STORIES. THEY were mainly about himself, but in one instance the story was about *his* father, whom I hardly knew, and who died from cancer when I was six. In fact, my only clear recollection of my grandfather Morris—a memory forever sharpened with remorse—is that when I was six, he sat on my favorite record of the Seven Dwarfs singing *"Heigh Ho, Heigh Ho (It's off to work we go...)"* and broke it. And that I yelled at him, protesting the injustice with all the force my small lungs could muster, as if my yelling could make the record whole. And that, shortly afterwards, they took my grandfather to the hospital—and I never saw him again.

It was nearly fifty years ago that my grandfather vanished. I am sitting now in my own home, leafing through a photo album I inherited from my parents' house. The album is encased in red velvet and embroidered with white roses. Its latch is broken and its edges are frayed. The front cover is inlaid with porcelain, and there is a scene showing two lovers eternally holding hands in a Victorian garden. Inside, there are rotogravure photographs of stiffly posed children and adults—some with Semitic features, some with high Slavic cheekbones and Oriental eyes. They are smartly outfitted, but in different national styles: some have waistcoats and high collars and look Americanized, while others wear Russian blouses and boots. The facial resemblances could be to either side of my family, but they look more like what I imagine my mother's forebears to be.

I am probably mistaken, however. On other pages the photos have fallen out of their frames, exposing the white backing, and there are pencil marks in a child's hand. They spell out the words *Fivel Anna Fivel Anna Fivel Anna*. This is my father's name and his mother's. It is as though my father had written them to practice his English script, suggesting that the pictures are not my mother's relatives, but his. *Who were these people?* I don't know. I do not see my grandfather Morris, or his wife Anna, or anyone else I can recognize. There is not a single name in the album that is familiar to me, and no one is left who remembers who these people were who can tell me.

What else is this life about but vanishing? We come and go as strangers. We disappear even in advance of our deaths. Do we ever know ourselves? I can remember swearing as a youth of twenty that I would never become the man I eventually was at forty. *Who could be more surprised at the way my life turned out than I?* There is more than enough pain in the memories I have left behind me, yet I seem to have become accustomed to these losses, to see them as necessary and—in some cases—even beneficial.

My mother is now the last survivor of everyone who preceded me. Past eighty and no longer coherent beyond a sentence or two, she has developed her own mantra to answer the questions for which she has no answer: *Life is a mystery*. I expressed this thought to my father once, when I was a college student encountering mysticism for the first time. He was a Marxist, and apparently could not face the possibility that life might be a puzzle without a solution. The words sent him into a rage, like a pious man confronted by blasphemy. Having embraced the truth of Marxism, he was convinced he had discovered the key to life's important questions, and did not want his son to throw it away.

Political utopians like my father had a master plan. They were going to transform the world from the chaos we knew into a comfortable and friendly place. In the happy future they dreamed about, there would be an end to grief from life out of control, life grinding you down and smashing your gut when you expected it least. Human cruelty would go out of style and become a memory in the museum of historical antiquities. In my father's paradise there would be no strangers. No one who felt like an outsider, *alienated* from others and at odds with themselves.

For thirty-five years I followed my father's footsteps and believed in his earthly redemption, until a day came when I realized that there are tragedies from which one cannot recover, and alienation that no revolution can cure. That *we* are the mystery, and this is the only truth that matters.

My grandfather Morris was a wraith of a man, barely five feet tall, with doleful eyes and a shock of white hair that fell mournfully to one side. His real name was Moishe—Moses. Like his namesake, my grandfather had escaped a kind of slavery in the Pale of Settlement on the western verge of the Czarist Empire. With his wife and two infant children he had left Russia in the exodus of 1905, coming to America with thousands of others who were fleeing the pogroms of the *hetman* Petlura. Like the Hebrews of *Exodus*, they crossed the sea and made their way to a promised land.

Only my grandfather was not at all like Moses. He had led no one; indeed had been led (by the nose, if my mother told the story) by his wife, Anna—a short, abrasive woman with thick, braided hair that she knotted in a bun. It was Anna who had created the family, marrying Moishe to save him from the Czarist conscription. Anna's word was law in their household, just as—in a more covert way—my mother's word was law in ours.

They had started out in Mazyr, a city located in the western Ukraine, where my grandfather was a tailor. The immigration officials at Ellis Island had translated his surname which was probably Gurevitch to "Horowitz," and he had accepted the change, like the other circumstances of his life, as an unalterable fate. Arriving in America, they had settled in the Delancey Street section of the Lower East Side in Manhattan, where my grandfather found employment in a sweatshop which paid him three dollars a week. Like other immigrants, he was often required to work until after dark, sometimes so late that he had to sleep under his sewing machine on the shop floor.

Not only was my grandfather Morris unable to stand up to his wife; he was finally too timid to become an American. Like Moses, he was allowed to see, but not to enter, the promised land. Its competition and dynamism intimidated and finally overwhelmed him. My grandfather was not a Moses, as everyone in the family knew, but a mouse.

It was this fact that was the center of the story my father told about him. One evening, Morris came home from work later than usual. The dinner his wife had prepared was already cold when he came in silently, as he always did, and sat down to eat. Even though Anna knew that the circumstances that had made him late were beyond his control, her fury was already at white heat. It was this fact itself that inflamed her. She had fled from her *shtetl* prison in the Old World only to arrive in another prison in the New. A mouse could no more lead his family out of poverty in America than he could out of slavery in Russia.

All the passion that Anna could not express in her marriage was invested in her rage against the unhappiness of her life. The prison of her circumstances, her loveless household, the meagerness of her existence in an alien world, were the *leitmotifs* of the tirade that was set off now by a dinner that had grown cold. As Morris continued to eat in wary silence, his wife's pent-up grievances flooded their containing wall in a cataract of complaint. Then an extraordinary thing happened. This man, who had borne his wife's rages with the same equanimity that he did her coldness (as he bore all the injuries of his unfortunate life), snapped. With a violence that still shocked my father when he told me the story half a century later, my grandfather stabbed his fork into the plate in front of him with a force that shattered it to pieces. It was the only rebellion my grandfather Moses ever made against his condition that anyone could remember.

I never really was able to match this image with my own memory of the old woman in the shapeless print dress I knew when I was young. She seemed merely intimidated by the strange American energies that swarmed into her apartment on the occasions when my parents took me to visit. Yet it was she who had propelled her little family across continents and oceans, leaving a Ukrainian backwater of thatched houses and horse-drawn carts, thrusting them into a modern wilderness of skyscrapers and motor cars. Her ambition was so strong that she didn't stop there but soon moved them out of the comfortable familiarity of the Lower East Side to Yorktown Heights, where Jews were scarce and their antagonists numerous, but her children might have a better chance to step up and out. Because the terrors of this world were very real to her, she kept her brood under close rein. When my father and his sister went out to play in the cobbled streets, they were not allowed to stray beyond the reach of her voice. The perimeter of his mother's fear formed another of the invisible ghettos that circumscribed his young life.

One day when he was flying his kite in the street with the neighborhood boys, my father heard his mother's voice come keening through the tenement canyons. "Fivel, *Fivel!*" she shouted. My father froze, stricken by the sound. "FIVEL!" He knew instantly the meaning of the summons. Reeling in his kite as quickly as he could, he hurried home, hot with a shame that was still burning the day he told me the story sixty years later. His embarrassment flamed from the fact that he had taken his mother's only pair of underwear and shredded it to make the tail of his kite. When my father confessed this to me, his voice grew pinched, as though someone was standing on his chest. Sixty years had not provided him with the absolution necessary to release him from his guilt.

My father bore visible scars of his childhood which, in the political romance that enveloped our lives, became marks of a social distinction. He had bandy legs, from a case of rickets that a poverty-induced diet had caused. This was the physical aspect of him that was most personal, allowing me to spot him at a distance when no other feature was clearly discernible, like a brand that made him mine. His calves and thighs were muscular over the damaged bones, and he had an athletic build. I loved to touch his brawny arms and rounded shoulders—and yet, when occasionally he hugged me, it seldom provided the comfort and pleasure I was seeking. His embrace was more of a squeeze than a sheltering warmth, as though he was afraid of his feelings and did not want them to leak too obviously to the surface.

I came eventually to see that his parental "no's" were inspired by a fear that had begun in his own childhood and never stopped. In his family's errand into the American wilderness, he had been volunteered as the company scout. His mission was to cross the boundaries that hemmed them in. In these uncharted territories the family Yiddish was not spoken, and my father was called by his English name, Philip. Confined to their ghetto by language and culture, it was as though his parents were still in another country. What could they understand of the difficulties he encountered, and the dangers he faced? What guidance could they give? I came to see that my father's "no's" were a language of self-preservation directed not so much at me as at himself. Denial defined a zone of safety: Nothing ventured, nothing lost.

When he was thirteen, my father was sent with other academically gifted youngsters to Townsend Harris, a special high school where students were taught Latin, and graduated in three years, and where my father felt hopelessly out of his depth. Although his academic performance was miserable, he managed to conceal his poor grades by hiding the report cards his teachers sent home in his care. When he grew desperate, he would even alter them, his parents' inability to decipher the English making the deception relatively easy. But he could not hide them from himself. The fear that my father could never escape was, finally, the fear of being found out. He was in perpetual fear of someone discovering that he was not where he belonged. But that was wherever he was.

It was my mother—a dark-haired, handsome woman with pursed lips that always seemed to be withholding something—who spoiled me. If my father constantly set limits, it was she who undid them, persuading him in their private negotiations to countermand his own orders. Other times she would go behind his back to produce the result I desired. One of my most vivid memories is opening the front door on my eighth birthday, to find my father holding a red and blue chain-drive bike in his arms. (My happiness was doubled because he usually begrudged me such extravagances, as when he refused to buy me Foto Electric Football, a board game that was the latest rage among my peers.) I was an adult before my mother finally revealed the truth of this event. My father was old and ailing then, and perhaps my mother was out of sorts with him for something I have forgotten. Or perhaps she had just grown tired of manipulating so many appearances and occasions for others that she decided it was time to end her charade. But, thirty years after the fact, she informed me that she had fought him for a week to get him to purchase that bike.

The irony was that my mother's indulgences also came from a denial of self. Like my father, she too felt like a swimmer out of her depth. But unlike my father, she wanted me to have what she could not, and to achieve in life what she was afraid to attempt. Just as my grandmother had pushed my father into uncharted seas to feed her own unrequited hungers, so my mother was the silent thrust behind my trajectory into the American unknown.

My mother's family had emigrated from Russia, in the middle of the Nineteenth Century, to a town in Rumania called Vaslui. Their name was Braunstein, but in the New World the family halves split into "Browns" and "Stones," anglicizing the names to hurry their ascent. In 1898, at the age of seventeen, my grandfather Sam, who was one of seven brothers and sisters, walked all the way from Vaslui to Amsterdam, to catch a boat to America. His father, Chaim, was a wine merchant who followed his son shortly thereafter because of government laws that barred Jews from owning land. The family's passage was paid by the Baron De Hirsch Settlement Fund, which relocated Jews to become farmers in southern New Jersey. Soon after arriving, Chaim left the farm with his wife and children for New York.

At five-foot-eight, my grandfather Sam was not only the tallest of our lineage, but also the only one with a bristly mustache, a shining round forehead, and a cigar permanently clenched between his teeth. He began his career in a brass factory and then went to work as a sales clerk in a mail-order house. Around 1900, one of the Stones opened a chain of 5-and-10-cent stores, and in 1910 my grandfather became the manager of their New Haven outlet. His parents lived with them on Maple Street, made sacramental wine in their cellar and kept the Jewish laws—the last to do so in our family.

These facts about my family's progress have been passed to me on a typewritten sheet prepared by my grandma Rose, who was the family archivist. Her notes also record that in 1918 my grandfather became a buyer for the Stones' chain, and nine years later acquired one of them as his own. The information stops there. Recently, however, I received a letter from one of my grandfather's nieces, Betty Tomar (whom I have yet to meet) who still lives in South Jersey, which fills in some of the blanks: "In 1929 the business failed and the family scattered. I think your grandfather Sam, who was a committed Communist, went to Russia." I knew my grandfather Sam was a freethinker and a socialist, but not this. Perhaps it was one of the secrets my mother held behind those pursed lips. On the other hand, perhaps it is only the embellishment of someone who doesn't really know.

The same letter from Betty Tomar advises me: "I think if you write your autobiography, the evolution of the intellectual New York Jews from Second Avenue to affluence to Communism to Hippiedom to mature members of the community is normal and probably the story of all our sons and daughters." She adds: "I understand that's happened with you. But in a capitalistic society anyone who doesn't believe in capital is probably a shnook." Betty Tomar was definitely from the Brown side of the family.

In 1907, my grandfather Sam married Rose Abramowitz, who was only seventeen years old. She gave birth to my mother a year later. The baby was named Blanche, which my mother always thought pretentious, what with its French air, and somewhat of an oxymoron: Blanche Brown. Rose was my favorite grandparent. A small woman with high cheekbones and kind eyes that looked out through stylish frames, she had a curiosity that made her seem young. (At sixty she went back to school to earn her high-school diploma.) Always full of useful information and advice, she admonished me to chew food exactly twenty-three times before swallowing, and not to put a knife in my mouth (even to lick off peanut butter) because I might hurt my tongue—as she had. After giving this advice, she would stick out her tongue for me, as a warning, to show just where it had been cut.

But what I loved best about my grandma was a tune she had made up, and would sing to me when I was very young and she tucked me into my bed before I went to sleep:

And grandma loves her David,
And David loves his grandma,
And grandpa loves his David,
And David loves his grandma,
And daddy loves his David ...

And so on, down the whole family line—mother, sister, cousins, aunts, uncles, Horowitzes, Browns, Stones—and then friends, until she had gathered in and exhausted the whole world of people that surrounded me beyond the dark. I loved these moments when she sang me to sleep. It was like being connected to a world that was mine, and being able to hold on to everyone in it for those sweet moments she was with me. No one else, not my mother or father, ever was so intimate, or did anything so comforting for me.

When my father was sixty-four (ten years older than I am writing this), he sent me a letter that I kept and never reread. When I took the letter out to look at it, recently, it turned out to be a plea for communication between us. Characteristically, it also predicted that this would never happen. He wrote it on his birthday in 1968, when I had just returned from Europe, where I had lived for nearly five years with my wife and three children. I guess he was missing me:

February 16, 1968

Dear David,

There is an irony in everything, I suppose. My guess is that at some time when you were very young, you felt that sometime when you were older, you would get to talking things over with your father in a way that was too hard at the time to do. I did, too. Both of us are older now, and the older we get, the less possible it has become to talk—just talk. To wonder how and why and what's gonna be. As "father" I've been self-conscious too long now to hope for the thawing out of it. Perhaps it's because when my father was as old as I am today, he had been so long silent watching his son change into an educated man that he feared to be talked down to.

I'm afraid that I was well aware of how more time given and more thought spent would have drawn a great deal out of his life that I could add to mine—a life that somehow found occasion to hum and even sing revolutionary songs whenever he had a piece of sewing to do; deep hurts and pointless quarrels with my fiercely unhappy mother, whose disappointments with our lives became the arsenal which she drew on during their quarrels, as if bringing him down would clear the air ahead and make the road behind comprehensible. I was well aware and fond of the things he bore within him, that I discovered as I grew older, and my mother's picture of him faded before the reality of a man small, weak, kindly, and with a sense of humor that sprang from his keen insight into the disproportion between human boasts and their actual achievement.

I do not remember how I received this letter as a self-absorbed young man of twenty-nine. Its intimacy probably embarrassed me, or seemed merely burdensome before I put it aside. Today, twenty-five years later, when my father is dead and I cannot speak to him anymore, I am impressed by the pathos of it all, the incomplete connections, the circular rhythms of our lives, the wisdom we earn through sweat and pain and cannot pass on. The continuing disproportion between human boasts and achievements.

In thinking about the men who have preceded me in my family, I can't help noticing also my father's quotation marks around the word "father," as though he was not quite sure he *was* my father, or perhaps what a father should be; and the picture of my grandfather mouse sewing away and singing revolutionary songs in a fantasy of the power he would never acquire.

Soon I will be the age my father was when he wrote me this letter. Yet it seems hardly yesterday that my grandfather Morris sat on my record and went away to die. I can still see the armchair with the crewel pattern under the old carved mirror where I had left my treasure, its center marked with a yellow sticker so that I could pick it out from all the others. It is fifty years since all this took place. My grandparents and my father are dead, and my mother is in a retirement home where the past doesn't matter anymore, her memory erased by too many strokes. I am the teller of stories now. I am the grandfather, too. *Heigh ho, Heigh ho...*

RUSSIA

WHEN MY FATHER WAS FIFTEEN, HIS CAREER AS THE FAMILY SCOUT propelled him through the gothic portals of City College. Perched on the heights above Morningside Park, City was the poor man's Ivy League, a school for immigrant sons excluded by birthright from Harvard and Yale. But though he had begun to distance himself from the ghetto his parents would never leave, my father felt as much an interloper in his new environment as he had at Townsend Harris before. Even his classmates who shared similar roots seemed to him like inhabitants of a different country.

His best friend, Maurice Valency, was pursuing a career in medieval literature, and another, Ernest Nagel, was an aspiring philosopher. They all studied logic together with the school's most famous teacher, Morris Raphael Cohen, and after classes reprised the great intellectual debates, and assessed the treasures of world literature and art. My father got to press his nose against the glass of a life that stretched far beyond the world he had known. But he was never able to get past the threshold and enter it with the rest. When the four years were up, "Val" and Nagel went on to graduate school, eventually to write books, and to pursue distinguished academic careers at Columbia University. My father stayed another six months to get his high-school teaching credential and, at nineteen, went to work.

"It was like a sentence," he said about receiving his first job. "It was a day of absolute misery when the sky went black." He made a stab at explaining his feelings to me, but failed when he could not name the career he had been forced to relinquish. Perhaps he recognized by then that he lacked what it took to achieve his dream, which—it became apparent to me—was to be a writer. What he actually said was, "I loved the wind and the sun and wanted to go to sea."

The theme of escape recurs often in the notes my father left behind. I found them in a file along with a diary and letters and other papers, which I have read only now, writing my own story. I am struck by a passage from a letter written when he was wooing my mother and was trying to explain the difficulty he had in making a commitment. Its broken syntax seems to me only another expression of the discomfort that was a permanent aspect of his being, like a desire to exit his own reality:

> Travelling like this with home in danger of being lost behind the veil of distance was once a relief to me. It still is strong in me to face forward instead of looking to where I came from which is profoundly my way of thinking. I don't feel safe unless I deny myself the pleasure of thinking about home.

In 1923, my father reported to work as a teacher of English to immigrant children, beginning—it seemed to him—an indentured servitude from which only death would set him free. The pittance that his father earned could no longer support their household. Although Anna was a talented seamstress, she refused to work, as though unwilling to relinquish her last remaining prerogative as a bride. As a result, it fell to my father to support them both. Every month he deducted half his pay and set it aside for his parents' allowance, continuing to do so for the rest of their lives.

As if in response to his existential trials, my father was afflicted with allergies and a childhood asthma, that would not go away. These appeared almost as a somatic imprint of the burdens that already weighted his spirit, requiring constant medication and occasionally causing his body to swell so badly that he was bedridden for days. The asthma particularly seemed a metaphor for the conflict in his soul: a gasping for life that he felt was constantly being choked off.

My father's literary ambitions inspired him to style his prose, and to adopt the salon look that was popular with writers of the "Lost Generation." He affected a suave air in handling the cigarettes he smoked almost chain-style, despite the fact that they aggravated his asthma. Fashionably slim, he grew a mustache to offset his silky black hair and wounded brown eyes. When he was just shy of thirty, he noted in his diary:

> To the doctor today to corroborate my conclusions. Looking over the record, he found years of misery there which explain for him my present state and from which, we both understood, recovery would be fairly impossible. I am not ill; I am ailing, but I will be sick soon permanently.

The one bright feature of my father's melancholic life was his dedication to a worldwide movement for human renewal. Sometime in the Twenties he had joined the Communist Party and given himself to the dream of a socialist revolution. In a folder I discovered in his file cabinet after his death, I found the notes he had saved from the study groups he attended as a Party novice:

> Upon the different forms of property, upon the social conditions of existence, rises an entire superstructure of distinct and characteristically formed sentiments, illusions, modes of thought and views of life. The entire class creates and forms them out of the material foundations and out of the corresponding social relations.

A man could grow spiritually calm just reading formulations like this and absorbing their sense of Olympian certitude.

I do not really have an answer to the mystery of origins—to what, in particular, had set my father and eventually, therefore, myself on the radical path; to what had inspired the dream of a revolutionary future that shaped all our ends. All I have to answer this question are the notes he left me from his youth, among them a diary he kept in the summer of 1932, when he made a pilgrimage to the promised land.

The trip was arranged by the New York Teachers Union, an organization the Party controlled, and was a *tour d'horizon* of the revolutionary ferment that was sweeping the capitals of Europe. There were stops in Berlin, Paris, and Moscow, and my father kept track of his observations in a school copybook he brought with him. In reading this journal, I am struck by the fact that he doesn't seem to have made any attempt to depart from the official itinerary of his trip to visit

Mazyr, or the Pale of Settlement, to inspect his point of departure. For years, he had been escaping the tribal self that identified him with his childhood ghettos. By now there was no trace of an accent, in his perfectly executed English. While he could still speak Yiddish fluently and used it as a *lingua franca* on his European stops, my father considered himself an "internationalist," a missionary in humanity's cause. The first entry in his diary reflects this self-image while reporting an incident on board a German liner to Hamburg, his port of entry:

July 1

Three Russians in the cabin. One small, second fat, third big and bony. All three smiling, friendly and talkative but not humble. Wishing to learn the Russian for "I am," I asked the small one how to say "I am a Jew." He said, "No Jew, no Christian. After Communism, all people."

The same diary entry contains a jarring note in recording his annoyance when a "comrade" insists that he join a table of six teachers in order to recruit them: "This proselytizing zeal makes an otherwise honest person look more cunning than a crook. I replied sharply that I preferred to stay where I was." My father had other provocative observations:

July 2

To be spoken to as an equal by a steward is surprisingly disagreeable apparently. The unconscious desire is much stronger than the thought. One wishes other than one thinks. Thinking is far ahead and perfectly hollow till desire creeps up to understanding. Real Communists, therefore, are as rare as ships on this vacant sea. Those who see clearly and therefore fight for Communism do not yet feel clearly, nor will they in this generation. But sobriety will come.

One wishes other than one thinks. At the very outset of his journey, my father had stumbled on a truth that would be fatal to the dream of revolution he had embraced: the cunning of human desire. It was the paradox over which St. Paul had agonized in his famous *cri de coeur*: "I do not understand my own actions. For I do not do what I want, but I do the very thing I hate." On this human fault line the entire edifice of my father's utopia would one day fall to ruin. But he could not follow his own perception. Wracked by inner torment, he clung to the faith that reason would rule desire and sobriety would come.

From Germany he went by train to the Russo–Finnish border, reporting "the somewhat sacred thrill of seeing the Red Army soldiers standing along the tracks" as he entered the country. When he arrived in Moscow, the Mecca of the revolution, the sights conformed to his expectations:

July 17

Workers everywhere. No dwellings to point to and say "there live the wealthy." Workers, peasant faces, clad incredibly shabby, knowing no meat and little sugar and butter or potatoes, but workers all subject to no threats from bosses, with clubs of their own and sanitariums and parks and theaters all for them and their children.

My father was not unaware of the harsh realities that already prevailed in the socialist state, but he attributed the repression and shortages to the civil war that had followed the revolution. "All this but ten years ago!" my father exclaimed, referring to those events. "The world is full of idiots and the most idiotic those who dare criticize conditions today, forgetting this brief moment of ten years just passed."

Soon after his arrival, he was taken ill with an attack of bronchitis and grippe. Wrapping himself in blankets and drinking six cups of tea at a sitting, he recorded his impressions of the Park of Culture, which he found similar to an American amusement park, "if we substitute educational amusements and pastimes for idiotic ones." He was impressed by the crowds of workers that swarmed to take advantage of the cultural offerings, which included a play he described as "for workers, by workers, about workers and their work." The play addressed the problem of motivating people in the socialist state to actually produce. My father noticed that the audience was not very interested and indeed only half-filled the theater, but he did not pursue the implications of the observation. Afterwards, he joined a group of young workers in a circle dance around an accordion player. The thoughts this inspired come as close as anything he wrote to an explanation of his radical commitment:

All of this draws me. I feel as if all of my life I have been preparing myself for such a rich group life. I felt the same learning group singing last night. Also, listening to a concert of blind musicians and doing handstands with a couple of promising athletes. This is life; because it is not isolated, it is fruitful; because it springs from the group, it can never be sterile.

Two days later he was again waxing lyrical about the collective rebirth that he saw in the revolution, and about what this might mean for him:

Dawn reddening faintly, and along the far ridge of spires and domes silhouetted searchlights shining powerfully into Red Square. Before Lenin's tomb two Red soldiers at attention. So—fusion and unity. And with it strength as well as understanding: For now begins the ending of the breaking out from a life of sterility...

Fusion and unity—this was the cry of my father's Communist heart. His unquenchable longing to belong.

The following day, he visited a school with the other members of his teachers' delegation. He noted the pride of the administrators in the achievements of their institution, and imagined the USSR as one big family:

But what is more impressive is the sense of common ownership in everything in the USSR. They are at home. Everything is theirs. No event or place is too remote for their concern, no person in the USSR beyond their concern.

It was the same feeling that moved him at a surprise feast to which their hosts invited them that night. They sat at a long table in a lavishly decorated dining room in what was formerly the home of a wealthy furrier. It had silk-lined walls, a carved mantelpiece with a gold clock, and a fireplace, "the sort of set used by movie directors to make proletarians gape in the movies of America." When the guests asked guiltily about the opulence of the meal that had been provided, the answer only increased my father's admiration for the Soviet state: "Proudly they told us the government refused them nothing, and this feast was the result."

Afterwards, their hosts asked them about their own working conditions, and then entertained them with facts about industrial production in Moscow, and the newly completed Dnieper dam of *"their* USSR." It inspired in my father a flight of self-pity:

> All this made me feel isolated, reduced—the poor teacher looked down on in America, the poor slave, owning nothing, looking to nothing but his pay, unable to be proud of anything. For nothing in America was his, no, not the children whom we were training to become able, skilled slaves for those who owned and possessed what belonged to all Russians from now on, but which only a handful owned in America.

On leaving the Soviet Union, he visited a Communist neighborhood in Hamburg, recording a last vision of the revolutionary future:

> It would be difficult indeed to forget these people who have taken us into their home as one of them. Here we say du. Here we are truly at home. We are their people and they are ours. One feels constantly on the edge of dream. But one day all else will seem nothing but dream and story. Their lot is hard here in Germany, but their vision is great, vast. Such things and Russia—and there is never again turning back. For here is strength. And significance at last.

I never asked my father about his trip to Russia and he never spoke to me about it. Was he too embarrassed by the time I was old enough to listen? Would he have had too much explaining to do by then: the Moscow Trials, the purges, the Nazi-Soviet Pact? Were there too many layers to get past in order to reach the bedrock of his feeling, the bond he had discovered in the home of the revolution? Or did he sense that its meaning was too deeply embedded in his own inner torments to be intelligible to me?

Struggling for air, my father concentrated on the black hole beneath him and tried not to be swallowed up by it. But all around him there were other black holes he was unable to see—the deepest and widest of which was Russia itself. The year my father went to the Soviet Union the country was ravaged by one of the most terrible famines on human record. But my father did not see it, while others who did concealed it. Walter Duranty, the Moscow correspondent of the *New York*

Times, whose job it was to be the eyes and ears of the American public, was one. Like my father, Duranty considered himself a progressive. While millions perished, he purposely kept their fate from view in order to protect socialism from its taint. The cause of the famine was not hostile capitalists or foreign invaders, as my father had been told, but the "workers' government" he admired.

Three years earlier, Stalin had launched a collectivization drive "to bring socialism to the countryside." Troops were dispatched to confiscate the peasants' land and goods, in an effort that became an all-out war. When the troops came, the peasants resisted. Rather than surrender the crops they had grown, they burned them. Rather than give up their farming tools, they disabled them. Rather than lose their livestock, they slaughtered them. Thirty million cattle (nearly half the nation's total) and a hundred million sheep and goats (two-thirds of the total) were destroyed in this fashion. Ukrainians were singled out for special punishment. Their confiscated grain was shipped out of the republic, leaving the population to starve. By the time my father arrived at the Finnish border on his way to the socialist future, the workers' state had killed more than ten million people and put another ten million in slave-labor camps. The "mass annihilation of completely defenseless men, women and children," as the Bolshevik leader Bukharin described it in his secret diary, had transformed the comrades into "cogs in some terrible machine." My father had found a home in Russia in the year that Stalin consolidated the totalitarian state. The haven he imagined was in fact a prison, the comrade-owners he envied only its trustees.

The illusion my father had given himself to was all-encompassing, and yet it still could not repress the feelings of emptiness that had become the undercurrent of his life:

> *Stayed overnight and came back today—to a sickening day and IT all over again. The illness is still there. That it seized me here in Moscow proves conclusively that it is as permanent as my asthma which has also appeared. I must learn to bear it.*

My father drew a lesson from this: "So, one can never leave behind the past." It was a revealing fatalism for a man who wanted to change the world.

BLANCHE

M Y FATHER RETURNED TO AMERICA AND NORMAL LIFE IN AUGUST 1932, and his first diary entry described the return of his symptoms: "There is once again that unbearable, lingering loneliness of heart, echoing, beating pain." This depression continued through the winter; there were self-admonitions to develop the will to "fight," which only betrayed his continuing weakness. He imagined a day when he would be able to put his misery completely out of mind, and then declared, "but my body will always remember, always." He described one of his "outbreaks," the eruptions that signaled to him the disturbance of his being: "...a blind fury which boiled and boiled, feeding on each moment of its poisonous existence, till it spurted vainly in swearing and saying nasty things to my mother." He wondered whether he would ever be rid of the episodes, and what the cause might be. A helpless passivity prevailed. "I have been silent for eight hours," he noted in a June entry, as though the silence had been imposed by some external force. But, in another, he recorded a flurry of dating and a burst of male optimism, fused with the hope of transformation which seemed to provide the only possibility of rescue: "My cock drives ahead. How swell it is to know that there can be no return. For while said cock glides headstrong down the same swift channel, my life has gathered momentum with the heavy speed of the present, bolting toward revolution."

The following spring he met my mother, a fact not noted in the diary until six months later, when he recorded a resurgence of his interest, and the possible birth of love: "And now, just yesterday, the weekend with her and the seed flourishing, throbbing faintly like a pulse. And not yet certain. But growing, the signs appearing—desiring to call, to write, and then calling."

It was chance that brought my mother, who was a teacher of stenography and typing, to Seward Park High, the school on the Lower East Side where my father taught English. "You must hear Phil Horowitz," someone had said to her one day when he was scheduled to speak at a union meeting in the school cafeteria. It is not hard to understand why my mother was smitten by the political agitator she saw that day. The public persona my father had developed was a far cry from the suffering private man. The Marxist formulas he had absorbed provided him with verbal hammers, while his voice accumulated force from the deep passions that seethed inside. Unlike his regular teaching job, the Party constantly pushed the envelope of his talents, making him the union spokesman at his school, and summoning him for a national mission that spring.

I have no record of the speech in the cafeteria that won my mother's heart. But in my father's file I found a letter, written only a few months later, which preserves a picture of his political self. The letter is dated December 10, 1934, and is addressed to an instructor at Columbia Teachers College, where he was taking a course in Education and Public Opinion. My father clashed with the instructor over a state law that required teachers to take an oath of allegiance to the Constitution. The president of the Board of Education, Dr. George S. Ryan, had also endorsed the oath, while the Communist Party had made opposition a key point in "the struggle."

My father criticized the position his Columbia instructor took in the dispute, which was that the oath should be made more specific, to avoid abuse, and that it should be directed at everyone—not merely radicals. This quest for a middle ground failed to satisfy my father.

> An oath of allegiance is a bad thing, not because it is incomplete or "not sufficiently specific." It is bad because bad men make it up for specific bad purposes—to put it crudely. Hearst, the DAR, fascist Dr. George S. Ryan—these are the representatives of the forces that have designed the instrument for their own class purposes....

In this letter my father emerges as a tiger, attacking his own instructor without apparent fear of consequences:

> The evil of taking your position is even greater than I have indicated.... You will be splitting the fighters against the bill by your position that it is desirable if "improved." You will weaken the real opponents of the bill by attacking them as unpatriotic.... In the meantime, the forces of fascism drive ahead blow on blow, organized, clear as to their purpose. There is little time left. It is dangerous to waste it. The enemy must be exposed brilliantly to the teachers, and then efforts should be made to organize them to wipe out the enemy. How else can one save "the good life"?
>
> Sincerely,
> Philip Horowitz

I look at my father's words *wipe out the enemy* and marvel at the power he has been able to suck up from the silences and defeats of his life. The Party had given him this strength and made him a man. Yet his new power remained firmly in the Party's control. Without it, he was nothing. In his heart, my father knew this. A memo dated August 16, 1934, provides an intimate view of his relationship to the Party he had joined and now apparently wanted to leave:

Balance Sheet:

To remain in the Party means for me:

1. That I take the leadership in a mass organization because I am by now fitted for it, and therefore, necessarily cannot refuse to do my plain duty.
2. That I take assignments, attend all demonstrations, etc., within the unit.

Both options, he concludes, are impossible: "In the mass organization, I duck the responsibilities of leadership. I am afraid of both." He doesn't like his Party assignments or demonstrations, and feels dishonest in accepting them, a "four-flusher," which makes him miserable. It has begun to affect his thinking. He writes of his fear of "dangerous tendencies" to rationalize his position. He detects symptoms of hypochondria, but also ones that are real: "My health is in fact affected already, having at this point shown a ready response to the psychological contradictions;... there is every reason to expect the situation to become pathological." But there is no exit from his dilemma because the consequences of leaving the Party are more dire still.

To resign would mean:

1. To lose all my friends, and more perhaps.
2. To lose the basis for all of my thinking, to have no direction for any of the ordinary activities of daily existence; in brief, to stagnate and then degenerate mentally as well as intellectually.

The Party has become so much my father's personal salvation that without it the possibilities of life itself vanish.

The memo was written just a few months after he met my mother in the cafeteria at Seward Park. In his letters to her, my father was candid about the insecurities that haunted him:

Dear Blanche,

When a guy asks what do you think of him, it's really a confession, not a question.... It means simply, something like this: "Don't you see that great yawning gulf of weakness in me? I hope you don't, but it would relieve me if you did and said so." That's all the question means.... Now when a dame like you begins to look "that way" at him, he feels like saying go 'way, you're wasting time, skip it, find a nice guy, etc.

My mother had met a man powerful and passionate in his commitment to a cause, yet floundering in a tide of hidden fears that threatened to pull him under. The attraction proved irresistible. His warning went unheeded.

When she came to hear my father speak, my mother was twenty-six and also a Party member. That summer she had made her own pilgrimage to the Soviet Union, where she attended a lecture by the Hungarian Marxist György Lukács, and visited the Black Sea. Despite a law degree from Hunter College, my mother had become a teacher of typing and stenography. She explained this to me once, saying she was afraid to step out into the competitive world during the Great Depression. Yet she could have gone back to the law when conditions changed, or sought other employment more suited to her talents.

Throughout her life, my mother remained determined and forceful, yet unsure of herself. When she was eighty, she said to me apologetically, "We didn't know how to be parents." As if anyone did. The security my mother was eventually able to achieve came, I realized, from a combination of denial and control. Before my father, she had suitors who were stockbrokers and lawyers, but—in a kind of reverse snobbery—disdained them. My mother's secret was to find situations in which she could exert her own superiority. Among these, her marriage was the most important of all.

"You never knew what she was feeling," her oldest friend said to me once. I already knew this from a lifetime of trying to guess. The one exception seems to have been her desire for my father, which she recorded in a batch of letters I found with his diary. They were sent in the spring and summer of 1935, when my father was traveling out west on a mission for the Party, and were always signed "B," as though she was hiding her full self.

Sunday February 26

Who said ole dear,

That I wouldn't know you were gone until the weekend? It's not true, not in the least. In the first place, I've buried my jigger [I take this to be her diaphragm] in a place where no one can see it—something I always intended to do, but now I don't have to get at it in a minute's notice. Ah, sweet symbol of a well-ordered life. I almost felt like placing a rose on it, but that would seem too much like marking the spot for anyone who chances into my closet. In the second place, my telephone rings until I get good and ready to answer it because it can't possibly be you.... How do you like that for fidelity? You've been gone two whole days and I still love you.

B

She followed this letter with another:

I've looked over the horizon and I'm not surprised to find that you're still the only one in sight. Of course, you're practically at the vanishing point and I'm going to be terribly out of breath when I finally catch up to you...

But my father was elusive even when caught. In his effort to protect her, he seemed almost incapable of directly expressing affection: "Your instinct to follow me to the coast was correct. I mean we were both right in seeing the importance of continued contact for a correct working out of the problem which we two started. Don't misunderstand—stop palpitating. What I mean is that I'm lonesome. Under such circumstances, it's hard to see clearly what I'm lonesome about. I think it's you, but how the hell can I tell...?" My mother's response was pained but controlled: "I wish you'd stop thinking of me as a problem just until the summer and then you can start all over again if you want, but it's too much to deal with in letters."

He had taken a sabbatical for the spring term in part because his asthma and hay fever were kicking up and he thought the trip west to a drier climate might help. He was on the aforementioned Party mission to organize teachers against the loyalty oath in the Midwest, and to agitate against American "militarists" who wanted to arm because of the German threat. His ultimate destination was Palo Alto, California. "You'll love this place," he wrote when he arrived, "although it has the usual repellence that all swanky places have." He was going to work with Holland Roberts, the president of the American Russian Institute, a Communist front. Assigned to help Roberts write a tract on Soviet education, he was to draw on his own trip to Russia as a source.

Before reaching California, my father traveled by bus through Colorado, which inspired emotions of estrangement that were the direct opposite of those he experienced on his Russian journey:

I've had a feeling, riding on the buses, that I'm in a foreign land. And it strikes me that unless we learn the people in this country of ours so thoroughly so that we won't feel that way, we won't get anywhere.

I'm afraid that most of us aren't really "patriotic," I mean at bottom deeply fond of the country and the people.

The message the Party had instructed him to take to the "masses" isolated him further. "I heard about the Hitler business after I left Chicago," he wrote, referring to Germany's repudiation of the Versailles Treaty. In the eyes of the Party, the Nazi threat was a myth invented by the capitalist ruling classes for their own agendas (a line that would be reversed in 1936 with the Popular Front and again in 1939 with the Nazi-Soviet Pact). My father even detected collusion in the news reporting of the local papers: "They're building up the myth about our having the smallest army and about our keeping peacefully away from European troubles. And they're convincing, too, to the people out here, let me tell you. There's no talking any other way; they just don't understand you when you try."

Meanwhile, my mother was getting "awfully fed up with this letter business. I sometimes feel like saying 'come home,' only it seems wrong somehow. I don't know exactly why." My father responded:

You speak of saying "Come home." And I have thought of it often. In my mind, the reasons against it are just as vague as in yours. I have failed to do any work here, utterly; I have not appreciably improved in health; I am sometimes desperately lonesome....

And yet, there were reasons not to go home, even though he was not about to divulge them. "Thinking of B.," he confided to his diary, "it was plain that I could never write sweet lyrics to her, that I could never seek to rest in her. And it was again plain that I needed her vitally for this living, for this thinking that must be done in the rest of the life that is mine.... Vaguely, I see that it is not toward rest, toward home and mother that I head; it is toward motion and change."

My mother was motion and change. The advent of May had brought on an attack of spring fever ("I'm so excited I can hardly write"), making her alternately joyous and then suddenly bereft when a meeting or a party disbanded and she found herself alone. Four days later, she took a desperate step:

Saturday, May 4

Listen darling,

And listen carefully. Your last three letters have made a tremendous difference. I think I'm right now when I say "Come home".... Sell your car or just leave it and take a train and stop this nonsense. Don't stop in the south and don't stop in Chicago... I want a night letter by the end of the week. I don't want an explanation.... Decide whatever you want as long as you decide to come home. This is your chance to make good. Don't slip up on it.

B

Overbearing as this letter is, I identify with it totally. I identify with what it reveals about my mother—her powerful will; her need that refuses to be deferred; her willingness to take risks; her blindness to every signal warning her of the dangers she is courting in reckless pursuit of her desire.

My father returned home just before Memorial Day. By September their long dance was over. "*Nu*, it's done," he wrote to a male friend. "Look at the address. It's mine and Blanche's. And I'll be married sometime this week. Stop! It'll be too late for you to rush to save me. The best thing that I can say about this is that it grew. There was no explosion, no rosy sunburst. She had to have an apartment and I had to get away from the enlarged family. So, we carried over the summer into this." It was just like my father to make such a momentous passage seem a matter of convenience—escape from life with his parents.

My father thought of himself as a revolutionary. He looked forward to the day when the world would be transformed through a singular act of collective will. But when I look at these texts, what I think about is how he could not, in the course of an entire lifetime, take charge of his own fate, or alter his own character, to the smallest degree.

Even understanding this, I find it disheartening to read a diary note he made a year into the marriage:

Put it simply: I am unhappy. Have been so for a long time. Did not face it. Blanche. Is it she? Would I have done better to have stayed alone? Still alone. As never even in those days when I faced dead white walls.

Five years later, my parents were spending their vacation at a Party camp in Jewett, New York, where the conversational buzz was about the German invasion of the Soviet Union a month before. Overnight, Party members who had been denouncing the war as an "inter-impe-rialist" squabble had become advocates of America's involvement in the "anti-fascist struggle," embracing the very "militarism" they had previously attacked. My father was sitting up in bed, unable to sleep. He was composing a letter addressed to no one. In his melodramatic style, he explained, "I have none who can meet me as a friend in the darkness which grows daily deeper." My mother was in the bed beside him, unconscious of his unhappiness. Looking on her sleeping form, he reflected on how lost he was, and on his inability to break the shell of isolation that had become the normal condition of his earthly existence. He turned inward and, in ruthless introspection, identified the cause of his misery as himself:

> *Up here at camp I am heartily disliked by many people who ordinarily would be pleasant irrelevancies in a summer vacation. The signifi-cance is twofold. Subjectively, it means that I'm becoming sharp and nasty and arrogant. There's never a good reason for this. Objectively, I'm becoming useless as a political teacher, guide, organizer or what-ever the situation demands.*

It was the old problem he had described in the memo years before. Afraid of leading, he had assumed a background role, but then resented those who stepped forward: "Having set myself apart from the group, sort of pushed aside my real function as leader (by experi-ence and training) the quality turns into its opposite, that of potential distemper: from leader to arrogant punk. What a transformation!" The political situation afforded him some relief. Reading reports about the war front in Russia in the *Daily Worker*, for instance, was a welcome distraction. But, in the end, it was not enough to take his mind off himself:

> *I read hungrily the tales of Soviet heroism and the diary of that Communist in the Finnish-Soviet war. But daily enjoyment is more*

and more marred for me, as shame for my thinking and inactivity
intrudes itself and spoils the page before me.

Inner rage still consumed him. "I'd do murder, but for my background," he confessed alarmingly to the silent page. The actual
outbursts, which vented such feelings, never resulted in physical violence. But his expression would become black, and the timbre in his
voice so sharp that the pain inflicted was hardly less than if he had
actually hit you. He had become enclosed in his own darkness, where
the only ray of light was his revolutionary fantasy, now reduced to a
desperate personal quest:

> *I have come now to the single hope that I do not give way altogether*
> *before the task that has been assigned to me in the great struggle.*
> *That I can strike a good blow to the vile enemies that face us. Partic-*
> *ularly do I wish to strike one that shall not only not discredit me,*
> *and so those about me, but one that will inspire them even if only a*
> *little. I must!*

This note conveys the elements of my father's angst. It is the
unanswered cry of the adolescent: *notice me*. His friends, the revolution, life, were leaving him behind. Two years before, my birth in
a Brooklyn hospital on January 10, 1939, had made him a father. He
was thirty-five years old, still a young man. Perhaps my arrival was the
reason he felt that it was all slipping by him.

PART 2

COMING OF AGE
(1940-1956)

Little David, play on your harp
Halleloo, halleloo

—NEGRO SPIRITUAL

SUNNYSIDE

PERHAPS IF I HAD KNOWN THE CONTENTS OF MY PARENTS' SECRET file, or if they had been able to disclose to me some of these private dimensions of themselves rather than hiding behind the safety of parental walls, I would have felt closer to them and more confident of their authority in areas of the heart, a subject about which we seldom spoke. Perhaps I would have been able to draw a deeper strength from the counsel they tried to give me. Perhaps the course of my life would have turned out differently. Who can know?

The war and their marriage, now more than a decade in duration, seemed to have erased every trace of my parents' bohemian youth. Three years after my own arrival, my sister Ruth was born on February 1, 1942. One of the earliest memories I have is being wrapped in my favorite brown and red plaid blanket, to be driven with my mother to the hospital. By then, my parents had settled into a middle-class existence, outwardly following a path never too distant from their non-Party neighbors. My mother, in particular, was impelled by a powerful need to appear respectable to the community and not to give offense—to avoid a "shame for the neighbors," a homily her father had passed on to her. Typically, she had anglicized and bowdlerized it from the Yiddish—a *shanda* for the *goyim*. We attended no synagogue, and did not dress up for the Jewish Sabbath, but my mother coaxed us to look nice on Sundays, when the Catholics of the neighborhood trooped off to Mass at Saint Teresa's church on Skillman Avenue.

The decor of my parents' home was commonplace except to the eye that could spot a Gropper print or a Käthe Kollwitz etching, and understand its significance. Other clues were provided by the volumes from the Book Find Club: *Red Star Over China*, which documented the wonders of the revolution in the East, the Soviet fiction of Sholokhov and Ehrenburg, and the novels of Party writers like Shirley Graham and Howard Fast. More obvious giveaways, such as the green volumes of *The Little Lenin Library* or the red companion set of *The Works of J. V. Stalin*, were cached out of sight in a basement closet lined with shelves.

My parents' political choices were carefully hidden behind their middle-class facade, and their political opinions artfully couched in sanitized phrases. In part because they took themselves seriously as revolutionaries, they never broke a law or committed a violent act, or gave any public indication that they would. To a stranger encountering them, they were idealists and registered Democrats who did their citizen part, volunteering in tenants' councils and PTAs, and working for goals that ordinary people could understand and support. But these organizations were fronts for other, more serious purposes, serving them as recruiting grounds for the agendas they only revealed later on.

Their real politics were conducted far from view, in the neighborhood cell meetings of the Communist Party. It was in this subterranean activity that the romanticism of their youth finally got to express itself. Here they lived outside the norms of other mortals, breathed the intoxicating air of a world revolution, and plotted their impossible dreams. In the cell, they were given secret names for the day when the Party would go underground and the illegal business of the revolution begin—as they all believed it would. My mother's Party name was Ann Powers, which sounded like the heroine of a dime-store romance. In their daily routines and to all outsiders, however, they remained scrupulously conventional and law-abiding, as bourgeois and proper as anyone would expect school teachers to be.

My parents were living in an apartment house in Forest Hills when I was born, but during the following year they moved into a two-story redbrick on Bliss Street, in a neighborhood called Sunnyside Gardens—a ten-block development of English row houses in Long

Island City. The name was like an emblem of the radical fantasy they would impart to me the way other families transmitted a religious faith. Its designers were urban planners who built the Gardens in the Twenties as a model housing development for working families. The promotional flyer described it as "a garden community" and "a reproof to capitalist chaos" not "a row of houses in a block marred by varied operations of individual builders." Lewis Mumford praised it as being "framed to a human scale with opportunities for spontaneous neighborliness." The planners had grouped the row houses along streets lined with sycamore trees, arranging them in rectangles separated by hedge-lined alleys. They had set the kitchens on the off-street side, opening their back doors into small yards that abutted a commons. These lush green plots shaded by willows and mulberry trees were formed by taking forty-year easements on the private yards, whose remaining segments were separated by a path from the commons itself.

The forty-year period was a biblical term. According to the rabbinical commentaries, the Hebrews had been made to wander in the desert in order to prepare them for entry into the promised land. In that time frame, the generation raised in slavery would be replaced by another bred in freedom and thus morally able to complete the passage. It was the planners' idea that surrendering property rights to provide a safe play area for their children would bond the Sunnysiders into a permanent community. But, like many other noble designs, this one proved unworkable. By the time we moved in, fifteen years later, the residents had already put up a wire fence to preserve the lawns and keep the children out. When the easements expired a quarter of a century after that, the residents claimed their portions and closed off their lots. Fences and hedges now crisscrossed the commons, making a patchwork where once there had been an open space. Fifty years after its creation, Sunnyside was designated a Planned Community Preservation District—an unintended notice of the way history had left its utopian premise behind.

While the working-class inhabitants of Sunnyside were exercising their property rights to claim their own, the Communist Party was identifying the Gardens as a target of opportunity and moving its activists in. Among these colonists were the painters Moses and

Raphael Soyer, the educator Edwin Berry Burgum, and Lillian Hellman's secretary, Selma Wolfman, who was a close family friend. Another friend, Sol Abramson, was an editor of the *Saturday Evening Post* and then the *Daily Compass*. Their migration from Manhattan to Queens caused Sunnyside to become known in Party circles as "the maternity ward of Greenwich Village."

The original advertisements for the Sunnyside units had announced that for $475 down and $64.75 a month a family could buy a six-room house with four tons of coal in the cellar and "a mortgage that never comes due." But the offer was made during the boom years of the Twenties, and when the Depression hit, the developers were forced to renege on their promise. As the owners began foreclosing the mortgages that had gone into default, the political residents fought back. A mock funeral cortege was organized down 48th Street behind a coffin filled with mortgage papers. Eleanor Roosevelt, a director of the City Housing Corporation, which had financed the development, led the procession herself.

At the time my parents moved into the Gardens in 1940, they could have purchased the house on Bliss Street for $4,000—less than its original price. But, as radicals, they had scorned the opportunity to own property and moved in as renters instead. Seven years later, the Gardens were acquired by new owners, who decided to sell off the individual units, including our house. A Sunnyside Tenants' Association was organized to resist the sales. The Association was a front that the Party created with my mother as its secretary. It mobilized the community to oppose the evictions, posting the following warning in the window of every house that would take it:

NOTICE TO BUYERS
This house is about 20 years old.
The price is highly inflated.
INFLATION
Hurts all of us. You are being Victimized and so are we.
We have joined with our neighbors to
STOP EVICTIONS.

We will apply for the
FULL STAY
Allowed by Law:
A YEAR OR MORE.
SUNNYSIDE TENANTS' ASS'N
B. Horowitz—Sec'y

My parents and their Party friends had no real understanding of how the market economy worked. It made no impression on them that the country was in the midst of a postwar expansion, and that the baby boom had increased the demand for family housing and pushed up its value. They did not even consider that Sunnyside houses were still a bargain at $10,000, and that ownership (which they could have afforded) would benefit them, too. My parents had no respect for the property rights of the existing owners, who wanted to sell the houses and realize the returns on their investments. To my parents and their friends, property was theft; the rights of owners did not exist in any reality they recognized.

The agent for the owners met with the protesters in an effort to persuade them to be reasonable and to stop intimidating potential buyers of the Sunnyside houses. As secretary of the Tenants' Association, my mother was its spokesman at the meeting: "Since you people intend to sell these properties at an exorbitant profit to yourselves and will essentially carry out the same practices as the former owners, we shall have to resort to the same tactics as heretofore employed which have resulted in a 100% batting average to our advantage." According to the petition filed before the State Supreme Court of New York, the agent appealed to her sense of fairness: "We are all nice people. Let's try to work this out in a friendly manner." But my mother was not about to be seduced by his earnest appeal. She replied: "You'll find out that we're not such nice people when we go to work on you."

Is *this my mother?* Is this the voice of the woman who nurtured and cared for me? In her political life it was. To my mother and her comrades, politics was class war conducted by other means. The agent, whatever else he may have been, was an instrument of the hated oppressor. It was this "objective reality," and not any contingent fact that he might have been a nice person, that determined the morality according to which they would treat him. The aggression displayed by my mother reminds me of my father's letter to his Columbia instructor: In her cause she had found an arena which freed her to vent the passions that elsewhere she was unable to express.

I do not know what happened to the injunction that the owner of the Sunnyside properties sought against the Tenants' Association. But two years later, my parents' house on Bliss Street was sold and we were served with eviction papers. In a last-ditch effort to discourage the buyer, the Tenants' Association organized a picket line in front of our house. It was a memorable event for me—all those adult friends of my parents marching up and down with their signs of protest and appeal. Yet the impression it made was ultimately disturbing: to see the adults I knew helpless to control the circumstances of their lives.

When their political efforts failed, my parents made a sudden turn that was typical of the politics they had embraced, and suggested how abstract it was. Not wishing to give up a situation they found congenial and convenient, they swallowed their principles and bought another property in the Gardens, two blocks away. The house at 39-07 44th Street was an identical two-story redbrick except that the floor plan was reversed because it was on the opposite side of the street. So powerful was the real-estate boom in America that the price of the houses had nearly doubled from what they had been a mere two years before. The new house was now priced at $18,000, more than four-and-a-half times what my parents would have had to pay for it nine years earlier, when they first moved into the neighborhood.

The Sunnyside masses had failed to join the vanguard in their protest. Whereas the vision of the progressives was to abolish property once and for all, the dream of the ordinary working people who lived in the Gardens was just the opposite: to own their own Sunnyside home. This was not the only issue that divided them. The progressives had names like Abramson, Adler, Heller, and Wolfman. They were like a tiny scouting party that had infiltrated the camp of an alien tribe, vastly superior in number, who were neither intellectuals nor Communists nor Jews. They were Irish and Italian, and their church was a pillar of the anti-Communist cause. Their names were Bradshaw, Canorazzi, and O'Brien, and the institutions of their

Catholic life were visible along Skillman Avenue, where the shops of the neighborhood were also arrayed. Here were the stations of sin and redemption that marked their mortal progress—the Shamrock Bar & Grill, the Amodeo family grocery, the storefront office of the Veterans of Foreign Wars, Saint Teresa's, and the Shea Funeral Home.

There was an irony in all this that was hidden to the Sunnyside progressives, who normally were alert to historical resonances. During the war just ended, America had been the only safe haven for Jews, and this goodwill had only increased afterwards. It was possible that Jews were more accepted, and felt more at home in America at that time, than they had in the 2,000 years since the destruction of the Second Temple. Yet it was at precisely that moment that the progressive tribe of Sunnyside, by dint of their own political choices, found themselves surrounded by hostile forces as intense as their forebears had faced in the past.

As soon as Germany surrendered in 1945, the world began dividing again. In the West the democracies demobilized their armies, while in the countries the Red Army had liberated in Eastern Europe, Stalin began subverting the regimes and replacing them with his own. In East Germany, Poland, Rumania, Hungary, Bulgaria, and Czechoslovakia, new Communist dictatorships proclaimed themselves "people's democracies." Land reforms patterned on Soviet collectivization were instituted, property was confiscated, and political opponents disappeared. On a visit to the United States in 1946, Winston Churchill declared that an "Iron Curtain" had descended across Europe "from Stettin in the Baltic to Trieste in the Adriatic," locking the inhabitants in. When the Western powers began to protest the new tyrannies, military blocs formed on either side of the political divide, and by 1949—when my parents purchased their home—the Cold War had already begun.

In the West, progressives rallied to the defense of the Soviet cause. Fellow travelers of the Communist Party, like *Daily Compass* columnist I. F. Stone, justified Stalin's conquests by explaining that Eastern Europe was ruled by fascists and class oppressors. New books appeared on my parents' shelves, like *Democracy With A Tommy Gun*, which defended the takeovers as a liberation. Our progressive community supported the new dictatorships and believed that the forces of justice were triumphing over reaction in Eastern Europe, even as they believed that good had triumphed over evil in Russia itself.

Many of the existing governments in Eastern Europe were Catholic. Another book on my parents' shelf—*The Vatican* by Paul Blanshard—explained how the Catholic Church was in league with corrupt privilege and was the world's biggest landowner. The Catholic Church had rallied the reactionary forces in the Spanish Civil War, and now was playing a similar role in Eastern Europe. When the Communists seized the government of Hungary, Cardinal Josef Mindszenty took refuge in the U.S. embassy and made himself a symbol of the anti-Communist resistance. In America, Catholic politicians, and clerics like Cardinal Francis Joseph Spellman and Bishop Fulton J. Sheen, became leading spokesmen of the anti-Communist cause. The inflammatory currents of the international civil war simmered in the Sunnyside air.

My parents' middle-class propriety was in part a direct response to this hostile environment. My mother even bought a Christmas tree during the holidays, to promote the idea of our normality. But the presence of this Christian symbol so upset her friend Isaiah Heller that he would not set foot in our home during the holiday season. It was not that Isaiah was a religious Jew, but that he felt my mother's act showed disrespect for those who had died in the Holocaust. The dispute spread into the Party, and led to the creation of a *shul*, which held classes in the afternoons. It was run by Isaiah and Ben Efron, the author of a history of the Jews called *People Without a Land*. The *shul* was designed to teach us our Jewish heritage from a radical perspective, without religion.

Even the Yiddish we were taught at *shul* was a way of dividing our tribe of radicals from nonprogressive Jews. At that time, the Hebrew language was being revived in the newly created state of Israel. Yet, to progressives like my parents, Hebrew was not an instrument in the revitalization of a people, but a language of the reactionary past. At the *shul*, the Jewish festivals we celebrated were each given a political interpretation. When we performed a play about the Maccabees for *Chanukah*, it was to showcase them as revolutionaries lifting the yoke of oppression. Playing the part of Judah Maccabee and refusing to bow before a Syrian idol, I declared: *"Jews never bend the knee."* Many years later, when I attended my first Jewish service, I was surprised to discover that not only did Jews bend the knee when they *davened*, but did so with fervor.

What my parents had done in joining the Communist Party and moving to Sunnyside was to return to the ghetto. There was the same shared private language, the same hermetically sealed universe, the same dual posture revealing one face to the outer world and another to the tribe. More importantly, there was the same conviction of being marked for persecution and specially ordained, the sense of moral superiority toward the stronger and more numerous *goyim* outside. And there was the same fear of expulsion for heretical thoughts, which was the fear that riveted the chosen to the faith.

This is my own conclusion. My parents never really discussed their decision to become Communists, or the factors that motivated them, with me. It was an unnatural silence because politics was in all other respects the currency of their lives. Almost all conversation in our household was political, other than what was necessary to advance the business of daily life. Despite our disdain for religious belief, the creed we lived by was not dissimilar from that of our ancestors, the "People of the Book" who were forever analyzing the meanings hidden behind the text of life. We had our own guide to these meanings which was not the Torah and the Talmud, but Lenin and Marx. The significance of a text, the meaning of an event, the value of a friendship were evaluated on a scale calibrated to a single standard: How did they measure up to the revolutionary goal?

My father was so secretive about the organization that was central to his life, that I can only recall a single conversation with him that attempted directly to address the subject. But this was long after he had retired and put political activities aside, and he expressed himself in formulations that were so characteristically oblique, that I was never sure of what he really had said, except that the Party had treated him badly in the end. I made a similar attempt with my mother once, but she also grew nervous as we approached the forbidden terrain. In explaining why she had joined the Party, she confined herself to generalities like "injustice," and "the Depression," as though anyone who was concerned about either would naturally have joined. It was a form of evasion that was familiar to me in the talk of all my parents' political friends who hid their real agendas in abstractions that were opaque, often even to them. Their attitude toward these agendas was not unlike the Victorians' toward sex, which they could approach only through indirection. My mother's answers did not begin to confront the obvious question: Why had they chosen to become *Bolsheviks* in America? After all, this was not their only option. If their passion was injustice, why had they not joined a movement that required less wrenching of their personal lives, and did not involve an allegiance so *alien* to everything around them?

As a consequence of their decision, they became permanent conspirators in a revolutionary drama. Secrecy enveloped everything they did that was important to them. Like the agents of a secret service, they operated on a "need to know" basis, making it a rule never to discuss their real politics, to identify their associates, or to reveal their Party activities to any outsider. Even my parents' correspondence was secretive. Initials like "H" and "M," which intruded among the real names in their letters, represented Party contacts. "H," for example, was the code for Holland Roberts, whom my father had gone to see on his trip west in 1934. Although Communism was the center of my father's passionate life, he never mentioned the Party by name, but would refer to it as "the Organization" or, on rare occasions, "the Party," without specifying which party it was. In fact, I never heard my father use the word "Communist" to describe himself or his political agendas. Nor was he alone in this. All my parents' friends were Party members, but in identifying themselves to the political *goyim* they invariably used the term "progressive."

By the time I was aware of it, this secrecy had become so ingrained as to be a matter of character rather than choice. Yet the rationale for their behavior was never far from the surface. If I had asked them about it, they would have justified the secrecy by the hostile environment in which they had to advance their cause; by the punishment they believed awaited them and their associates, just for holding their progressive beliefs. They would have invoked names like Sacco and Vanzetti, Tom Mooney, and Elizabeth Gurley Flynn, martyrs of their progressive cause. A congressional committee to investigate subversive and un-American activities had been created in the Thirties, and was a permanent fixture of national life. The scent of inquisition hovered in their political air.

And yet, what else could they have expected? Even before they had really sunk roots in America's soil, they had rejected its fruits. If the faith they had embraced was not "un-American," as the committee claimed, it was certainly alien to most Americans. Their speech was salted with usages that were unfamiliar and foreign, like "Bolshevik" and "dialectic," "cadre" and "comrade." In the land of Washington and Lincoln, their heroes were Marx and Lenin; in democratic America, their goal was to establish a "dictatorship of the proletariat." Instead of being grateful to a nation that had provided them with economic opportunity and refuge, they wanted to overthrow its governing institutions and replace them with a Soviet state.

As if this threat was not enough to create anxiety in the world outside their political ghetto, my parents and their comrades had also given their hearts to a foreign power. The Soviet Union was the land of their dreams, and they had pledged their allegiance to its political future. It was not my parents' idealism that elicited fear and provoked hostility from the *goyim*. It was their hostility toward the *goyim*, and indeed everything the *goyim* held dear, that incited the hostility back.

Of course, if my parents were right and America was as unjust as they were convinced it was, if its institutions could be changed only by violent means, if Marxism was the map of a rational future—then their persecution *was* inevitable, and they really had no choice. But my parents were incapable of entertaining the alternate possibility: that they were wrong about each of these points; that they could have lived different lives and still made moral stands; that the politics they had chosen was both a provocation and a threat. To the end of their days, they remained incapable of real self-reflection about the radical commitments that had defined their lives. In this they were typical among the inhabitants of the progressive ghetto, who believed in their truth with a ferociousness that left no room for dissent.

What was my own choice? In the beginning, I hardly had one. I understood early that my parents' political religion was really the center of their moral life. This meant—without their necessarily intending it—that the condition of their parental love was that I embrace their political faith. I would make my choices only later, after I had separated myself from them and set out on the path that every son takes—to become a person in his own right.

IDOLS

FREUD, THE GEOGRAPHER OF MEMORY, BELIEVED THE PAST WE FORGET is the one that counts. But what about the past we remember? The incidence of memory is like the light from dead stars whose influence lingers long after the events themselves. Would these fragments of our youth continue in the imagination if they were no longer important? And would we even remember them if they did not shape, in some luminous way, the contours of our souls?

When I was a year and a half old, probably as soon as I was able to walk and speak, my parents enrolled me in the Sunnyside Progressive School. It was a Party creation, housed in a three-story brick building located at the point where 47th Street sloped up to meet Queens Boulevard. Two long flights of stairs led up to the nursery level, whose classrooms had brightly colored walls, and painted blocks big enough to sit on, and a large wooden slide. I spent every weekday from 9 to 5 within these walls so that my mother could return to work. I don't know how much her decision owed to the necessity of supporting my father's parents, and how much to progressive ideas. But I do know that my mother had second thoughts about it, as she did with her decision not to breast-feed my sister and me. By that time it was too late to do anything about either. We never discussed the subject, but she said to my wife once, when we were parents ourselves: "The Left was wrong about how to raise children."

My mother suffered more from our premature separation than I did, at least judging from our conversations. Even in her eighties she would still occasionally voice feelings about her inadequacy as a parent. These apologies were discomforting to me, because in my eyes she had done well enough. I did not feel handicapped by some deficit in parental attention. Yet, who am I to judge myself in this matter? By leaving me in an all-day nursery and then going out every night to political meetings (as they did), my parents sent signals that may still be registering. I can remember only one time when their departure seemed traumatic. On that occasion I sobbed hysterically after they left, and locked myself in the bathroom until the babysitter persuaded me to come out. After that, the nights without my parents fell into a routine, and my adjustment, as far as I could or can tell, was normal.

Perhaps because of this accommodation, my mother expressed her parental guilt almost exclusively toward my sister, Ruth, who was unhappy at her preschools and periodically had to be taken out of them. My sister's childhood was crossed with episodes of emotional distress, and my mother's later introspection was without doubt partly inspired by Ruthie's willingness to draw attention to her unhappiness. Even as an adult, Ruth continued to express forcefully her feelings over what she felt was my mother's emotional denial. This roiled my sibling blood, but then I didn't feel myself the victim of emotional abuse in the way my sister did. Perhaps a Freudian would say I repressed it.

The creation of the Sunnyside Progressive School reflected the desire of its creators to shape human destinies. But my life there was made problematic by the permissive atmosphere its mission required: Another four-year-old, Tommy Finley, had taken immediate possession of the freedom it afforded. In order to play, we had to get Finley's approval and become a member of his "gang." If he didn't like something we had done, or if the whim merely struck him, he would announce "You're out!" and we would find ourselves irretrievably alone. It was like being sentenced to stand in the corner all day, a punishment our teachers would never have countenanced. When I recalled this memory to my mother, she sighed as if to say "What else could you expect from that school?" It was yet another of her second thoughts.

I hardly remember more than a few incidents from these preschool days, but I have a vivid recollection of the time I was purged from

Finley's gang. We were building an apartment house with wooden blocks, and as I reached through the window to right a toppled figurine, my elbow knocked others over. I can still feel the panic as I awaited the dread edict that would seal my fate. Not everyone reacted to the Finley terror in so abject a fashion: My two closest friends were, inexplicably, without fear. Danny Wolfman's little frame had grown too fast to coordinate its moving parts and, as a result, he was a constant infractor of the Finley code. This seemed to have accustomed him to his punishment and the solitude it entailed, which effectively put him beyond the tyrant's reach. Michael Colloms was a somewhat morose single child and a physical match for Finley. He established himself not as a rival, but as an independent force, as though he disdained the system itself. I admired them both for their power to resist the common lot, and was pained by my inability to muster the courage to either stand up for them or follow their example.

In retrospect my life at the Sunnyside Progressive School was interesting as an omen. The school had been designed by our parents to start us off early on the road to a new world, but we had acted out a Lord of the Flies scenario reflecting the immutable state of our nature instead.

When I was five, I entered kindergarten in public school, where my teacher was Miss Olha, a tall, blonde woman, who set Friday afternoons aside for group singing. After the victory over Hitler, racial tolerance had become a civic watchword, the focus of a national campaign of social uplift. Several of the songs we sang reflected these adult concerns: "Oh, the peach pit said to the apple core/The color of our skin doesn't matter anymore." Since Jews had been the primary victims of Nazi persecution, another explained: "Though you pray on Saturdays or Sundays/It is always music to His ears." When Miss Olha asked us for our favorite song at one of these sessions, I raised my hand and said, "The Pledge of Allegiance." There was a pause, during which Danny leaned over and whispered, "The Pledge of Allegiance is not a song." I'm not exactly sure what to make of this episode. But I can still feel the tremor of excitement elicited by the words and justice for all, and the deep attraction of the idea of allegiance to the flag of the United States.

While the idea of justice seemed to move me in the abstract, there was a family form of it that I was already finding onerous. This was my parents' sense that some principle of equality, as between my sister and myself, should be invoked to infringe my bedtime privilege. Despite the three years' age difference, my sister was allowed to stay up as late as I was. When I complained, my parents offered a compromise: If I was prepared to humble myself by sneaking out of bed without detection, I could reclaim my prerogative. Why did they decide on this unfair arrangement? My mother's guilt toward my sister was one probable cause. As the aggressive and achieving child, I was the focus of too much attention. My sister was volatile and sensitive, and often unhappy. Perhaps as progressive parents they felt it necessary to equal out all disparities. There was also a house alert for the vice of "male chauvinism," and it seemed inevitable that my mother—with my father dutifully following—should assume a protective attitude toward my female sibling, and that I should be expected to cooperate.

I precociously assumed other responsibilities of maturity as well and, at the age of 10, undertook my first political project. It was an attempt to change my immediate world. The sandlots alongside the Long Island Rail Road tracks, which ran by 39th Avenue, provided an arena for our neighborhood baseball games and other adventures. In the afternoons and on the weekends we congregated behind the fences and arranged our makeshift bases and diamonds, and roamed the "Sherwood Forest" on the other side of the railroad bridge. We had to conceal these activities from our parents, who were fearful of the dangers since one teenager had already been killed by a train. One of the few times my father punished me physically was when he caught me behind the railroad fence. A sharp clip to the back of the head greeted me as I came guiltily up to him. Perhaps it was this knock that gave me the idea of drawing up a petition to the city to build a park on a vacant lot on 43rd Street. I composed the demand on notebook paper, and tied the pages together with a string:

Dear Mayor,

We 46, 45, and 44th Street children wish you would do something about a park being built or a play-street for us. When we play hockey, the people chase us because: Somebody works at night and is trying to sleep or the baby is sleeping or sick. When we play

football or baseball, the people are afraid of broken windows. We
know all about the Sunnyside Park [on 48th Street]. It is crowded
with, 50, 49, 48, 47th Street children. The schoolyard of P.S. 150
is crowded with, 43, 42, 41, 40th Street children, will you help us?

I gathered signatures door-to-door, but never sent the petition to
anyone. The praise I received for my efforts was payoff enough, and
not too many years later the city built a park on the spot.

I did not receive instruction in the Marxist catechism from either of
my parents, although when I asked questions about "current events"
the answers always came with a preface encompassing the progressive world view. The view itself, however, was transmitted far more
effectively through a kind of osmosis rather than directly by homily
and lecture. My instruction was in the environment I moved in and
the air I breathed—the headlines in the *Daily Worker* carefully folded
under the *New York Times;* the titles of the political books arrayed on
the shelves (*Stalingrad, Scottsboro Boy, The Plot Against the Peace);* and
the adult concerns that surfaced in my parents' conversations with
friends. It emanated from festivities like a benefit for Spanish Civil War
vets, which would elicit simple explanations of the cause, and from the
epithets my father hurled at the "ruling class" enemy—*sonofabitch, hyp-
ocrite, bastard*—which, in a backhanded way, added up to a social creed.

To live up to my parents' ideals, I knew I had to take on responsibilities in the larger world. My school, P.S. 150, provided a microcosm.
Surveying my classmates, I imagined I could see the inequalities of
their future estates. I was only in the fifth grade, but the natural
hierarchy of the schoolyard already weighed on my socialist conscience—the gifts of beauty and grace and physical prowess that
seemed so unevenly distributed; the disparity that marked intelligence as we vied for classroom grades. It seemed unjust that some,
like myself, should excel, while others fell behind. I attributed my own
success to the fact that my parents were teachers and gave me help,
while the failure of others was due to the lack of such privilege. The
remedies I devised for these injustices were clichés of our progressive
culture. Physical ability was an accident of nature, emphasized too
much in a society "distorted" by competition. In the world to come,

athletics would be a recreational pastime rather than a contest, and everybody would be a winner. Likewise, beauty could be seen as a social myth, exterior to the individual, its standards shaped by the brainwashing influences of the commercial market. In our future, the standard would be based on inner qualities that would not leave anybody out. As a progressive I yearned for a *monde ideal*, where the True, the Good, and the Beautiful would be one.

Ponderous though they might seem for a fifth-grader, these ideas were indeed mine. Intelligence presented the thorniest problem, since it appeared to be inseparable from the self. But if one believed in the possibility of justice, and the shaping power of social forces, as I had been taught, unequal knowledge could be redressed by proper attention, opportunity, and hard work. In my developing political imagination, the schoolyard was full of mute, inglorious Miltons, deprived of their chances for achievement by a system that neglected or stunted them because it was concerned about profit alone. Socialism would provide the answer, leveling the playing field and bringing victory to all. As a result of the Marxist ideas I had already absorbed, I was thus able by the age of 11 to dispose of the enduring pathologies of our social condition.

At some deeper and more psychological level, however, I had also embraced an idea that contradicted these earnest conclusions. There was a way in which my own experience seemed to provide a paradigm of justice: If you worked hard and did right, you were rewarded. My parents' protectiveness added an even more powerful assumption: Conflicts could be referred to a wiser authority, and thereby resolved. It is a paradox to me that, well into adulthood, I acted regularly on these optimistic expectations in the areas that affected me personally. Rather than be suspicious toward others, or prepare for injustice (as Marxism would have predicted), I was trusting to the point of recklessness. As a result, I was constantly blindsided by events, until pain and disappointment eventually confronted me with our common fate: There is no inevitable reward for our virtues, and no authority to whom we can safely appeal.

Every summer my parents rented a vacation cottage in Hampton Bays, which was a stop after Riverhead on the Long Island Rail

Road. It was not really a "Hampton" in the upscale sense—neither a community of artists nor an enclave of the wealthy, like East Hampton and Southampton. It was more a social replica of Sunnyside, where a working-class population of Rileys, Cassinas, and Smiths had been colonized by our contingent of Communist Jews. Our first summer was in 1945, when a huge block party was held in the middle of town to celebrate V-J Day and the end of World War II. The war had provided the romance of my childhood, and fragments of it were visible in the Sunnyside streets. There were the soldiers in their khakis, marching down 39th Avenue, singing:

> The WACS and WAVES are winning this war,
> So what the hell are we fighting for?
> Hinkey-Dinkey Parlez-Vous ...

There were the civil-defense drills on 47th Street, at which air-raid wardens in metal helmets and Red Cross arm bands loaded the "wounded" on stretchers from apartment houses that had been "bombed." There were the squadrons of B-29s, overhead after the invasion of Normandy, which my father explained were on their way to liberate Europe. And now it was over.

In these summers, my father and I would go biking alone. Riding was a solitary recreation, free of the domestic complications that often befuddled and frustrated him. It was the only sport—besides occasional swims, when sometimes we would stand 20 feet apart and then dive down to meet and kiss underwater—that he engaged in with me. The long rides through the Shinnecock hills to Southampton, or sometimes even all the way to Water Mill and Sag Harbor, were a source of both pride in the achievement and of pleasure in being with him. We didn't talk much, except when we camped in some vacant field and broke out the bag lunches we had taken along. We would ride down to the docks on the inland bays and he would identify the different vessels, cat boats and sloops and yawls, as we examined the fishermen's catches. I had the sense that he enjoyed being with me, too—the father in command of the journey, his son's teacher and guide on the open road.

These male bondings and retreats proved a sore spot for my mother. Often, when she was taking up the cudgels for my sister over some family conflict, she would inexplicably add this to the list of her complaints, as though Ruthie had been excluded from the trips by a decision of the men. But my mother also had a bike and, when I was very young, she and my father would ride with both of us kids on seats fitted on the crossbars. For whatever reason, my mother had stopped riding, and I don't remember her taking the time to teach my sister, or either of them proposing to go on the trips we took. I sensed, even then, that there was something deeper in her complaints than the issue she raised.

In the conflicts between my parents, my mother was the one who seemed to prevail. While my father's anger was fierce, and often decided a skirmish, he lacked the staying power to win the war. When my mother unleashed her own anger, my father would sink into a smoldering silence and leave the house, disappearing into the neighborhood to lick his wounds. Hours later he would return contrite, and petition for forgiveness. Because the outcome of these battles was foreknown, they were often unnecessary. The near certainty of my father's defeats allowed my mother to set the guidelines for our family existence.

Even though my mother occupied the center of our practical life, my father retained an important authority in my imagination. This derived in part from his ability to provide lucid explanations of the world, the power of money, the evils of capitalism, and other ideas that seemed important to me. Not all his teachings survived scrutiny, however. For example, he once posed the question as to why more people were in error than found their way to the truth. His answer: There were many ways to be wrong, but only one way to be right. Along with this didactic talent, he had a manifest courage that provided me with feelings of security and confidence throughout my life. On one memorable occasion, we were walking together on the beach at Shinnecock Bay when we saw a crowd gathered at the water's edge. Two dogs were locked in combat, their snarls piercing the air with a terrifying sound. An aging white hound was getting the worst of the battle. By the time we came up to the onlookers, the other dog had already closed his teeth on the hound's throat and was slowly strangling him while the crowd, transfixed by the spectacle, waited for the end. Suddenly, my father strode into the circle of fury and grabbed both dogs by the scruffs of their necks, to yank them apart. As the jaws unlocked the victim bolted to freedom, but the conqueror, cheated of victory, sank his liberated teeth into my father's arm. The wound was deep, and we had to take him to the hospital for a tetanus shot. On the way, my mother fretted, allowing a tone to enter her voice as though he were a child who had to be constantly watched or get into trouble. These two images of my father—powerful, heroic, but also childlike, beaten—I could never sort out.

In the summer of 1947, my father could be with us only on week-ends in Hampton Bays. During the week he was in New York for radium treatments for the tongue cancer he had developed from smoking. About this time, he was overtaken by another form of disturbance. While swimming in Peconic Bay, he suddenly was seized with the fear that he would never get back to shore. Soon after, he developed a phobia of enclosed places so intense that he could no longer go down into the subway. When the fall came, he had to take the bus to Manhattan to get himself to work. The cancer cleared up after the treatment, leaving no trace of the disease, and eventually he was able to go down into the subways again. But the sense of fragility that the experience imprinted on his psyche never left him.

During the next summer a polio epidemic struck, and one of my friends was taken by ambulance to the city for treatment. Fear of the contagion introduced restrictions on my freedom. My mother was always worrying that I would get a chill, so we didn't go to movie theaters or public swimming pools which the government closed while the epidemic was raging. It was not quite as restrictive, though, as when I was three and was quarantined for several weeks with scarlet fever. I felt like a little monarch then, attended in my chamber by both my mother and a nurse.

Looking back, I see that there is a way in which my entire youth was a form of quarantine. There was the protective environment of our political community itself, a kind of hospital of the soul. We were embattled, surrounded by enemies, and this made the members of our tribe like family. There was instant recognition by others who shared our values and political commitments, and exaggerated estrangement on the part of those who did not. I was a sociable youngster, good at athletics and quick to make friends, but I was always separated by an invisible wall from the world of my peers. Even before I became close to a playmate, I knew that unless his family shared our politics (and the risks that accompanied them), we would always be strangers. It was not just that a whole area of my life had to be kept secret, but also that, if the wall were ever breached, I knew the friendship would end.

I lived in two worlds. One was filled with the currency of the common culture—favorite radio programs like *The Lone Ranger*, *Captain Midnight*, and *Ozzie & Harriet*, and on the exciting new medium of television shows like The *Texaco Star Theater*, *The Honeymooners*, and Ed Sullivan's variety spectacular. On Saturdays we went to the Bliss Theater, where my imagination was fired by cinema idols like Marlon Brando and John Wayne. In the "Movietone News" there were shots of my sports heroes in action: Joe Louis, Glenn Davis, and Doc Blanchard, and—towering over them all—the Yankee Clipper, Joe DiMaggio. But I had another, secret world that was lit by different stars, the likes of whom none of my friends outside our progressive circle had ever heard of. Among them were the folk singers Pete Seeger and Martha Schlamme, the writers Albert Maltz and Howard Fast, the Communist leader Elizabeth Gurley Flynn (an enormous woman who came to Sunnyside and shook my hand in the Abramsons' living room), and the politician Vito Marcantonio, who stamped his foot and yelled into the microphone at a rally I attended. Above them all was the enduring hero of my political youth, Paul Robeson, the Negro singer whose sonorous bass was like a great bell that made your bones resonate with its sound.

When this physically grand person appeared at the progressive rallies I went to, a palpable reverence filled the air. As he entered the room, a hush stilled the audience, virtually all white, which rose as one and began to clap rhythmically, Soviet style, to pay homage to the great man. When the Robeson voice boomed "*Go down, Moses*" and summoned the Hebrew leader to tell old pharaoh to "*Let my people go*," it was as if he was issuing a summons to free us all. Its sound filled every bosom in the room with a glow of satisfaction, as though his presence confirmed our truth.

In our political catechism, the suffering of the Negro people was always a central image. The crime against the Negro was like an American crucifixion, and we constantly used it to pierce the veil of American benevolence, revealing the inequality and oppression underneath. Both my parents stayed after school to conduct "extra-curricular" Negro History and Culture clubs for their students—my father at Seward Park on the Lower East Side, my mother at Girls' High in the Bedford-Stuyvesant section of Brooklyn. My mother's files contain an old note of commendation she received when her club put on a play about the "underground railway" and Harriet Tubman. These hidden heroes of "the struggle" supplied the material of my fantasy life. When my father and I took our neighborhood walks, he would explain to me how the streets were named for real-estate magnates and businessmen, and how, after the revolution, they would be renamed. I sensed there was something off in his claim, since I knew that many street names were those of presidents and military figures. But I took up the idea anyway, and began imagining revolutionary names that would replace the old. I began my list with Harriet Tubman, Frederick Douglass, and Paul Robeson.

My only real contact with Negroes, however, was with our housekeeper, Henriether Smith, one of seventeen children from a Tennessee sharecropper's family. She lived with us and took care of us when my parents were at work. My parents tried to help her get ahead by correcting her spelling and sending her to night school, where she learned how to read and write. Henriether was a devout Jehovah's Witness, and she took me once to a religious rally at Yankee Stadium. On another occasion my grandfather Sam engaged her in an argument about God and, to my great distress, ridiculed her religious beliefs. But Henriether just laughed, confident that he was the one who would eventually regret it. Henriether was a reserved, kind person who never had an angry word for us. When I married, she gave me a diamond ring as a present.

My instruction in the history of the Negro struggle included reading such books from my parents' shelves as Howard Fast's *Freedom Road*, and an account of the Scottsboro Boys, who had been falsely convicted of raping two white women, and whose case the Party had taken up. Another was *We Charge Genocide*, which the Party had published through one of its fronts, the Civil Rights Congress, and which contained a petition to the United Nations condemning America's "genocide" against Negroes. Paul Robeson had written the introduction, and the text was illustrated with a famous photograph—which I could hardly bring myself to look at—of Negroes being lynched by smiling whites. It was part of the Party's effort to help the Soviet Union by suggesting that the United States was like Nazi Germany.

In the pages of the *Daily Worker* there were always reports of injustices to Negroes that only our progressive community seemed to care about. Often these were Negro males charged with felonies the Party claimed they did not commit. These cases were referred to by collective names like "The Martinsville Seven" or the "The Trenton Six." In all these cases the issue of guilt remained unclear, but for us the general condition of racial injustice was enough to draw the appropriate conclusions. Linking these cases to the Cold War was a favorite Party strategy. After the formation of the NATO alliance, Robeson told news reporters that Negroes wouldn't fight if the United States found itself at war with the Soviet Union. After Robeson's statement, there was a riot at a concert he gave in Peekskill, New York. Sugar Ray Robinson, the middleweight boxing champion and a hero of my other world, told the press he would punch Robeson in the mouth if he met him. The incident left me feeling embarrassed for Sugar Ray.

After the Russian Revolution of 1905, the philosopher Nicholas Berdyaev analyzed Communism as a form of idolatry in a way that proved to be prophetic. Berdyaev traced the origins of what he called the Marxist "heresy" back to the tower of Babel. In that story, people had tried to achieve their own redemption—without a transcendent God—by building a ladder to heaven. Communists had a similar ambition. They had projected onto fallible beings godlike powers that would enable them to overcome their human fate. In doing so, Berdyaev warned, the Communists had created demons they would not be able to control.

Robeson's presence as a god in our midst seems prophetic to me now. In my radical generation, blacks would replace the proletariat in our imaginations as the Chosen People who were going to lead the rest of us to the Promised Land.

I first became aware of politics, in the ordinary sense, during the presidential election of 1948. My parents and their friends belonged to the Democratic Party and had voted for Roosevelt. It was what they called their "mass work"—going to where the people were, in order to lead them to something better. This had been the Party line since the days of the Popular Front, when, under orders from Moscow, the comrades abandoned their "ultraleft" position and stopped calling Roosevelt a fascist. "Communism is twentieth-century Americanism," the Party leader Earl Browder had said, promoting the spirit of cooperation during the war against Hitler. But the postwar conflict over Eastern Europe had changed all that. William Z. Foster had replaced Browder, and had summoned progressives to an all-out resistance to "fascist America."

As the election of 1948 approached, the Democrats split into three factions. On the right, the Southern Dixiecrats were angry at Truman's support for civil rights, and formed a new party behind the candidacy of Gov. Strom Thurmond. On the left, the Communists were upset with the Truman Doctrine, which promised support for "free peoples" who were resisting Stalin's conquest of Eastern Europe. They regarded Truman as a "warmonger" and formed the Progressive Party to oppose him behind the candidacy of Henry Wallace. The fact that Truman was a strong proponent of civil rights had been eclipsed in their eyes by his anti-Communist policies. Their allegiance to the Soviet Union took precedence over their concern for anything else.

That spring, I marched with my parents in the May Day Parade, which was organized by the Communist Party. In those days, the women wore dresses to political demonstrations and the men wore suits, carrying their jackets in the early summer heat. Our section marched behind a huge banner that said "New York City Teachers Union," and we chanted on cue:

> One, two, three, four,
> We don't want another war.
> Five, six, seven, eight,
> Win with Wallace in '48.

Along the sidewalks of Eighth Avenue, curious onlookers gathered behind gray police barriers with "N.Y.P.D" stenciled on them in black. Every now and then, I glanced warily at the crowds, encouraged when a few showed their support with applause. As our ranks approached

23rd Street, a group of teenagers in T-shirts and jeans were hanging over the barriers and chanting back:

Down with the Communists
Up with the Irish!

Forcing my eyes in their direction, I looked to see if there was anyone from my neighborhood among them. But there were only strange, jeering faces. My whole being wanted to shout, "We're doing this for *you!*" But my voice died in my throat. The memory has remained with me ever since as a symbol of the permanent alienation of progressives like myself who set themselves up as the people's redeemers.

Our relocation to 44th Street had been a move into enemy territory. The 44th Street Cardinals were rivals we played in stick ball and roller hockey. On Halloween night, they raided our block, carrying flour-filled socks which they used to pummel us if we were caught. I was fearful at first, but they seemed to accept me, and even allowed me to become a Cardinal. The star of the team was a black-eyed Greek named Pauly Vlachos, our cleanup batter and idol. Pauly had six younger brothers and sisters, and at Christmastime I took the allowance money I had saved, and bought each of them a present. But when I appeared at their house up the street, my arms loaded with wrappings and ribbons, they just looked puzzled—and there was no present from them to me.

In 1949, the New York Yankees were in a tight pennant race with the Boston Red Sox. With two games left in the season and the race still undecided, Joe DiMaggio was going to be honored with his own Day. The 44th Street Cardinals had planned to go to the game, and arranged to meet at Pauly's house at 7:15 in the morning. But when I arrived at the appointed time, one of Pauly's little brothers opened the door and, with that same quizzical look I had encountered at Christmas, told me they had already left.

Yankee Stadium was a long way from Sunnyside. I wasn't even sure how to get there. I had never ridden to Manhattan by myself on the subway, let alone to the Bronx. Asking my way of strangers, I took the IRT to Grand Central and then changed trains for the Jerome Avenue

Express. I arrived at the Stadium at 8:30 A.M., more than five hours before game time. There already were large crowds lining up to get in, but Pauly and the Cardinals were nowhere to be seen. I bought a ticket for $1.25 for the lower right-field stands, behind where the Yankee outfielder Hank Bauer would play, and sat myself down. Around 1 o'clock the Yankee Clipper appeared at home plate. He made a speech, and received a big car and other gifts. Then the players took the field and the Red Sox' Ted Williams hit a home run. But the day finally belonged to the Yankees, and I went home to happily report their victory to my mother. I was too embarrassed, though, to tell her what had happened that morning.

I couldn't talk to my father at all about Joe DiMaggio Day. Professional baseball, he had explained to me, was a form of capitalist exploitation, an elaborate scam to sell Wheaties as "The Breakfast of Champions," and other products. His disapproval made the game a guilty pleasure, although my mother's solicitous eye kept his censure in check. Rather than being eccentric, my father's attitude was typical, a fact I was able to confirm when I read *The Book of Daniel*, E. L. Doctorow's novel about the Rosenbergs. In Doctorow's book, the Rosenberg father attempts to teach his son, who is a Dodger fan, the same lesson about Wheaties and baseball as my father taught me. Later, the father is arrested for attempting to steal the secrets of the atomic bomb, and sentenced to death. His son Daniel visits him in Sing Sing. When the two are alone together, the father tries to make contact with his son by talking about the Dodgers. But the boy perceives the sudden interest to be artificial, and the ploy backfires. Politics creates a wall between them.

The Ethel Rosenberg character in Doctorow's novel is like my mother, in taking a softer view of her son's interest in sports. But her attitude is determined by her politics as well. She approves of the Dodgers because in 1947 they were the first team to break the color barrier by hiring Jackie Robinson to play second base. Robinson's first season was also the year I became a baseball fan. That fall, the kids on the block brought their radios out to listen to the World Series between the Dodgers and the Yankees. Just about everyone in the neighborhood was a Yankee fan—and when the Dodgers' Cookie Lavagetto broke up Bill Bevins' no-hitter in the fourth game, the passions were so contagious that I began rooting for the Bronx Bombers, too. But baseball was also political and, without realizing it, I had violated an important code. Once the Dodgers hired Robinson, no conscientious progressive could be a Yankee fan. The Yankees were the ruling class of baseball: They were lily-white and rich, and they always won. To root for the Yankees was to betray a lack of social consciousness that was unthinkable for people like us. My new allegiance had to remain an uncomfortable secret.

But it was in retrospect that this event had its most lasting impact. Long after, I told my mother what had really happened on Joe DiMaggio Day—how my Cardinal teammates had lied to me and left me behind. As usual, she was not the least surprised. She reminded me of the balls and bats I had loaned the team that had been "lost" and never returned. Now she told me they were not lost, and revealed the truth about other incidents as well. The team shirt I had to buy had been given free to the other Cardinals, paid for from the monies we had all raised selling raffle tickets door-to-door. My teammates were anti-Semites. My mother had protected me from this knowledge, and my own blindness had done the rest. My mother had kept this secret as she kept all others, with the best of intentions. But when she told me this as an adult, I felt more betrayed by her than by them.

Every morning, my father sat down at our dining room table, a cup of coffee and a stash of Uneeda biscuits within close reach, to read the *New York Times*. It was his most observed ritual, but the meaning of his devotion was still a mystery to me. Weren't the *Daily Worker* and other progressive papers, like the *National Guardian*, sufficient to determine what was going on? Yet I attempted to follow his example, and struggled to read the *Times* myself, gaining a currency with the headlines that made me want to know more. During the election campaign of 1948, my fifth-grade teacher set up a debate over the presidential candidates. Our class was mainly Jewish and also liberal. I volunteered to speak for Wallace, whom the overwhelming majority supported, while Danny Wolfman agreed to represent the Republican, Tom Dewey, since no one else would. Nobody volunteered to speak for the Dixiecrat, Strom Thurmond. The day before the debate, I sought out my parents, note pad in hand, and asked them to help me with my speech. They were in their bedroom, dressing for a political meeting. As they outlined for me the Progressive Party platform, its points seemed as simple and inevitable as the instructions they gave to be truthful and fair, and to clean up after myself. *We don't want another war.* Who could argue with that? If only the people were allowed to know the truth.

Like my other political lessons, this one reflected the core sense our community had of its political mission: *The world is cursed by ignorance, and the task of progressives like us is to set everybody right.* It was not too different from the liberal view that inspired the social agendas of P.S. 150. And the Hollywood films my parents took me to, like *Gentleman's Agreement* and *Home of the Brave*, promoted the same ideas. My personal favorite was *The Boy with Green Hair*, starring Dean Stockwell and Pat O'Brien. It was about an orphanage kid, played by Stockwell, whose hair turns bright green overnight, which makes him a target of his adolescent peers. In a futile effort to escape his tormentors, Stockwell shaves his head. A kindly priest (Pat O'Brien) comforts him and tells him that surface differences don't matter, except to the ignorant. Stockwell takes courage from this sermon, and decides to grow his hair back—green.

The moral of these progressive lessons seemed to be always the same: *Evil is the failure to understand.* And, of course, from our point of view it was. We were badly misunderstood. Terrible hatreds were directed at us because we were falsely perceived as spies, traitors, and defenders of tyranny; fifth-column supporters of the enemy camp. Whereas we were really progressives, friends of Negroes and the poor, partisans of peace, and patriots of a future America in which there would truly be justice for all.

From the moment 1 was given the election talk in my parents' bedroom, their political cause became my passion. It occupied my fantasies in the way that winning the World Series or marrying Rita Hayworth occupied the daydreams of my peers. 1 can remember walking in solitude on the ocean beach in Hampton Bays, in the summer of 1949. The sandpipers were running up from the foam and then following it down, as 1 walked along preoccupied with a speech 1 was preparing in my head to make to President Truman. It was a long speech, and 1 went over it again and again in order to memorize it. In

the speech, I explained to the Commander-in-Chief the misunder-
standings that had led to present world problems, beginning with the
failure of officials like him to see that the Soviet Union was no threat,
but a nation interested only in peace. Wall Street capitalists, ruled by
the profit motive, were the only people who could have an interest
in war, and were responsible for the misunderstanding. After this
discourse on international politics, I went over the progressive litany
of racial and social injustices in America. It was an elaborate appeal,
and I prepared it with a solemnity appropriate to the belief that at
any moment I might be presented with an opportunity to confront
Truman and persuade him of its merits.

I was just 10 years old, but I thought of myself as someone who
could lecture the President of the United States on the difference
between right and wrong, and thus change the course of history. I
was just starting out in life, yet was already suspended so high above
everyone else, was there anything I could do but fall?

LOYALTIES

As the rifts of the Cold War deepened, it became more and more difficult for me to straddle the two worlds of my childhood. There was some relief in the fact that the members of the 44th Street Cardinals went to parochial schools while their parents read the tabloids and moved in separate social circles from mine. But my public schoolmates, particularly the Jews among them, were not so safely segregated. Some of their parents were "social democrats" who had been under attack from progressives like mine. Their families read the *New York Times*, and when my father's name appeared in its news section, in 1952, as one of a group of teachers who had been suspended for not answering questions about their political allegiance, the secret world I inhabited was threatened with exposure.

But the actual event proved anticlimactic. Perhaps the issues were too overwhelming or too obscure for adolescents to handle. As a result a strange decorum prevailed, and the subject of my father's case was never directly confronted. Occasionally, however, a male classmate would accost me when we were alone, and offer a provocation ("Why don't you go to Russia?"), forcing me to fight to defend both honor and self. It occurred to me long afterward that the question was not altogether unreasonable. But it was not really put as a question. It was more like a threat to expel me from the gang. "Because I love my country!" I would yell back, lunging at my persecutor and pounding him with my fists.

Even within the borders of our own camp, the sharpening tensions of the Cold War created new burdens for me. One of our adolescent antics was shoplifting from Woolworth's on the way home from school. The items we pilfered were ridiculous knickknacks, like stopper chains for the tub. It was the *risk* that inspired us. One afternoon we were examining our take when Richard Efron's father poked his head inquiringly through the bedroom doorway. It was embarrassing to be caught with stolen stopper chains by Ben Efron, whose gentle, scholarly face, framed with wisps of gray hair, darkened as his lecture began: "I understand that boys will be boys, and you are good boys and I know you didn't mean any harm by this. But you two young men do not have the luxury of other children your age. Unlike their parents, yours have dedicated themselves to an important struggle, to make the world a better place for everyone. Because of your parents' choices, there are people who would like to hurt them, and would not stop at using you to hurt them. Especially you, David. That's why you have to set a better example than other boys your age. That is your special burden."

Until Ben Efron singled me out, I hadn't thought much about my father's situation. My parents had hardly discussed it with me. They hid so many things that I just accepted the blank spaces as normal, and became complicit in their denials. I felt resentful toward this "special burden" that I had been singled out for—and, at the same time, guilt at my unworthy reaction.

All the time his father was talking, Richard said nothing. (Richard *never* said much about politics.) Shortly afterward, the Efrons moved away from Sunnyside, and I lost track of him completely. But I heard a strange story from friends, later on: When Richard graduated from college, he changed his name and disappeared. For twenty years he didn't contact his parents, and no one knew whether he was alive or dead. Then he reappeared, and it turned out that he had joined the Navy and was engaged in some kind of military work that required high-level clearance. He had disappeared and changed his name because he didn't want his father's politics to interfere with his career. I always wondered how Ben dealt with *his* special burden.

For years my parents and their friends had been playing a cat-and-mouse game with their political enemies, and now they were being made to pay the price. They had postured as pacifists and then as anti-fascists in the Thirties, but then opposed the fight against Hitler as "an imperialist war" after Stalin made his pact with the devil. After Russia was attacked, they made *another* about-face. Becoming super-patriots, they turned on their former political friends who failed, in their eyes, to support America's war effort with sufficient zeal. When union leaders such as John L. Lewis refused to take a "no-strike" pledge, they accused them of "dividing the home front," of being "pro-Nazi" and "traitors." Negro leaders who organized demonstrations for civil rights, like A. Philip Randolph, were the targets of similar abuse. At the same time, my parents and their friends continued to present themselves to the public as Democrats and progressives, and nothing more than that.

Now that the war was over, the new conflict was with Russia, and *they* had become the targets of the patriotic crowd. Once again they had reversed themselves in a way that left them looking hypocritical and foolish: Having staunchly supported democracy during the war, they had become apologists for the new dictatorships that Stalin was creating in Eastern Europe. The old clamor from the political right about the danger on the left began to look plausible to liberals, too. And there were individual scores to settle. The union leaders, whom they had smeared during the war, now saw a chance to pay their tormentors back. When the Communist Party opposed the Marshall Plan to rebuild Europe, it was socialists like Walter Reuther who purged the "Reds" from the CIO. The Democratic Party they had infiltrated and betrayed began enacting loyalty programs to weed the Communists from their organizations, and from the government itself. While denouncing the Democrats as "warmongers," progressives found themselves accused of being "fifth columnists" whose loyalty was in doubt.

There was a basic truth to the anti-Communist charge. My parents and their comrades were indeed conspirators, as anyone could see who cared to look. Their secret names and secret organizations, the elaborate network of front organizations they created to camouflage their agendas, their practice of infiltrating and subverting liberal organizations, and the disingenuousness with which they presented themselves as "progressives" all added up to a suspicious case. And in their hearts they were indeed loyal to the Soviet state. Their allegiance to the socialist future was the root of all their political commitments. For them, Russia was the incarnation of the socialist idea. Their loyalty to Moscow was as inseparable from their faith as was a Catholic's belief in the authority of Rome.

One way I absorbed the family catechism was through the ritual of our family outings to the Stanley Theater, which showed the latest Soviet films. From *Cossacks of the Kuban* I discovered that jealousy was a bourgeois emotion, and from *The Fall of Berlin* that Stalin had been the real hero of World War II. A feature about the World Peace Conference that the Kremlin had staged in Warsaw in 1951 provided a guide to current events. Armed conflict had broken out in Korea during the previous year, and a film within the film "documented" germ-warfare atrocities which Americans had committed. I remember a particularly disturbing image of a dead Korean child, flies crawling across her eyelids as the Soviet writer Ilya Ehrenburg intoned his indictment of the United States.

By this time, the Cold War was so close to being a hot one that it was as though we were behind enemy lines. The only time I felt politically safe was during the two weeks I spent at Wo-Chi-Ca, a summer camp for children of the Communist Party. The Indian-sounding name was an acronym for "Workers Children's Camp." My buddies there were Billy Gerson and Freddy Jerome, whose fathers were "second string" leaders of the Party indicted under the Smith Act. Freddy's father, V. J. Jerome, was the Party's cultural commissar. I slept over at their house one evening when the dinner guests were the Negro scholar W. E. B. Du Bois and his wife, the novelist Shirley Graham. Du Bois was a sprightly 86 and charming. He was (like Robeson) an icon for us, and I had already begun to reverently read his book *The Souls of Black Folk*. My only disappointment in the evening was that—to the annoyance of everyone at the table—Du Bois' wife, who was much younger than he, constantly interrupted him.

Our camp life was flavored with progressive themes. Pete Seeger, Paul Robeson, and other Party artists made appearances, entertaining us with songs like "If I Had a Hammer" and "We Shall Overcome," which later became anthems of the Sixties protests. Every summer there would be a campfire dedicated to the ritual burning of comic books that were "imperialist" or had anti-Communist themes. Even when we engaged in adolescent rites, the consequences could assume political dimensions. Once, when the lights went out after taps, one of my bunkmates yelled "C-cup" into the darkness, provoking the response "Harriet," which was the name of a staffer. The counselor on duty came into the cabin to give us a lecture on male chauvinism.

At camp we could ventilate the political feelings and attitudes we were forced to mask the rest of the year. Yet here, too, there were limits. After China entered the Korean War and drove America's armies back to the 38th parallel, I sent my parents a postcard that contained a camp political joke: *The Americans are advancing in Korea. Backwards.* The postcard was intercepted by my counselor, who called me aside to lecture me, much as Ben Efron had. The FBI read the mail, he said, and my thoughtlessness would endanger not only my parents but the camp itself. There was a background to this warning that gave it an air of plausibility: After Robeson's public statement that Negroes would not fight for America against the Soviet Union, the camp became the focus of a hostility so intense that armed guards had to be stationed along its perimeter.

My father's suspension took place in January 1952, shortly after my thirteenth birthday. It was ordered, along with that of seven other teachers who were questioned about being Communists, under New York State's Feinberg Law. The law declared teachers "unfit" if they were members of either the Party or the Puerto Rican national-ist group that had shot and wounded several members of Congress. When asked if he was a Communist, my father refused to answer and was fired for "insubordination." He had taught English for twen-ty-eight years, all but four of them at Seward Park. This was only two shy of the amount required to qualify him for a pension, which he had to forfeit as a result of his refusal to answer.

My father was an excellent teacher. The very insecurities that were such a heavy burden for him personally made him a lucid expositor of ideas to others. He derived immense satisfaction from the authority he gained in transmitting the knowledge he had acquired. Did my father attempt to indoctrinate his students? An anonymous letter, which the inquiry turned up, accused him of this. But no other evi-dence survives that he had abused his trust. Long after he was dead,

I was presented with testimony that suggested the opposite. I had written a brief memoir about my political odyssey that mentioned his case. When it was published, I got a call from Arnold Beichman, a political journalist I knew, asking me if my father was the Phil Horowitz who had taught at Seward Park. I told him he was, and Beichman said, "Phil Horowitz changed my life." Then he explained: "I was just a poor kid from the Lower East Side and he encouraged me to become a writer. He had a journalism class that he taught on his own time after school. I was the only student who showed up, but he taught the class anyway. He taught me how to write and told me I could become a journalist if I wanted to. If it hadn't been for him I never would have had the confidence to try."

Beichman offered me the opportunity to answer the question at the heart of my father's case. I had followed Beichman's long career as a stalwart of the anti-Communist right, and was curious to find out from him whether my father had used his teaching position to recruit students for his political agendas. "Did my father ever try to indoctrinate you in his politics?" I asked. "No," Beichman replied, "he never said anything about politics. He just taught me how to write."

After his suspension, my father defended himself in a statement before the superintendent of schools which began by recalling his long years of service. No one, he said, had ever accused him of misusing his classroom or being "unfit to teach." He appealed to the fact that 70 percent of the teachers at Seward Park had signed a letter of confidence in him "in spite of the current threats of possible reprisals." But after this preamble, his statement attempted to explain why he would not answer the question about his membership in the Party. Here, the voice ceased to sound like my father and became a kind of verbal political cartoon. Even the syntax was distended, as though he had become suspended outside himself:

> *Your question, so closely resembling in its senseless monotony, the bigotry of the Inquisition, is by now seen clearly as a device, a gimmick behind which you have been working steadily for several years to subvert the school system for ends other than the use of the children of our city.... Your question is being used by you to screen from the parents and teachers with the smokescreen of anti-Red hysteria a*

conspiracy to refashion our schools from institutions for acquiring knowledge and skills for peaceful living, to institutions of indoctrination where students will be trained to accept unreasoning hatred for other nations against that time when the present war plotters will want to drive from the Cold War to a world war that will destroy us all. It is the same Red Scare behind which the German Nazis drove their people into a world war of conquest.

This was standard Party stuff: The United States was moving toward fascism and planning a war against the Soviet Union, just as Nazi Germany had before. Three years earlier, the Party had announced that fascism had already arrived in America. Its top officials were ordered underground to prepare the resistance. Bob Thompson, a Party leader from Sunnyside who had won the Distinguished Service Cross in the Philippines, talked behind closed Party doors about launching a "guerrilla war" in America. Then he and other Party functionaries disappeared. Our family friend Sam Coleman, who was the state Party chairman, vanished with Thompson on this quixotic mission, leaving his wife and two children behind. The guerrilla war never materialized, and the two were arrested several years later in a hideout in the Sierra Nevada mountains of California.

To make the parallel to Nazi Germany seem plausible, the Party played up the "Jewish issue" whenever it could. A leaflet distributed by the Teachers Union about my father's case gives the flavor of this campaign:

WHO IS LOYAL TO AMERICA, DR. JANSEN?

Is It Yourself and the Board of Education

OR

Is it the 8 Jewish Teachers you have recently suspended?

LET THE PEOPLE OF NEW YORK JUDGE!

IS IT "AMERICANISM" when there sits on the Board of Education a man like George Timone, described by the fascist Gerald L. K. Smith as "a follower of Coughlin," and backed for reappointment to the Board of Education by the notorious anti-Semite, Allen Zoll?...

FROM THE PRESS

JEWISH DAY: "There is in it a foul stench, which regardless of the perfume poured over it still gives forth the foul odor of anti-Semitism." (B. Z. Goldberg)

COMMITTEE FOR THE REINSTATEMENT OF THE 8 SUSPENDED TEACHERS

Teachers Union
Local 555

In public, my father sounded the required notes like a dutiful piper, but privately the ruse made him uncomfortable, even unhappy. Senator Feinberg—the author of the law under which he was fired—was a Jew, as were many of the Party's other opponents. My father knew very well that all eight of the suspended teachers were Party members, and that it was their politics and not their Jewishness that had made them targets. He had struggled his whole life to leave his ancestral past behind. To him, his Jewish identity represented a legacy of superstition and prejudice. The one sure source of pride in his life was that he was being persecuted because he was a progressive—because he had embraced the liberating and universalist ideas of Marxism and would not betray them. The Party had denied him this satisfaction.

Years later, I discovered that my father had left the Party at just about that time. He continued to be a faithful follower of its politics, but could no longer be part of an organization that had forced him to betray himself. A recent change in Party policy had made his quiet withdrawal easy. After their decision to go underground, the Party's leaders had ordered their rank and file to reregister, with the idea of weeding out those who were too weak for the coming struggle against American fascism. About a third of the members, my father among them, failed to do so, and were dropped from the rolls. Decades later, when I tried to talk to him about this, he was as evasive as ever. But a look of pain came into his eyes, as we sat in the basement by the closet where he kept his collections of Lenin and Stalin, and he complained to me about the bureaucrats who ran the Party and had treated him like dirt.

The leader of the anti-Communist "witch-hunt," as the Party was calling the campaign against it, was Sen. Joseph R. McCarthy, an artful demagogue and political opportunist. McCarthy was a late-comer to the anti-Communist crusade, which had begun in the early Thirties when the rise of Hitler and Stalin first made the totalitarian threat real. The House Committee on Un-American Activities had already been created, and congressional investigations launched. It was not until June 29, 1950, four days after the Communists invaded South Korea, that McCarthy seized the national stage. In a series of famous speeches, he turned anti-Communism into a weapon against the Democrats who had allowed the Party to infiltrate both its coalitions and the government itself. This liberal failure to appreciate the Communist threat had been highlighted by the sensational case of Alger Hiss, a top adviser to Roosevelt. Hiss had been allowed to keep his government position even after Whittaker Chambers warned the Roosevelt Administration that Hiss was a member of the Party's "Ware Group" and a Soviet spy.

While the senator was riding the wave of his success, the Left produced a dramatic satire about his crusade and put it on a long-playing record. In the narrative, McCarthy is killed in an accident and wakes up on the "other side," where he meets his heroes—Torquemada (the leader of the Spanish Inquisition) and Cotton Mather (the judge at the Salem witch trials)—before going to judgment himself. The Spanish Inquisition and the Puritan witch-hunt provide the historical frame in which the McCarthy episode has been viewed by the Left ever since. Watergate journalist Carl Bernstein, whose parents were also Communists, even described the era as a "reign of terror," pairing it with events in revolutionary France and Stalinist Russia in which millions perished.

What actually happened to my father and American Communists in general bears little resemblance to these lurid images. They were neither executed nor tortured, and spent hardly any time in jail. In the entire Cold War period less than two hundred leaders and functionaries of the Party ever went to prison, in most cases serving less than two years. This was not a small number or an insignificant price to pay for their political allegiances. But, considering the Party's organizational ties to an enemy power armed with nuclear weapons poised to attack America, it was not a large one, either.

My father was not a Party leader, and merely lost his job—but even this setback was temporary. Through Party connections, he immediately found other employment at an offset print shop. As a protégé of the shop foreman, who was responsible for getting him hired, he was even a privileged apprentice. My father was pleased to share his lot with the working class. But, as soon became apparent, he was unhappy working with others outside a school setting where his authority was secure. After a while, his relations with the shop foreman turned sour, and eventually became so bitter that he had to leave. Once again, though, he was able to find a position through Party contacts, this time teaching English at a school for troubled teenagers in Hawthorne, New York, where he remained until he retired.

My mother was also called before the superintendent of schools to answer the question about Party membership. Instead of fighting the case, she took a disability retirement as a sort of plea bargain. (Her disability was ascribed to "mental distress.") Unlike my father, who suffered outside the school environment, my mother thrived. She was free now to follow the path of her talents, and immediately found a job at the National Lawyers Guild, a Party front, where she became the executive secretary to its chief, Royal France. Later, the Party was able to get her a job at Planned Parenthood. At the age of sixty she went back to school, obtained a degree in library sciences, and founded the Margaret Sanger Research Library. Eventually she traveled to conferences in Thailand and Costa Rica, delivering papers on special research libraries. When she retired, she received the first Margaret Sanger Award in recognition of her contributions. Afterwards, she said to me that being fired from her teaching job during the McCarthy era "was probably the best thing that ever happened to me."

Far from being unique, my mother's experience was common in her circle of friends. Many who lost their jobs were even more successful in the new careers they found, and for good reason: They had all been first-generation Americans who had gone to work during the Depression and had gravitated to school teaching as a secure profession in uncertain times. When political circumstances released them into the competitive arena of the prosperous Fifties, they were able to

find far more lucrative and—in many cases—more fulf
for their abilities. After their suspensions, they brought
the Board of Education, challenging the constitutionality or the Feinberg Law and the legality of their dismissals, which they eventually won. As a result, they received not only legal vindication, but all the pension monies (with interest amounting to tens of thousands of dollars) that their premature retirement had previously cost.

They were vindicated in another, more important, way as well. When the radical upsurge of the Sixties shifted the American political spectrum to the left, "old Reds" like my parents became the heroes of the Cold War "repression." Celebrated in Hollywood films like *The Front* and *The Way We Were*, they lived to see their antagonists become the arch villains of the era. The Party's own morality play had become a national myth.

Just as the Party characterized its nemesis as American fascism, so it had presented itself as a champion of democracy, and its members as First Amendment patriots. In his statement to the superintendent of schools, my father had sounded the Party theme:

> *I have never taught one thing in the classroom, and held to a different course of conduct for myself outside. I could not now betray my numerous discussions with my students about the sacredness of the first ten amendments, about how our forebears fought and died for these, without betraying them, without betraying all the adult years of our lives as free Americans before these witch-hunts began to destroy the Bill of Rights.*

Neither my father nor the Party, of course, believed these patriotic pieties. The liberties they were willing to invoke in order to defend themselves, they elsewhere dismissed as "bourgeois rights" designed to protect the rich. The sole rights that mattered to them were "economic rights" which, they believed, were the bases for all others. My parents and other progressives would not think of invoking the political rights that had protected *them* in behalf of the millions that Stalin had imprisoned in the Soviet Union whose only crime was to hold the wrong beliefs.

In fact, the Party had supported the very Smith Act that was used to jail its leaders, when the government first invoked it against

Trotskyists before the war. Moreover, within its own house the Party treated dissenters with an inquisitorial ruthlessness that was unavailable to a United States senator like McCarthy. John Lautner, the security chief for the Party's underground apparatus, had been falsely accused of being a government agent. The charge had been made by Bulgarian Communists fighting an internecine battle in their own Party. Lautner was tied up in a Cleveland basement, as part of his Party interrogation, then threatened at gunpoint unless he confessed. Lautner was so embittered by his treatment that he went directly to the FBI and exposed the Party's entire underground.

A more widely known incident involved the novelist and screenwriter Albert Maltz, one of the so-called "Hollywood Ten," who had gone to jail for refusing to answer questions before a congressional committee. While this public drama was unfolding, Maltz was hauled before a secret Party tribunal over an article he had published about artistic matters. V. J. Jerome and other Party officials had deemed his views to be politically incorrect. Before his comrades and peers, and with no camp of supporters outside the courtroom, Maltz was convicted of thought crimes, forced to confess his ideological sins and renounce his deviant ideas.

Another case, even closer to home, was that of Bella Dodd, a New York school teacher and leader of the same Communist union as my parents. After working for the Party for twenty years, she decided she wanted to return to the Catholic Church. But she was unable to make the break with her comrades, and so the Party made the decision for her. At her "trial" she discovered that the twenty years she had devoted to the Party suddenly counted for nothing:

> I found myself with only a few shabby men and women, inconsequential Party functionaries, drained of all mercy, with no humanity in their eyes, with no good will of the kind that works justice. Had they been armed I know they would have pulled the trigger against me.

Bitter and disillusioned by the treatment she received, Dodd became a political adversary and a public witness against her Communist past. It was because of defectors like Bella Dodd, who were able to identify Party members, that my father was unable to escape his fate.

But the story of the McCarthy era that made the deepest impression on me was one my mother told me, involving a small incident in the scale of events. She told it to me thirty years later with a sense of guilt that lay heavily on her even then. The episode had taken place at the height of the Cold War, before the Party's decision to go underground. A daughter of one of the comrades had brought a Paul Robeson record to kindergarten class to share with her classmates. It was right after Robeson's inflammatory statement about Negroes' unwillingness to fight against the Soviet Union, and the Peekskill riot his words provoked. The kindergarten teacher recognized Robeson's name and refused to play the record.

When the incident was reported to the Sunnyside cell, its members took up the matter as though it were an issue of great political moment. After careful deliberation, they decided that the mother herself should go to the kindergarten teacher and demand that the record be played. After the meeting, the mother had second thoughts; she could not bring herself to perform the mission. The reasons for her resistance were not political but personal: She felt it would put too much pressure on her child to make an issue of the matter, and did not feel up to the task herself.

The cell reconvened to take up the new crisis. Refusal to carry out a Party order was considered a serious matter at a time when the Party was facing a "fascist" threat. After more deliberation, the members decided to expel the rebellious comrade. In keeping with Party rules, this meant not only that the woman would no longer be a member of the Party, but that no Party member could speak to her, on penalty of also being expelled. In her heart the woman was still a Communist, and believed in the Party's cause and its truth. But now, at the height of the Cold War, with no place of refuge in sight, she was cast out with her family, and cut off from her closest friends and political comrades. It was a fate far worse than losing one's job, a nightmare greater than any the McCarthyites could inflict.

A bachelor friend of my parents, Henry Danielowitz, set up my own encounter with the passions of the time. On Saturday mornings, I would go over to Henry's apartment on 43rd Street, across Skillman Avenue. He would greet me at the door in his undershirt and boxer shorts, his belly protruding over the waistband to reveal a scar where his gall bladder had been removed. Gingerly, I would step between the piles of books and sheet music and dirty laundry scattered over the floor, and sit down at his Steinway, where the lesson would begin. Once, instead of having the lesson, we walked across the Queensborough Bridge to a music store on Second Avenue, where he bought me some blank sheet-music. When I got home, I sat down to compose my "Opus One, Number One"—a piano concerto. I carefully wrote in the names of the orchestral instruments, using the German abbreviations I had picked up from the scores he had shown me, and, after finishing the first page, asked him to play it. Suddenly, the room filled up with notes, exciting me for a moment with what I had wrought, until I realized, as the music went on and on, that he was improvising it all.

Henry also gave me trumpet lessons that led to a position in the school band and a chance to play "Pomp and Circumstance" at graduation. At one rehearsal, I was standing by myself at a side wall of the school auditorium, trumpet in hand, waiting for the teacher in charge to call the assembly to order. Suddenly, I found myself surrounded by five or six seniors I didn't know who were bigger than I was. The leader of the group grabbed my arm and shoved me against the wall, while another took the dangling cord of a huge auditorium drape and slipped it around my neck. Pulling the cord tight, he shouted: *"His father's a Red. String him up!"* Another hissed: *"Send him back to Russia!"* I struggled to free myself, but was too embarrassed to cry out. Nobody among the hundreds of people in the room seemed to be aware of my plight. Nobody cared. *You could die without anyone noticing.* But then one of the teachers called the assembly to order and, like obedient children, my tormentors released me.

My ordeal was not more painful than the manhood rites that others went through as a matter of course. But for me, it was the worst moment of the McCarthy era.

About the time my father was being called before the superintendent of schools, my childhood hero Paul Robeson made a trip to the Soviet Union. While in Moscow, he arranged to meet with an old friend, the Yiddish poet Itzhak Feffer. Like Robeson, Feffer was a Party stalwart who had deployed his art as a weapon in the political struggle. During the war, Feffer had come to the United States as a member of the Jewish Joint Anti-fascist Committee, which Stalin had created to help his relations with the Allies in the West. While visiting the United States, Feffer met many American artists and became friends with Robeson.

Now the poet was fighting for his life. The cause of his danger was Stalin's latest purge. Since the 1930s, when Stalin first instituted the Terror, wave upon wave of internal "enemies" had been disposed of in the chambers of the secret police. War had interrupted the slaughter, but when it was over the killing resumed. Lifting a page out of Hitler's book, Stalin decided to launch his last liquidation campaign against the Jews. It began without warning in the winter of 1948 with the killing of a friend and colleague of Feffer, the actor Solomon Mikhoels. An alleged plot to murder the Soviet leader was used as the pretext for a full-scale pogrom. As the new persecutions got underway, Jews began to vanish into the vast concentration-camp system that Stalin had built along with the other construction feats of the socialist state. Among those arrested was Feffer.

In America, the question "What happened to Itzhak Feffer?" entered the currency of political debate. There was talk in intellectual circles that Jews were being killed in a new Soviet purge and that Feffer was one of them. It was to quell such rumors that Robeson asked to see his old friend, but he was told by Soviet officials that he would have to wait. Eventually he was informed that the poet was vacationing in the Crimea and would see him as soon as he returned. The reality was that Feffer had already been in prison for three years, and his Soviet captors did not want to bring him to Robeson immediately because he had become emaciated from lack of food. While Robeson waited in Moscow, Stalin's police brought Feffer out of prison, put him in the care of doctors, and began fattening him up for the interview. When he looked sufficiently healthy, he was brought to Moscow. The two men met in a room that was under secret surveillance. Feffer knew he could not speak freely. When Robeson asked him how he was, he drew his finger nervously across his throat and motioned with his eyes and lips to his American comrade. *"They're going to kill us,"* he said. *"When you return to America, you must speak out and save us."*

After his meeting with the poet, Robeson returned home. When he was asked about Feffer and the other Jews, he assured his questioners that reports of their imprisonment were malicious slanders spread by individuals who only wanted to exacerbate Cold War tensions. Shortly afterward, Feffer, along with so many others, vanished into Stalin's Gulag.

It was not that Robeson had not understood Feffer's message. He had understood it all too well. Because it was Robeson, near the end of his own life and guilty with remorse, who told the story long after Itzhak Feffer was dead.

MARTYRS

UNDERNEATH THE ORDINARY SURFACES OF THEIR LIVES, MY PARENTS and their friends thought of themselves as secret agents. The mission they had undertaken, and about which they could not speak freely to anyone but each other, was not just an idea to them. It was more important to their sense of themselves than anything else they did. Nor were its tasks of a kind they could attend or ignore, depending on their moods. They were more like the obligations of a religious faith. Except that their faith was secular, and the millennium they awaited was being instituted, at that moment, in the very country that had become America's enemy.

It was this fact that made their ordinary lives precarious and their secrecy necessary. If they lived under a cloud of suspicion, it was the result of more than just their political passions. The dropping of the atomic bomb on Hiroshima had created a terror in the minds of ordinary people. Newspapers reported on American spy rings working to steal atomic secrets for the Soviet state. When people read these stories, they inevitably thought of progressives like us. And so did we ourselves. Even if we never encountered a Soviet agent or engaged in a single illegal act, each of us knew that our commitment to socialism implied the obligation to commit treason too.

As everyone knew, Lenin had created the Communist International over this very issue. Marx's *Communist Manifesto* proclaimed that workers had no country, and nothing to lose but their chains. It called on them to unite across international boundaries in order to win a new world. But in 1914 the socialist parties of the Second

International, which had been created by Marx, ignored this call and supported the war efforts of their respective governments, pitting themselves against each other. They had preferred patriotism to the proletarian cause. It was this betrayal that inspired Lenin to create a Third International which would put class above nation. When the moment of truth came, Communists would be ready to betray their country for the revolutionary cause. This was what made them *Communists* and not "social democrats."

This fantasy infused the very ordinary lives of our Sunnyside community with extraordinary possibilities of political romance. In 1944 one of my parents' closest friends was summoned for a secret mission. Ann Colloms was a schoolteacher, no more than five feet tall in her stocking feet. She was the mother of my nursery schoolmate, Michael, and had never broken a law in her life. The Party asked her to take a sealed envelope to Mexico and deliver it to a contact. It was a call she could not refuse. She was instructed not to tell anybody about her mission, and had no idea what the envelope contained.

Mexico had been the last refuge of Leon Trotsky, the great Bolshevik adversary of Stalin. Trotsky was a hero of the revolution, but had lost the power struggle afterwards and fallen from Bolshevik grace. In exile he produced endless manifestos accusing Stalin of betraying the revolutionary faith. Expelled from one country to the next, he was finally granted asylum by the Mexican government. From behind the walls of a fortress in Coyoacan, he created a Fourth International to wage a final battle against the Soviet tyrant and his monster state. In 1940, Stalin decided that this unpleasant thorn had to be removed from his side and sent an agent to Mexico to execute the deed. To reach Trotsky in his American fortress it had been useful to enlist the help of trustworthy American comrades on whose services he could call. Ann Colloms was such a comrade. The mission for which she had been chosen turned out to be a botched attempt to help an agent named Ramón Mercarder escape from a Mexican jail. It was the same Ramón Mercarder who, on Stalin's orders, had entered the compound at Coyoacan and put an ice pick in Leon Trotsky's head.

Although the code of secrecy kept me in the dark, there was a Trotsky sympathizer in our family midst. It was my mother's younger brother, Harold, who was a teacher at the High School of Music and Art. Harold had a high forehead, unkempt hair, and a gravelly voice that sounded as if he had just rolled out of bed. I never knew anything about his politics, except that he was the family maverick. A talented musician, he had studied with Nadia Boulanger, and written a symphony that Leonard Bernstein was scheduled to perform. But Bernstein wanted him to change the last movement, and he refused.

Harold was the only person I knew who was divorced. His first wife, Lucy Robison, was a concert pianist and friend of my mother's who remained close to our family afterwards. Later, he married Nancy Clemens, a photographer who was kind to me and took our family portrait. But Nancy was not a New Yorker, not Jewish, and not political. I didn't know anyone else in our circle like her. I was drawn to my uncle because he was so different, and his opinions seemed to make everyone else in the room uneasy. He would voice them with a defensive humor, acknowledging that he was outnumbered and letting out a scratchy laugh that defused conflicts when they became too intense. What drew me to him was his courage in expressing ideas that were heretical, and the fact that I never knew what he was going to say next. It was only after his death that I learned from Nancy that there were years in the Thirties when my mother didn't speak to him because he believed Trotsky was right. Later she relented, and it became a rule with her that family was more important than politics.

After my graduation from junior high school in 1952, Harold helped me gain entrance to the High School of Music and Art, which was a special school for artistic talents in uptown Manhattan. I joined the radical club Harmony which, like the Sunnyside Young Progressives, was a group connected loosely to the larger network of Communist Party organizations. Harmony met after school to discuss political issues and to decide what we, as a social vanguard, could do about them. That year, the big political cause for progressives like us was the campaign to save the Rosenbergs.

The Rosenberg case made our secret mission real to me, as it quickly became the centerpiece of our moral drama. Four years earlier, when the Rosenbergs were first arrested, the Party and its organizations had remained cautiously aloof. Even during the Rosenberg trial, the Party had remained in the background so as not to be drawn into the net of suspicion. But once the Rosenbergs were convicted, its attitude changed. After the death sentences were handed down, the defendants had steadfastly maintained their innocence and concealed their Party membership. Their silence convinced the Party that it might be safe to get involved. With the Party's resources behind it, the "Save the Rosenbergs" campaign became international, the "Dreyfus Affair" of the Cold War era, as the Party's propaganda presented it. Famous scientists and intellectuals, the president of France, and even the Pope pleaded for clemency for the couple, until the case seemed to engage the attention of the entire world.

At this time, Stalin had begun a purge in Eastern Europe in which leading Communists, many of whom were Jewish, were summarily executed for political crimes by his satellite regimes. World sympathy was directed toward the victims. A campaign against America's decision to execute two Jews for their political beliefs—which was how the Party framed the case—would provide an opportunity for the Stalinists to neutralize this concern.

It was the familiarity of the Rosenbergs that made their fate so terrible to me. They were a little Jewish couple who looked like everyone else we knew and made the same progressive gestures, like standing up for Negroes and collecting money for the Abraham Lincoln Brigade. As the execution date drew nearer, there were more and more events arranged to drum up support for the clemency appeal. In the spring of 1953, Henry and I hiked across the Triborough Bridge to a Rosenberg rally on Randall's Island. At the rally, the Rosenbergs' lawyer spoke. Sophie Rosenberg, Julius' mother, and the two little Rosenberg boys, Robbie and Michael, were also there. But what I remember most from that afternoon was a moment when Henry and I stopped in the middle of the bridge to discuss a passage that disturbed me in a text he was explaining.

My Saturday sessions with Henry always included political lessons along with the music. The texts were Marxist classics like the *Preface to a Contribution to the Critique of Capital* or Engels' *Origins of Private Property, the Family and the State*. That day it was a pamphlet written by Lenin about Party organization. The passage that concerned me was a statement that it was necessary to lie in order to advance the revolutionary cause.

This was a logical position for revolutionaries to take. If you rejected the system, you rejected its norms and standards as well. Yet, I did not want to accept this. I had never previously challenged the propositions that Henry put to me, but this one seemed wrong, and I was determined to resist it. How could we make a virtue of lying, and still advance the cause of truth? Would the Rosenbergs lie about their innocence? But Henry was adamant. He even seemed amused by my distress. "Aren't there things you keep from your parents?" he asked. "No," I said. But even as I said it, I knew that I did. I had recently begun to have sexual feelings, and couldn't even think about discussing the subject with my parents. I *did* conceal things, even from them. In my heart, I still felt that Lenin's instruction to be dishonest was wrong, but I had been caught in the web of my own deception and could not discover a way out. We began walking again, but the sense of moral rectitude I had, setting out to join the Rosenberg protest, was gone.

Shortly after the rally on Randall's Island, the Rosenbergs' time ran out. President Eisenhower rejected their appeal, saying that as a military commander he had learned the utility of making public examples. On June 18, a last-minute stay by Justice William O. Douglas was vacated by a hastily convened Supreme Court, and the execution was set for the following day.

At sundown on the evening of June 19, I went along with ten thousand others to 17th Street in Manhattan for the final deathwatch. The headlines in the evening editions of the tabloids screamed *Spies Fry Tonight*. Grown people were crying hysterically in the streets. From a platform truck, the speakers were raising the crowd's passions to an even higher pitch by talking about new appeals and hopes. Then, at eight o'clock, a woman's voice announced, "They have just taken Julius and Ethel Rosenberg into the execution chamber...." At this signal an unearthly wail went up from the crowd, a terrible keening, trapped and amplified between the darkened skyscrapers, creating the most awful memory of my youth.

As the wailing went on, the police began breaking up the demonstration. Someone pulled the plug to the microphone while a Negro woman was singing "Let my people go." The demonstrators began moving out of 17th Street to Union Square, where monitors directed them to march down to the Lower East Side. But the march had only progressed about 10 blocks when mounted police rode up onto the sidewalk to break up the line. I scrambled with the others to avoid the hoofs of the oncoming beasts, thinking: *This must be fascism.* Afterwards, I wrote a story about the demonstration, describing these events. I had already learned something about the chemistry of our political romance, and interspersed my description of the police charge with lines from the defiant song of the Warsaw ghetto, "Zog Nisht Keynmol." I showed the article to friends, who praised it, and even submitted copies to the *Daily Worker* and the Party's literary journal, *Masses & Mainstream*, both of whose editors returned them with polite rejections.

Among the friends I showed it to was Ellen Sparer, whom I had come to know through the Sunnyside Young Progressives, a club we had formed in junior high school. She had a quizzical expression and a long neck, with a scar from a childhood tracheotomy that flamed at the little indent above her clavicle, like a mark of vulnerability. Ellen had written a poem for the first issue of our club's newsletter, the *Sunnyside Young Progressive Reporter*. The issue featured my editorial call-to-action for social justice and peace, which began "We the youth of America ...," along with Ellen's poem about Willie McGee, a Mississippi Negro who was to be executed for rape. *"Did he have a fair trial?"* her poem asked. *"NO,"* it answered in reply to its own question. *"The only proof they had was that he was a Negro."*

There was a virginal quality about all of us, but especially Ellen, which made her poem jarring. After I distributed it to our ninth-grade English class, our teacher, Miss Montrose, a spinsterish lady with a prim mouth and gentle eyes, summoned me into the hall for a "conference." Didn't I realize—she asked—that rape might be a disturbing subject for young people? I didn't know what to answer.

Perhaps it was the sexual element that Ellen's poem had put into the air that filled me with the desire to get closer to her. At first, I had no idea how to accomplish this, since I had no experience to guide me. But after I finished my story about the Rosenbergs, I phoned to ask if she would like to read it, and then if I could come over to her house so that we could discuss it. Even as I conducted these maneuvers, I was filled with misgivings. I knew enough about Ellen to gauge the slimness of my chances, no matter how inspiring my prose. She seemed to like tall boys who were older than I and had a doomed air about them. Her first boyfriend, Richie Sperber, was a morose fellow everybody liked but who committed suicide shortly after his eighteenth birthday. His successor, a tall and amiable Negro named Kenny Gaines, never seemed to be able to put his own life in order, either.

On the appointed evening, Ellen and I sat on her bed and talked about my story of the Rosenberg demonstration. She liked my story and admired my "courage" in speaking out in public for what we believed. This surprised and flattered me, because her poem, with its mention of rape, had seemed a far more daring act than any I could muster. But when these political subjects were exhausted, I didn't know how to shift the discussion to other matters. Between abrupt pauses and awkward stabs at conversation, the evening dragged painfully on until the silences became so long that I ended them by saying I had to leave.

Three months before the Rosenbergs were executed, the Soviet dictator Stalin died in Moscow. I learned the news while riding home from school on the Seventh Avenue subway. As I looked at the headline, I thought: *"What will become of us without him as our guide?"* A few days later I received an anonymous note in the mail which said:

> *The greatest momseh that ever lived is dead.*
> *How's Carol (the one with the pimples) and*
> *your other commie friends?*

The term *momseh*—bastard—indicated that it was from one of my Jewish schoolmates, but I never discovered who it was. "Carol" was Carol Pasternak, one of the editors of our SYP *Reporter*. Her father, Morris, was the Sunnyside cell leader, a small, humorless man who exercised his authority as though he was a real commissar in a Communist state. The note was mean and upsetting. Who could have sent it?

After Stalin's funeral, my father tried to sum up the great man's achievement for me. In the course of eliminating his rivals, Stalin had acquired five offices, including General Secretary of the Communist Party, President of the Soviet Union, and Generalissimo of the Red Army. Now his successors had apportioned the same posts among themselves. My father said: "You see what a genius Stalin was. It took five men to replace him."

After Stalin's death, his successors made approaches to the West with the idea of creating a détente in the Cold War. In 1955, a summit was held in Geneva, the first time in a decade that the leaders of the two sides had met. Soon, artists from the Soviet Union began coming to the United States on concert tours. My parents took us to Carnegie Hall twice, first to see David Oistrakh and later the Moiseyev dance troupe. I remember my excitement when Oistrakh walked onstage. I thought: *This is a man from the future*. When he spoke a few words to the audience, I strained to hear the difference it made. After the Moiseyev concert, we waited at the stage door for the artists to come out. As they pushed through the crowd, I caught the attention of one of the dancers and repeated a phrase I had memorized for the occasion: "*Mir y druzhba*"—peace and friendship. I wanted him to know that he had friends in America who were not Cold Warriors and did not hate the Soviet state. What I got back was the iciest stare I had ever seen.

After a year at Music and Art, I decided to transfer to my local high school in Queens. At M&A I felt outclassed by the talents of my fellow students, and isolated by what I regarded as their social snobbery. In the fall of 1953 I entered William Cullen Bryant High, whose most famous alumnus was the Yankee pitcher Whitey Ford, and whose students were drawn from the working-class neighborhoods of Astoria and Sunnyside. I presented the move to my progressive friends as a decision to get closer to the people.

In 1955 I graduated from Bryant and entered Columbia College. My father took me up to the campus for the orientation session, where I was given a freshman beanie and provided with a dorm room for the weekend. I was awed by the classic facade of Butler Library, which was inscribed with the pantheonic gods of Western culture: Homer, Sophocles, Lucretius, Shakespeare, Dante, Cervantes, and Goethe. But I noticed that my father was not responding to the pride I felt at my achievement in becoming a part of it all. It occurred to me that perhaps he was disappointed that I had not followed his path to City College. (It had seemed too ordinary, to me, to go there.) But I also knew it was more than that. Although he would not say so directly,

I sensed that he regarded my choice as a betrayal. Columbia was an Ivy League school for the social elite. It was the school where his old City classmates Valency and Nagel had gone on to worlds that were forever closed to him. Entering its gates, I was crossing a boundary into enemy terrain, and leaving him behind.

For years my father had felt he was losing me. The feeling had begun with the Saturday sessions with Henry, who, by introducing me to the Marxist mysteries, had supplanted my father as my teacher. It had developed over innumerable unintended slights, starting with when I showed my Rosenberg story to others for approval before showing it to him. It had reached a kind of climax, a year later, when I organized a reading of poems by Aragon, Éluard, and other Communist writers. I had compiled a script, and organized some of my friends to participate in the reading (including a flute player to add a musical touch). I made certain to invite my parents' friends, and the evening proved a success in their eyes. But I had not solicited my father's advice, and this in an area—literature—which was *his*. My intention had been to surprise him with my growth and independence, but he reacted to this occasion, as he would to each of my unsolicited self-assertions, as an unmanageable threat.

These conflicts came to a head in my seventeenth year. While other sons declared their independence in confrontations over dating and the use of the family car, my test of will was provoked by Columbia and the *New York Times*. I had remained at home during my college years, where the dinner table was a zone of political engagement. School friends who visited were enthralled by the passions displayed in its conflicts, which, paradoxically, formed a powerful bond between my father and me. But in the spring of my sophomore year we had a fight that was qualitatively different from all the others, and which touched issues we both sensed would not be resolved. I had come home from a class in Contemporary Civilization, which was part of Columbia's famous "core curriculum." In it, we had read *The Communist Manifesto* alongside Nechaiev's *Catechism of a Revolutionary*, and the juxtaposition had disturbed me. Nechaiev seemed to advocate a bloodthirsty terrorism I associated with hostile caricatures of radicals, rather than the radicals I knew in our progressive circles.

Was there something I didn't know? I hoped my father would provide reassurance about our cause.

My question was probably put in a provocative way because his mood grew instantly black. He was sure my Columbia professors had linked the two texts to discredit the Left and mislead his son. As I defended their good faith, my words only confirmed his deeper suspicions, until I heard him ask: "Do you believe everything you read in the *New York Times?*" My father read the *Times* every day from cover to cover, so I did not realize that I was being given a test. "Not all of it," I answered impatiently, "but about 90 percent is probably right." The "90 percent" was a further provocation. As the words left my mouth, his anger turned white, and he launched into a jeremiad about "the ruling-class press." For an instant, it almost seemed as though he was going to hit me, until my mother intervened. In those desperate moments I felt the ground under us give way, and I knew that my life as his son would never be the same.

This schism had a dimension that reached far beyond our family circle. A month earlier, the *Times* had published a report from the Kremlin describing a secret speech by the new Soviet premier, Nikita Khrushchev. It had been smuggled out of the Kremlin by the *Mossad*, the Israeli secret service. The speech made headlines all over the world because it was about crimes that Stalin had committed. Until then, Communists and progressives everywhere had denied such crimes ever took place, and had denounced the reports as "anti-Soviet" propaganda. Over the next months the story was confirmed, even by Communist sources, and in June the full text was published in the *Times*, and then in the *Daily Worker* itself.

The Khrushchev Report, as the speech came to be known, was an attempt by the Soviet leadership to normalize the totalitarian state. The terror they had instituted against the "enemies of the people" had assumed a life of its own and become a threat, even to them. The situation was summed up in a famous statistic: Of the 130 members of the Party's Central Committee who had attended its 1934 Congress in Moscow, all but 40 had been shot by 1938. Fueled by Stalin's paranoia, the revolution had devoured its own, killing both the enemies of Communism and Communists alike. By speaking openly among themselves about these crimes, Stalin's successors thought they could "de-Stalinize" the system they had helped to create.

In his secret speech, Khrushchev identified the "cult of the individual"—the glorification of Stalin which had made him so powerful that he could not be opposed—as the source of their problems. "Individualism" was, of course, the hated philosophy of their political adversaries. Identifying it as the root cause of the terror was a clever way of blaming capitalism for the crimes of socialists, as though a vestige of the past had tripped them up on the road to utopia.

The publication of the Khrushchev Report was probably the greatest blow struck against the Soviet Empire during the entire Cold War. When my parents and their friends opened the morning *Times* and read its text, their world collapsed—and along with it their will to struggle. If the document was true, almost everything they had said and believed was false. Their secret mission had led them into waters so deep that its tide had overwhelmed them, taking with it the very meaning of their lives.

Peggy Dennis was the wife of the Party's general secretary and the mother of Gene Dennis, Jr., one of my campmates at Wo-Chi-Ca. In her autobiography, she described her reaction to the Khrushchev Report: "The last page crumpled in my fist, I lay in the half darkness and I wept.... For Gene's years in prison ... For the years of silence in which we buried doubts and questions. For a thirty-year life's commitment that lay shattered. I lay sobbing low, hiccoughing whimpers."

In the Thirties, Peggy and Gene Dennis had spent years abroad in Moscow and the Far East as international agents for the Kremlin. Peggy had been a courier carrying sealed envelopes to Spain, where the Party was conducting a liquidation campaign against Trotskyist dissidents. But when Peggy and Gene prepared to leave Moscow and return to the United States to become leaders of the American party, the Russians informed them that they could not take their son, who was five years old, with them. The reason they were given was that it would be politically unsound for them to be seen with a child who spoke only Russian. The real reason was that the Soviet leaders wanted him as a hostage, so that his parents would not reveal what they knew.

In the American community of the faithful, the Khrushchev Report was a divisive force. Forty-year friendships disintegrated overnight, and even marriages dissolved as one partner would decide to quit the Party, the other to keep its faith. The very future of American Communism was put in doubt as activists deserted its ranks and were cut off by those they left behind. In the two years that followed, more than two-thirds of the Party membership dropped from its lists. One poignant testimony of excommunication was given by a Party leader's wife to the writer Vivian Gornick, who included it in her book *The Romance of American Communism:*

> *The morning after we quit I went to the grocery store to buy some milk and bread and I ran into a Party member on the street. When he saw me coming toward him he veered in his tracks and crossed the street... I had become—literally overnight—non-existent. The only people who remained our friends were the people who quit with us: at the same moment, in the same way, over the same issues. Everyone else disappeared.*

My Uncle Harold's first wife, Lucy, was one of those embittered by the humiliation and waste of the years she had spent serving a lie. She turned her back on both the Party and the Soviet cause. My parents were among those who struggled to find solace in the thought that while "mistakes" had been made, remedies were being taken. But even as they tried to remain true to their ideals, they were paralyzed in practice, as though stunned by a blow from which they could never recover. My parents had attended four and five political meetings a week for as long as I could remember. But in the years following the Khrushchev Report, although they remained faithful in their hearts to the radical cause, they were never really active in politics again.

The Communist world continued to unravel, and in October 1956 a revolt erupted in Hungary, whose Communist leaders declared their independence from the Soviet bloc and announced their intention to take a "new road to socialism." The Kremlin regarded these declarations as sedition, and condemned the revolt as an attempt by fascist elements to restore the past. Soviet tanks were sent to crush the rebels, and thirty thousand Hungarians were killed in the battle. Some American Communists, including the editor of the *Daily Worker,* sided with the Hungarians; others, like my father, defended the intervention, believing the Kremlin's lies. The conflict with my father had grown into a confrontation of radical generations. If his generation thought that the Hungarian rebels were abandoning socialism by taking a "new road," mine wanted to give them a chance. Why should the revolutionary future be encumbered by the revolutionary past?

On the anniversary of Khrushchev's speech, the Party held a special convention to address the crisis. Three factions appeared at the gathering: the hard-line Stalinists who were suspicious of Khrushchev; the reformers who wanted to renounce violence and the "dictatorship of the proletariat"; and the centrists whose primary concern was to avoid a break with the Kremlin rulers. The centrists were led by Eugene Dennis, whose position won the day. Following the convention, an article appeared in an official Soviet journal, outlining the Kremlin's view of what had happened. It hailed the victory of the Dennis faction as a defeat for the "revisionists" and a triumph for "the vital force of proletarian internationalism." The article was written by Timur Timofeyev, the director of Moscow's Institute of the World Labor Movement. The name Timur Timofeyev was self-chosen and meant "Tim, son of Tim." This was the son whom Dennis had been forced to abandon in Moscow, twenty years before.

My father had already quit the Party because of his personal difficulties with its officious functionaries, and in the wake of the Report my mother left, too. She had always had a broader grasp of the issues anyway, and was able to accept the possibility that perhaps history could not be accounted for by a theory, even as advanced as Marx's. She was convinced that the Party theoreticians had lost touch with any reality that might connect them to a viable future. Although bitter toward the Party bureaucrats who had mistreated him, my father still clung to the idea that they possessed a secret that would lead him and the other faithful to their promised land at last.

I was not sure of what to make of it all. Monstrous crimes had been committed, and much else had gone terribly wrong. But did this mean it was necessary to abandon socialism? I was not ready for that. The socialist vision provided the only way I knew of looking at the world that would distinguish right from wrong that gave hope for a better future. Socialism was the desire for justice. I did not see how I could give that up.

In the next few years I concentrated on my studies, and did not attempt to find answers to the questions that the Communist debacle had provoked: How had it happened? How had socialist ideas and Marxist economics produced Stalin and his crimes? How could such disasters be avoided in the future? How should socialists relate now to the Soviet state? It was only after I graduated from Columbia and went on to Berkeley that I became seriously concerned with politics again. When I did, it was in conjunction with others of my generation who were forming a "New Left" out of the ashes of the old. We did so out of the conviction that the original passion could be born again, and that we could create a new socialist vision free from the taint that Stalin had placed on the movement our parents had served. When the New Left finally appeared, however, its members ignored the history that had shaped those beginnings. Unwilling to confront the legacy they had inherited from the past, they regarded themselves as offspring of a virgin birth—self-parented and self-invented, just like Eugene Dennis's son.

ELISSA

What I had learned from my parents was this: it is *ideas* that are important. If you had put yourself on the progressive side of the important issues, you had done what was necessary for a worthy life. It was ideas that identified friends and distinguished enemies, separating those who could be trusted from those who could not. I didn't notice at the time, but my parents' catechism was a strange inversion of the Marxist thesis: Ideas make you what you are. Consciousness determines Being.

As a consequence of my parents' political choices, I inhabited a Platonic universe. In this setting, the Ideal Forms of things were always present at the back of reality, to point to where everything (and everyone) should be headed. This perspective had a profound influence on my conduct in the real world. *My* task in life, as I understood it, was to point myself in the direction that would realize the socialist ideal, and to point others in that direction as well. As a result, the actions of people I encountered along the way appeared not as expressions of character—ineluctable facts of their being—but attitudes that the right information could alter. When I faced opposition, it never had the same weight for me as it did for those who didn't share my assumptions. I was inclined to discount what people said, and often even what they did, since reason could persuade them to do otherwise. Nor was this indifference to the gravities of human nature a quirk peculiar to me. It was the heart of the radical belief. In the eyes of radicals, society was not a reflection of the needs and desires of those who inhabited it, but an imposition on their natures that politics could change.

This view led, over the course of time, to consequences for me that were eventually destructive. In the beginning, however, the benefits seemed to outweigh all else. Discounting the specific gravity of others' characters imparted force to my own, while believing that nothing human was rooted in nature made almost anything seem possible. I was able to cross boundaries that others found impassable, and to achieve more than I probably should have. But the confidence that lay behind my successes eventually worked to undermine them as well. At crucial points in my journey, it resulted in a blindness to dangers I could have avoided, and disarmed me before enemies I should have foreseen.

Others have noted the paradoxical effects of the culture that shaped me. The writer Anatole Broyard, who habituated Greenwich Village in the 1940s, was impressed by the Promethean ambitions of the progressives he met there. But he was also struck by the disabling effects of their intellectual virtues and Platonic conceptions. It was as though the intoxication with ideas had deprived them of their senses:

> They were blinded by reading. Their heads were so filled with books ... that there was no room for the raw data of actuality. They couldn't see the small, only the large. They still thought of ordinary people as the proletariat, or the masses.

My character was formed in a rite of passage akin to that of a religious instruction. Like a novitiate in the priesthood, I was preparing myself for the next life. I was still innocent of any real experience, but I felt I had the significant answers. This attitude denied me the tests of self that served as educational passages for my unprogressive peers. I had no room for such experiments. I was too intent on preparing myself for the revolutionary future. But, even as I hurried toward my destination, I failed to notice how isolated I had become. A diary entry records the following complaint from a girl I dated when I was seventeen: "You don't *live* an experience, because you're too busy *analyzing* it."

By this time, ideas had made me an outsider even to myself. I was a Jew whose ancestors had fled from persecution in Rumania and

Russia, yet I was describing myself to peers as a "Christian romantic." A disjunctive posture like this was not unusual for Platonists of the Left. My philosophical fantasy was hardly more peculiar than thinking of oneself as a Bolshevik in America, the way all progressives did. It was just another way that consciousness could determine Being. The Christian idea I had adopted was my response to the Stalinist horrors that Khrushchev had unveiled. It did not signal that I was a believer in the divinity of Christ. I was searching for the ethical truth that Marxism lacked. My thinking was this: Even if progressives were not directly responsible for these crimes, the ideas that had made the world intelligible to us had been insufficient to prevent them. I was shaken by the confusion of my parents' generation, and by their demoralization in the face of what Khrushchev had revealed. I was looking for a moral compass that would help mine to avoid their fate.

I thought I had found such a compass in a small volume in the bookstore at Columbia. It was Tolstoy's *Confession*. In it, the great Russian writer described the crisis that confronted him when he arrived at the pinnacle of success. He was world-famous, wealthy, and artistically fulfilled, yet he was thrown into a depression so profound that he had to lock his hunting rifle in the closet so that he would not use it on himself. Searching for an answer to his suicidal despair, he turned for counsel to the great philosophical texts—but came up empty. Then he asked himself the following question: Why did the poorest peasants working his estate seem to possess the happiness that eluded him? The answer he found was their belief in the Christian gospel of salvation, which provided their solace and their strength. In this insight, Tolstoy was able to find an exit from his black hole. He gave up all his worldly possessions and went to live among the peasants he admired, even adopting their faith.

I found Tolstoy's story compelling. It paralleled the Marxist romance in which the poor and the meek would inherit the earth, but added a moral dimension that seemed necessary to prevent the crimes that Marxists had committed. In reading *Confession* I also identified with Tolstoy's loneliness and his desire for connection. I wanted connection too, but felt insulated from my experience. It was as though I was encased in a plastic bubble, like one of those children for whom the environment has become dangerously toxic. The political abstractions I was struggling to live by formed an invisible membrane separating me from others, controlling even my relations with the opposite sex. The political was also personal. While taking my adolescent steps toward manhood, I wanted to be a worthy bearer of the progressive faith, to live in the image of "socialist man."

My Parents had urged me to study science as "the knowledge of the future." To appease them and please myself, I took mathematics courses alongside my literary studies. The purity of mathematical abstractions appealed to me. In keeping with my radical outlook, I liked the way the truth of a proposition could be grasped without the distraction of a clutter of facts. But a natural inaptitude for mathematical thinking soon resulted in declining grades as the courses became more advanced. I would have failed Galois Theory, except that the professor passed me for merely attending the class. Rather than acknowledge the innate character of mathematical intelligence and the natural hierarchy it implied, I blamed my failures on poor instruction. Just before graduating, I drew up a ten-page indictment of the department, along with a program for reforming the curriculum, and delivered them to the dean:

> Until the Math Department can demonstrate beyond the shadow of a doubt that there is a mathematical section of the brain that allows some people to proceed without instruction, while others cannot learn no matter how intelligent they are, nor how much instruction they receive, it does not seem to me just that they should proceed with this assumption and allow many good students who probably would make competent mathematicians and certainly excellent teachers to go down the drain.

The map of justice I had made in the schoolyard was still my guide. My education at Columbia appears to me now also as a series of missed opportunities. As part of the sequence for English majors at Columbia, I took a seminar with the department's most famous professor, Lionel Trilling, who had come briefly under the spell of Communism in the year my father went to the Soviet Union. I was unaware of this link, although I knew Trilling had written a novel about Communism called *The Middle of the Journey*. I didn't read the novel, and Trilling's demeanor did not invite my trust, so I never asked him about his experience.

Trilling was a brown study. He hunched over the seminar table, in an angular pose, cold and remote from his students, and kept his secrets. Circles under his doleful eyes, and hair gone prematurely gray, suggested existential worries that could not be expressed. This reserve provoked a certain resentment among members of the class, who had enrolled in the seminar to get close to the great man. Although the seminar was small, he did not grade our papers, but left the task to his mustachioed young assistant, Steven Marcus. In conducting the classes, Trilling could be cutting in a way that was both surgical and cruel. Once, when I expressed a preference for a poem by Coleridge, he retorted sharply: "Anyone who prefers Coleridge to Wordsworth has a tin ear."

One of the seminar members was a taciturn junior named Mark Zborowski, whose flaming red beard seemed a natural rebuke to Trilling's neurasthenic pallor. During a session about Wordsworth's "Prelude," Zborowski was asked about the meaning of a passage. "I don't think it has any meaning," Zborowski mumbled sullenly. "Come, come, Mr. Zborowski," replied the irritated professor. "Surely it must have *some* meaning." Zborowski was another missed opportunity. I never pushed to discover the sources of his resistance, which seemed a not-so-subtle rebellion, but against what? Years later, I discovered that his father, a famous anthropologist, had been one of Stalin's American agents, far more important than Ann Colloms in arranging the assassination of Trotsky.

The most powerful influence on my intellectual development at Columbia was Andrew Chiappe, a professor as obscure as Trilling was famous. Where Trilling was almost gaunt, Chiappe was rotund, with soft pink skin, a vanishing chin, and a penguin nose that he habitually pointed into the air. When you sat in Chiappe's office, his walleye floated into the distance, as if fleeing intimate contact. But unlike Trilling's remoteness there was an intense affect in Chiappe's gesture, as though even this proximity was too much for him to handle.

Chiappe presided over the Shakespeare course that Mark Van Doren had established, covering all thirty-six plays over two semesters. His lectures were lyrical performances, introducing me to dimensions of language and experience about which Marxism had given no intimation. What I was drawn to in the texts themselves was the way in which symbolic orders were seen by Shakespeare and the Elizabethans to shape societies and individual lives. By participating in these orders, human beings had the possibility of ascending or descending a Great Chain of Being that stretched between the extremes of angel and beast. In a famous passage in *Troilus and Cressida*, the character of Ulysses describes what happens in an age of relativism, when there is a collapse of these orders—when right and wrong "lose their names" and force becomes the sole social arbiter. Then "everything includes itself in power, power is included into will, will into appetite,"

> *And appetite, a universal wolf,*
> *So doubly seconded with will and power*
> *Must make perforce a universal prey,*
> *And last eat up himself.*

This was not a bad description of what had happened under Stalin.

Elissa Krauthamer was sixteen when we met on a blind date in the late summer of 1957. We had been introduced by Michael Colloms, who was seeing her best friend Florence Luftig. The two girls had just graduated from Music and Art, and we invited them over to his apartment, when his parents were away, and made them dinner. I entertained everyone with intellectual jokes I had learned at Columbia, and then we went to the movies.

I was in love with Elissa the moment I saw her—drawn by her shy, passionate eyes that alternately smiled into mine and searched the air beneath her, as if looking for a place to hide. I loved the way her brown hair, which she had put up with pins, kept tumbling in falls from her head. She had an innocent, vulnerable look, and milky skin which made her lips seem redder than they were; and soft, full breasts that I wanted to bury my face in. I felt when I talked to her that my words went straight to her heart.

Although I never would have asked her then (I seemed always in pursuit, and she constantly vanishing into herself), I did inquire long afterwards what it was that she had seen in me when we were young and first met. She said, "I loved your bones and your neck; you were the cutest boy I ever dated. I remember standing with you on a Broadway train platform and you quoted Byron: 'Every man has a moment of truth when he's 19 and in love.' And then you said: 'And I want to live in that moment forever.' How could I resist?"

Falling in love with Elissa put an end to my career as a Christian romantic. Unlike me, she never worried her judgments. Her reactions were spontaneous, and seemed to spring fully formed from a core of her being. It was such a relief from my own intellections that her feelings quickly came to exert a force on me that was something akin to a magnetic field. "That's ridiculous," she said when I told her how I regarded myself. "It's so un-Jewish."

I proposed to her three months after we met. We were sitting on the bed in my room, when a hoarseness entered my throat as I began to tell her how important she had become to me—how she had filled my life with a new sense of possibility and meaning. She was wearing a black wool dress with a crescent neck, her legs curled under the skirt. Her head was bent down and her fingers nervously worked her falls as she listened to my buildup and anticipated what was to come. Finally I asked, *Will you marry me?"* I hadn't calculated the terrifying silence that might follow the question. But then she quickly rescued me, saying *"Yes. Yes."*—repeating the word with such passion that I felt myself blessed.

We were practical enough to realize that we couldn't get married until I graduated and was able to support us, and so our courtship continued along with our studies. She was attending Columbia's sister college, Barnard, and we would arrange to see each other at lunch hours on the steps in front of Low Library. As she approached along 116th Street, her nearsightedness caused her to tilt her head to the side and squint before she would give a little skip and then hurry forward to meet me. On weekends, I drove my parents' blue Dodge across the Triborough Bridge and up the Major Deegan Expressway to Yankee Stadium and then Jerome Avenue, where she lived. We would take her dog Terry for a walk in the park in front of her apartment house before going to a movie. In between these trysts, I wrote her poems in the style of Paul Éluard:

In you I discovered
New reasons for being.
Speaking to you
I seemed to myself
To be speaking
For the first time.

Elissa had a passionate connection to animals and plants that fascinated me, not least because I could not understand it. I bought her the biggest gardenia plant I could find, relishing the pleasure it would bring her as I waited for her to open her door. She was gratifyingly overwhelmed, but her apartment had no light, and soon the plant began to wither, until she became distraught to the point of tears, and I had to take it back. Her passion was oxygen to me. It pumped energy into my soul, until I felt I couldn't breathe without it. But I also worried that her happiness should be so fragile and so dependent on vulnerable things outside my control, even as my happiness was becoming so dependent on her.

I was always impatient with the pace of things, and could hardly wait until we set up house together and became parts of a single life. We set the date for the marriage—June 14, 1959—right after graduation. But when we announced our plans, I discovered that my parents were opposed to the wedding. Perhaps they thought we were too young. Perhaps my mother had ambitions for me that she thought the marriage would not support. But she never said a word; she sent my father instead.

The confrontation took place in the same bedroom where my parents had instructed me in the Progressive Party platform, when I prepared for my fifth-grade election debate more than ten years before. He began by asking me why I wanted to get married. The question seemed absurd. I was in love, I said. Why else would anyone want to get married? "The only reason for getting married," he corrected me, "is to hang out a shingle that you intend to have children." I found this annoying. "I love her," I repeated. "Of course I want to have children with her." But I had only provided him with another opening, as he launched into the theme of how expensive families were. How did I intend to support mine? I reminded him that I was going to graduate school at Berkeley, and had no intention of starting a family just then. The teaching assistantship in English Literature I had been awarded would provide the two of us adequate support. But my father had not been sent on a mission that could be satisfied by reasonable answers. "How are you going to afford Kleenex?" he asked. "How are you going to buy toilet paper?" *Toilet paper?* My life was going to be put on hold because of a detail like this? A chasm had opened. For me, the discussion was over. My father had set out to dissuade me from my course, but he had ended up convincing me that I no longer had anything to learn from him.

I could never forget this confrontation with my father. It was a cutting of the filial cord that had made him my mentor and guide. How could I take seriously any advice he might offer about the life I had embarked on, when he had derided its beginning with such bizarre objections? But now that he is gone and the letters he left have afforded me a glimpse of his own passionate youth, I have been forced to look at this confrontation again. How much he had to tell me! If only he could have found the courage to speak. Probably nothing he could have said that day would have swayed me. But if he had been able to open his own life to me, his confidence might have helped me in the years ahead when my life took unexpected and wounding turns, and I could have used his wisdom and support. Yet when the moment presented itself for him to confront me man-to-man, he was unable to do so. He could not let me inside his intimate self to share what life's pain had taught him. He could only talk to me about Kleenex and toilet paper.

In searching for a clue to my father's silence, I turn to the letter he wrote me about his own father, and the silence that had developed between them: *"Perhaps it's because when my father was as old as I am today, he had been so long silent watching his son change into an educated man that he feared to be talked down to."* Perhaps my father was silent because he feared his own vulnerability in the face of his self-confident son.

Elissa and I were married in a Jewish ceremony in Yonkers, according to the wishes of her parents. My mother's attitude was practical. As she put it, "Weddings are for the parents." (Perhaps this was what she had learned in reflecting on her own wedding, which took place, without parents, at City Hall.) The Krauthamers were not religious, but rather comfortable in their identity as Jews, and it would have been unthinkable to them not to have had a rabbi preside over the ceremony. My mother readily acquiesced. She was always willing to accommodate others' beliefs, as though she was so certain of her own that theirs didn't matter. My father "went along."

In her bridal innocence, Elissa was ravishing. She wore a low-cut white gown and a corsage of phalaenopsis orchids whose subtle palette reflected her tastes. Knotting my tie in the bedroom mirror before leaving for the ceremony, I was so nervous that my fingers trembled. We stood under the traditional canopy, and I placed the ring on her finger and said in Hebrew the 2,000-year-old vow I had memorized for the occasion: *"Harei at mekudeshes li b'tabaas zu k'das Moshe v'Yisrael"*: "With this I marry you by the laws of Moses and Israel."

Just before the marriage, my father had a private talk with Elissa. The subject was his son, who was now stepping into his own domain. As in the totality of my father's communications, he proceeded by indirection but his words were clearly inspired by my ambition to conquer all worlds that lay before me, and my refusal to heed his advice. His impulse was probably filial concern, but he revealed also his resentment at the force with which I assaulted my future. Pulling her aside, he asked: "When David comes down, do you think it will be slowly, or all at once?"

PART 3

NEW WORLDS

(1957–1967)

The times they are a-changin'

—Bob Dylan

BERKELEY

W ITH THE MONEY WE WERE GIVEN AS WEDDING PRESENTS, I bought a used Volkswagen "bug," and we jammed Elissa's plants and our belongings into it and headed west. In my fantasies, California was the closest thing to an American utopia. I imagined Berkeley as a university town set among redwoods and overlooking the ocean. Typically, I never looked carefully at a map to check my assumptions. In fact there were no redwoods, and the ocean was off in the distance, beyond San Francisco Bay. We arrived in late August, just two years after our first date, and rented a one-room apartment in a brown stucco addition in the flatlands between the university and the water.

Elissa had dropped out of Barnard in her freshman year, and was entering "Cal" as a biology major. I was enrolled in a master's program in English literature, which was a kind of alternate path I had taken to avoid a direct confrontation with the political past. It was part of the compartmentalization I performed after the Khrushchev Report. I never viewed my literary studies as a career in itself, nor had I given much thought to what I would do to earn a living. Perhaps I would teach. It didn't really matter. In a strange way, my radical upbringing had made me unworldly. I had a sense of mission that drove me forward without regard for the practical considerations that seemed to preoccupy everyone else. Like others enrolled in literary studies, I had developed an ambition to be a writer. But even this was secondary to pursuing the path I had embarked on as a very young man, which was to know a revolutionary truth and make it real.

At Berkeley, I assisted the Shakespeare professor Jonas Barish, teaching the sections after his lectures. But I chafed at the scholasticism of my graduate studies, longing for the intellectual journeys of my Columbia education. In my second year, dissatisfaction led me to seek refuge in a new subject, classical Chinese. I had taken a senior seminar in Oriental philosophy and literature at Columbia, and was lured to the subject now by the prospect of studying with a legendary professor named Peter Boodberg. A linguist who knew dozens of European and Asian languages, Boodberg challenged traditional scholarship. For example, the Chinese character for the knowledge of sages was generally regarded as depicting a sun and moon—hence "illumination," "brilliance." In Boodberg's view, characters were not merely pictograms, but incorporated phonetic codes as well. As he interpreted it, this character for knowledge represented the numinous surface of the dark oval of a crescent moon, an incipient light, "intuition."

Boodberg was the son of a Russian count, and still held a Czarist passport. His sister was the translator of Pasternak's *Dr. Zhivago*, which had been published during the Khrushchev thaw and became a Cold War *cause célèbre* after Pasternak was awarded his Nobel Prize and then forced by the Kremlin to refuse it. Boodberg had a rich experience in the real-world consequences of my revolutionary aspirations, and could have opened vistas onto the Soviet experience for me—had I been able to ask him. He was another missed opportunity.

In Chinese philosophy and culture, I pursued the ethical theme that had attracted me in my studies in English literature: the connection between the form and content of social life. There was an affinity between the aristocratic code of the Confucian world and the ideal of order exemplified in Shakespeare's plays, as indeed in art itself. Aesthetic order was even more intrinsically an order of *creation*, and thus connected to the revolutionary idea. In one of my papers in Boodberg's class, I quoted Wallace Stevens:

> There is, in fact, a world of poetry indistinguishable from the world in which we live, or I ought to say, no doubt, from the world in which we shall come to live, since what makes the poet the potent figure that he is...is that he creates the world to which we turn incessantly and without knowing it and that he gives to life the supreme fictions without which we are unable to conceive of it.

The third influence I came under was that of the contemporary Jewish thinker Martin Buber, and his philosophy of dialogue. In his most famous work, *I and Thou,* Buber spoke to my desire for connection, and in his Hasidic writings to my need for life to have order and meaning. By treating ordinary life as holy—by "hallowing the everyday"—we could redeem our existence from its ordinariness, liberating the "divine sparks" within all creation. For me, this was another form of the ethos that lay at the core of the progressive faith: the redemptive possibility of human action. A lecturer in the English department knew Buber, and sent him a paper I had written about his work. The philosopher wrote back from Jerusalem, saying I had been faithful to his text, and expressing interest in my work. I was so flattered by this attention that I could hardly bring myself to read the little note, and never wrote back.

Finally, I was inspired by the recent publication of Marx's *Economic and Philosophical Manuscripts,* an early work that had been suppressed by orthodox Marxists after his death, and then by the Russians, as too Hegelian. The new edition came with a long introduction about Marx's "humanism" by the left-wing psychologist Erich Fromm, and a new title: *Marx's Concept of Man.* It also introduced a new word into the vocabulary of the Left: *alienation.* According to Marx, man was alienated from the world of his own creation by private property and capitalism. The essence of the Marxist project was to humanize the world by eliminating property, thereby enabling human beings to possess the fruits of their own labor. I did not realize it at the time, but this was really a secular version of the parable of the Fall. Marx envisaged an original state of "primitive communism" where human beings treated each other as members of one family who shared what they created. Then came the forbidden apple: Private property made possible the exploitation of labor, and the expropriation of the results of that labor in the form of profit. As a result of humanity's fall from grace, there was a long historical travail through a valley of tears. Finally, the historical process reached a point that made possible a revolutionary redemption: the creation of real Communism and the end of alienation—the restoration of man to his "true self."

I attempted to tie these philosophical threads together in a long essay on Shakespeare that I wrote for my doctoral seminar with

Professor Barish. The piece was called "Imagining the Real," after a line in Buber: "Man's heart designs designs in images of the possible, which could be made into the real." This summed up for me the revolutionary passion as I understood it. The secret of Marxism's appeal was, ultimately, its conjuring power, its fantastic vision that there could be a world different from the one we inhabited—from "all hitherto existing societies"—and that it could be *ours.* Marx expressed this idea in the most famous sentence of his *Manifesto:* "The workers have nothing to lose but their chains—they have a world to win." The revolutionary idea was not to attain a new place in the old order of things, but to change the world itself. Marxism was about a new creation that would begin with a "new man" and "new woman." It was about remaking the world. About going back to Eden and beginning again. It was the romance to end all romances.

Others arriving in Berkeley found it a wholly unusual American place, a city of social argonauts setting out on uncharted seas. Nine months earlier, Fidel Castro had led his army of *barbudos* into Havana, proclaiming the liberation of the island and a new socialist era in the West. The political torpors of the Left that had followed the Khrushchev Report seemed about to lift. Political groups proliferated, and the atmosphere was filled with a strange ideological air. There were anarchists, beatniks, old Trotskyites, and Communists holding forth in the cafés around the university campus, and the chatter was about organizing student protests and "revolution."

For me, however, Berkeley was more like a larger Sunnyside where the aliens were fewer in number and our tribe greater. On arrival, I immediately became part of a group of "red diaper babies"—the designation we used to identify ourselves as children of the Communist left. We met regularly to discuss socialist ideas, and eventually to put out one of the first journals of the Sixties, *Root and Branch.* The phrase expressed the totalism of our agenda to transform the world. Two members of our group, Bob Scheer and Maurice Zeitlin, would soon write one of the first books celebrating Fidel as a New Left hero, and defending the Cuban Revolution as a liberation not only from American capitalism but from Stalinism as well. Another group member, Sol Stern, would join Scheer as an editor of *Ramparts* magazine, the flagship publication of the New Left. In 1966, Sol would write the *New York Times Magazine* profile that would make the Black Panthers a household name. Another member was Susan Griffin, who would become a well-known author and prominent figure in the radical feminism of the next decade. It was also our little group that in 1962 organized the first demonstration in America against the war in Vietnam.

One of the first political issues we discussed among ourselves was the coming presidential election of 1960. For us the first question was not whether to vote for Richard Nixon or John F. Kennedy, but whether, as radicals, to vote at all. We organized a formal debate, and I volunteered to defend the idea that we should vote for Kennedy as "the lesser of two evils," which would have been my parents' position. With the rest of the Communist left, they had supported Democrats until 1948, when the outbreak of the Cold War and their loyalty to the Soviet Union caused them to turn against Truman. In 1952, the Progressive Party backed San Francisco attorney Vincent Hallinan, but by 1960 the Communist left had virtually disintegrated, and there was no progressive candidate to support.

Taking the position that we should not vote at all was Bob Scheer, an economics major from CCNY. Scheer had grown up in the "Coops," a cooperative apartment complex in the Bronx which, like Sunnyside, had been colonized by the Communist Party. Bearded and ursine, Scheer gave the impression of an unfinished human being. He had a bohemian charm, but was prone to gestures of gratuitous rudeness. He was said to have lost his master's thesis off the back of a motorcycle, failing to get his degree as a result. A compelling raconteur, his appeal was perversely fed by the way he retained the habits of an ill-bred adolescent. He would enter a house and announce his own arrival with the greeting "Anything to eat?" and proceed directly to the refrigerator to help himself. A camp follower of the Beat Generation, he did not however qualify as a beatnik due to a position he held as lecturer in the economics department at Cal. His style was self-consciously that of a political hipster, and his speech was salted with allusions to Charlie Mingus and Allen Ginsberg, along with Marx and Lenin. Despite his boorishness he possessed an arresting intellect, and the position he took in our debate proved to be prescient for the decade ahead.

Scheer declared the electoral system a sham because both parties were controlled by the "ruling class." Rejecting the idea of the popular front, the tactic under which the Old Left had supported Democratic candidates, he warned that Kennedy was a greater threat than Nixon because he would "co-opt" the progressive agenda. The path to real change was not through elections, but by means of demonstrations and direct action. The revolution was in the streets.

It was exciting to hear the Marxist categories revived by someone who affected the style of the Beats and was at home in the popular culture. The Old Left had a snobbish disdain for mainstream entertainments, which it viewed as corrupt expressions of "commodity capitalism." Scheer connected the political failure of the Old Left to its ghetto mentality. To hear him speak of a coming revolution in images that were not those of a marginalized subculture was exciting. It offered us the prospect of inclusion into the American mainstream while at the same time rejecting it. It was the have-your-cake-and-eat-it-too attitude that provided much of the New Left's appeal.

The same attitude has worked to obscure the real origins of the movement we created. After the Sixties, many New Left rebels went on to comfortable careers in the academic and political establishment, where they proceeded to rewrite the history they had made, in order to render it more palatable to their peers. Sometimes their revisions were as bald as misrepresenting the actual politics we embraced. Todd Gitlin, for example, was an early president of Students for a Democratic Society (SDS) who always seemed to aspire to a "nuanced" reasonableness in his political pronouncements but never had the courage to stand for these convictions in his political practice. A taut individual with eyes that peered out from behind thick-rimmed glasses, Todd was a spectral presence on the edge of the decade's events. Now an eminent professor, he has assumed center stage as a media pundit explaining them to others. In his widely read text *The Sixties: Years of Hope, Days of Rage*, Gitlin pretends that we viewed Kennedy as our leader rather than our political enemy. Gitlin contends that it was Kennedy's assassination that took away our innocence and *made* us radical. But even I, who argued that we should vote for Kennedy in 1960, was never innocent in the way

Gitlin suggests. We were Marxist revolutionaries when we began the New Left, and would have scorned *anyone* who supported Kennedy in the way Gitlin suggests.

In June 1962, for example, our radical group in Berkeley organized the first demonstration to protest the growing American presence in Vietnam. Kennedy, whom we held responsible for this intervention, had been invited to Berkeley to receive an honorary degree, and we picketed his appearance. In addition to the imperial adventure in Vietnam, Kennedy had launched an invasion of Cuba in order to reverse its revolution. (When the news broke, Scheer said, "It's right out of Lenin," prompting me to get a copy *of Imperialism: The Last Stage of Capitalism* and read it for the first time.) We regarded Kennedy as an arch Cold Warrior, a liberal agent of the imperial ruling class. Our picket signs protested: "Kennedy's Three R's: Radiation, Reaction, and Repression."

Sometimes the historical rewrite is not so brazen, but as subtle as an altered word or a suppressed understanding. James Miller, also a passive intellectual and veteran New Leftist, is an honest reporter, where Gitlin is not. But his account of the origins of the New Left, *Democracy Is in the Streets,* suffers from a similar desire to sell the Sixties to more sober times. Miller's title, for example, bowdlerizes the famous Sixties slogan, substituting the innocuous word "democracy" for its original "revolution," which was the way we actually spoke of our political agenda.

Miller's book describes the career of SDS, which was launched in 1962 via the "Port Huron Statement" and soon became the largest student organization of the New Left. In writing this statement, its Marxist authors made a self-conscious attempt to "speak American," as Miller accurately notes. Its key concept, participatory democracy, was a term coined to obscure its radical provenance. The concept was intended as a challenge to "bourgeois democracy," the kind of political democracy the Marxist left had always disdained as a sham because it did not touch the basic inequalities of class and power. Participatory democracy was really a code for what our parents' generation would have called "soviet democracy." The "soviets" were workers' councils through which "the people" were supposed to rule directly. Miller's book is honest enough to recall that the phrase "participatory democracy" was understood by the SDS founders to be a code for socialism, and that the architects of the Port Huron Statement—with one important exception—were scions of the Communist left. But he avoids the implications of these facts in his analysis of the decade.

Port Huron would get credit for creating the New Left, but the crucible of the movement was Berkeley itself. Our group regarded the Port Huron Statement as timid and disingenuous. We were proud to be socialists, Marxists, and revolutionaries. We scorned the Old Left's dishonesty in hiding its agendas behind liberal and progressive masks. Liberals were the real enemy; "progressive" was a mealy-mouthed camouflage for a revolutionary agenda. When the "Yippie" leader, Jerry Rubin, was called before the House Un-American Activities Committee, later in the decade, he did not take the Fifth Amendment or pretend he was a civil-liberties democrat, the way the Communists called before the McCarthy committees had. He appeared in knee-breeches and a three-cornered hat, and said he was an "American revolutionary" and proud of it. This was the authentic—if brief-lived—voice of the New Left.

Tom Hayden, the principal architect of the Port Huron Statement, was one of the few important figures in the SDS leadership who was not a red diaper baby, and had no radical upbringing. Instead, Hayden's radicalism seems to have sprung full-blown from what Irving Howe once described as an "obscure personal rage." The son of an alcoholic father with whom he was not on speaking terms, Tom was indeed an angry man who seemed in perpetual search of enemies.

Hayden's inner angst was given political shape by the radicals he encountered at the beginning of the Sixties. In his autobiography, *Reunion,* he records how he came to Berkeley, which he calls "the Mecca of student activism," to get a political education two years before Port Huron. But then his memory becomes vague and selective. "The Bay Area was radiating with a utopian spirit," he writes, as though the activists he met were innocent of Stalinism rather than having grown up in its political crucible. In fact, while Hayden was in Berkeley he stayed in the apartment of Mike Tigar, whose radical upbringing was just like mine. The "experienced activists" who, Hayden says, functioned as his teachers, learned what they knew as a result of growing up in the Communist left.

The real politics of the Port Huron Statement was announced in the sections on anti-Communism that were written by Hayden's mentor, Richard Flacks, whose parents were Communist schoolteachers, and members of the same Party-controlled union as mine. In the beginning, the most sincere expression of the New Left's attitude vis-à-vis Communism could be seen in its stance toward *anti*-Communism, since it was politically safer to oppose the one than to support the other. The SDS statement defined anti-Communism as a "major social problem" for anyone wanting to create a "more democratic America," rather than as a worthy struggle against a totalitarian creed. In the section about Communism, Flacks wrote: "The Communist Party has equated falsely the 'triumph of true socialism' with centralized bureaucracy." In other words, the Soviet failure did not implicate "true socialism," whose realization would be the task of the New Left. What Miller, Gitlin, and Hayden sought to obscure in their recollections of the past was this: From its beginnings, the New Left was not an innocent experiment in American utopianism, but a self-conscious effort to rescue the Communist project from its Soviet fate.

At the time the Port Huron Statement was written, to be identified with socialism was still embarrassing, which was why its authors hid their agendas behind cumbersome phrases like "participatory democracy" and double negatives like "anti-anti-Communism." It took several years and the onset of the Vietnam War for SDS to openly proclaim its Marxist agenda, which could then be justified as a response to America's "imperialist aggression." In the meantime, most activists employed liberal euphemisms to describe their politics, concentrating their attention on issues they framed in an American voice. But, as a contributor to the SDS publication *New Left Notes* observed at the end of the decade:

> You have to realize that the issue didn't matter. The issues were never the issues. You could have been involved with the Panthers, the Weather people, SLATE, SNCC, SDS. It didn't really matter what. It was the revolution that was everything... That's why dope was good. Anything that undermined the system contributed to the revolution and was therefore good.

The first of these New Left issues was unfinished business from the McCarthy era. In May 1960, the House Committee on Un-American Activities decided to hold hearings in San Francisco. It was a miscalculation by the Committee that became a made-to-order opportunity for us. We decided to organize a protest, feeling confident that we could win support for our opposition to the hearings. In the years since my father was fired, the political atmosphere had undergone a sea change. McCarthy's attempt to investigate the Army for "coddling Communists" led to his own censure by the U.S. Senate in 1954. Three years later, he died in disgrace. Meanwhile, the Supreme Court struck down the Smith Act convictions of Communist leaders, declaring them unconstitutional, while "de-Stalinization" in the Soviet Union and the progress of *détente* diminished the specter of an external threat. We no longer had the vulnerability of our parents. As members of a new radical generation, our political identity was virginal: We had the benefit of *everybody's* doubt. We could position ourselves as radical critics of American society without having to defend the crimes committed by the Soviet bloc. We could present ourselves as concerned civil libertarians without having to answer for the ghosts of Stalin's victims. And we could express our moral outrage at Communist excesses. Even Khrushchev had done that.

The first days of the San Francisco hearings were interrupted by protests in the gallery. They were led by a local Communist whose ejection from the hearing room triggered a melee in the hallway outside. When the police turned fire hoses on the students who had come to protest, the Sixties left was handed its first political cause. Afterwards, the Committee compounded its mistake by producing a film called *Operation Abolition,* which purported to uncover a Communist plot behind the events. Since we regarded the Communist Party as a political relic, and intended that our own movement supplant it, we were easily able to refute this charge. We were even insulted by the imputation, an outrage that was shared by nonradical students who had joined us as civil-liberties liberals and did not regard Communism as a significant threat. It was this alliance that made the New Left. We obtained copies of the film and showed it all over the country, using its exaggerations to discredit the Committee and the anti-Communist cause.

I wasn't there to participate in the City Hall episode, which we dubbed Black Friday, because I had classes I couldn't miss. But on the next day, Elissa and I crossed the Bay to march with the pickets around City Hall. In the months that followed, the movement seized on similar issues to swell its ranks—issues that did not require us to articulate our real politics or to justify the revival of a leftist tradition that had resulted in so much misery and death. In our campaign for the moral high ground, we demonstrated against nuclear-weapons tests by *both* Cold War camps, although our actions, of course, impacted only the politics of testing in the West. We demanded "Fair Play for Cuba" after Kennedy launched the Bay of Pigs invasion to overthrow the Castro regime, but our real desire was to see a Marxist revolution succeed. We held vigils at San Quentin, to protest capital punishment and the execution of convicted rapist Caryl Chessman (and were joined by the actor Marlon Brando just before the execution took place), and we lent our support to the struggle for civil rights in the south.

Civil rights for Negroes was the cause through which we felt most morally ennobled and politically secure. At Columbia I had been a member of the campus NAACP, and gathered signatures on a petition for a federal anti-lynch law. Like other radicals, I followed the progress of the Montgomery bus boycott and the early sit-ins, and was pleased when my mother indicated in a conspiratorial tone that Rosa Parks was "one of us." Civil rights was the cause we supported that felt most consistently right. But it had an ambivalent aspect at its core. The injustice we protested—legal segregation—was an offense to the very principles of American democracy. But in that very fact, we realized, this issue was also the one most easily co-opted. If our efforts succeeded and segregation was ended, we would have confirmed the virtue of the hated "System." In securing justice, we would have proved the efficacy of democratic reform. It was only at the end of the Sixties, when Black Power activists redefined civil rights as a "liberation struggle" *against* the System, that its politics became reassuringly radical.

Before then, the most radical issues involved military policy. When Kennedy announced that the United States would resume nuclear testing, I led a campus protest. Standing under the "speakers' tree" in

Dwinelle Plaza, I harangued students about the dangers of radioactive fallout, and the dark forces in Washington that were leading us to "a universal grave." While I was speaking, I noticed a man rocking to and fro in an agitated manner at the back of the crowd. Afterwards, I was told that this was Edward Teller, the architect of the hydrogen bomb, whom I had identified in my speech as a prince of darkness in the nuclear debate.

In organizing the rally, we had deliberately violated university regulations that required three days' notice before a demonstration, and a signed permission from university officials. Several of us were summoned before the faculty committee on student conduct. "Because I knew the campus regulation," I told the reporter for the *Daily Californian*, "I was faced with a choice when I heard the news about the President's decision on nuclear testing. That choice was between the dictates of my conscience and the directives of the administration. I made my choice believing that the genius behind the democratic ideal is the hope that institutions can respond to such individual calls as mine and become more effective instruments of social justice. I trust that the committee before which I am to appear will take that view." It did, and I was not punished. This reflected the reality that would become more apparent as the decade progressed. In our attacks on the "repressive" institutions of the university culture, we were pushing largely on open doors.

My most important political activity, at the time, was as an editor of *Root and Branch*, the first issue of which appeared in early 1962. We collected money from our group to pay for the printing and had a "collating party" to assemble the pages. The contents of *Root and Branch* reflected the concerns of the emerging New Left: the Cuban Revolution, black radicalism, "alienation," and the Third World. A member of our group, Maurice Zeitlin, had been to Cuba, where he interviewed the revolutionary icon Che Guevara. For us, the Cuban Revolution embodied first of all the hope of breaking with the tainted Stalinist past. Fidel inspired this hope by declaring that the revolution would not be a dictatorship of the Left or Right, and that its colors would be "neither red nor black, but Cuban olive green." We thought of Fidel as one of us. He was making a revolution that would be indigenous to Cuba and freed from the incubus of the Communist past. One member of our group, an engineering student named Paul Friedman, even emigrated to Cuba, to run a cement factory for the Castro regime.

Unfortunately, Maurice's interview revealed Guevara to be a hard-line Stalinist, committed to the totalitarian path that the revolution had already taken. Maurice questioned Guevara about the incipient Stalinism of the regime—its decision to outlaw internal dissent and to regard opposition to the party line as treason. Guevara seemed merely annoyed by Maurice. He defended the outlawing of opposition factions as a form of revolutionary democracy. Maurice responded by invoking the fateful specter of the Bolshevik past:

Zeitlin: It was by labeling all who disagreed with the prevailing line of the Party..."counter-revolutionaries," or by accusing them of "factionalism," that the worst aspects of Soviet politics emerged....

Guevara: I prefer not to discuss the internal politics of the Soviet Union.

Cuba's great break with the revolutionary past was obviously going to be no break at all. Another Communist dictatorship was clearly in the making, a fact which we all intuitively understood. Yet, despite this blow to our expectations, we remained staunch partisans of Fidel, and defenders of his revolution, telling ourselves—despite the evidence—that its dark turn was the work of the United States, rather than the Cubans themselves. It never would have occurred to us that it was Fidel's *intention* to turn Cuba into a Communist state, though to others that was clearly the case. We were sophisticated enough to see what was happening, but we still clung to the illusion that if America's opposition were neutralized, the revolution would reform *itself.* In this way, we discounted the negative acts of the Castro regime—and even credited them to its opponents. The same double-ledger accounting shaped our support for the Communists in Vietnam.

At one of the campus rallies we organized to defend the Cuban Revolution, a black law student named Donald Warden delivered a passionate speech. "I'm for Castro," he declared, "because Castro's for the black man." I contacted Warden about writing a piece for *Root and Branch,* called "The Black Negro," which became our lead article. It began:

> *If the liberal white Northerners who are crusading to end segregation in the South think that their efforts will solve "the Negro problem," they are sadly mistaken.*

The idea that problems were insoluble under the present System was exactly what we wanted to hear, and what we tried to persuade others to believe.

Warden's piece went on to rehearse themes that would eventually come to dominate the civil-rights movement under the slogan "Black Power." These included the psychological oppression of blacks by white values (here he invoked the virtually unknown Black Muslims), the essential conservatism and irrelevance of Martin Luther King's movement for integration, and the status of black America as an "internal colony" whose liberation was linked to revolutionary movements in the Third World. Even Warden's use of the term "black" as opposed to "Negro" anticipated political developments in the movement by nearly five years. Warden was soon to become the political mentor of Huey Newton, an Oakland street hustler who would found the Black Panther Party and make it the New Left's officially anointed "revolutionary vanguard."

An article by Scheer in the second issue of *Root and Branch* prefigured developments in a way that was even more central to the success of the Sixties left than its stands on particular issues. This was its stylistic radicalism—its "in your face" tactics and its ability to fuse Marxist agendas with the anarchic spirit of American mischief. This innovative style was what allowed the political left to join a burgeoning "counterculture" and "youth rebellion" that was much larger than itself.

The New Left did not start out with this rebellious style. The anti-HUAC pickets in San Francisco, for example, were given instructions by the organizers which contained these prudential admonitions:

> *We strive to achieve respect for the dignity of man. Thus, we must act in accordance with this ideal if we want others to respect it. All persons who participate in this line are expected to show good-will and to be*

polite, calm, and reasonable to everyone, including police, hecklers,
the public and other picketers. Do not show anger and do not use
abusive language....

Scheer's *Root and Branch* article, "Notes on the New Left," was a
calculated challenge to this left-wing propriety, and prefigured the
hallmark excesses to come. He began by dismissing the press organs
of the Old Left for speaking a Marxist language that made them irrelevant to everyone else in America. He went on to damn the two other
New Left magazines, *Studies on the Left* and *New University Thought,*
for being too stuffy and academic. What the Left needed was not only
a "reconstruction" of its theory, he wrote, but a spirit that reflected
the "sense of desperation" inherent in the revolutionary idea: "Reasonableness, responsibility, scholarliness are words with meaning to
those who do have something to lose, those to whom a slip or an error
could be costly." But our small band of leftists, he argued, could come
alive only through ferment that was "necessarily chaotic, divisive,
confused, impulsive and erratic.... We must set off explosions which
will make us relevant to this society which will disturb it and change
it." These words proved to be prophetic.

We were, in our own eyes, the self-conscious vanguard of a social
revolution, not a collection of spiritual idealists. We managed to
carry along with us "fellow travelers" who did respond in idealistic
ways to the issues we engaged, and to the high-minded slogans we
managed to contrive. But the action belonged to us and was driven
by our self-conscious political agendas. The reason for this was
simple. Among the protesters, we had the superior political experience and were able to provide convincing analyses that explained the
social mysteries to those who joined us on impulse. Others tended
to evaluate issues on their merits, prompted by judgments that were
individual and diverse. By contrast, we made our decisions collectively, and had a religious fervor toward the positions we took and the
slogans that defined them. (Lenin, as we never forgot, had split the
socialist International on the basis of a single idea). In preparing for
political actions, we identified the correct political "line," and united
behind it in a force that was able to overcome most opposition. "Hands
Off Cuba!" and "Bring the Troops Home!" were slogans designed to

consolidate majorities, but also to achieve agendas that would never have been defended by most of the people who eventually supported them. Thus, if the troops were brought home from Vietnam (a pacifist or merely meliorative hope), America would be defeated, and the Communists would win—a revolutionary gain.

In addition to soliciting "The Black Negro" from Warden, and editing Scheer's rough prose, I took on the task of acquiring art and poetry for the magazine, an editing responsibility in keeping with my literary background. I did not write a political article myself, but contributed a review of Fellini's new film, *La Dolce Vita,* which I turned into a moral indictment of capitalist consumerism. I also wrote a Buberian essay called "The Question About Meaning," whose theme strikes me now as uncannily close to the feelings that had impelled my father to join the radical cause: "The question about the meaning of life, which men have in their hearts so centrally in our era, is but another sign of the homelessness that man, himself, experiences in his social and cosmic dwelling place." Socialism would provide a home.

By the second issue, which appeared in November 1962, I had reintegrated myself into the political culture, writing a lengthy critique of the new Soviet Party program. Khrushchev had announced that the USSR would achieve the transition from socialism to Communism by 1980, overtaking the United States in production and wealth. In boasting about this prospect, he had made his famous "We will bury you" remark, which provoked a predictable reaction in the West. The program was the official plan for achieving this goal.

My essay, "The Roots of Alienation," criticized the Soviet plan for not dealing with the question that I had come to feel was at the heart of the revolutionary project, which was to restore humanity's control over its own destiny. I drew on Marx's *Economic and Philosophical Manuscripts,* and also invoked Buber's *Paths in Utopia,* which argued for a decentralized socialism. Like the rest of the New Left, I praised the socialist "base" the Soviets had created, but decried the absence of political democracy. "Since its inception," I wrote, "the socialist movement has had a two-fold impetus: the desire to redistribute the wealth of society on a more rational and equitable basis, and the vaguer and in some sense more compelling urge to liberate the spirit of man." In their new program, the Soviet leaders had rejected Stalinism as a "cult of the individual." But this, I argued, was a most un-Marxist formulation. Marxists did not normally attribute historical causation to the action of individuals or to psychological factors, but to structural forces anchored in the mode of production. The Soviet leaders' program did not have "a single proposal for the restructuring of socialist society which would insure the presence of real democracy in a communist one."

Unlike many of my New Left peers, I had doubts about the future of the new revolutions in Cuba and Vietnam. Not wanting to repeat the embarrassments of my parents' generation, I did not travel to either, and kept a certain distance from the revolutionary enthusiasts who did. My hope for the Communists was that eliminating private property would make their transition to political democracy less difficult than the transformation that lay ahead for capitalist states. In a small circle of the New Left, we even developed a *bon mot* about this. The first socialist revolution, we said, would take place in the Soviet Union.

In the spring of 1962, I published a book about the HUAC demonstrations titled *Student*. It was the first book to appear in print about the New Left, and also the first, written by a New Leftist, to present the ideas of the movement to a larger public. *Student* appeared in May, and sold 25,000 paperback copies. Twenty years later, I met Mario Savio, the leader of the Berkeley "Free Speech Movement," which organized the first demonstration to shut down a campus. Savio told me he had seen *Student* on a rack in a New York drugstore and read it almost in its entirety before he left the shop. When he finished, he said to himself "Berkeley is the place," and made up his mind to come out west.

The immediate inspiration for *Student* was a tragic incident on the Berkeley campus. On January 18, 1961, a deranged ex-student named John Harrison Farmer entered Dwinelle Hall carrying a sawed-off shotgun and looking for "Communists." Stopping at the office of English professor Thomas Parkinson, with whom he had once taken a course and whose door was carelessly ajar, he fired twice, killing teaching assistant Stephen Thomas and wounding Parkinson in the face. The crime was doubly alarming to us, because we were still embattled with the pro-HUAC forces over *Operation Abolition*, and didn't know what other reactions its incitements might provoke.

I wrote to various newspapers, hoping they would do a story on Berkeley to correct the impression that student activists were pawns in a Communist plot, and diminish the possibility of future vigilante attacks. In desperation I wrote to Ballantine Books, which had published a passionate defense of Castro (*Listen, Yankee!*) by the radical sociologist C. Wright Mills. I proposed to edit a collection of articles by participants in the Berkeley events. An encouraging reply came back from Ballantine. It was signed by Saul Landau, a friend of Mills and an editor of *Studies on the Left*. I had met Saul in 1957, when he and his wife Nina came to Sunnyside to speak to our political club, as representatives of the Labor Youth League, which was a Communist youth organization. The Landaus had just returned from the Moscow Youth Festival and China, and I remember how, in response to a question about capital punishment in the People's Republic, Nina explained that socialist executions were different from capitalist ones since they were conducted on behalf of the "people."

In the summer of 1959, Saul spent three months in Cuba, where he met with Castro and other Communist officials and formed a working relationship with them. On his return to the States, he set up the national Student Fair Play for Cuba Committees and went on a tour of campuses, telling his audiences, "Fidel made the revolution without the Communists and against them." This was an important contribution to Castro's propaganda campaign against U.S. policy, which was based on the claim that Cuba's revolution had been hijacked by Communists bent on taking Cuba into the Soviet orbit—which Castro soon did. It was only after Cuba had been a Soviet satellite for thirty years that Landau—who was still a supporter of the dictator—felt it was safe to admit that Castro had been "a Communist from the beginning and we always knew it."

With Landau's letter in hand, I sat down to write the introduction to *Student*, and set deadlines for the other contributors. I regarded my effort as a political action rather than a literary project, but when the deadlines came and the others failed to deliver their chapters, I ended up writing the book myself. This was not difficult, however, as my passions were immediately engaged by the subject. In the introduction,

I indicted the university as a bureaucratic enterprise that reduced the students to cogs in a machine. I quoted the poet Kenneth Rexroth, who had described Berkeley as the "Rouge River of the Intellect," a reference to the site of Henry Ford's vast automobile production plant in Dearborn. Quoting a book on college careers which said "The most important product you'll ever have to sell is yourself," I objected: "A man is not a product, nor is he an IBM record card." My indictment of the university as the symbol of an oppressive corporate culture found its way into Mario Savio's most famous outburst during the Free Speech crisis:

> *This is a firm, and if the Board of Regents are the board of directors,... then...the faculty are a bunch of employees and we're the raw material. But we're a bunch of raw material that don't mean ... to be made into any product.... There's a time when the operation of the machine becomes so odious ... you've got to put your bodies upon the gears and upon the wheels, upon the levers, upon all the apparatus, and you've got to make it stop.*

The concluding chapter of *Student* was called "New Politics" and outlined the political vision of the emerging New Left. It identified our difference from the Communist left in our commitment to a democratic politics, including free speech, the abolition of capital punishment, and self-determination. In defending this last principle, my conclusion equated America's intervention in Cuba with the Soviet invasion of Hungary, a common position among us. Behind our agendas, I explained, was a "philosophy that puts human beings in all their complexity first, that denies the existence of a single True Path in politics" and that establishes "respect for others" as the cardinal principle of social action.

In keeping with other common attitudes of our New Left group, I also criticized economic determinism and the idea that socialism had to mean a centralized plan. In its penultimate paragraph, I even took a guilty—if still elliptic—look at the concealment of our Marxist assumptions and socialist agendas. I attributed this lack of candor to the atmosphere of intimidation that McCarthyism had created. I tried to turn it into a virtue by suggesting that there was a natural connection between our radicalism and our defense of such liberal issues as free speech: "Only those who have something to say in the first place will risk defending the right to say it. Only those who are really concerned with society can be really concerned for freedom." This strikes me now as just another instance of the arrogant nature of our politics, as though progressives like us had a monopoly on caring.

I dedicated *Student* to Justice Hugo Black, the First Amendment absolutist on the Supreme Court, and sent it to him along with a gushing letter telling him that his views had inspired in me a "love" for America's heritage of freedom: "While I have not relinquished my socialist beliefs, nor my critical stance, they have been infused and transformed by a new and equally revolutionary stream,... [which] is the life element of my native land." The notion that democracy was a revolutionary idea for America itself was a characteristic radical subterfuge that Black missed. He wrote back: "I agree with you that there is no reason why a 'socialist of one kind or another' cannot be, as you are, a passionate believer in the freedoms embodied in the Bill of Rights," and added: "I hope you will continue to have the same fervent devotion to your country that your letter indicates you have because I agree with you that our country is worth that kind of devotion."

The Communist Party's west coast paper attacked *Student* for what it regarded as my concessions to the anti-Communist cause. But Dorothy Healey, a Party leader, wrote me a personal letter dissociating herself from its attack. My mother also wrote, noting each of our progressive friends who was pleased with the book plus those, like Henry Danielowitz, who were not. (Henry was offended by my critical remarks about the Party.) In another letter she advised me that it was important to promote the book. The *National Guardian,* a progressive paper, also attacked *Student,* so I wrote to its editor, James Aronson, who wrote back a two-page reply. To my mother this was a sign of his respect. She added that I should not expect this respect to find its way into print in the *Guardian's* columns, and warned me not to take this to heart:

> *David, don't be like us oldsters. You were the one who said you are interested in dialogue and here it is. One thing we of the Left used to do (and I don't think we had a monopoly on it) was to argue a point to the last word and everyone had to be committed by the time*

the last word was reached. Then, of course, once we were committed,
there was no retreat. Well, now I know better. For my own part, I am
quite sure that the Guardian is going to be very slow in changing any
of its ideas, if it ever will. But to me that is very unimportant. What
remains important, and has remained so for all the years I have been
in disagreement with them, is that we are both on the same side and
they are doing a noble job.

My father, as usual, let my mother do the talking at first. Then I
got a letter from him which avoided the conflicts I knew were there,
because I had been so conscious of his looking over my shoulder, especially when writing the last chapter, which contained my criticisms of
the Party. He began by bestowing a welcome fatherly praise, albeit one
that still seemed to contain an ambivalent note: "I must say that it's a
great piece of work, and that I'll not shy away from accepting my 'due'
as a proud father when others congratulate me as I've tended to do in
the past through a feeling that the praise was a general kudo for having
a son who had written a 'book' and had it published." Then he said he
wanted "to quote from something that reflected the central situation
in your book in much the same way that you see it." There followed a
passage from an article comparing the Thirties and the Sixties. "Now
who do you suppose said that?" my father asked. It turned out to be
Gus Hall, the General Secretary of the Communist Party.

I wrote *Student* when I was studying for my master's orals. It was a
calculated distraction from the work I should have been doing, but
I did well on the exams anyway. Elissa and I had moved into a little
stucco house on Acton Way, where we had a one-bedroom apartment for sixty dollars a month. We had acquired a white cat with tiger
markings whom we named Minnelouche, after a poem by Yeats; and
a German Shepherd we called Andy Chiappe. When kittens arrived,
it was difficult to get them "adopted" and we began to accumulate
a sizable menagerie. At one point I counted twenty-seven cats and
three litters in our tiny household. But nature quickly asserted itself
as the rival mothers drove each other out, killing their newborns and
even eating their own.

In our second year, Elissa became pregnant. This was not exactly planned, but neither was it entirely an accident. We had never used any contraception except the rhythm method, which was an uncertain precaution at best. Like the vegetarian regimen we had adopted after arriving in California, this was a decision Elissa made and I was happy to follow. In declaring her rejection of other contraceptive methods, she might have said something to me like "It's unnatural." But it was not really an idea as she presented it, and there was no argument offered to justify it. She did not think programmatically in that way. It was more like an instinct or feeling.

Once I yielded to her will, on the other hand, I felt the need to convert it into a principle. When I had worked it out as a formal position on contraception (pretty much against), I incorporated it into my *Root and Branch* article on meaning. But when I presented the text to Scheer, he responded with a smirk and pretended not to understand the argument at all. His subtext was transparent: *Only a reactionary, probably only a Catholic, could have a point of view so perverse.* The subject itself was so personal that I was embarrassed to defend what I had written. I removed the explicit reference from my text, and approached the matter obliquely. "A sign of the uncertain footing of this generation in the world," I wrote, "is the reluctance to bring new being into it."

When Elissa told me she was pregnant, my response was ambivalent. It was not that I didn't want a child, but having one seemed impractical at the time. She had not yet completed her degree, and I felt that by getting her pregnant I was jeopardizing her studies. She was a bright student scheduled to graduate in less than two years. I felt at once protective and guilty. As the male and the sexual aggressor, I was sure that I was the source of the conflicts she now had to face. A maternal state was part of woman's oppression. I had made it harder for her to become independent and achieve a status beyond motherhood. This progressive but abstract understanding prevented me from entertaining the idea that her will might be as forceful in this situation as mine. Or that her adamancy on the issue of contraception, and her insistence on an unreliable method, might have constituted an important factor in our dilemma. Or, more importantly, that it was an indication of a powerful desire.

Years later, after we had three of our four children, Elissa confronted me over the lack of emotional support I provided at the onset of her pregnancies. I was bewildered. I wanted children, and I also wanted her to feel that I stood behind her. But my guilt at "getting her pregnant" had caused me to let her down. I had done the "right" thing, but somehow it had turned out wrong. For the first time, I began to resent the progressive ideas that had shaped my reactions and, in this instance, separated me from her.

I was allowed by the doctor to be present at the birth of our child, whom we named Jonathan. The drama was increased by the fact that he came into the world feet first, a breech birth. The anticipation of his exit from the womb was overlaid by the anxiety that his umbilical cord might be wrapped around his neck and strangle him as he emerged. But the real excitement flowed from the primal sense that here was something alive, a being whom I had a part in creating and who would depend on me and be linked to me forever.

Jonathan's arrival shifted the center of our little universe. We were no longer children, but parents responsible for another life. In the first few months, we took this responsibility to its natural extreme, checking periodically on the infant in his crib, to see that he was still breathing. Even without such attentions, our life now revolved around his. Elissa breast-fed him on demand, nursing him in the rocker we bought for the purpose. She did not want to feed him formula from a bottle, so there was no relief from this routine. In a moment of frustration, I calculated that these attentions occupied her eight hours a day. Inevitably, this played havoc with her studies. When she had classes, I would baby-sit and she would feed him before she left for school. Three hours later, I would pack him in the back of the car and race to pick her up before he woke. Once I got a ticket for running a red light, and always thereafter would dread his waking before she returned. This arrangement became more and more untenable, and soon Elissa was forced to drop out of school again, a move which caused me a new bout of guilt.

Yet this birth provided me with an answer to the loneliness and lack of fulfillment I had felt, fusing the bond between Elissa and me, and providing a powerful pull into the future. In my *Root and Branch* essay I even made it the answer to the philosophical question I had posed about the meaning of life:

> *Man's life is cluttered with purposes, but his own has none.... The mystery that the heart seeks, the renewal, the spring of renewed living that keeps lived life in its course, is the mystery of creation, of bringing into being.... The question about meaning is answered in the face of creation, where all question disappears.*

But, of course, in "lived life" having a child was not the sufficient answer to anything. It was more like the beginning of new questions.

By the spring of 1962, I was again restless. My academic career had reached an impasse. The professional field of English literature had been mined by too many intelligent scholars for too long. The subject had been over-analyzed and over-researched, leaving little that would justify another thesis-length study or book. I could envisage no scholarly exercise to qualify me for a doctoral degree that would not feel like intellectual death. I had enrolled in a doctoral seminar with Professor Barish for the purpose of writing my dissertation, but had handed in the long paper on Shakespeare that I had called "Imagining the Real," instead. It made no pretense to being a contribution to scholarship. Professor Barish chuckled when he handed it back to me and said, "What do you propose to do with this?" I understood that I had to leave.

LONDON

STUDENT OPENED WITH A QUOTE FROM INGMAR BERGMAN'S FILM *The Magician*—"I have prayed just one prayer in my life: Use me." I thought of it as a plea my generation might have addressed to the void at the center of the American cornucopia. I had inherited this indictment of American culture from my father, but it was a cliché of the Left. Even in its taste for films (that most American of art forms), the radical mind affected a snobbish disdain for the national product. At the south end of the campus, the Telegraph Avenue Cinema showed the latest features of Fellini, Godard, Bergman, and Truffaut, making it a mecca for Berkeley's New Left. It was the impact of these films— especially Bergman's, with their portentous quests for meaning—that triggered a desire in me to go to Europe, where I would find "real" culture. Jonathan's tender age and Elissa's reluctance to pull up roots meant that any move would be difficult. But, as so often in my life, I was impelled by forces I felt I couldn't ignore, and, once the idea took hold in my mind, I was prepared to drag everyone along to follow it.

I had received a $500 advance for *Student*—exactly enough for two air tickets—and, with savings of roughly $2,000, I was confident we could support ourselves for a year. In April 1962 I walked into the Dwinelle office of a Norwegian political scientist named Christian Bay, who served as a faculty adviser for the Left, and asked him for contacts in Norway and Sweden. Another contact I could count on was Lionel Colloms. While attending a conference of leftists in Spain, he had fallen in love with an Englishwoman named Brenda Collins, and had never come back to his wife. With these resources assembled,

I was ready to pack up our Berkeley house, relocate the animals with friends, and set off for a new world.

On arriving in London we touched base with Lionel and Brenda, in their flat near Primrose Hill. When they asked me my plans, I told them I intended to write a book about Buber and Marx. It was going to be my attempt to make up the theoretical deficit in Marxism that had led to the Stalin debacle. In *Paths in Utopia*, Buber had suggested a way of joining the ethical schemes of the utopian socialists with what I saw as the more realistic Marxist assumptions about power. By chance, the head of Tavistock Books lived in a flat upstairs from the Collomses, and they arranged a meeting. I left him with the essay I had written on Buber, and a book proposal, and he said he would contact me when he had read them.

London was dreary, and the weather foul. Every day it rained. Jonathan, an active infant, refused to ride in his stroller, crawling on all fours wherever we went. During a tour of the Tate Gallery, his hands and feet became coal black, and we anxiously tried to keep his fingers out of his mouth. We had made the mistake of taking a week's lodging near Paddington Station, in a gloomy bed-and-breakfast, whose proprietor cooked everything in large quantities of grease. When the seven days were over, we decided to give up on England and push on to Sweden, which had been my agenda from the start. The prospect of being in a setting that was even partially socialist had an irresistible attraction. As if that was not enough, there was the added pull of a culture that had produced Ingmar Bergman. Perhaps I expected the Seventh Seal to open when we arrived in Stockholm.

Traveling by train to Edinburgh, and from there to Newcastle, we boarded an ocean ferry. Following a turbulent overnight passage across the North Sea, we landed in Bergen just in time for the summer solstice. The Norwegian light was magical, the sun hanging high in the evening, far into the night. Even the bed-and-breakfasts were a comforting contrast to England, offering sumptuous buffets *sans* grease. After a few days, we pushed on to Oslo, where Professor Bay had provided me with a contact named Luggen Mowinckel. The eight-hour trip from Bergen was billed as the most beautifully scenic train ride in the world, but I had to take in the view from between the cars, where I stood holding Jonathan, who was teething, so that the noise of the wheels would drown his cries. From this vantage, I did notice the huge warehouses along the route that had the letters MOWINCKEL emblazoned across them. Arriving in Oslo, we discovered that Luggen was a scion of one of the great Norwegian shipping families, and that his grandfather had been prime minister. Luggen was a gentleman adored by his wife and towheaded son, but there was a cloud of tragedy over his family. His father and grandfather had committed suicide, and a few years after we left Norway, the cloud enveloped Luggen, and he too took his own life.

Luggen was bemused by my innocent enthusiasm for his country, which he regarded as a backwater at the edge of the significant world. When I expressed my admiration for the statuary in Frogner Park (the famous sculptural display that had been financed by the Norwegian government), Luggen remarked wryly that its muscular celebrations of humanity reminded him of fascist monuments. I was taken aback by his observation: I had regarded the park as a socialist use of public space.

With Luggen's help we put an ad in the Oslo paper, offering to do work in exchange for room and board. Within a week it was answered by a farmer, one Trygve Fruhaug, who wanted me to serve as a working hand. Elissa was to help his pregnant wife with her chores. We soon found ourselves living in a 200-year-old farmhouse overlooking the Tjieri Fjord, about an hour's train ride from Oslo. The setting suited my romantic expectations, but the rigors of the farm routine were severe. The workday began at four in the morning and went practically straight through until eight at night. By that time, I was so tired I couldn't lift the ax with which I was supposed to be stripping logs as the last chore of the day. Whether I would have adjusted to the rural life was rendered academic when Elissa became enmeshed in a conflict with the farmer's wife. Our permissive ways included letting Jonathan crawl about in the house naked, so that the air might heal his diaper rash. This was incomprehensible to its mistress, particularly when he peed on the floor, which was promptly scrubbed with boiling water. "He must have a playpen," she said, "a place where he stays." In her mind, the incident was clearly the symptom of a larger issue: Children were to be ruled, not to rule.

We left the farm and returned to Oslo to say goodbye to the Mowinckels, heading for Uppsala, where another contact waited. Sven

Hamrell was a political scientist, an important figure in Sweden's tiny political elite, who ran the Liberal Party's publishing house, Verdandi. Hamrell found us a cottage on the banks of Lake Mälaren, a twenty-minute bus ride from the center of town, and offered me a modest contract to rewrite *Student* for a Swedish audience. It was already autumn, and the woods on the route to the Carolingen library, which I visited twice a week, were a kaleidoscope of colors. The cold came so suddenly that I could map the changes in the leafy palette on trips to town. Half jokingly, I asked our landlord if the lake, which stretched sixty miles to Stockholm, froze in the winter. You could drive a car on its surface all the way to the capital, he answered. In fact, it eventually became so cold that you couldn't be outside more than ten minutes without a fur hat to cover your ears, or the physical pain would be too much to bear.

Fortunately, our cottage was made of walls a foot thick, which kept the cold out once we had lit a fire in the wood stove. It was a cozy time for our little family, although the uncertain financial future imposed invisible deadlines on my writing project, so that I buried myself in newspapers and books as soon as we were up. We never laid down a bedtime rule to Jonathan, whose energy seemed inexhaustible. Our hours got later as the days grew shorter, until we were rising at noon, and "night" was falling less than three hours after. The cellar of our cottage was filled with apples from the orchard surrounding it, prompting Elissa, who had become an inventive cook, to use them for pies, sauce, and other treats. Reluctantly, we had to expand our vegetarian diet to include fish when we discovered that, besides potatoes, there were hardly any vegetables available. Since the cold kept us indoors except for brief sojourns to the local store, meals and the preparation of meals became the principal events in our days, and the center of our family life.

Shortly after we settled in, an international crisis began building in the Caribbean over the placement of Soviet missiles in Cuba. The United States blockaded the island. As Soviet ships headed toward collision with the American fleet, I watched the television images at our landlord's house, and tried to decipher the stories in the Swedish press. During the weeklong crisis, I walked the banks of Lake Mälaren, watching the northern light play on the spectacular autumn canvas, thinking how wonderful life was with Elissa and my new son, and wondering if it was all going to end.

My Swedish version of *Student* had transformed itself into a full-scale history of the Cold War. When the crisis was resolved, I took the scare as an inspiration to put even more energy into my new book. I was still operating under the illusion I had when I was ten years old—that I could influence history if given the chance. I also wanted to understand the origins of the conflict that had dominated world events since I first became conscious of political issues. I even told myself that I was ready to consider the possibility that Stalinism was its cause. But it did not take me long to convince myself that this was not the case. I relied heavily on two writers who shared the progressive view that its origins lay in America's opposition to the Russian Revolution. D. F. Fleming, the author of *The Cold War and Its Origins,* was a longtime Soviet sympathizer, and Carl Marzani was a Communist whose tract about the early years of the Cold War was called *We Can Be Friends.*

In my preface I adopted an Olympian pose, taking both sides to task for creating self-justifying myths that obscured the facts. It was the same doctrine of moral equivalence with which the drafters of the Port Huron Statement had masked their deeper commitments to the socialist camp. Unlike Marzani, I was critical of many Soviet policies, including the establishment of satellite dictatorships in Eastern Europe. But it was also clear in everything I wrote that America and the "Free World" were the prime movers of the conflict, and had provoked the Soviets to react.

I called the book *The Free World Colossus* and set up its argument by revisiting the Cuban Missile Crisis. U.S. spokesmen had attributed the conflict to a "remorseless Soviet expansionism" that began after World War II. "No one can question that Chairman Khrushchev has altered many things in the Soviet Union, ..." Ambassador Adlai Stevenson declared before the UN, "but there is one thing he has not altered—and that is the basic drive ... to destroy the hope of a pluralistic world order. ..." Against this official perspective, I marshaled the views of liberal and left-wing writers like Walter Lippmann and P.M.S. Blackett. Following Lippmann's seminal articles, I argued that the Soviet Union had *not* expanded after 1945, but had merely failed to withdraw its armies from the line of truce.

Like other left-wingers, I attributed this failure to the West's unwillingness to provide aid to Russia and thus make its leaders feel secure. Of course, making the Kremlin feel secure meant strengthening the Soviet dictatorship and its grip on Eastern Europe. A great deal of faith was required to believe that supporting Stalin would encourage him to relinquish his wartime gains. But, in this area, I remained a party liner—believing that Stalin's actions were motivated by fear, and that his interventions in Eastern Europe had merely "distorted" an indigenous process that was "in the last analysis" progressive and would advance the cause of social justice. With other radicals, I believed that the real drama of the Cold War was *not* about a truce line in the middle of Europe. It was about an epochal conflict between rival social systems. The term "Soviet expansionism" was the West's code for the spread of revolution; "containment" was really a policy of counterrevolution.

When it was published, *The Free World Colossus* became the first account of the Cold War written from a New Left perspective. Its long middle section—"Leader of the Free World"—was devoted to what Movement radicals would soon be referring to as the American empire, and helped create the standard radical litany of America's global crimes. Separate chapters dealt with the CIA-engineered *coups* in Iran and Guatemala, the CIA-orchestrated invasion of Cuba, and the U.S. intervention in Vietnam. It concluded with a peroration, in cumbersome prose:

> *When America set out on her post-war path to contain revolution throughout the world, and threw her immense power and influence into the balance against the rising movement for social justice among the poverty-stricken two-thirds of the world's population, the first victims of her deeds were the very ideals for a better world—liberty, equality and self-determination—which she herself, in her infancy, had done so much to foster.*

Like much New Left rhetoric, this was overwrought but effective. When the book came out two years later, it received praise from such reviewers as John Leonard (soon to be editor of the *New York Times*

Book Review), John Gerassi, an editor at *Newsweek*, and Dwight Macdonald, a charter member of the New York intellectuals who should have known better, but wrote: "The best survey I know of the historical background of our present foreign policy—clearly written, fully documented, and so moderate and reasonable in tone that defenders of our post-war crusade against 'Communism' won't know what's happened to them until they try to sneeze." My father's old Palo Alto comrade, Holland Roberts, who had moved his American Russian Institute to San Francisco, sent a letter of congratulations: "How happy I am with you at David's remarkable creative development."

Some critics refused to join the general approbation. A notice by Harry Howe Ransom in the *Saturday Review* was headed "Aren't We Doing Anything Right?" and observed that the book failed to take into account "the Marxist-Leninist basis of Russian and Chinese policies." Robert Hazo wrote, in *The New Republic*: "Mr. Horowitz' posture is that of a bearer of 'possible enlightenment from within' who dispassionately is examining the slogans and clichés of the current consensus before the tribunal of serious history. [But] once the calm cautions of the Preface are out of the way, like so much ritual before the slaughter, Horowitz proceeds to prosecute the United States at every possible turn." Hazo described me as a member of "a new breed of American ideologue, the anti-anti-Communist," and agreed with Ransom that I had failed to treat the Soviet Union as an active force in shaping events: "There must be some mysterious cosmic joke in Horowitz's failure to mention, even in passing, theoretical Communism's explicit intent to convert the world into its own image." *The Free World Colossus* eventually went into several printings, and was translated into French, German, Spanish, Norwegian, Swedish, Dutch, Hebrew, and Japanese—a tribute to the international network of the Left. In America, it became a handbook for the emerging movement against the war in Vietnam.

Ransom and Hazo were, of course, right that I had ignored the dynamics of Soviet policy and its international agents and supporters, and that I had discounted the active role of the Soviet rulers in shaping Cold War events. By making many critical observations about Soviet society and socialist practice, however, I had gained a credibility that writers like Marzani and Fleming could never have achieved.

These criticisms caused me concern as to the possible reactions of my parents and their friends. To soften any blow from what I had written, I sent them chapters of the work in progress.

My father responded in a letter dated March 31, 1963, which began reassuringly:

> Your [chapter], dispassionate as it may seem to you, certainly makes plain which side we are on, and as long as we are on the side of the people, "just poor people" as Abe Lincoln put it in the play, as we have been for as long as you can remember—all of our lives, there will be no gap or hostility until nuclear destruction or threat of it destroys us all.
>
> Your letters pile up on my desk kept there by my very best intentions to reply to each. And I do......in the silence of the afternoon ... my thoughts are rapidly typing their way through a long reply in praise of the vast job you've done, in recognition of your great strides and in great delight and pride in sweep of the journey that you and your little family have undertaken.

I was not prepared by memory for the generosity of these paternal blessings. Rereading them, after so many years, my first reaction was to reflect on whether we are simply destined, as children, never to get enough. But as I read further, my original feelings of rejection returned. The praise seemed now, as it did then, typically abstract and general, while the rejection that followed was particular and concrete. Along with the pages of the manuscript I had sent him the second issue of *Root and Branch,* which had appeared with my article on the Soviet Draft Program:

> *Root and Branch* struck me by the complete absence of anything that was critical of this capitalist-imperialist world. Bob Scheer's brittle brilliance was expended in a fury against the left with only a side glance here and there, perfunctory it seemed, against today's main enemy. Your article "The Roots of Alienation, A Critique of the Soviet Draft Program" struck me as leaning too heavily both on Buber and Fromm. Your quotation from Fromm estranges the discussion from economics to ethics, and by tying in Buber no help is given to the reader toward understanding why the Soviet

program fails to abolish alienation. It's confusing rather than clar-
ifying, and it seems overstuffed and pretentious.

Overstuffed and pretentious. That was the way my father really saw
me. He had directed his attack right to the place where my ambition
was centered, and where I was going to make my "contribution"—as
a Marxist.

I still had no American publisher. While I was wondering what to do
about this, a notice appeared in the *New York Times,* announcing
that the famous philosopher Bertrand Russell, then in his nineties,
was forming a new Peace Foundation in London. I wrote to ask if his
new organization might help in publishing my book. Meanwhile, the
Tavistock publisher I had met in London came through Stockholm.
He told me that the psychologist R. D. Laing, author of *The Divided
Self,* who was the editor of a Tavistock series on existentialism, liked
the essay I had written. He offered me a contract for the book I had
proposed to him on Buber and Marx.

The prospect of writing a book for Tavistock strengthened the
decision Elissa and I had already made to move back to London. We
had hardly any contact with anyone in Sweden, aside from rare visits
with Sven Hamrell and his wife. I was so absorbed in my work that I
barely noticed the isolation of our Swedish stay, but it was hard on
Elissa, who was pregnant again. Her condition made me sensitive once
more to the conflict between my ambitions to explore what life had
to offer, and my responsibility to provide a stable environment that
would nurture the life we were creating. Our new home in England
would be the third in Jonathan's two years of existence. I worried
about the impact of these dislocations on his development, even as
I regretted the added stress that it meant for Elissa. London seemed
more likely to offer a setting where we could make some friends. I had
no financial means or prospect of getting us back to the United States.

In London we located a one-bedroom basement flat on Rosecroft
Avenue, near Hampstead Heath. I had secured a position as a lecturer
with the University of Maryland's overseas extension, which had a
degree program for U.S. servicemen. Twice a week I took the train
for Greenham Common and other military bases, to teach English

composition to the airmen. Some of my assignments were on Strategic Air Command bases, whose B-52s loaded with nuclear bombs were on readiness alert. The atmosphere was tense enough so that on one occasion, when I was sitting with my students in the canteen after class, a test alarm went off and one of the officers at our table jumped with such a start that he spilled his coffee.

In the course I taught, I often introduced political themes into the essay subjects, once inviting the students to write on the question of whether the United States should withdraw its military forces from Vietnam. It was one of only two occasions on which my views in class produced any conflict, the other being my affirmative answer to the question of whether I would marry a Negro. An Air Force captain regarded my Vietnam views as treasonous, saying that if I were under his command, "I would shoot you dead." But in general my students, and especially the noncommissioned officers (mainly southerners from working-class backgrounds), were friendly, and we got along well.

While I labored over *Capital* and other Marxist texts in preparation for my new book, our little family gradually adjusted to an English routine. Jonathan, we discovered, had a musical aptitude. At three he could identify all the instruments in the orchestra by sound. I took him to a concert featuring five contemporary concertos, where he sat rapt for two and a half hours while he sucked on his pacifier. He had a flair for drawing as well, and could construct recognizable facsimiles of such complicated scenes as an Irish sword dance. Elissa, who had been an art student at Music and Art, would sit and draw with him for hours on his little bed in what otherwise would have been our living room, while I wrote in the bedroom or was off teaching at a base. When I came home, I would bring back toy replicas of the Queen's guards and other soldiers, which he and Elissa would use as models.

My first meeting in London was with Bertrand Russell's secretary, Ralph Schoenman, who had answered my request for help in publishing *The Free World Colossus*. When we met in his London office, however, Schoenman switched the subject abruptly, proposing that I ghost a book about "the rise of the Fourth Reich" instead. It was clear that he wanted such a book in order to tar the West German government with the Nazi brush. I had no appetite for this. I was doubtful of the claim, and anyway didn't know German, so declined the project.

Schoenman was an angular American with a Lincoln beard, a slash for a mouth, and eyes that burned right through you. A saccharine smile made his manner aggressive and ingratiating at the same time. He was only three years older than I was, but as Russell's emissary—as he quickly informed me—he had already visited fifty-seven countries and been received by thirty-five heads of state. It was impressive to watch him pick up the phone in our basement flat and put in a call to "Jimmy" Baldwin in Paris, to commiserate over the assassination of Malcolm X. He was the only New Leftist I ever met who I felt could live up to our revolutionary rhetoric about "seizing the state." I could easily imagine Ralph walking into the War Room of the Pentagon to announce "We're taking over."

At the time I met him, Ralph had just spent more than a month in Ghana making himself an American Rasputin to its dictator, Kwame Nkrumah. In Ralph's probably exaggerated account, the chief minister would arrive at his suite in the morning for marching orders. He did show me a speech he wrote for Nkrumah, however, which called on the Organization of African States to expel the UN forces from the Congo. On a trip to China, Ralph had been closely watched by government agents, while Premier Chou En-lai kept him waiting several days for an audience. Fuming over this treatment, Ralph picked up the hotel phone and shouted into the receiver "Chairman Mao is a sacred cow," to get their attention. Taken boating on the lake in the Forbidden City, he removed his clothes and went for a swim. When he finally gained an audience with Chou En-Lai, the premier warned Ralph that if he continued to misbehave, they would put him in a cell four feet by six.

Arriving in England in 1958 at age 22, Ralph had approached Russell with a plan to turn the Campaign for Nuclear Disarmament into a civil-disobedience movement called the Committee of 100. Russell embraced the idea, and the CND split into two warring factions. Then, at aged 90, Russell participated in a sit-in in Trafalgar Square, was taken to jail, and made headlines. Ralph's irrepressible energy had transformed a revered figurehead into a leader of men. But there was a price to be paid, as Ralph took an increasingly important role not only in shaping Russell's pronouncements but also in steering him into situations where he was at the mercy of the younger man's judgment. From then on, it was difficult for outsiders to know where Ralph left off and Russell began.

Both men shared a passionate moralism that was principally directed at America and the West. But as Schoenman took over the philosopher's public persona, an extreme note entered his declarations, unleavened by his customary wit. After Schoenman's entry into his life, Russell thrilled his young antinuclear disciples, while shocking their elders, by saying: "We used to call Hitler wicked for killing off the Jews, but Kennedy and Macmillan are much more wicked than Hitler.... We cannot obey these murderers. They are wicked. They are abominable. They are the wickedest people who have ever lived in the history of man and it is our duty to do what we can against them." Stylistically, this was of a piece with Ralph's own pronouncements. As a fledgling member of the Campaign for Nuclear Disarmament, he had said: "Aldermaston and the rocket bases are Britain's Auschwitz and Buchenwald."

Russell would have been marginalized even more than he was by these statements, except for the fact that Khrushchev recognized they could be used to his advantage. During the Cuban Missile Crisis, Schoenman had Russell fire off telegrams to both superpower leaders. To Kennedy he declared: "Your action desperate ... Ultimatum means war ... End this madness." To Khrushchev he wrote: "I appeal to you not to be provoked by the unjustifiable action of the United States." The Soviet dictator immediately made Russell an intermediary in negotiating an end to the crisis.

Later, when he became disillusioned with Ralph, Russell confided in a memorandum that the younger man's power over him owed much to his own vanity: "I am by no means immune to flattery," he wrote a year before his death. "It is so rare as to be sweet in my ears." The flattery to which the author of *Principia Mathematica* fell prey was a siren song that seduced many an intellectual before and after, including myself. Schoenman had convinced him that through the force of his intellect he could shape historical events.

Other acts of devotion completed Ralph's conquest. Above all, he demanded that Russell be given his due when others treated him as the irrelevancy he had become. Famous artists had been asked to donate their works to raise money for the Foundation. When Picasso failed to deliver his promised canvas, Ralph went to his house in France and announced at the door that he was Russell's secretary and had come to collect the picture. He then lay down in Picasso's driveway for three hours until the item was produced. Subsequently, he waylaid Richard Burton and Elizabeth Taylor, jumping out of an elevator in a hotel in Scotland to demand their performance on a similar promise.

Like all good salesmen, Ralph believed his own pitch about being at the center of world events. One night I was roused from sleep in our basement flat by his call. His voice was urgent—he couldn't talk over the phone, and I was to come immediately to the Foundation's office. It occurred to me that something terrible had happened. Perhaps there had been a bombing; perhaps Russell had died. I arrived at the office at 1 a.m.

The Foundation occupied two bare rooms in a small building in central London. Despite the impressive names on its stationery—which included Nkrumah, Nehru, Elizabeth Queen of the Belgians, Haile Selassie, Pablo Casals, and Albert Schweitzer—it had virtually no funds, and no influence aside from what Russell's dwindling reputation could command. The other staffers were a Trotskyite printer named Pat Jordan; Russell Stetler, a young American who had organized something called the "May 2nd Movement" at Haverford College in Pennsylvania; Chris Farley, a youthful aide to Russell; and Pam Wood, a secretary to Schoenman. When I arrived, they were there with Faris Glubb, a Schoenman hanger-on whose father, Sir John Glubb, had been the last commander of the Arab Legion, but who himself had no special claim on anybody's attention. When we were all assembled, Ralph opened the meeting with these words: "There's been a *coup* in Oman. What should we do?"

Ralph's megalomania was manifest in other and more worrying ways. At one point, before leaving on a trip to Kenya, he showed me a fifty-page plan he had written for a *coup d'état* against the Kenyatta regime, complete with instructions for taking over communications centers and the airport. He intended to put the document in the hands of Oginga Odinga, the country's leading left-wing politician and Kenyatta's tribal rival. On the same trip, Ralph had an audience with the dictator himself. He urged Kenyatta, who was then head of the Organization of African Unity, to issue an ultimatum to the

Western powers to leave the Congo or face war. As Ralph pressed his point, Kenyatta leaned over and said something in Swahili to Ralph's escort. Shortly afterwards, the audience ended. When Kenyatta was gone, Ralph asked: "What did the old man say?" The escort answered: "He said 'Get rid of this man, he's dangerous.'"

I was beginning to have similar feelings, though not strong enough to extricate myself from my entanglement with Schoenman. Not for the last time in my life, I discounted the destructive elements in someone's behavior as an excess of good intentions. Like Russell, I admired his courage and his outrage at injustice. Ralph was not only ready to risk others' lives, but his own as well. The massacres in the Congo, which he facilely attributed to the Western powers, inflamed his political passions and led him to write a brief on the atrocities, which he distributed at the UN. Later, he visited the Congo in person, clearly a dangerous undertaking. These acts of personal bravery partially disarmed my doubts. But I was still uncomfortable with his behavior, and increasingly with his attempt to transform Russell into a Marxist. Because of this concern, I could no longer work on the speeches he wrote for Russell. Ralph didn't really see himself as a facilitator, but saw Russell as an opportunity to serve himself.

Even when Ralph was out of the country, the Foundation proved a surreal environment. Once I had to stand in for him, to orchestrate a meeting between Russell and the American folksinger and antiwar activist Joan Baez. When I arrived at Russell's Chelsea flat he came to the door himself—a thin, spectral figure in large felt slippers, his white mane translucent in the morning light. Frail as he was, he would not let me help him, and insisted on pouring tea from a pot that seemed as heavy as stone.

Baez had not arrived yet, but the meeting already gave me forebodings. Its agenda, as Ralph had explained, was to raise money for the Foundation from the wealthy American star. It seemed demeaning for Russell to be put in the position of begging for support, and I understood my task as making this unnecessary. Unfortunately, the moment Baez stepped gracefully out of her stretch limo, her familiar black tresses wafting about her cheeks, it was clear that she had no interest whatever in the Bertrand Russell Peace Foundation. She was there to have an audience with another Sixties celebrity.

When the introductions were made, it became apparent that neither of them really knew who the other was. Communication was further complicated by Russell's hearing aid, which kept whistling, much to his annoyance, so that the proceedings had to pause at intervals while he took it out for adjustment. During one of these pauses, I made an earnest effort to explain to Baez whom it was she was talking to, but she remained obstinate in her disinterest in anything that came from me. As a result, I had to look on helplessly while she babbled on about her experiences with transcendental meditation and a Santa Cruz guru named Ira Sandperl—all this to the last surviving exponent of nineteenth-century rationalism, a man whose disciples included Wittgenstein and Moore, and whose godfather was John Stuart Mill. In the middle of this distracting *pas de deux,* I neglected my task, leaving it to Russell to painfully extend his wrinkled palm in behalf of our work. The singer pretended not to understand the request. Escorting her on her way back to the limo, I attempted to retrieve the situation by repeating the appeal—again to no avail. I resolved never to let Ralph put me in such a predicament again.

Fear of public embarrassment over Ralph's antics issued from a nerve center of my political being. My formative experience in politics had been the humiliation of my parents by the Khrushchev Report, whose revelations had undone their life's work. I never wanted to be involved in a similar complicity that would compromise my intellectual efforts. My life's work had already taken shape in my mind as the reconstruction of socialist theory after Stalin. This was the reason I was at the Foundation. When Ralph offered me the job, I told him I would accept his offer only with the understanding that he was hiring me to carry on the enterprise I had already begun. I did not intend to involve myself in the daily operations of the Foundation. In fact, I rarely went to the office, except to attend an occasional directors' meeting or give my political advice.

Having my work discredited by some indiscretion of Ralph's became an escalating concern. To insulate myself from the possibility, I carved out an independent niche, which I called the Bertrand Russell Centre for Social Research. I had separate stationery printed, and kept Ralph at arm's length from my projects. Under the umbrella of the Centre, I conceived a series called "Studies in Imperialism and the

Cold War," that I would edit. Two volumes were published under the titles *Containment and Revolution* and *Corporations and the Cold War.* My correspondence over these volumes put me in touch with New Left intellectuals all over the world, including Martin Bernal, Marcel Liebman, Ernest Mandel, and Andre Gunder Frank. The volumes themselves included essays by such young writers as Todd Gitlin and James Weinstein, as well as the father of New Left historians, William Appleman Williams.

Before we left Sweden, Sven Hamrell had set up a contact for me at the London School of Economics. He informed me that my London flat was situated next door to the house of Ralph Miliband, a lecturer in sociology. A large man about fifteen years older than I, with black hair and a full, sensuous mouth, Miliband was one of the leading Marxists of the Labour Party Left. Like his friend E. P. Thompson, he belonged to the "generation of '56," which was made up of Communists and sympathizers who had broken with the Party over Hungary and the Khrushchev Report. Miliband was a serious intellectual with a great respect for scholarly method and decorum—a refreshing contrast to Schoenman.

I soon discovered that Miliband had a brittle personality. Once he did not speak to me for a week, until his wife induced him to relent. My sin was not having introduced him to my parents, who were visiting. I had actually thought it would be an imposition. Or, perhaps, it was that I had reached that stage in my youthful career where I would just as soon be thought of as being on my own and not having parents. Miliband was starting his own family late—his much-younger wife Marian was pregnant—and he took great pleasure in my son Jonathan. When Jonathan would work himself into a tantrum over some minor mishap, Miliband lectured him sternly: "Milk spills, cookies crumble but life goes on!" At the sound of Miliband's deep voice and the oddness of the adult address, the tears would stop.

Like me, Miliband viewed his intellectual mission as an effort to rescue Marxism from the Stalinist debacle. He had written a book titled *Parliamentary Socialism,* a history and critique of the Labour Party's reformist politics. Now he was writing a book that would reformulate Marx's class theory of the state. The problem he had to solve was the paradox of democratic rule: How could the state be "the executive committee of the ruling class," as Marx had claimed, yet be controlled (as it was in England) by a socialist party whose political base was the working class? Miliband developed a sophisticated argument to explain how, in the "final analysis," Marx's view of the state was right. To amuse him, I trained Jonathan, who was just learning to speak, to answer the question "What is the state?" with a quote from Marx: "The state is just the instrument of class oppression."

Miliband took me under his wing, providing me with contacts in the British left and even helping me to secure the services of a literary agent named Deborah Rogers. But it was Miliband's bookshelves that proved the biggest influence on my education. They provided a library of texts in the development of Marxist thought with which I attempted to fill in my intellectual gaps. I read his files of the *New Reasoner,* which was the precursor to the *New Left Review,* and especially the long theoretical articles with titles like "Out of the Moral Wilderness," by Alasdair MacIntyre. I also borrowed the works of Isaac Deutscher and began systematically reading through them. Deutscher had been a follower of Trotsky in the Thirties and was now an intellectual hero of the New Left, appearing as one of the principal speakers at a "Teach-In" against the Vietnam War in Berkeley. Deutscher's name was familiar to me because of a slim volume, *Russia in Transition,* which I had seen in my parents' bedroom in the period following the Khrushchev Report. In my eyes, this gave him a kind of political imprimatur. I borrowed Miliband's copies of the Deutscher biography of Stalin, and the three-volume trilogy on Trotsky, and Trotsky's own *History of the Russian Revolution.*

Through Miliband I met Perry Anderson and the other editors of *New Left Review.* Miliband had created an annual called *The Socialist Register,* and I watched him mediate an intellectual dispute between Anderson, easily the most brilliant thinker of the *New Left,* and the historian E. P. Thompson, who had been purged from the *Review* by Anderson and a group of young turks. With one or two exceptions, I found the *Review* editors, who all seemed to be products of Eton and Oxford, intellectually snobbish and aristocratically remote. They were partial to neologisms like "problematizing," and were always invoking French obscurantists like Althusser and Sartre, never wanting to address political questions and the divisive issues of the Communist legacy.

While I continued to steep myself in the history of Communism, I was also devouring books on Keynesian economics and the labor theory of value, in hopes of finding a way to revise Marxism and move its economic theories out of the sectarian closet. I read Keynes' *General Theory of Employment, Interest and Money*, and the works of his disciples Joan Robinson, E. D. Domar, and J.R. Hicks. I also read Marxists like Piero Sraffa, Michal Kalecki, Oskar Lange, and Maurice Dobb, and out of my readings put together a book called *Marx and Modern Economics*, which was published in England and America, and in an Italian edition. The introduction quoted Robinson: "If there is any hope of progress in economics at all, it must be in using academic methods to solve the problems posed by Marx." I added: "It is the Marxists, alone, who have been ready to take up the challenge." To pursue these studies and acquire an academic credential, I also entered a Ph.D. program at the London School of Economics, where my advisers were Mark Blaug and Ernest Gellner, the latter a friend of Miliband's. I never finished the doctorate, but the essays I wrote on subjects like "Marx, Keynes and the Accumulation of Capital" were published later in a volume called *The Fate of Midas and Other Essays.*

The more I progressed in my studies, the more my interests shifted away from the Buber aspect of the book I was writing for Tavistock and toward the problems of Marxist theory. My original idea now seemed unfeasible, so to fulfill the contract, I proposed a new book based on the Shakespeare paper I had written at Berkeley, "Imagining the Real." I decided to supplement it with a new section called "The Bonds of Human Kindness," taking the word "kindness" in its dual meanings of "nature" and "compassion." This was inspired by what I took to be socialist sentiments in the plays, especially *King Lear,* but which were in fact merely Christian.

About this time I met my editor at Tavistock, the existential psychiatrist R.D. Laing. A pale, intense, almost haunted man, Laing would drop in at our basement flat unannounced, and in a lyrical Scottish burr describe a dream he had the night before, in which he had visions of hidden worlds and "tessellated marble," while neither Elissa nor I had the slightest idea of what he was talking about. Laing was in the throes of a divorce, having left his wife and five children for a 30-year-old disciple. His wife had taken revenge by selling off his personal library—a lifetime accumulation of texts on psychology and Eastern mysticism, including a rare edition of *The Tibetan Book of the Dead*. She sold the volumes to different used-book stores so that he had no possibility of ever retrieving them.

Laing took an interest in my Marxist studies, and invited me to give a lecture to a group of economics professors at Kingsley Hall, a facility where he dealt with patients who normally would be institutionalized, testing his theories that the insane really were visionaries responding to an irrational world. The subject of my lecture was *Monopoly Capital*, the theoretical *summa* of the American Marxists Paul Baran and Paul Sweezy. I quickly realized I was over my head with these professional economists, but was partially saved my embarrassment by the fact that during my talk one of Laing's schizophrenic patients loped around our little circle like an ape, making loud simian noises.

I dedicated my Shakespeare book "To Elissa, who brings grace to my world." I'd wanted to call it *Shakespearean Grace*, but when I mentioned the title to her, she thought it "too Christian," and I changed it to *Shakespeare: An Existential View*. Later I came to regret this, because the original title was more appropriate, and this was the only book I managed to write in those years that I can reread comfortably today. It didn't receive much notice, although the chapter on *Much Ado About Nothing* was anthologized in a "20th-Century critics" series, while the stage director, Peter Brook, was impressed enough to summon me to an audience so that he could look me over. Apparently I failed whatever test he was giving, however, because that was the last I heard from him.

Our second child, Sarah, was born at home in England on January 4, 1964. We gave her the middle name Rose after my grandmother, who had recently died in Florida, where she and Sam had retired and where he had died of stomach cancer ten years earlier. When Rose was felled by her fatal stroke, I was notified by my Uncle Harold because my parents were traveling in Europe on their way to see us. Her last words to the doctor called to the scene were, "Don't bother my children, they're too busy."

Elissa and I found the idea of a home birth attractive because it was more "natural" than a hospital setting. But we had also been warned that the state of British hospitals under the National Health Care was so poor that it was actually safer to use a midwife at home. When Sarah was born, we noticed that she had an extra fold of skin on her neck. A specialist was called in to look at her. He immediately discovered that her hips were dislocated. At first the specialist suspected that she was missing two vertebrae, which introduced the possibility that other things might be wrong as well, and caused us considerable distress. Meanwhile, the dislocated hips required splints, which had to be removed and replaced daily, and Sarah's legs had to be constantly bathed in a special solution, to heal her skin sores. As I watched Elissa patiently and lovingly care for this infant, and nurse her toward what we hoped would be a state of health, I was grateful all over again to have married such a woman.

When the doctors had completed their diagnosis, we learned that Sarah had Turner's Syndrome, the result of a missing chromosome. This meant she would be shorter than average, and hard of hearing—and would never be able to bear a child. At the time, it was thought that some Turner children would be retarded, an idea which extended the period of anxiety for us—especially for Elissa, who was as inclined to pessimism as I was to the conviction that things would work out. I seem to have inherited, from sources I cannot identify, a sense of positive destiny. In my life, things would go well; the tragic and inexplicable would not happen.

Sarah began speaking late, passing from incoherent babblings to complete phrases without an intervening period of words—so, in the end, my optimism was justified. Meanwhile, our having two children now was proving a challenge of growing proportion. In addition to the extra work, there was the problem of managing the interactions between them. Jonathan had been the center of our universe but now was abruptly displaced. "Jon is very resentful of all my attentions to Sarah, especially feeding of course, and is worse when David is not home," Elissa wrote her mother. "Of course I try to understand, but it is very hard to go on smiling when they are both screaming at the tops of their voices and I am attempting to get dinner started." These difficulties were often attributed by others to our parental methods, which elicited the same disapproval in England that we had encountered in Norway. Shortly after our arrival, Lionel's new wife, Brenda, wrote a critical report to my parents: "About two Saturdays ago [David and Elissa] came to a film and social fundraising evening at an old friend of ours, who lives in the next road. Johnnie came too, of course, from about 9:30 to 11 P.M. He was good, but again of course on his terms. Johnnie was delightful, but of course he has his parents at his constant beck and call. He doesn't content himself and play for very long on his own—his parents are his playmates on his level. One cannot blame him. This is the result of the whole theory of his upbringing, but I can't help feeling it means that much of the time David could be writing, he has to spend playing with Johnnie."

I certainly did spend a lot of time with Jonathan (we never called him "Johnnie"), and did do my share of changing and rinsing diapers (while sure that neither Shakespeare nor Marx had ever done the same). Notwithstanding such distractions, however, my work went well. I had a capacity for focus that allowed me to concentrate even while the children were playing—or screaming—around me in an "office" that was merely a cluttered table in our bedroom. Occasionally the stress would get to me, naturally, and produce a surface explosion that I quickly regretted.

There were other causes of stress in our lives, as I seemed driven to seek out more projects than I could handle. There were my University of Maryland papers to grade, and the books to edit for the Russell Foundation, in addition to the Marx and Shakespeare projects. I was also writing an article on the Alliance for Progress, for Miliband's magazine. *The Free World Colossus* still didn't have a publisher, and our financial situation was precarious. And then there were the children. It did not help my equilibrium that the baby was up every night, or that Elissa and I never had a day or an evening off from the household—the latter situation only partly attributable to the difficulty of finding sitters. Elissa did not want to leave the children with anyone, and also did not really enjoy socializing. And I didn't care to introduce further tension into our lives by making her discomfitures an issue.

Without either of us realizing it, a fissure had developed in our marriage. My ventures outside the cocoon of the household through my work had created pulls that she found threatening. From my side, it seemed as if the passion in her that had so attracted me when we first met had gone into the children, and exhausted itself in the tedium of the family chores. Living in two small basement rooms on a minimal income didn't help. But there was also the clear emergence of divergent attitudes. Elissa seemed overwhelmed by the circumstances we found ourselves in, while I wanted more out of life (and out of *our* life) even though I could not have said at the time what it was.

The dissatisfactions simmering inside me came to a head one evening as we discussed over the dishes the affairs of one of her female friends. Elissa always seemed to have a romantic view of other lives, even as she had a resigned attitude toward the responsibilities imposed by ours. The drug-and-sex culture of the Sixties had begun, and her friend had plunged headlong into its excesses. It would be hard to imagine anything farther from Elissa's own character and tastes than the adventures she was relating to me without apparent censure. Feelings of betrayal rippled inside me.

We had chosen our lives as rational individuals. I was convinced, at least, that I had chosen mine. It was important to me to think I had. I had chosen a life that I also thought would please her. Part of the shame I experienced in fighting desires that did not fit our life was the thought of how she might look at them. Her apparent approval of her friend's behavior was inexplicable, wounding. Almost ferociously, I said: "Well, if you like that life so much, why don't we live it?" Without seeming to hear my distress, she answered "Oh, I wouldn't want to live that way."

This answer, which seems perfectly reasonable to me now, seemed impossible then. How could she endorse a life and not live it? Angry and helpless, I stormed into the night, almost running for blocks at a time, as though heading for a new existence. But I did not want another life, without her. I wanted only to come back and be made whole again. With each step I felt anxiety and guilt at the worry my absence was causing, and frustration with my own impotence. A sudden recognition brought me up short: *This was what my father had done.* How many times had I seen him, defeated in some conflict with my mother and unable to take control of the terms of his happiness, leave the house like this? On those occasions, he would walk the neighborhood streets for hours until, resigned once more to the terms

life had set for him, he would return home. *I had become my father.*
The idea was unnerving.

In 1965, a year after Sarah was born, *The Free World Colossus* was
finally published in England and America. I had taken on the project
without any background in history, and it showed in the difficulty I
had in locating a publisher. There were too many passages cited from
other books, and I was too tentative in my authorial voice. My mother
had located an editor for me—her boss at Planned Parenthood, who
was part of the progressive community—and, under his guidance, I
revised the manuscript. Just prior to the book's release, I wrote two
articles to publicize it. The first was my half of a debate with Michael
Walzer over the nature of the Cold War, which appeared in the pages
of *Views* magazine; the second was an article in the *Tribune* about the
dropping of the atomic bomb. I repeated the argument in my book,
based on the writings of the pro-Soviet strategist P. M. S. Blackett,
that the Bomb was dropped on Hiroshima to keep Russia out of the
Japanese peace.

Shortly after the *Tribune* article appeared, I received a phone call
from a man with a thick Russian accent who said he was with the
Novosti Press Agency and wanted to have lunch. I remember clearly
that his first name was Lev, because I immediately associated it with
Trotsky. But the whole experience caused me to block his second
name, and there is no way now for me to retrieve it. After it was over, I
discussed the affair with Schoenman and discovered that Lev was the
third man in the Soviet embassy, a post usually reserved for officers
of the KGB.

A man of medium height with thin white hair and a pasty Slavic
complexion, Lev wore the badly tailored black suits favored by Soviet
officials. He always used a pay phone, a precaution I accepted as
natural. This was not because I presumed from the outset that he was
a spy, but because it was normal in the Left to assume that phones
were tapped, and thus that "sensitive" political matters should be discussed in person. The fact that Lev was a Soviet official merely made
the discretion seem particularly prudent.

Our trysts took place in London's more expensive restaurants, like
Prunier's, where I sampled my first *coquilles Saint Jacques* and other

elegant cuisines. My reaction to this treatment was a mixture of plea-sure and guilt. It seemed rude to bring up to my host, nor did I want to lose an opportunity to present my views to an influential official, but in my private thoughts I deplored the way the Soviet government seemed ready to squander wealth that properly belonged to Soviet workers on such luxuries. My host routinely ordered a bottle of wine, a potion which I did not hold well, so that by the middle of the meal I was always a little tipsy.

The topics of our discussions were wide-ranging, and I did most of the talking. I took it as my mission to convert Lev to New Left ways of thinking. I advised him that it was important to publish Trotsky's writings in the Soviet Union, and tried to persuade him that it was counterproductive to incarcerate dissidents in psychiatric institu-tions (the then-current Soviet practice). Repressive methods may have been necessary, I suggested, during the period of "primitive accumu-lation" when the Soviet Union was catching up with the industrial powers. But now that Russia was a superpower, the controls could be relaxed. I knew how hard the Soviet line was on this issue, because I had already gone to their embassy as an emissary of Russell, to protest the psychiatric incarceration of a young dissident.

The focus of our discussions often shifted to the subject of Russell and his secretary. Lev wanted to know the answer to the question on everyone's mind: How influential was Schoenman in shaping the phi-losopher's political stands? Russell had made some public statements that the Russians didn't like. Did they reflect his views, or Ralph's? Later I discussed these conversations with Ralph, and he gave me some background to Lev's curiosity. The Johnson Administration had recently begun bombing military targets in North Vietnam. At Ralph's prompting, Russell issued a public appeal to Moscow to supply MIGs to the North Vietnamese, so they could shoot down the American planes. The Soviet consul general had summoned Ralph to a meeting. After explaining to him that sending Russian planes would mean war with the United States, the consul warned: "Mr. Schoenman, people who advocate World War III are either crazy or working for the CIA, and they get into trouble."

When Lev was not asking me questions about Russell and Schoen-man, I lectured him on how the Soviet future could be reshaped. He didn't try to discourage me from the belief that I was making an impression. At the end of the second or third session, he gave me a Parker fountain pen. It was still in the store box, and wasn't wrapped like a present. I didn't know how to refuse it without insulting him. The next time we had lunch, it was raining and I was wearing my trench coat. As we walked into the street at the end of the meal, he stuffed a thick white envelope into my left pocket.

I knew instinctively what was in the envelope, but was so frightened that I didn't dare remove it until I reached home. Without taking off my coat, I went into the bedroom and closed the door, laying the envelope on the bed. Inside were 150 one-dollar bills. I was not so much surprised as dumbfounded. How could these people be so stupid in their own interest, and so reckless with mine? *The Free World Colossus* was the first left-wing history of the Cold War that could *not* be tainted as the work of a Soviet apologist. It had taken me years to develop this perspective, which was far more effective in persuading readers that America was responsible for the Cold War, and far more valuable to the Soviets (if they wanted to look at it that way) than any information I might be able to obtain as an intelligence asset. Yet they thought nothing of putting my work (to say nothing of my life) in jeopardy by attempting to recruit me as an agent. The thought enraged me.

I returned the envelope at our next meeting, and told him never to give me another. He was disappointed, but not discouraged—especially since I agreed to go on with our lunches. But, a few sessions later, it became apparent that my rejection of the money had prompted a more drastic test. When we left the restaurant, he brought up my teaching job and asked me if I would be willing to obtain information about NATO for him. We were standing in the middle of the street, but I screamed at him: *"You're crazy. I'm not going to spy for you or anyone else. Get the fuck away from me and don't ever contact me again."* I walked away, and never saw him again.

I was not the only radical courted by Lev. I had seen him with a Marxist economics tutor at the LSE. I had discussed him in a veiled manner with the editor of *Views,* who had also been having lunches with him. Members of the *New Left Review* crowd knew him, as did activists I recognized from the Labour Party left. How many had failed to reject him as I did? How many had become suppliers of information to the KGB?

One afternoon when Elissa and I were invited to Miliband's for tea, his other guests were Isaac Deutscher and his wife, Tamara. Deutscher was a Polish Jew—a short, intense man with a Trotsky goatee who spoke with a heavy accent, though in such well-constructed sentences that he might have been reading from a text. After we became friends, I learned that he had dictated his massive biographies to his wife, who typed them on the page. Listening to Deutscher was a literary experience. His talk was richly allusive and informed by a lifetime engagement with the ideas and events that had shaped the modern world. He had been an activist in the Marxist left in Central Europe between the wars, and was now an exile from both. There was a bitterness attached to his present independence and the isolation that accompanied it: He was a professor without a classroom, and convinced that the critic Isaiah Berlin had interceded to deny him a chair at Oxford that would have freed him from his financial insecurity.

As I quickly discovered that afternoon, Deutscher did not brook the opposition of those he considered his intellectual inferiors. When we arrived, he was holding forth on the schism that had developed within the Communist world, forcing every party to choose between the rival centers of Moscow and Peking. As a result of the split, there were now (as he put it) two popes in the revolutionary camp. The very existence of such hostility between socialist powers was a challenge to Marxist theory, which explained national rivalries by the competition for markets. Deutscher, however, was no simple economic determinist, and argued that the conflict was in fact ideological.

I had written about the Sino-Soviet split in *The Free World Colossus,* attributing it to the nuclear disparity between the two powers. The Soviets had a shield against the American threat, which the Chinese did not, causing their interests to collide. With all the enthusiasm of a neophyte, I jumped into the conversation, hoping Deutscher would be impressed with my ideas. But my intervention had the opposite effect. Did I think that Luther's Wittenberg theses were inconsequential to the Reformation? he snapped. How, then, could I suggest that the ideas of the Chinese and Soviet Marxists had no bearing on their conflict? Mine was the thinking of a *cheder* Marxist (in effect, a schoolboy), he finished acidly, turning his back so that I was cut off in midsentence.

The next time we met he seemed to relent. Perhaps Tamara, who worshipped him but also tended him like a mother hen, had said a word on my behalf. In any case, our relationship developed progressively from that point until we became quite close. He lived in a redbrick Tudor on Kidderpore Gardens, which was only three blocks away from my flat, a proximity that encouraged the bond. Another, and more important, factor was that Deutscher's only son, Martin, who was then about 13, was slightly retarded, and this left a painful gap for a man who was so obviously in search of intellectual heirs. Our relationship took a leap forward when I gave him an essay I had written which attempted to locate the origins of the Cold War in the Western response to the Bolshevik Revolution, and was heavily indebted to his work. He read and annotated the text, and encouraged me to expand it—until eventually it developed into my next book.

Deutscher was an intimidating guide, given to stern and unforgiving admonitions. You cannot understand Marx, he lectured me one day in his living room, unless you have read *Das Kapital* and *Die Grundrisse* in the original. For my edification, he would casually dismiss New Left heroes like Fidel Castro and Stokely Carmichael as "stage-hall comedians" unworthy of a place in the radical tradition. Despite these Eurocentric prejudices, Deutscher had a powerful impact on the New Left, as he had on me. The ultimate source of this power was his ability to explain the tragedy in Russia as a consequence of the environment in which the revolution had taken place, rather than any flaw in the Marxist argument. In Deutscher's view, however perverted the revolution's ends had become, it had created the base of an industrial democracy, a possibility which the next generation might realize. This restored our faith in socialism without forcing us to close our eyes to its unhappy Russian fate. Because Deutscher faced squarely the crimes the Soviets had committed, he was denounced in *Pravda* as "a troubadour of imperialism," while his continuing faith in the Marxist future caused his work to be characterized by Western critics as "a transmission belt to Stalinism."

The book I wrote, under Deutscher's inspiration, was *Empire and Revolution: A Theory of Contemporary History.* Its ambition was large. It set out to be a reinterpretation of Marxism, and a theory of imperialism, Communism, and the Cold War. It was the culmination of my efforts to rescue socialism from its tainted past, and to reconstruct a Marxist theory that would guide the revolutionary future, and it ended with this challenge: "The struggle which the Bolsheviks began more than half a century ago is still in its early stages—indeed, in a sense, is just beginning.... Liberation is no longer, and can be no longer, merely a national concern. The dimension of the struggle, as Lenin and the Bolsheviks so clearly saw, is international: its road is the socialist revolution."

I owe you this. My father had written me a letter. It was about *The Free World Colossus,* which had just appeared and, like so many communications between us, it was shunted in transmission into a channel that caused me to receive it as another of his oblique disapprovals:

> Speaking of images, you have written a gigantic book for your age and circumstance. But you should beware of accepting the images of giant. When you were very little, David, you did think you were a little Mozart once, and you did with charming naivete inspire yourself to write a "concerto." Sartre makes clear in The Words how the biography of one is created by the family he is surrounded with in childhood. I'm afraid we, too, are guilty, as guilty as his grandfather was in creating for him the image of a writer of classical serious and ponderous tracts—when indeed he would sooner have romanced his way thru life.
>
> This is your Achilles heel. This your great danger to your self. To put it plainly, I think, David, you often, too often, are permitted by friends who love you and parents who dote on you, to play your "part" successfully—your "part" is to be genius—a treacherous concept—a faithless support. "To thine own self be true, etc." To find it and not lose it in the "parts" which are created for you by fellow ideologues, publishers, teachers, parents etc.—a monstrously difficult task.

I reacted negatively to this admonition. *Giant, genius.* He was taking an ambition that I would never have expressed to anyone and exposing it on the page in a way that made it seem obscene. I had to admit even then that it contained sound advice: Don't take yourself too seriously. But the whole struck me as merely another attempt on his part to belittle my aspirations and thwart my desires. It was no different from when he sought to deny me the Foto Electric Football game I wanted as a kid: "You can't have this." *Why not?*

And yet, reading his letter now, from a vantage at the other end of the story, I am struck by my own obtuseness. It is difficult to see around the corners of ourselves. From this distance, his words do not seem that far from the truth, and I can hear in them another voice that I did not hear before:

> I owe you all this because I have failed to guide you or to contribute directions with any decisive firmness in the past. I am tempted to go on, David, but I shouldn't. However, I must corroborate your own impression that I'm not well—this is the way one has to put it today. That is that more often than not my observations and impressions are tinted by my own emotional disturbances. I know, unfortunately a great deal about playing a part—losing sight of my self. Clarity and accuracy of judgment about it have come pleasurably to me at times but not often enough to have prevented the damage and ache which have distorted much of my life. This and my love for you have made possible tonight's sally into a "Chesterfieldian" foray. I love Jon and Sarah Rose and Elissa, too, very much; but more of that on another morning.
>
> Da

I should have heard this voice: *I owe you all this. ... I must corroborate your own impression that I'm not well.* I don't know what I made of the words at the time, or if they were even intelligible to me. Had I given him such an impression? I certainly don't remember it. I don't remember thinking my father the prisoner of inner demons. I thought of him as stubborn and hard to penetrate. Despite the praise, his approval still felt elusive.

While I was writing *Empire and Revolution*, our next child arrived. When the midwife, a large German woman, came to our house,

Elissa was vacuuming the floor, even though her waters had already broken. After setting up shop, the midwife watched Elissa as she moved on to the next room, and then started out the door herself. "Where are you going?" I asked. "To lunch," she said. "Don't leave me!" I begged. A few minutes later, our second son was born. The English law allowed the baby to go nameless for six weeks. On the last day of the allotted time, I went to the birth registry with two first names and, as I walked through the door, decided that he would be Benjamin.

The two rooms on Rosecroft Avenue were already too small for the four of us. My mother stepped in and bought us a larger flat on Laurier Road in Highgate, near the cemetery where Marx was buried. She bought us a washing machine, too, ending our arduous treks to the washeteria. I say "my mother" did this because it was she who handled the household finances and made such decisions. I don't believe my father had ever reconciled himself to the purchase of property, just as he never reconciled himself to her pampering of his son.

The Highgate flat was roomy enough to have an office for me, where I could lay out my books and typewriter on a real desk. But, despite the new space, I was as tense as ever. Three children were proving much more of a handful than two. We rarely went out, reluctant as ever to leave the kids with a babysitter. The normal turmoil of the household alone, and the financial pressures I'd long labored under, had some time since combined to create a somatic resonance. Like my father, I had suffered childhood allergies, and these had returned when we settled in London. The dank climate proliferated lung ailments like bronchitis and catarrh, whose symptoms were difficult to distinguish from asthma. One autumn I had such difficulty breathing that I thought I would suffocate, and ran out in the street gasping for air. After that, I was never without an inhaler until we returned to the United States, where the symptoms disappeared.

A stream of friends arrived from America—among them Ron and Alice Radosh, who came over on a summer visit with their daughter Laura. I had met Ron when we were both 13 and I was recruiting contributors for the "Youth Page" of the *Daily Worker*. I spoke to a meeting of his section of the Young Progressives of America, and we stayed friends after that. Radosh had gone on to the University of Wisconsin at Madison, which was a center of radical activity, and had become an editor of *Studies on the Left*. Together we made a kind of pilgrimage to Marx's grave in Highgate Cemetery, and had ourselves photographed in front of the great bronze bust on the headstone, our fists raised in the Bolshevik salute.

My Sunnyside friend Carol Pasternak, whose father was the Party cell boss and who had been attacked in the unsigned note I received after Stalin's death, came with her new family, too. She had married a young historian, and they also had a daughter. The last time I had seen Carol was at the wedding of Ellen Sparer, who had written the protest poem about Willie McGee. Ellen had married a teacher who did not have "our politics" and of whom Carol and our other friends disapproved. "Ellen is such a rescuer," Carol said.

In the spring of 1966, Schoenman decided that the Foundation would put on a "War Crimes Tribunal," to try America for its intervention in Vietnam. I had misgivings from the start about the new project. The Foundation had just launched a "Vietnam Solidarity Campaign," whose manifesto I wrote. The point of the campaign was to support the National Liberation Front, not to pose as a peace movement that was neutral between the sides. But how could we run a "tribunal," purporting to judge impartially America's conduct of the war, when we had already declared our partisanship for the enemy camp? Such questions did not seem to bother Ralph, who had just returned from North Vietnam, where he'd made a speech to American troops over Radio Hanoi:

> I speak to you today from Hanoi as one American to another ... Brothers, you know what kind of war we are fighting against the people of Vietnam. It is barbaric. It is an aggressive war of conquest that all of us hate and few of us understand ... We are the cannon fodder. We are the ones they deceive into killing Vietnamese, attacking, occupying, using gas and chemicals, bombing their schools and hospitals—all this horror to protect the empire of our rich men ... The brass-hats and money-boys at home have made us their victims. These new Hitlers use us to carry out every war crime in the book.

These remarks were made in February 1966, just eight months before the official opening of the tribunal in London. Much as I opposed the American presence in Vietnam, much as I wanted the National Liberation Front to win, this kind of attack made me queasy. America was not Hitler Germany, and I did not like the idea of addressing troops on the field of battle with thinly-veiled incitements that might cost them their lives. Yet, like so many others in the "antiwar" movement faced with similar issues of conscience—some who genuinely wanted peace, not a Communist victory—I did not break ranks with people like Ralph, and in fact facilitated their agendas.

Although my political reservations caused me to take no part in the activities of the War Crimes Tribunal, I was instrumental in making the tribunal possible. Shortly after my arrival, I realized that the Foundation had almost no funds. Beyond the modest expenses of its small staff, there was nothing really available for a project like this. I had noticed, however, the huge advances that publishers were beginning to pay for autobiographies, and knew that Russell had completed such a manuscript of his own. This prompted me to approach Ralph with the idea that Russell's autobiography might be worth hundreds of thousands of pounds, and to suggest that he contact my agent, Deborah Rogers, for her advice. Deborah went with Ralph to Wales to meet Russell, but this interlude in Schoenman's company was enough to cause her to walk away from the deal. She recommended another agent, who was able to get nearly £200,000 for the rights.

With the new funds in the bank, Ralph was in business. Typically he made decisions first and sought counsel afterwards. When we met with Deutscher to solicit his advice and invite him to serve on the tribunal, the plans were already set. As a political concept, Ralph's choice of format was simple enough. It would be immediately associated in people's minds with the Nuremberg Tribunal, and America's actions would thus be connected with Nazi war crimes. Merely announcing the tribunal would be a political *coup*. America would be "convicted" by its very existence. But Deutscher did not think the matter so simple. Because the Nuremberg Tribunal had been created by the victors, its legitimacy could not practically be challenged. To establish the credentials of *this* tribunal, on the other hand, would be an almost impossible task. The tribunal idea itself, moreover, was a bourgeois legalism. The tribunal members would be bound by bourgeois rules of jurisprudence, including the notion of judicial neutrality. There would inevitably be calls for the tribunal to investigate war crimes committed by the Communists, as well as by the United States.

Warming to his subject, Deutscher argued that the legalistic framework of the tribunal would limit its conclusions and blunt its historical impact. He suggested that it should be called instead a "commission of inquiry," modeled on the group that the American philosopher John Dewey had headed to investigate Stalin's charges against Trotsky. It should be, he said, a *revolutionary* commission of inquiry that would conclude by issuing a "manifesto" calling on the masses all over the world to resist American imperialism and follow the example of Vietnam. As Deutscher grew more and more passionate, Ralph became visibly dispirited. The vision that Deutscher put before him matched exactly his grandiose sense of himself and the mission to which he aspired. He wanted to do what Deutscher was proposing, but he had already publicly committed Russell to the tribunal concept and it was too late to change.

Yet I could already see that this was not going to faze him. Even as he sought to mollify Deutscher and persuade him to serve despite his reservations, Ralph was hatching a solution to his dilemma. By the time we discussed it later, he had convinced himself that he could accomplish both ends—an impartial tribunal, and a revolutionary forum. The judges he had hand-selected were a formidable group, some even world-famous, but they were all radicals and he was confident he could manipulate them. The prospect reminded me of a remark his teacher at Princeton had once made: "You have an innate capacity," he told Ralph, "for erecting brick walls and using your head as a battering ram against them."

Of course, Ralph revealed none of his *real* plan to Deutscher, who finally agreed to sit on the panel alongside Stokely Carmichael, Jean-Paul Sartre, Simone de Beauvoir, James Baldwin, Vladimir Dedijer, and others. Staughton Lynd, a radical historian who had also received an invitation from Russell, declined, saying that he was concerned that only one side would be in the dock. He hoped the tribunal would take care to weigh the evidence impartially, so that it could not be accused of applying double standards. Meanwhile, Sartre, a consummate sophist, attempted to solve the problem in advance by declaring that the Communists were by definition incapable of committing war crimes: "I refuse to place in the same category the actions of an organization of poor peasants ... and those of an immense army backed by a highly industrialized country...." Of course, the NLF—the "organization of poor peasants" to which Sartre referred—was created by the Hanoi regime, whose own army, supplied with high-tech weapons by the Russians and the Chinese, was America's main opponent in the South. But these facts were ignored by Sartre and ourselves.

Months before the preliminary session took place in London in November 1966, I traveled with Ralph to Russell's home in Plas Penrhyn, situated high above the Glaslyn estuary, to celebrate the philosopher's ninety-fourth birthday. When we arrived, I was immediately struck by the character of the gathering. There were twenty or so guests, all connected to the Foundation or in some other way to Ralph's activities. All were under 25 years of age. They were Marxist activists, mainly Trotskyists, reflecting Ralph's most recent political enthusiasm. One, a shallow American named Karen Wald, was typical. She eventually made her passage through a series of New Left sects to a position as a flack for Fidel Castro. I once heard a broadcast interview she did for public radio from Havana in the 1980s, defending Castro's policy of incarcerating homosexuals who had contracted AIDS.

The extraordinary scene in Russell's home reflected the fact that the great man had outlived himself. All his friends were dead, and the world that had been his was gone. Now, there were only these children whom Ralph had gathered, who neither were Russell's friends nor had any connection with him, other than the political utility they saw in his name. The cruelest account of the London opening of the War Crimes Tribunal appeared in the *New York Times Magazine*, under the byline of Bernard Levin, and captured this truth: "A stir, a bustle, a craning of necks; he comes! *He* comes? Say rather, without disrespect, *it* comes ... The man who has now become the holiest relic the international left possesses is to be unwrapped and shown to the populace."

I attended the London session, where Deutscher made a spontaneous and eloquent tribute to Russell for his courage, and for the inspiration he provided. After the session, we packed ourselves into a car with the editors of the *New Left Review* and Jean-Paul Sartre in the back. An ugly little man with a famous walleye, who was now in his seventies and whom we all revered (I had wrapped my copy of his *Being and Nothingness* in a special plastic cover, to preserve it), Sartre was on his way to a tryst with a young woman.

Stockholm had been chosen as the site for the actual hearings because the British and French governments had refused the necessary cooperation. (The Labour government would not issue passports for the North Vietnamese, saying the tribunal would make a peace settlement more difficult.) Once the sessions began, tension developed between Ralph and the tribunal members, just as I had feared. Ralph had appointed himself "director general," and from the outset was determined to use the tribunal as an incendiary device. While tribunal members strained after the appearance of impartiality, Ralph held inflammatory press conferences condemning the United States and invoking Russell as his authority to do so. This raised a protest from Sartre and the others. One evening at dinner, Ralph became so acrimonious under their attacks that the Yugoslav Dedijer, who could have been an American football tackle, lifted him bodily by the arms and shook him until he shut up. But it was Sartre who had the last word: "*Monsieur* Schoenman!" he said in exasperation. "You cannot have Lord Russell in your pocket and hide behind his back at the same time."

I attended none of the sessions in Stockholm, and kept myself relatively ignorant of the goings-on. After the meeting with Deutscher, I had removed myself psychologically and in every other way possible from the event. It was not that I did not believe the United States was guilty in Vietnam. But I didn't want our cause to be compromised by dishonest agendas in the way the Old Left's had been, and I saw the tribunal as a formula for accomplishing just that.

While the sessions were in progress, *Ramparts* magazine, a slick monthly that had become the flagship publication of the radical movement in America, appeared on the newsstands with a portrait of Russell on its cover. The story inside featured an interview with Russell and a sympathetic, if critical, account of the War Crimes Tribunal. In exculpating the organizers from charges of bias for neglecting the war crimes of the Communist guerrillas, the reporter embellished Sartre's sophistry, observing that no one would have expected the Nuremberg Tribunal to inquire into the conduct of those who defended the

Warsaw ghetto. But the article also recognized that the tribunal had been unable to achieve its mission:

> The Tribunal has to date failed in its potential for confronting America with the enormity of its actions in Vietnam. The responsibility for this failure must be traced to the poor organization of the Tribunal, which has fallen into the nightmarish world of little left sects and, in the center of all the confusion—and apparently enjoying every minute—is Ralph Schoenman.

The article was written by my old *Root and Branch* comrade Bob Scheer, whose interview with Russell had been arranged by me when Ralph was conveniently in North Vietnam. It was both a gesture of rebellion on my part, and an attempt to correct the course that Schoenman had set. I did not want the movement dragged down by Ralph's political manipulations, and I knew Scheer would be shrewd enough to establish an appropriate distance while promoting the tribunal's political agenda. When I received his call from San Francisco, telling me he was an editor of *Ramparts* and wanted to interview Russell, I had no hesitation in offering to help.

Ralph regarded my act as a personal betrayal—as I knew he would. He detested Scheer, whom he had recently met in Cambodia when both were on their way to North Vietnam. Scheer was sitting by the pool at the Hotel Intercontinental, hanging out with American embassy officials and reporters, or—as Ralph put it—"with the CIA pigs." To Ralph, Scheer was just another ugly American sipping daiquiris in the sun while his countrymen rained napalm on the hapless Vietnamese. Schoenman saw to it that Scheer's request for a visa was denied by Hanoi.

The two men provided a study in the contrasts of the Left. Ralph's demeanor was moralistic and intense, Scheer's cynical and smug. While Ralph's political aggressions were displayed on his sleeve, Scheer kept his concealed. Where Ralph instinctively sought the political margins and the outlaw status that would prove his authenticity as a man in revolt, Scheer headed toward the comfort and cover of the social mainstream.

In the years since I had seen him, Scheer had put behind his beatnik phase, cut his hair short, and was now wearing three-piece suits. Ignoring the case he had once made against electoral politics, he was running for Congress in the Democratic primary, against a liberal incumbent. As a *Ramparts* editor, he ostentatiously traveled first class, and stayed in the finest hotels. He had even joined the Berkeley Chamber of Commerce. He was rebelling again, this time against the street politics of the New Left, and he was just as eloquent in justifying his new choices as he had been in defending the old. The Communist left had failed, he argued, when it allowed itself to become marginalized. Instead of the in-your-face politics he had once advocated, he now proposed that the Left should advance under the colors of the liberal establishment and "bore from within." Scheer's instinct proved prescient once again when this became the Left's political style in the next decade. For the present, however, he was far enough ahead of the pack to make himself vulnerable to attack by radicals like Ralph.

Scheer had found the political style that suited his personality. He was an illegitimate child—occasionally even referring to himself, when in a self-punishing mood, as "the bastard." His mother, a Russian Jew and a Communist, had brought him up in the radical Coops, but his father was a Lutheran who had another family on the side. The new face Scheer had put on, and the taste for luxuries and respectability he cultivated while rebelling against the system that provided them, were almost perfectly designed to solve his family riddle.

Scheer's article on the tribunal appeared in May 1967. When Ralph discovered my betrayal, he was beside himself. But his anger, normally of armor-piercing intensity, was blunted by circumstances his own antics had created. The tribunal was in open revolt against him, and its members had moved its headquarters to Paris, beyond his reach. A second session had been scheduled for Copenhagen in November, and Ralph soon left for Vietnam on another "fact-finding" mission. The Foundation was in financial crisis, having exhausted the advance from Russell's autobiography. But when Ralph returned, instead of attending to this crisis he embarked on a new plan to realize the agenda whose seed Deutscher had unwittingly sowed. Even my familiarity with Ralph's outsize ambitions did not prepare me for the scheme he now presented.

The continual escalation of revolutionary ambitions had led to a conviction among radicals that the time was at hand to spread the guerrilla war from Indochina to other regions. The peripheries of the American empire were going to rise up against the center. Ralph was planning to have Bertrand Russell, Fidel Castro, and Ho Chi Minh announce the formation of a "Fifth International" to compete with the Communist and Trotskyist ones, which had failed to ignite this conflagration. He would launch the new force with a revolutionary manifesto based on Che Guevara's call to "create two, three ... many Vietnams." He had already discussed the matter with Ho Chi Minh on his recent trip, as well as with Russell, and was on his way to Cuba to persuade Castro to sign on.

In October, however, Guevara was captured and killed while trying to open a guerrilla front in Bolivia. At the same time, Régis Debray, the Frenchman whose theory of guerrilla *focos* provided an intellectual gloss for Guevara's efforts, was arrested in Bolivia and put on trial. As if compelled by some gravitational force, Ralph went directly to La Paz, abandoning the Foundation to its financial crisis. He surfaced in the courtroom where Debray was being tried, denounced the ruling military junta, was arrested and swiftly ushered out of the country. The British government seized the occasion to rid itself of its meddlesome pest by withdrawing Ralph's visa. This episode effectively ended his public career. Two years later, he did manage to sneak into England and have himself photographed in front of the prime minister's office at 10 Downing Street. But he was soon apprehended while riding in a minicab in Hyde Park, and deported. Shortly thereafter, Russell, who felt abandoned and used by his secretary, removed Ralph from the board of the Foundation they had created, and issued a public statement severing their connection.

After Scheer's article appeared, he offered me a job at *Ramparts*, and I accepted. It seemed an appropriate time to leave. Deutscher had died suddenly at the age of 60, of a heart attack. His death had a tragic overtone because he had just begun what he regarded as his life's great work, a biography of Lenin—the leader who, in his view, had gotten the revolutionary formula right, but had not lived to carry it through. I helped to put together a memorial evening, and edited a tribute volume called *Isaac Deutscher: The Man and His Work*. In the introduction, I described him as a "link between revolutionary generations," having devoted his life to solving the puzzle posed by the Bolshevik fate. I compared him to Akher, a figure he had made emblematic in an essay called "The Non-Jewish Jew" Akher was the heretic-stranger who gave lessons in theology to Rabbi Meir, the great pillar of Mosaic orthodoxy, but on the Sabbath crossed the ritual boundary into forbidden territory. He was for Deutscher the model of the revolutionary critic, faithful to the revolutionary ideal while remaining outside its orthodoxies. "Deutscher [I wrote] was no less the heretic-stranger, who appeared to be in Communism and yet not in it, to be of Communism and yet not of it, who, like Akher, showed a curious respect for his pupil's orthodoxy, and a care lest he wander beyond the boundaries of Marxism and of Communism and become lost." Deutscher himself was an emblem of our new radical generation. We wanted to be in the radical tradition, yet escape implication in its crimes. We wanted to eat from the radical tree of knowledge, yet not bear its taint—to know a radical truth without having to pay its heavy price.

Deutscher was buried in December. In January, Elissa and I packed our belongings into tea chests and, with our three children, boarded an ocean liner for the United States. When we arrived in New York, I called Scheer to tell him we were headed for California. In a tone that was both distant and superior, the voice on the other end of the line asked: "Did you get a haircut?"

PART 4

REVOLUTIONS

(1968–1973)

Break on through to the other side...

—The Doors

POWER TO THE PEOPLE

When we returned to Berkeley in January 1968, the change was everywhere evident. People even looked different. Peace symbols and crystal pendants had replaced crucifixes and Stars of David as emblems of religious conviction. Clothes were tie-dyed and bucolic, colors psychedelic, and hair long. (I immediately felt betrayed by Scheer's orders to get mine cut.) To liberate themselves from the old sexual order, women were going bra-less, a protest whose immediate effect was to raise the libidinal pulses of everyday life. At the south end of campus, hippie craftsmen had transformed Telegraph Avenue into a street fair, where musicians and jugglers "doing their thing" attracted crowds for the tradesmen. It all had the air of a medieval pastoral, like the Forest of Arden in Shakespeare's *As You Like It,* where there were no menacing creatures, or hungers that could not be satisfied.

Shortly after our arrival, I took Jonathan to a local school to hear a band called Purple Earthquake. It was the first time I had been exposed to electric instruments in a live setting. Booming through huge amplified speakers, the sound enveloped us and produced an effect something like entering a new dimension. I looked around at the dreamy faces of the audience. They were wearing the insignias and uniforms of the new counterculture that had blossomed from under the American surface while we were gone, and I experienced an unmistakable, strong kinship with them. Like my father in Russia thirty years before, I felt: *A new world is possible.*

Searching for writers for the Russell Foundation series, I had turned up a radical named Bob Fitch, who was the author of a book on imperialism in Ghana. Once my family and I were settled, I invited him to our new house. It was a two-bedroom stucco in the low hills of North Berkeley, with a picture window view of the Bay. We had bought it for a modest $3,000 down, plus mortgage payments of $240 a month. As Fitch and I exchanged information about the political scenes in London and Berkeley, he twirled his red mustache with a nervous energy so intense it caused his pupils to flutter. Like many radicals, he was a self-exiled son of the middle class. During our talk, he ridiculed an uncle of his named Philip Klutznick—one of the largest real-estate developers in Chicago and a Democratic Party bigwig. I had the impression that he did this less to emphasize his radical credentials than to make me aware of the social connection.

The date of our meeting was February 17, which also happened to be the birthday of Huey Newton, the leader of the Black Panther Party and a man who, unknown to me then, was destined to have a profound impact on my life. Newton was in jail, accused of murdering an Oakland policeman, and the Panthers were holding a public celebration in the Oakland Arena, with speakers like Stokely Carmichael, the radical leader of the Student Non-Violent Coordinating Committee (SNCC), Eldridge Cleaver, the Panthers' "Minister of Information," and the Panthers' chairman, Bobby Seale. I planned to attend the celebration as my first political event on returning to Berkeley. Fitch and I were standing on my new front porch in a brilliant sunlight, looking out at the Bay, when I mentioned this to him. "Oh, you don't want to go, David," he said in a tone conveying absolute authority. "They hate whites. The blacks are gonna come up here one day and burn your house down." His eyes had a Mephistophelean glitter as he said this, and the violent image caught me off guard. I had been out of touch for so long, I was unable to distinguish the reality from Fitch's personal malice. Reflecting on my responsibilities to Elissa and our three children, I decided to take the prudent course and stay home.

I had been hired by Scheer to run *Ramparts'* book-publishing projects, and to take charge of a volume about the CIA, which the magazine had contracted. Two young radicals from Boston—Michael Ansara and Danny Schechter—were working on the project, but seemed unable to produce anything more than lists of guilty associations and scattered incidents of dubious intent without any apparent connection. By this time, the CIA's fortunes and those of *Ramparts* had come to seem inextricably entwined. The magazine had been launched as the brainchild of a liberal Catholic named Edward Keating, who had married the wealth to finance his ambition, and then hired a flamboyant, one-eyed Irishman named Warren Hinckle as his editor-in-chief. Hinckle wore patent leather pumps, and a patch over his bad eye, and drank heavily to type. A baby-faced exuberance and an absence of scruple enabled him to float above the gravitational forces that made everyone else seem earthbound by comparison. I learned quickly that you could never count on his word, but could not decide whether he was sold on his own hype. He had bankrupted every newspaper he had edited since high school, and *Ramparts* was to prove no exception.

Hinckle hired Scheer as his "political editor," and Scheer brought the staff of his congressional campaign on board, shifting the magazine's viewpoint dramatically to the left and raising his own status to almost coequal. It was only Scheer's combination of laziness and disinterest in the practical side of the business that kept him hostage to Hinckle's whims. By the time I arrived, the duo had already thrown Keating over the side, having subverted his moderate political agenda and exhausted his wife's dowry. A major factor in Keating's financial woes had been Hinckle's decision to convert the quarterly into a monthly. This characteristically failed to produce the slightest stirring of Hinckle's conscience. When the tearful publisher confessed that he was bankrupt, Hinckle was incredulous. "I thought you were rich," he said to Keating in the bar of New York's Algonquin Hotel. "I was," replied Keating, "but now I'm broke." Hinckle then signed the check for the drinks they were having. "Thank you Warren," Keating said, genuinely touched. "What are you thanking me for?" Hinckle replied. "I just signed my room number. You're paying the hotel bill."

Beginning in 1966, a series of sensational *Ramparts* stories drew a national spotlight and expanded circulation to 100,000 readers, making it the largest publication of the Left. The stories featured the CIA and its global intrigues. The first had come to *Ramparts* courtesy of Stanley Sheinbaum, an obscure assistant professor of economics at Michigan State who had participated in a CIA-funded program to train police in South Vietnam. Sheinbaum's story revealed an explosive connection between the campus and the war. When a student came to *Ramparts* with information that the CIA was funneling secret funds into the National Students Association, a further link was established. This scoop led to revelations about the Congress for Cultural Freedom and other liberal institutions that had been created to oppose the Communist offensive. In the hands *of Ramparts'* editors, a moral equivalence between Russia's police state and America's democracy was established. In the absence of similar stories about KGB operations among the organizations of the Left, or of links between the antiwar movement and the Communist forces in Vietnam, the *Ramparts* articles seemed to confirm the New Left view of the world.

One of the writers who worked on these stories was Sol Stern, a member of our old Berkeley group whom Scheer had hired to be assistant managing editor. In 1968, *Ramparts* sent Sol to Bratislava, along with Tom Hayden and an SDS delegation, to meet Madame Binh and other leaders of the National Liberation Front. For the radicals attending, this was not just a fact-finding mission. The organizers allowed Sol to be present only after *Ramparts* agreed that he would not report on the "sensitive" political discussions taking place. Long afterwards, Sol told me what these were: "The SDSers held a seminar with the Communists on how to conduct their psychological warfare campaign against the United States." According to Sol, Hayden was particularly vocal in making suggestions on how to sabotage the American war effort. He also tried to get the group to publicly endorse the Communist line on the war, but Sol and the sociologist Christopher Jencks, who was also present, objected, and Hayden's proposal was voted down.

Their dissent had consequences. Following the Bratislava meeting, members of the group were scheduled to go to North Vietnam. Hayden had already been there, publicly proclaiming that he had seen "rice roots democracy" at work. As a consequence, he so enjoyed the confidence of the Communist rulers that he had become one of their gatekeepers, screening American radicals for his hosts. To punish Sol and Jencks, Hayden saw to it that they were denied permission to go on to Hanoi with the others.

Hundreds—maybe even thousands—of similar contacts and arrangements were made with the Communist enemy both during the Sixties and after. Yet only a handful of New Leftists have ever written or talked about them. Few had the high-level contacts of Hayden, and only one, Carl Oglesby, was able to tell his story and remain a leftist in good standing. Others, like Phillip Abbot Luce and Larry Grathewold, made their revelations as "renegades," and were attacked as "government agents," a stigma that warned anyone else not to follow their example. Even after the collapse of Communism made its evils difficult to ignore, the cover-up by veterans of the New Left continued. Memoirs and historical monographs by New Left historians painted a virginal portrait of radical protesters, rewriting the history of the period on a scale that would have seemed impossible outside the Communist bloc. In his own memoir, Hayden includes pages of excerpts from his FBI file interspersed with disingenuous presentations of his political career that keep his readers in the dark about many of the far-from-innocent activities he was actually engaged in. The effect is to make the FBI's surveillance seem both gratuitous and malign at the same time.

Another source of *Ramparts'* growing influence was its promotion of the Black Panther Party as the new vanguard of the black struggle. When Newton founded the Panthers in 1966, he was a young street felon attending Oakland's Merritt College. On campus, he came into contact with Scheer and other white student radicals, and became familiar with their theories that criminals like him were "primitive rebels" who intuitively grasped the socialist idea that property is theft. As members of America's most oppressed class, black hoodlums—in this view—were taking the only avenue of revolt open to them. Newton became a leader of the new generation of activists, who were turning their backs on the nonviolent, integrationist preachings of Martin Luther King, just as Don Warden had predicted they would in the first issue of *Root and Branch.* Led by Stokely Carmichael and the Black Muslim leader Malcolm X, they identified themselves as "blacks" and called for "Black Power," reserving the word Negro for "Uncle Toms," among whom they included Martin Luther King (whom the Panthers referred to as Martin Luther Coon). Malcolm X called King's historic march on Washington "ridiculous" and predicted that white America would never grant the full citizenship that had been promised. Malcolm's racist doctrines and violent solutions made him marginal to the civil-rights struggle, and caused him to be shunned by its leadership. King himself had refused to appear with the Muslim leader in public. It was only in the year before Malcolm's death that he broke with the Nation of Islam and appeared to moderate his stance on race by holding out the possibility of a revolutionary alliance with radical whites.

On the surface, at least, Fitch was wrong. The Panther leaders, who claimed to draw their inspiration from Malcolm X's last year, did not appear to hate whites. One of their attractions to the *Ramparts* audience, in fact, was that they had publicly distanced themselves from so-called cultural nationalists like Leroi Jones (a.k.a. Amiri Baraka) and Ron Karenga, the leader of "US" (United Slaves). These "nationalists" adopted African names, wore *dashikis*, and were racially hostile. By contrast, the Panthers quoted Marx and actively sought alliances with the white left. While several items in the Panthers' "Ten Point Program" were racially specific—exempting black men from military service, and freeing all blacks held in prison—these seemed justifiable compensations for special oppression. The other Panther demands for land, bread, housing, education, clothing, and so on, were issues of class.

While no one would publicly say so, it was the Panthers' violent image that provided their real attraction to the New Left. Blacks would seek liberation, Malcolm said, through the "ballot or the bullet," but no radical believed that the System could be changed by peaceful means. After founding the Panthers, Newton had assumed the title of "Minister of Defense," declaring that blacks were "already at war with the racist white power structure." This seemed a plausible reading of the riots that had erupted in Detroit and other American cities during the summer of 1967. As a street predator, Newton had studied law at night to develop his craft. Among his discoveries was that the law allowed citizens to bear firearms in public. Dressing his recruits in menacing uniforms of black leather jackets and berets, he invoked

Mao's dictum "It is necessary to pick up the gun." Armed Panther "field marshals" patrolled neighborhoods to monitor arrests, making local police nervous and angry, and inspiring legislators to propose a change in the law. In the summer of the riots, the Panthers marched into a session of the State Assembly in Sacramento, shotguns aloft, to oppose legislation that would remove the privilege. Their demands were ignored, and the law about firearms was quickly changed.

In articles that both defused the alarm their violent message aroused, and presented their case in a positive light, *Ramparts'* editors showcased the Panthers and their agendas for a national audience. Their stories appeared in other places besides *Ramparts*. Sol Stern wrote the first major press account of the Panthers for the *New York Times Sunday Magazine,* where it acquired an authority that *Ramparts* could not have provided. His profile described a street-comer meeting the Panthers held in San Francisco's Fillmore district, where Newton told a crowd: "Every time you go to execute a white racist Gestapo cop, you are defending yourself." When Sol asked Newton if he was ready himself to kill a cop, he answered he was—and that he was also ready to die. Sol then explained to the *Times'* readers: "To these young men, the execution of a police officer would be as natural and justifiable as the execution of a German soldier by a member of the French Resistance." He added: "To write off the Panthers as a fringe group of little influence is to miss the point. The group's roots are in the desperation and anger that no civil-rights legislation or poverty program has touched in the ghetto."

Sol's article appeared in August 1967. In October, Newton was arrested for killing an Oakland police officer named John Frey, who was attempting to arrest him. The officer had been shot in the back from a distance of 12 inches. Immediately, the New Left denounced the "frame-up" of this young black leader, and organized support for his defense. World-famous intellectuals—Sartre and Russell among them—-joined the appeal. By the time I arrived at *Ramparts* three months later, the Minister of Defense had become a *cause célèbre*, an example of America's continuing injustices to its black citizens. A giant photograph of Newton sitting on a wicker throne—spear in one hand, shotgun in the other—adorned college dorm walls across the nation, becoming the most famous political poster of the decade. The

Panther chant of "Free Huey/Off the Pig" was taken up at movement rallies on campuses everywhere. In the eyes of the New Left, it was not Huey Newton who was on trial in the Oakland courtroom, but "racist Amerika."

With the Panthers' ascendance, Martin Luther King's hope of including blacks in the American dream was replaced by a new and intransigent racial vision. For radicals, the war in Vietnam provided the true metaphor for social conflicts like civil rights. In its prism the goal was no longer integration but "liberation," the destruction of the existing social order and its replacement by another. Police were regarded as a colonial army occupying the ghetto and defending the status quo. The epithet "pig" identified them as an alien force. A lone dissent to this term was offered by Staughton Lynd, the radical historian who had cautioned Russell to make the War Crimes Tribunal impartial and fair. Lynd objected to "pig" as dehumanizing, and pointed out that policemen were workers doing a job. But he had no supporters for his views. I had an uneasy feeling about the term, but forced myself to take the hard line defending its use, convinced that this was the mark of a serious revolutionary. If the police were the armed forces of the class enemy, to shrink from calling them "pigs" was to shrink from the task itself.

The quest for authenticity preoccupied white radicals like myself who made up the bulk of the Movement, and was the key to the Panthers' charisma. In a seminal article titled "The White Negro," Norman Mailer had cast America's blacks as Rousseau's "noble savages," representatives of humanity in its pristine state. These were the "oppressed" of the radical imagination. The Panthers' roots in the ghetto were the primal symbol of social injustice. Their will to violence was the mark of their revolutionary spirit. A memorable incident outside *Ramparts'* San Francisco offices crystallized the attraction. Malcolm X's widow, Betty Shabazz, had arrived for an interview, accompanied by a Panther honor guard, fully armed and led by Newton. When the police ordered the Panthers to put away their weapons, Newton leveled his shotgun at the commanding officer and pumped a round into the chamber. The officer retreated. Eldridge Cleaver later wrote an article for *Ramparts* called "How I Fell in Love With the Black Panther Party," describing the confrontation as the moment of truth that won his allegiance. In an introduction for a planned Newton autobiography, he characterized Huey as "the baddest motherfucker ever to set foot inside of history." The line, however, was not written by Eldridge, but by a white *Ramparts* editor named Peter Collier.

While Newton was in his Oakland cell awaiting trial for the shooting of Officer Frey, a profile appeared in *Look* magazine under the byline Joan Didion. Her signature skepticism had penetrated the screen of Newton's rhetoric, revealing the street hustler underneath. In her portrait, the Panther Minister of Defense appeared as little more than a young hood who had added Marx to his hustler's bag of tricks. I read the article with mounting rage. If intelligent people like Didion failed to understand the social reality, and did not lend support to the movement to change it, there was no hope. I decided to appeal to her directly. In a terse note, I expressed my dismay at her failure to take Newton's words at face value and validate his plea for the oppressed. It concluded: "If there is a race war in this country, you will be one of those responsible for it." Didion's reply was even briefer. It came in the form of a postcard containing a single line: "I thought radicals wanted a race war."

Her reply was even more distressing than the article itself. How could anyone be so cynical? I could not find the words to respond. Years later, I saw that if I had been able to reflect rationally at the time, I would have recognized the truth in what she said. Radicals like Fitch, it was clear, could hardly conceal their hope for a race war. In promoting the Panthers' violent rhetoric, *Ramparts* was doing its bit as well. In December, Scheer finished editing Cleaver's writings for a book that Random House was going to publish. He changed the title of Cleaver's article "How I Fell in Love With the Black Panther Party" to "The Courage to Kill," and concluded his introduction with the words: "Right on, Eldridge." Radicals like Fitch and Scheer simply assumed that if the Panthers were the vanguard, the targets of the coming war would only be racist whites who profited from oppression and defended its privilege.

Ramparts occupied something of an ambivalent place in the imagination of the Left. Its glossy, four-color format was in striking contrast to the newsprint tabloids of the "underground press," and aroused suspicion in a movement that rejected the symbols of capitalist success. The personal styles of its editors reinforced these doubts. Scheer lived in a spacious two-story brown shingle on Benvenue Avenue, in a posh section of the South Campus area. He paid himself an annual salary of $25,000—three times that of staff writers like me, and five times what the black receptionist made. Hinckle set a pace that was even more flamboyant. Three-hour, six-martini editorial lunches at Vanessi's Restaurant in San Francisco, junkets at the Algonquin Hotel in New York, and first-class fare wherever he and Scheer went, added fodder to the Left's indictment. On the other hand, *Ramparts'* radical credentials could not be so easily dismissed. Its campaign against the CIA, its Black Panther franchise, its publication of Che Guevara's diaries—approved personally by Fidel—were *bona fides* that commanded respect.

Once again I found myself in a setting where I didn't feel entirely at home. I had no trouble living modestly, nor any interest in doing otherwise. I considered myself a revolutionary theorist, and I identified with the activists who criticized the *Ramparts* style. But I did not share their scorn for the efforts of Scheer and Hinckle to reach into the popular culture. Nor did I regard these as "selling out." The street radicals who denounced the magazine lived like permanent undergraduates in "communes," where several adults shared a house, usually minus children. I had a growing family, and couldn't afford the luxury of their self-imposed indigence.

I attempted to ease the discomfort of my situation by keeping to myself and avoiding settings where I would represent the magazine to activists. I also avoided joining any radical groups. When Fitch tried to recruit me to a Leninist SDS faction called the Revolutionary Youth Movement, I said no. I did not want to put myself under the discipline of a "vanguard" that would expose me to my parents' fate. And, when *Ramparts'* editorial staff went to the Democratic Party Convention in the summer of 1968, I did not accompany them to Chicago.

Tom Hayden had called for a demonstration at the convention, to protest the Vietnam War. Everybody knew that it meant a confrontation with the Chicago police that could prove bloody, and Hinckle decided to put out a "wall paper," as Mao's Red Guards had during the cultural revolution in China. I knew that *Ramparts'* intrusion into the political fray would be resented by the radicals, and it immediately was when Hinckle made the Pump Room of the Ambassador Hotel his editorial office. But this was not my only reservation. Like the majority of the Movement, which failed to respond to Hayden's call, I didn't understand his objective at the time. If the two-party system was a sham, as we claimed, why draw attention to the convention as though it was important?

Chicago's Mayor Daley had recently ordered his police to shoot looters during the riots that followed the assassination of Martin Luther King. A radical street protest would put people's lives at risk. Because of considerations like these, Hayden failed to get an endorsement of his plan from SDS or any other significant organizations, and attracted only two or three thousand people to Lincoln Park. It was "the smallest [number] of any demonstration we ever had," one of its organizers, Dave Dellinger, wrote afterwards. It was a dismal failure by *any* measure in a period in which 100,000 protesters would not have been unusual at a national demonstration. But it was enough to generate trouble, which was Hayden's real agenda.

The ensuing melee changed the shape of American politics. The television shots of demonstrators being bloodied by police, and the chaos on the convention floor, destroyed the presidential chances of Hubert Humphrey and moved the Democratic Party dramatically to the left. Humphrey's inability to control his own party created a vacuum that the antiwar protesters, led by Tom Hayden, moved in to fill. Four years later, they provided the push behind the antiwar candidacy of George McGovern, and the changes in Party rules that propelled the rise to power of the Party's left wing.

When the dust in Chicago cleared, Hayden and seven other radicals, including the Panthers' Bobby Seale, were indicted for conspiring to create a riot. During the trial, the defendants turned the courtroom into a theater of protest, creating a near-riot in the chamber itself. Seale was so obstructive that the judge ordered him bound and gagged. The picture of a black man in chains was a made-to-order script for the radical melodrama. All of the defendants were eventually acquitted, but the "Chicago Conspiracy Trial" became a symbolic cross in the progressive book of martyrs—another triumph of political fiction over historical fact.

One of the conspirators, Jerry Rubin, admitted as much a decade later, in a column written on the occasion of the trial judge's death. The prosecution had been right, he admitted; the organizers' objective in luring activists to Chicago was to create the riot that then took place. This explained Hayden's choice of venue, and his determination to proceed with the demonstration after failing to get movement support. It also made sense in terms of the general strategy Hayden had laid out for me in our private political discussions. If people's heads got cracked by police, he said in more than one of these sessions, it "radicalized them." The trick was to maneuver the idealistic and unsuspecting into situations that would achieve the result. When Hayden disclosed these ideas to me, I found their cynicism disturbing, and didn't respond. But in the Chicago events I saw his design inexorably at work. It was the extrapolation of a familiar radical idea: "The worse, the better." The ascendance of Nixon would create a greater potential for the radical agenda than the election of Humphrey, which would pose the danger of "co-option." It was the same logic that had caused the Left to choose Malcolm X over Martin Luther King.

The call to the demonstration had been issued under the auspices of the "MOBE," an acronym of sorts for the National Mobilization to End the War In Vietnam. It was an ostensibly pacifist group whose organizational shell had been delivered to Hayden by Dellinger, who was on its executive committee. I learned this from one of its members, Sid Peck, who told me with some bitterness, after the fact, that Hayden had been "extremely deceptive" in outlining his agenda, assuring everyone that his intentions were nonviolent. Hayden's duplicity continued throughout the event, causing Staughton Lynd to comment: "On Monday, Wednesday, and Friday [Hayden] was a National Liberation Front guerilla, and on Tuesday, Thursday, and Saturday, he ... was on the left wing of the Democratic Party." Anyone who knew Tom immediately knew which one was the real Hayden. His own self-exculpation afterwards was this: "Many traditional pacifists worried that we wanted to initiate violence. Our answer was that we *expected* violence from the police and federal authorities, but we would not initiate it ourselves."

Having secured his pacifist cover for the event, Hayden then went to the most radical elements in the Left—those who actively advocated violence as a political tactic—and proposed that they provoke the conflict. According to his own retrospective account, he warned one group in New York that "they should come to Chicago prepared to shed their blood," and told his co-organizer, Rennie Davis, that he expected twenty-five people to die. He recruited the Yippies (formal name: Youth International Party), a group organized by Abbie Hoffman and Jerry Rubin, whose idea of politics was creative provocation, and who alarmed Chicago officials by immediately threatening to put LSD in the Chicago water supply. Before the event, Hayden met with the Weatherman faction of SDS, which had issued a call for "armed struggle" in American cities. As one of the Weather leaders, Gerry Long, told me later, Hayden proposed to them that "It might be useful if someone were to fire-bomb police cars." He gave Bobby Seale a platform in Lincoln Park, where Seale addressed the crowd with this suggestive exhortation: "If a pig comes up to us and starts swinging a billy club, and you check around and you got your piece, you got to down that pig in defense of yourself! We're gonna barbecue us some pork!" Once the violence started, while Dellinger and others sought to calm people down, Hayden defiantly incited the crowd to "make sure that if blood is going to flow, it will flow all over the city."

During the melee, Hayden himself went around in a mask and wig, certain of the dangers he had arranged. At one point he attempted to have a tape recording of his voice played over a loudspeaker from the Hilton, where the Democratic Party delegates were assembled. On the tape he proclaimed: "This is Tom Hayden. I'm inside the Hilton. The Hilton has to be taken by any means necessary." It was a call to certain bloodshed, except that the intended messenger, Geoffrey Cowan, refused to play the tape.

Years later, when Hayden was composing his autobiography, he asked me what I thought he should include. "Why don't you write the truth?" I said. By then, twenty years had elapsed—enough time to establish a distance from the events. What was the point of a memoir if not to help the next generation understand what had happened? But Tom was still enmeshed in the politics of the Left, and to write truthfully about his past would have closed options for him in the present. Except for inadvertent revelations which no memoirist can avoid, his account merely reiterates the myth of innocence he fabricated at the time.

Sometimes avoiding the danger zone where *Ramparts* interfaced with the Movement proved impossible. On one occasion, Scheer asked me to take charge of an article Eldridge Cleaver had written, "The Land Question." Cleaver was the magazine's most celebrated writer. He was serving nine years in prison for rape when his radical lawyer brought him to the attention of *Ramparts'* editors, who intervened to secure his parole. Scheer and Hinckle provided the prisoner character references, public support for his parole plea, and a job. In addition, they put together what proved to be a best-selling collection of his prison essays, *Soul On Ice.* The nihilistic view of himself that Cleaver promoted in this book fit snugly into the radical outlook. To the suggestion that he might owe something to society for his crimes, he replied: "I'm perfectly aware that I'm in prison, that I'm a Negro, that I've been a rapist....

> *My answer to all such thoughts lurking in their split-level heads, crouching behind their squinting bombardier eyes, is that the blood of Vietnamese peasants has paid off all my debts....*

It was the moral standard we applied to all criminals who happened to be black; and ultimately to ourselves.

One day, Cleaver appeared in my office in a *dashiki,* squinting through his own bombardier eyes in a way that made me extremely nervous. He had come to discuss the article I had been given to edit, which was exactly the kind of piece I wanted to see published—a theoretical analysis in the Marxian vein. But it was also the kind of article that *Ramparts* was *not* going to publish, lest the magazine become (as Scheer was constantly warning) a political "rag" like *Studies on the Left.* When I urged Scheer to print it anyway, he eyed me in disgust. "Why do you think I gave it to you in the first place?" he growled. "If I wanted to publish it, I would have edited it myself." I had become caught in exactly the dilemma I had tried so hard to avoid. I didn't have the authority to say yes to the article, and I couldn't bring myself to say no to Cleaver. Instead, I delayed a verdict and avoided his calls. For weeks my agony dragged on as Cleaver left messages to call him about its status, and I searched for excuses to put him off. Then, one morning, Scheer came breathlessly into my office and said, "Eldridge has been shot. Do we have anything by him?" I handed him "The Land Question," which appeared in the next issue.

The shooting took place two days after the assassination of Martin Luther King and quickly became another Movement cause. Cleaver was arrested, eventually fleeing the country to avoid prosecution. The episode was an important template in the Movement's turn away from non-violence. The Panthers' version of the incident, which we all accepted, was composed by Cleaver himself. Scheer included it as "Affidavit #2" in the book of Cleaver's essays, which he edited after the arrest. In a headnote, he explained that Cleaver had been dictating an essay—"Requiem for Non-Violence"—after the King assassination ("Malcolm X prophesied the coming of the gun, and Huey Newton picked up the gun, and now there is gun against gun"). In the midst of the dictation, Cleaver received a call from Panther headquarters, and left the *Ramparts* office without finishing the article. The call, according to Cleaver, was in connection with a barbecue the Panthers were planning:

> I think that the so-called shoot-out on 28th Street was the direct result of frantic attempts by the Oakland Police Department to sabotage the Black Community Barbecue Picnic, which the Black Panther Party had set up for April 7th in Defremery Park.

Cleaver went on to describe how the "pigs" normally harassed the Party members when the Panthers held community events. All week, the "pigs" had been tailing the Panthers' automobiles as they made their innocent arrangements and picked up supplies for the barbecue picnic. On the evening of April 6, Cleaver was leading a caravan of three cars when he stopped in order to relieve himself in the street. The "pigs," who had been tailing them until then, pulled up and started firing—unprovoked. The Panthers retreated to a house for safely. Two policemen were shot, and Cleaver and another Panther were wounded; a third, Bobby Hutton, was killed. Hutton was apparently attempting to surrender when he tripped and dropped his hands, triggering a hail of gunfire. Wrote Cleaver: "Eldridge Cleaver died in that house on 28th Street with Little Bobby Hutton, and what's left is force: fuel for the fire that will rage across the face of this racist country and either purge it of its evil or turn it to ashes." Eldridge's words resonated through the community of the Left and inspired white radicals farther along the road to revolutionary authenticity and violence.

Twenty years later, when hardly anyone remembered the incident anymore, Cleaver told reporter Kate Coleman what really happened. After King's death, he had issued an "executive order" to Panthers to assassinate policemen as a retaliatory measure. Cleaver himself had driven to San Francisco with some other Panthers and personally ambushed a police car, wounding two officers and leaving one with metal fragments permanently in his cheek. The attempted arrest of the Panther caravan and the fatal shoot-out followed this assault. It was far from the lynching of innocents he had described in 1968.

The principal way I sought to rescue myself from the predicament that *Ramparts* created was to stay out of the office, doing as much work at home as possible. This method was also suited to my temperament. Perhaps as a consequence of my early separation from home when I was sent to the Sunnyside Progressive School, I always felt a tug of anxiety when I crossed the bridge to San Francisco to go to work. I liked being near Elissa and around the children, despite the distractions. We had shared so many trials by then, and so many rewards of family life, that we were now as much like brother and sister as we were husband and wife. The completion I had sought in her when we first met had developed into a jointly inhabited world that was almost separate from everything outside. I felt this particularly on weekends, which I spent at parks, playgrounds, zoos, and other children's entertainments, while my colleagues at *Ramparts* were at political meetings, or hanging out in rock clubs like the Steppenwolf and the Fillmore. The plants, animals, and children with which she had filled our lives answered a need in me I'm not sure I would have known how to satisfy without her. Her focus was life-centered, present-oriented, and outside herself. This provided a discipline and counterpoint for my own impulses, which were interior, intellectual, and relentlessly toward the future. It seemed as though I was always under pressure from ideas that needed to be spelled out, arguments that required completion, books I had to write. Without her, I felt sometimes I might have missed Buber's "lived concrete," the rich pleasure of the family the two of us had created. The poet Yeats had said that one must choose perfection of the life or of the work. I felt that through Elissa's intervention I had been given the possibility of both.

When I conveyed the news of our third pregnancy to my father; his reaction was unexpectedly negative. "You've broken the mold," he said cryptically. It took me a while to decipher what he meant. Roz Baxandall, a historian of the Left and a friend whom I turned to for advice, observed that in our parents' generation no progressive had more than two offspring. Her mother had told her that in the Twenties, when the Party line was ultraleft, it was considered reactionary to have *any* children, since they would be obstacles to the revolutionary mission. When years passed and there was no revolution, people became frustrated with the situation and began to start families. But even then a ponderous rationality prevailed, and two children were regarded as a practical limit. More than two indicated a lack of political focus, a surrender to the forces of self-indulgence. I had the sense that this was the way my father saw me.

In his *Symposium,* Plato suggests that lovers are two halves of the same person in search of each other—a yin and yang of desire. I felt that way about Elissa's and my life together. Even the chores generated by our toddlers and pets, which sometimes seemed endless, became a bond between us. I felt integral to the fabric of the life we had created, and not only in emotional ways. Elissa did not know, for example, how to drive—and wouldn't learn. Yet we lived a mile from any stores, and driving was a necessity to maintain the household. There were other practical ways in which she had made me indispensable. As a result, I was also needed in a traditional sense as the man of the house. The idea was politically retrograde, but it resulted from Elissa's choices.

Like a dutiful husband, I pressed her to attend a "consciousness-raising" women's group, when this became a radical fashion. The group included Berkeley's feminist elite—among them Scheer's wife, Anne Weills; Susan Lydon, who had written a famous *Ramparts* article titled "The Politics of Orgasm"; and other political worthies. To distinguish their radical outlook from that of the then-moderate National Organization of Women and other liberal groups, they called their agenda "women's liberation." Elissa came home from the first session in a state of agitation, vowing never to return. "They hate me because I'm a mother," was all she said. Years later I learned from other members of the group that they had berated her for allowing me to "oppress" her by "making" her assume the housewifely role. They also told me that within a year of the group's formation, every marriage in it had dissolved.

The umbilical cord of the family kept a close rein on me. On January 9, 1969, I was giving a lecture, "Imperialism and Revolution," to two hundred UC students in the Pauley Ballroom, when someone came up to me and said, "Your wife's having a baby." I raced out of the hall, and drove home as fast as I could. The plan had been to leave the three children with Elissa's mother, who was visiting. But Benjamin let up a squall when he saw us leaving, and we had to take him along. I dropped Elissa off at Alta Bates Hospital on the south side of town, and raced back home with Benjamin (who finally had calmed down), and then hurried back again to the hospital only to find that our fourth child, Anne, had already been born.

Four children proved to be far more than a handful. Jonathan, who was now eight, had become a self-starter, off with his friends when school was over. He was an intelligent and engaging kid, still jealous of the prerogatives he had to give up when Sarah was born. Elissa was hard on him, I thought. When he didn't meet her standards, she was uncharacteristically sharp. Perhaps because she had spent so many lonely hours with him in Sweden and London, and he was such a precocious child, she expected more than he could deliver. Sarah had grown into a lovely, quiet child with a permanently quizzical look. This was a result of the partial deafness her Turner's Syndrome had caused. Her quietness made her easy to manage—something we were both grateful for, given the excess of energy on either side of her. But Elissa and I sometimes worried whether she wasn't *too* easy, often lost in her own space, and slow to engage with the flow around her. Benjy—the name itself suggested his vulnerability—was thin, milk-toned, and freckled. I have an image of him sitting on the crook of his mother's hip, head rested consolingly on her shoulder, soaking up comfort. But he had a worrisome side, too, a tendency to panic when things went wrong, as though he feared the space in front was already too crowded, and the one behind was being stripped away.

We attempted to stay in control of the household, but it was often a fruitless endeavor. The family dynamics were especially trying for me on the vacations we took to Yosemite and other distant destinations. We would pack everybody into our Volkswagen bus and head out on one of California's endless highways. Not long into the trip, the tedium of the road would trigger activity inside the van. Anne would set off Benjamin, Jon would pick at Sarah, and a chorus of howls would ensue. Soon Elissa would be in distress, until I came down hard on the most available. Often it would end up with Elissa frowning at me over my heavy-handed response. Stress seemed to go hand-in-hand with family pleasures.

My physical absence from the office could be made to seem almost reasonable, since my editorial responsibilities related to books, and I did not have to meet any magazine deadlines. But it was resented nonetheless. "How come he doesn't work?" Collier asked Scheer one day. "Oh, little Davey Horowitz," came the reply, "he's odd; he works at home." *Little Davey Horowitz*. It was Scheer's tag for me, a reflexive put-down that I chafed under. But Scheer's ascription of a kind of innocence to me was not wholly off the mark.

The cocoon-like ambiance of our nuclear family set limits to my experience. Outside, the cultural revolution, with its new attitudes toward drugs and sex, was well underway. Along with political calls-to-arms, the "underground" press ran sexual personals, and invitations to Dionysian rituals like the "Human Be-In," one of which had been attended by 100,000 enthusiasts in Golden Gate Park. At the "Be-In," which took place during the summer before we returned from England, Timothy Leary told the assembled: "Turn on, tune in, and drop out." Political radicals like Hayden welcomed the subversive element in the counterculture, its challenges to prevailing norms, and—in the case of drugs—open defiance of the law. Such attitudes were creating a disaffected generation that, given time, could be recruited for revolutionary goals.

Immersion in the routines of family life insulated Elissa and me from these events in the world at large. This was not a problem for Elissa, who never seemed to peer over the edge of the path she had chosen. There was in her something of the attitude I had noticed in my mother, as though the life they found themselves in was difficult enough without taking on the trials of another. But for me it was different. I had no special sense of difficulty, or that other choices might possibly entail more pain than pleasure. If I held back, it was because of my unwillingness to risk what I had—but also because my life's ambition was to champion a moral ideal.

As a result, when I moved in the world outside our household, I often felt like a traveler in a strange land, uncertain of the local customs and folkways, never sure where a zone of danger might lie. I was spending a lot of energy repressing unruly desires. The increasing visibility of the female body under the new cultural dispensation was distracting enough. Now, aggressive sexuality was becoming a mark of liberation. I was nervous around good-looking women. I wanted to be faithful to my wife, in imagination as well as the flesh, but there was no help for me in radical precepts. No amount of "consciousness raising" could suppress the elemental responses I was feeling, or make them go away. Others seemed better able to handle the problem. One day at *Ramparts* I was standing in the corridor with Peter Collier when an attractive blonde from the art department appeared in a dramatically low-cut blouse. I took my normal stance, attempting not to notice, but Collier went right up to her to confront the unavoidable. "Will you tell us when you're going to bend over, Mary?" he asked in a cheerful voice. This defused the sexual tension and converted the occasion into a kind of compliment. I envied his *savoir faire*.

My sexual guilelessness made me impervious to many of the undercurrents in the office, and caused me to misinterpret others. A storm had erupted over the January 1968 issue of the magazine, which attempted to boost feminism with a feature on the new women's movement. The article had a self-serving element, profiling Scheer's wife, Anne Weills, along with other better-known activists, and attempting to make the point that they all were pretty (not merely griping) females. But the real furor was provoked by the cover photo of a headless woman in a low-cut bodice. She was wearing a button that said "Women Power," as if that power emanated directly from her cleavage. Most of the heat of the reaction was directed at Scheer, as political editor, who was furious with Hinckle for having exposed him this way.

Yet there was a poetic justice, too, as Scheer provided a snug fit to the "male chauvinist" profile. When I first met him in Berkeley, he was married to Serena, a savvy Jew from Brooklyn whom he treated with a kind of annoyed concern, as if she were a pet that had been left in his care. Serena was the distaff wife, the kind of woman his mother would have approved of. The *new* wife, Anne, was her polar opposite. A picture-perfect blonde, she was the daughter of a telephone company executive, a fact that Scheer used to distance himself publicly from his new family. Scheer could be personally brutal to this wife as well. On one occasion, he summoned me to the bedroom in his home for an editorial meeting. Anne was present as he discussed a prospective trip to England for an interview with Vanessa Redgrave that he thought I might help to arrange. Turning to Anne, he said apropos nothing: "Doesn't Vanessa have little breasts like you?"

When I arrived at *Ramparts* in January 1968, the office was abuzz about an affair Scheer had while in Cuba with Michelle Ray, the journalist who secured the Guevara diaries for publication. If I had been privy to it, I would have found this information distressing, but my outsider status on such matters kept me safely in the dark. Adultery, I felt, was politically unacceptable. As radicals, our personal values ought to be consistent with the values we were trying to introduce into the world. That same month, Scheer assembled the magazine staff in his office to discuss the "women power" issue. There were thirty people present, including Anne. At one point in the discussion, she volunteered her own opinion, dissenting from a view Scheer supported. Suddenly he snapped at her, "Shut up, you don't know anything," which threw the room into embarrassed silence. I was appalled along with everyone else. What I didn't understand was that Scheer's anger was provoked by his discovery that Anne was having a retaliatory affair with Hayden. She had even trumped him politically: While his tryst with Michelle Ray had taken place in Cuba, hers had been consummated on a trip to Hanoi.

It was not just sexual monogamy that kept me apart from my peers. After much hesitation, I had tried marijuana with some of the office staff. The drug seemed fairly harmless, and the experience was seductive—but I remained skittish, and did not pursue it. One reason was that Elissa would not consider drugs at all, and to indulge such an illicit pleasure without her seemed like a betrayal. There was probably a more compelling psychological ground to my anxiety, in particular the fear of disappearing into some radical abyss. But, also, I could not be sure drugs were harmless, and did not want to put my rational faculties at risk.

My outsider status was crystallized by a radical named Michael Lerner, who had sought me out because he felt my *Ramparts* connections might be useful to him. Lerner was a graduate student, an unkempt individual whose appetites seemed always about to burst their ample envelope of flesh. He was constantly badgering others to satisfy these needs, being so utterly self-absorbed with his own agendas that he seemed oblivious to the fact that the impression he made was irritating, and often ridiculous. The pampered son of a chairwoman of the New Jersey Democratic Party, he had been a theological student at Columbia before coming to Berkeley to pursue the revolution. When his sister married a Cravath Swaine attorney, the guests included the state's governor and senior senator. This proved too tempting an opportunity for Lerner. He interrupted the celebration with a speech denouncing the guests as "murderers" with "blood on your hands" because they had failed to stop the Vietnam War.

When it came his turn to marry, however, he was not about to share the stage with anyone. Napoleon had crowned himself at his own coronation; Lerner was both rabbi and groom at his own nuptials. The bride, a doe-eyed brunette who was nearly ten years his junior, was dressed in traditional white. The daughter of a conservative military man, she had sought Lerner out when he was the leader of an organization he had created, the Seattle Liberation Front. "If you want to be my girlfriend," he told her when she approached him for a date, "you'll have to organize a guerilla *foco* first." In the wedding ceremony, held on his back lawn, the couple exchanged rings made from the fuselage of a downed American aircraft. The bride had brought them back from North Vietnam. Their wedding cake was inscribed with a Weatherman slogan: "Smash Monogamy." The marriage lasted less than a year.

Lerner personified the reasons I had come to see myself as an alien in the New Left. On one occasion he sought my help in getting a book published, but our partnership foundered when I discovered how intellectually slovenly he was. He had written sentences like "America is a hopelessly imperialist country," and refused to revise them, unable to see that it mattered. To me, intellectual rigor *did* matter. The business we had undertaken was deadly serious, and required as much precision of thought and responsibility of action as we could achieve. It was for this reason that I did not like the Hegelian obfuscations of the *New Left Review* crowd in England. If we were going to encourage people to risk their lives for our agendas, we should be clear about what we were telling them to do, and why.

Alienating me even more from radicals like Lerner was the fact that they were disconnected from family and real community. A friend of mine with a Freudian bent observed of Scheer that he "projected onto the socialist future the human connection he had failed to achieve in his own life." I had the same intuition about Hayden, who was not on speaking terms with his own father, and seemed to have no fixed home address. But it was Lerner, having turned his sister's wedding into a political melodrama, who illustrated the syndrome best. Soon after their marriage, he and his wife had a child. The young family went east, where Lerner took a job teaching philosophy at Trinity College in Connecticut. When the couple separated shortly thereafter, mother and son went to live in Boston. Lerner, however, returned to Berkeley. "Michael," I said, distressed that he would leave his infant behind: "How can you leave your son in the east to come to Berkeley? He needs you." Without hesitation, Lerner answered: "David, you don't understand. I *have* to be here. Berkeley is the center of the world-historical spirit."

It was Lerner who also made me understand that drugs were far more central to the consciousness of the Movement than I had realized. On discovering that I had never taken LSD, he gave me an incredulous look. We were standing in the middle of Shattuck Avenue after a protest and, in the same urgent tone he had used to insist on Berkeley's significance, he said: "You *have* to take LSD. Until you've dropped acid, you don't know what socialism is."

Events in the spring of 1968 were moving in a direction that seemed to lend credence to the radical apocalypse. In Vietnam, the Communists had breached the perimeter of the U.S. embassy, making the impossible dream of a "liberation" seem real. The episode excited public sentiment against the war, and swelled the demonstrations. Following soon after, the assassinations of Martin Luther King and Bobby Kennedy made the liberal option at home seem doomed, as well. When Lyndon Johnson announced that he would not run for reelection, many activists concluded that they had the power to topple presidents. Hayden's riot at the Democratic Convention was almost an inevitable hubris of these events.

So was the election of the new leadership of SDS. Until then, the organization had incarnated the ethos of the New Left—spontaneous and antiauthoritarian. But the new SDS president, Bernadine Dohrn, announced on taking office that she was "a revolutionary Communist," while with calculated and (to me) repellent pride, her vice president, Billy Ayers, declared that he had not read a book in a year. Learning from the past seemed to me the only way progress was possible. I had read through shelves of books in an effort to find out why previous revolutions had gone wrong. Now, the anti-intellectualism already present in the Movement had become a revolutionary badge of honor.

Shortly after their election, the new leaders dissolved SDS into "Weatherman," Dohrn's political cult which preached a Marxist version of race war. They issued a manifesto inspired by the Maoist doctrine of "people's war," and predicted the coming of a global Armageddon in which the Third World would take revenge on "Amerika" by "bringing the war home." American radicals could atone for their "white skin privilege" by serving as a fifth column inside the enemy camp.

For me, these developments were profoundly depressing. The hopes I had that the New Left would avoid the tragedies of the past were being overwhelmed by the primitive passions the war had unleashed. It had become apparent to me, since my return to the States, that no one in the Left gave much thought to the problems that had preoccupied me until then. As Fitch summed up the prevailing attitude: "Vulgar Marxism' is 95 percent correct." I expressed my concern in a *Ramparts* article titled "Hand-Me-Down Marxism and the New Left." It was a commentary on the 1969 SDS convention, which had come to a halt when the Progressive Labor Party faction began chanting "Mao, Mao, Mao Tse-tung. Dare to Struggle, Dare to Win" and the majority countered with a chant led by the Harvard SDS: "Ho, Ho, Ho Chi Minh. The NLF Is Gonna Win." In my article, I attempted to remind activists that "the New Left grew out of two bankruptcies—not just liberalism, but old-line Marxism as well." But no one was listening.

Weatherman and the Panthers were the vanguards of the hour. Even Hayden, one of the few radical leaders actually able to engage serious ideas, had surrendered to the "Vietnam Metaphor"—the prism through which the New Left had come to interpret all events. He was writing articles in the *Berkeley Barb* advocating guerilla warfare and the creation of "liberated zones" in American cities through armed force, and calling the Panthers "America's Vietcong." He had created a Berkeley Liberation School with his own "Minister of Defense" who trained its students in the use of weapons, including explosives. At one point, Hayden and his activists even conducted a training session in an emergency clinic in Los Baños, posing as doctors and para-medics, practicing on unsuspecting patients. "Fascism is coming," he announced on a visit to the *Ramparts* offices. "By the end of the year they're going to put us all in jail." About this time, Michael Lerner approached me with the idea that I should buy a gun. "Michael," I said in disbelief, "this is no revolutionary situation. The people aren't with us. You couldn't even describe a scenario in which there was a shoot-out with the police that we could win." Hardly pausing, he said, "Then you have to buy a handgun and give it to someone else for use in assassinations."

I had seen it coming on election eve the year before. The Peace and Freedom Party nominated Eldridge Cleaver and Jerry Rubin for its presidential ticket. There was a "Pre-Erection Day" (sic) celebration in the Berkeley Community Theater, and Rubin came on stage wheeling a live pig in a shopping cart. This was "Pigasus," the Yippie mascot, he informed the crowd, and then announced that he was turning over his vice-presidential spot on the ticket to the pig. Then he lit up a joint. Eldridge took the microphone and began a rant in which he said the Left had to unite with the Machine Gun Kellys and John Dillingers of the world. He talked about "pussy power," and said that he would kill San Francisco mayor Alioto and his children and grandchildren.

I was sitting in the audience with Fitch, sinking deeper and deeper into the plush upholstery in a vain effort to hide. To avoid the humiliation of my parents, I had been careful not to join any party. I had given myself to a movement that was free-spirited and democratic and that I thought would advance the cause of human enlightenment and social justice, and now I was deeply embarrassed.

BRING THE WAR HOME

AFTER DISPENSING WITH KEATING, HINCKLE HAD FOUND ANOTHER angel to support Ramparts' extravagant style—a graduate student in Aztec Civilizations named Fred Mitchell, who was heir to a Pennsylvania iron fortune. For weeks, Mitchell left phone messages at the office saying that he would like to put money into *Ramparts,* but Hinckle and Scheer hadn't returned his calls. "Anyone who would call up *Ramparts* and volunteer money can only be a crank," was Hinckle's comment. Mitchell was not so much a crank as a spoiled WASP who was burdened with ancestral guilts that seemed to invite the muggings Hinckle and Scheer took pleasure administering. When the two finally went to see him, they hardly got to their pitch before he offered to write them a $100,000 check, thus increasing their contempt. Shortly afterward, they brought Mitchell into the office and gave him the title "publisher." Insults behind his back alternated with weekly visits to his office to request new gifts to cover the magazine's escalating expenses. These included a move to new, sleeker offices on Fisherman's Wharf, and larger print runs—which Hinckle ordered to counter any impression that the enterprise might be failing. After $800,000 had disappeared down *Ramparts'* leaky drain, Mitchell's wife, alarmed that her children might be stripped of their inheritance, turned off the spigot.

When my paycheck bounced, the shock sent me hurrying to the office of *Ramparts'* business manager, Bob Kaldenbach, a dark man with a cynical take on life. I did not get the reassurance I was looking for, but Kaldenbach and I became friends, commuting across the

Bay Bridge to work every morning. These trips provided me with an opportunity to question him about the magazine's operations. I soon learned the players, and acquired a basic knowledge of the business—including the information that Hinckle and Scheer had gone to New York in search of a financial bailout. When their mission failed, Scheer came back, complaining that Hinckle had used the trip to raise funds for an entirely new magazine he intended to call *Barricades.* Since Hinckle was the president of the *Ramparts* corporation, this betrayal raised the possibility of a stockholders' suit if his behavior became known. Scheer wanted no part of Hinckle's new enterprise or liability, and chose instead to remain with the sinking ship. In October 1968, *Ramparts* published its last issue. A picture of Huey Newton behind bars adorned the cover.

As a kind of farewell party, Scheer invited a small group for drinks on the back porch of the Bateman Street cottage he had acquired when his marriage to Anne finally collapsed. In a nostalgic mood, he talked about the contribution that *Ramparts* had made, suggesting that in a few years we might think of starting another magazine. At this point, I interrupted. The magazine was too important to be allowed to die, I said with passion. It had captured a wide audience and secured national newsstand distribution—something that no other radical magazine had been able to achieve. Moreover, there was a way to save it.

In our conversations, Kaldenbach had described a version of bankruptcy known as "Chapter Eleven," under which a corporation could escape its obligations by offering creditors a few cents on the dollar while attempting to resume its business. Under Chapter Eleven, *Ramparts* wouldn't need to raise much money to pay its $3 million debt, but could focus on the amount required to sustain the operation, perhaps a twentieth of that sum. Scheer looked quizzically at Kaldenbach to see if there was anything to what I was saying. When Kaldenbach confirmed there was, Scheer's demeanor abruptly changed and he began to talk about reviving *Ramparts* according to my plan. Over the next few months, he raised $180,000 from Stanley Sheinbaum and two other investors. (Sheinbaum had married Betty Warner, an heir to the movie fortune.) In April we reappeared with a new issue whose cover featured a Huckleberry Finn-like six-year-old holding a Vietcong flag.

The caption said: *Alienation is when your country is at war and you want the other side to win.*

Outwardly, there was little to distinguish the new *Ramparts* from the magazine that Hinckle and Scheer had run, but in the process of bankruptcy the institution itself had undergone a sea change. The plush Fisherman's Wharf offices had given way to funky quarters in an old Victorian on Union Street; the $200,000 monthly budget had been slashed to nearly a quarter its former size; and the staff had been reduced from fifty to nineteen, leaving only six of us to put out the editorial product. As a result of the increased workload, the staff's tolerance for the old managerial style had disappeared. But Scheer was now enjoying exclusive command of the magazine for the first time, and was not ready to relinquish the privileges that Hinckle had previously established. While he was able to do without the large expense accounts that would advertise his power, he was unwilling to surrender the editorial prerogatives that expressed it. He reserved, for example, the ability to change the contents of the magazine after its deadlines had passed.

The first stirring of revolt came from our assistant managing editor, Jan Austin, a "Goldwater girl" from Iowa who had graduated to the New Left and Tom Hayden's Liberation School. Jan did our copyediting, and was variously responsible for articles at every stage of their development. When Scheer ignored editorial deadlines and changed the mix after the book was set, it was she who bore the brunt of his excess. As the deadlines fell due, Jan would proof the copy and hand-deliver it to the typesetter across the Bay, picking up galleys for additional edits. The trips were often taken in the middle of the night, following a full day on the job. Scheer's changes after deadlines meant she had to do this work all over again. When we were putting out the third issue of the new magazine, Jan came to me and said she wanted to quit.

I temporarily succeeded in dissuading her by promising to see that the situation would change—and soon discovered that she was not alone in her plight. David Kolodney, our managing editor, was a gaunt former philosophy student who fidgeted with his beard when he was entertaining a thought. Since he worked closely with Jan at every stage of the process, he felt the burden almost as much. Another victim of the spreading malaise was Peter Collier, the literary member of our small editorial group, who had begun to have what he called "a *fin de siècle* feeling," and was considering returning to the graduate studies he had left.

The collective dissatisfaction came to a head over an article by Susan Sontag in the July issue. It had been solicited personally by Scheer and was titled "On the Right Way to Love the Cuban Revolution"—which in her view was to adopt a double standard toward the suppression of human rights in Third World countries, like Cuba, that America "oppressed." Our problem was not with Sontag's sophistry, but with the way Scheer had conducted business with her. He had failed to hold her to the deadline, or perhaps hadn't even told her there was one. We couldn't be sure, because he insisted on being her only line of communication to the magazine. When the piece arrived a week late, it was 18,000 words, more than three times the longest article anyone could remember. We had not reserved enough space, and would have to drop several other articles that had already been edited, proofed, and set. The final straw was the discovery that Scheer had promised Sontag a $1,500 fee, which amounted to our entire editorial budget. In the past such extravagance was readily overlooked, but now circumstances were so tight that we were fearful of not being able to pay our own modest wages.

A crisis meeting was called, where we announced these grievances. Scheer appeared adamant in his own defense, even outraged. Through gritted teeth, he accused us of mounting a vendetta to destroy him. "This is a personal attack on me," he snarled as he began his bill of particulars. We were out to damage his relationship with Sontag, destroy his credibility, and challenge his authority over the magazine. When Scheer finished, Kolodney was shaking. His eyes were dark and his face reddened as he itemized Scheer's editorial sins, his contempt for our efforts, the personal hardship he had inflicted on Jan, and his arrogance in denying it all now. "You disgust me," Kolodney ended, and then left. The room sank into an awkward silence, and shortly afterward the meeting adjourned. When Collier and I were alone, he said: "Well, I guess it's over." The finality distressed me. I believed in *Ramparts'* mission and wanted the magazine to survive. In my mind, its demise would represent a political defeat. But I didn't know what to do.

The conflict with Scheer came to a head during the preparation of the next issue, which was devoted to the battle over what was referred to as People's Park. Owned by the university, this was an empty lot on Telegraph Avenue that activists had grassed over and were attempting to "expropriate." Local authorities had called in police forces from neighboring cities to contain the protesters, and Governor Reagan had sent the National Guard. Our cover story was a comprehensive account of the events. The byline was given to Scheer, but (like so much else that went out under his name) the article was written by staffers—mainly Collier and Kolodney. In keeping with the outlook of the Left, the account constructed parallels between the Park and Vietnam. It called the intramural playing field that the university was planning to create in the disputed area "a 'strategic hamlet' of clean-cut soccer players—a positive deterrent to subversion—in the very heart of the enemy camp."

When the crews arrived to fence off the park from its would-be liberators, Scheer and I found ourselves standing side-by-side on Telegraph Avenue, watching the events. Feelings of communal solidarity were in the air, and the moment struck me as an opportunity to try to dissuade him from further confrontation. I told him that the conflict at the magazine was not good for anyone, and reminded him that we had all come to *Ramparts* because of him—Peter, David, and Jan from his congressional campaign, and I from our old *Root and Branch* group. None of us had any ambitions to challenge his leadership, but he had to help us if we were going to be able to continue to serve him. I reiterated the way the circumstances had changed, now that the staff was small, and pleaded with him to try to understand our position. Kolodney had been his right hand since joining his campaign for Congress. Now Kolodney could not stand to be in the same room with him because of the tensions that had developed. I urged Scheer to reconsider his refusal to accommodate our needs, and pointed out how we were helping him to write the feature about People's Park that would appear under his name. When I finished, Scheer looked me in the eye and said, "*You* can't write."

This little bullet fixed my resolve. I outlined a plan to Collier and Kolodney under which we would devise a set of rules to help make our work lives bearable, and present them to Scheer as a set of nonnegotiable demands. Under the new order, Scheer would no longer be able to ignore deadlines, or speak for the magazine in public without consulting us, or force us to implement his agendas without our approval. I knew that Scheer would never agree to this plan, that his refusal would provoke a confrontation which could only be resolved by a vote of the board, and that if we lost, we would be fired. However, because of some earlier maneuvering, the odds for victory were not impossible.

While Scheer had been paying his usual inattention to the business side of the magazine, Kaldenbach and I had secured positions on the board for ourselves and Collier. We had persuaded Scheer that these seats were needed to counterbalance the votes of outside directors, six of whom resided on the east coast. The meeting would be held in San Francisco. If enough didn't show, we could win.

My plan proved a surprisingly hard sell to Collier, who had decided to leave without a fight. I urged him to stay, stressing the political importance of the magazine, and our responsibility to save it from the certain destruction toward which Scheer's leadership was heading. Collier looked at me oddly. It didn't matter, he said, whether *Ramparts* survived or not. It had had its moment, and that was over. I had no idea what he meant. But I persisted, and to my great relief was able to persuade him. Much later, he explained to me how: "I wasn't optimistic, because I never thought we could raise the money to finance the magazine the way Scheer and Hinckle had done, and I didn't have your urgency. You were a kind of Martian Marxist. Your reality was alien and impenetrable. But the political *zeitgeist* had shifted so dramatically toward the Marxist myth that it made us think you had a kind of insight that was important." At the time what he said to me was: "All right, I'm with you. But it doesn't really matter what happens to *Ramparts*. I'm only staying for the fight with Scheer, to punish him and see some justice done. Then I'm out of here."

Scheer rejected our set of rules, dismissing them as an attempt to destroy him. Then he began a lobbying campaign, telling the staff that I was conspiring with the board to turn *Ramparts* into a Zionist tract, while, alternately, he told board members I would transform the magazine into a "Trotskyite rag." He used his personal woes to advantage as well, confiding in one staffer that the breakup of his marriage and the crisis at the magazine had caused him to think of suicide. I didn't know whether to feel sorry for Scheer, or to fear him. "Nobody ever hated me like this before," I complained to Kaldenbach. "That's because you never did anything before," he said.

The staff voted for our proposal 17-2, with only the art director and Scheer opposed. That set the stage for a vote of the board, which met in September in the Union Street offices. Five of the eastern directors failed to attend. During the proceedings, Scheer was in a dyspeptic mood. At one point he was provoked by Collier, who was distractedly snapping bubbles from a wad of gum. "If you don't stop that," Scheer growled, "this meeting is over." When the showdown came, we won by a single vote.

But after the vote Scheer refused to quit. For weeks he had maintained that he couldn't work under the proposed rules which were designed to destroy him. Now he blithely announced he was now ready to live with them. We knew all this added up to a ticking bomb, and resolved to defuse it as quickly as possible. Officially, Kaldenbach was president of the *Ramparts* corporation. He had been elevated to the position for legal reasons so that he could testify at the magazine's bankruptcy proceedings. When Scheer gave an unauthorized interview to an underground paper, thus violating our rules, I told Kaldenbach to fire him. Scheer was incredulous. "You can't fire me," he said. "Oh, yes, I can," Kaldenbach replied.

Months later, a note from Ralph Schoenman arrived in the office, addressed to Scheer. It said: "I, too, know what it is to have energized an institution and then have others do what anthropologists tell us they will do." The meaning was clear: *Kill the father.* It annoyed me that Schoenman, who had exacted so much guilt from me because I had allowed Scheer to interview Russell, would now suck up to him so shamelessly. But I had the satisfaction of having stood up to the two of them and beat them both.

After the victory, we set out to institute the revolution we had promised. There would be no single editor to replace Scheer. Instead, a board of equals would rule collectively. Whereas Scheer's salary had been $25,000 a year under the old regime, and the black receptionist had received only $4,000, we announced that everybody's salary would be equal at $500 a month. We had instituted socialism in one magazine. We hoped, in part, that this would lift the taint from *Ramparts* in the Left and establish our revolutionary credentials. At the same time, we were mindful of the flaws in the equality we had created. Most of those who received the $500 wage had no family, while others—Collier and myself in particular—had several children. We told ourselves that eventually we would make an allowance for "need," but we were never able to figure a way to do it. Meanwhile, Collier and I took pride in bearing our special burden, failing to acknowledge to ourselves that this was an important inequality, too.

Why were we ready to carry an extra weight, unless we felt there was something superior in our position? And there was. It was Collier and I who effectively made the decisions that were crucial to the magazine's operations. The seed of the new inequality had been sown in the revolution itself. Collier and I had engineered the change of power, and carried it through. Neither Jan nor Kolodney nor anyone else would have confronted Scheer or contested his authority; they would just have quit. Everybody recognized this fact, and acted out of that recognition—just as everyone recognized that *Ramparts'* success or failure depended on its editorial product, and that its editors had to be the governing body of the magazine, which *ipso facto* made them a part more equal than the rest.

And within the editorial board we were more equal than the others. This was because Collier and I were the only editors besides Kolodney who could write the articles and generate the story ideas that made the magazine work. But Kolodney did not have the stomach for making decisions, or for the personal conflicts that were inevitable to running an enterprise. As a result, he also deferred to us. The net effect of the formal equality we created, therefore, was not to share the power but to increase the workload on the two of us, and—when challenged—to force us to expose the underlying reality that established our position. You could not dictate the policies of the magazine unless you were prepared to run it. That was the inescapable fact that underpinned our rule.

Of course, without a formal hierarchy, every issue that came up had to be debated. The need to justify decisions was not only time-consuming for us, but at times cruel to others. This was impressed on me when we attempted to reduce the mailroom budget and were confronted by a political revolt. The mailroom was staffed by members of Newsreel, a radical collective that had made promotional films for the Black Panthers and the Vietcong. They had no respect for our political *bona fides,* which they still regarded as suspect. The revolution's pecking order had again shifted to the left (as it was always bound to), and we remained unable to overcome the view that *Ramparts* was part of the power structure that needed to be overthrown.

Originally, we had hired just one Newsreeler to do the mailroom work, but he had taken on more and more part-time help, featherbedding for his revolutionary comrades. When a point was reached where the mailroom budget exceeded that of the editorial department, we decided that things had gone far enough and that we had to cut their hours. But no appeals from us to the common good made any impression. They saw *Ramparts* as their gravy train rather than their cause, and refused any cuts at all. To them, we were the ruling class and they our rebellious peons.

Because every decision had to be justified collectively, we assembled the entire staff, and in an all-day session hammered at the recalcitrants' deficiencies and derelictions, summoning other staff members to testify against them. The session went on for eight hours, escalating as the embattled mailroom crew resisted. Because of their obstinacy, it became necessary to expand the charges and sharpen their personal edge. What had begun as a move to institute economies that would save all our jobs turned into a prosecution. Accusations of laziness, dishonesty, and exploitation of fellow workers were hurled at the hapless defendants. In the end, they were made to feel so bad about what they had done that firing them was almost a mercy. It was a collectively supported, brutal exercise, necessary for us to prevail. Privately, this experience made me recognize the utility and compassion inherent in the principle of hierarchy we had overthrown.

Being a manager provided me with other lessons about human nature. Collier had little interest in the business side of the magazine, whose oversight fell mainly to me. I quickly learned how soft a science magazine economics was. Because of the complexities of accrual accounting, it proved difficult to get reliable forecasts. At one point, I received flatly opposing projections as to whether we were going to have a cash surplus or go belly up in three months. In despair, I asked for a weekly report that would tell me how much cash was available for the next issue. It seemed like a simple question, but no answer was forthcoming. Every Monday, a young man named Carl came faithfully to the staff meeting with a report that didn't give me the information I wanted, and every week I grew more frustrated with his inability to satisfy my requests. I understood that the numbers would be problematic, but I could not understand his failure to grasp what I needed, and to make some accommodation to satisfy me. He was inarticulate in his own behalf and it was painful to watch him sweat under the pressure. But I couldn't let go. Week after week he nervously came back for further punishment and futile instructions, until finally Collier took me aside and said, "David, it's his *protoplasm.*"

Collier's intuition that we would not be able to raise the money to finance the operation proved correct. We were too homebound to travel out of town in search of investors, and had an aversion to the high profile that Hinckle and Scheer had cultivated. In keeping with the New Left's anti-elitism, we had even arranged the masthead in alphabetical order, instead of featuring ourselves at the top. People didn't really know who we were, and consequently had no reason to want to back us. We also lacked the talent for hyperbole that seemed to be another crucial element in raising funds. Hinckle had thought nothing of holding expensive parties at the Algonquin when the magazine was verging on bankruptcy, in order to bolster its self-important image. He understood that no matter how radical their self-understanding, potential funders still wanted to be associated with glamour and success. To differentiate ourselves from the tainted past, Peter and I even attempted to sell our product by emphasizing our virtues. Under our leadership, we made it known, *Ramparts* was both fiscally responsible and politically serious, and its staff was making personal sacrifices to keep it going. But this was not the kind of message that got anyone excited.

Unable to raise new funds, we began to develop scams that were borderline criminal, but which the reigning rhetoric of the Left encouraged us to think of as a kind of civil disobedience. Abbie Hoffman, the Movement's resident anarchist, had written a tract called *Steal This Book*, which promoted this "political" strategy. We had printed an excerpt in the magazine under the title "America On Zero Dollars A Day." In it, Abbie advanced the idea that "ripping off the system" was a revolutionary act, advising readers on various ways to get something for nothing. It was a prefiguring of the communist future in which everything would be free. Abbie's idea was that people should take according to their needs. Like most radicals, and indeed Marx himself, he gave no thought as to how things would be provided. Our contribution to this "propaganda of the deed" was to put half the *Ramparts* staff on unemployment, so that they could collect their "paychecks" from the government. When the government allowance expired, we would put them back on the payroll and lay off the rest. But even this subsidy proved insufficient to sustain our operations, and we soon found ourselves again hundreds of thousands of dollars in debt with no foreseeable means of payment.

At this precarious point, Kaldenbach came up with an ingenious solution. We would abandon the corporate shell and sell the name *Ramparts* to a new entity. That corporation could publish the magazine and be freed of its debts. We called the new corporation Noah's Ark. The principal stockholders of the old corporation voted for the plan because they knew they were never going to recoup their investments, and wanted the magazine to survive. The scheme seemed foolproof—and we almost got away with it. One day, however, I answered a knock at my door, and there was a process-server with court papers announcing that Collier, Kaldenbach, and I were being personally sued for $400,000. The suit had been filed by the one investor we had recruited on our own, a Silicon Valley entrepreneur named Larry Moore. Fortunately, we had secured Moore's original investment by allowing him to use the *Ramparts* name for a book-publishing operation, so that he, too, would have a stake in its survival. Moreover, we were so lacking in assets ourselves that he couldn't hope to gain satisfaction through his suit. After a negotiation, he agreed to settle with us in exchange for a dozen free ad pages for Ramparts Books, and a contract with me to publish my collected essays under the title *The Fate of Midas*.

If financing the new *Ramparts* confronted us with unexpected challenges, shaping its contents provided rewarding compensation for our efforts. We stayed abreast of the Movement and its progress, carrying features that ranged from a report on the Panther trial in New Haven (the cover of the magazine pictured an electric chair and the caption "They Are Planning to Kill Bobby Seale") to the Indian occupation of Alcatraz (here we featured an Indian woman who had just graffitied a wall with the slogan "Better Red Than Dead"). Our most famous cover showed a color photograph of corpses at My Lai, in the middle of which a sign had been planted that read "Re-Elect the President." To cancel out Scheer and Hinckle's gaffe of the "Woman Power" issue, we ran a cover feature on "The Politics of Rape" by the feminist writer (and former member of the *Root and Branch* collective) Susan Griffin. We presented another, on the new ecological movement, with a photograph of a Bank of America in flames, emphasizing in our cover line that the profit motive was the enemy of the environment: "The students who burned the Bank of America in Santa Barbara may have done more towards saving the environment than all the Teach-ins put together."

We published an excerpt from Jerry Rubin's book *Do It,* and one from Kurt Vonnegut's *Breakfast of Champions,* and Herbert Marcuse's *Essay on Liberation* (our cover headline proclaimed: "Utopia Now!"). We ran a celebrated account of the Rolling Stones' American tour by rock journalist Michael Lydon, and interviews with Huey Newton (by Angela Davis), John Lennon (by two editors of *New Left Review*), Clifford Irving (by Abbie Hoffman), and Jean-Paul Sartre. We also interviewed Abbie after he went underground following his drug bust. Michael Lerner badgered us into allowing him to write up the May Day demonstration in Washington (the last of the Vietnam War), although we did so with a bad conscience because he was the organizer of the protest, and his account was so obviously self-serving. We published articles by a blue-ribbon roster of the Left—Noam Chomsky, Alex Cockburn, Andrew Kopkind, Allen Ginsberg, Harry Edwards, Marlene Dixon, Seymour Hersh, Peter Dale Scott, Todd Gitlin, Ellen Willis, Francine du Plessix Gray, Edward Sorel, Cora Weiss, Jonathan Kozol, Staughton Lynd, Carl Oglesby, and Tom Hayden (among others), and hired James Ridgeway and Brit Hume to write for us from Washington.

Our most dramatic bid to establish Movement credentials once and for all was to publish the entire text of Tom Hayden's *The Trial,* his account of the Chicago conspiracy case and his prescription for the coming revolution. Hayden demanded—and got—our entire $1,500 editorial budget as payment, saying he needed it to buy gas masks for the Panthers. Our decision to run the excerpt was made in June 1970, just after Nixon ordered American forces into Cambodia to cut off the sanctuaries the North Vietnamese were using to infiltrate and invade South Vietnam. The national response to this was unexpectedly dramatic: An estimated 80 percent of America's universities were shut down on the day of protest called over the incursion. More than a million people participated. It created a sense of new and radical possibilities. It also created the climate in which Collier and I succumbed to the Vietnam metaphor.

The last chapter of Hayden's book called for the establishment of "free territories" in America whose purpose, in a famous SDS slogan, was to "Bring The War Home." Inside these free territories, radicals would consider themselves "citizens of an international community" of revolutionaries. They would harbor political fugitives, train activists in weapons and "self-defense," oppose "occupying police," and put "all imperialist institutions (universities, draft boards, corporations) in or near the Territory ... under constant siege." Collier had written an editorial statement introducing the issue, which called Hayden's book "A Tract For Our Time." It said:

> We are now facing a whole range of crises, any one of which could permanently and profoundly alter the course of American history and threaten our individual lives and liberties. Together they constitute a social crisis so pervasive and profound as to lift the prospect of revolution from the realm of utopian speculation and raise it as a real political alternative. We believe such a revolution to be necessary. For this reason we have opened the pages of the magazine to the thoughts of one of the country's most serious revolutionaries and to a book which we feel is one of the most important literary and political events of our time.

The editorial concluded with this flourish: "The system cannot be revitalized; it must be overthrown. As humanely as possible, but by any means necessary." I had inserted the phrase "as humanely as possible" after Collier drafted the original. The whole sentiment seemed over the top, but I endorsed it anyway because I was swept along by the euphoria of the political moment, and also by the power of the relationship I had begun to have with my new partner.

Peter Collier did not, like me, come from the Marxist ghetto. He had that dough-faced Christian look of the 44th Street Cardinals who had tormented me as a youth. Perhaps I was even drawn to him because of this. His parents had been New Dealers and then Goldwater Republicans, whose family had migrated from Alabama to southern California. He had become radicalized in the civil-rights movement of the early Sixties, but, unlike Jan Austin, had not become a political ideologue in the process. The intellectual tropisms that distinguished "socially conscious" people from everyone else were absent in him. He had a curiosity about normal life that allowed him to tap the *Zeitgeist* at will, a talent that made him our editorial compass and our authority on the choice of features that would fuel our newsstand sales.

Collier seemed to have entirely different sensory organs than mine, hearing voices that I was unable to hear and seeing things that were obscure or opaque to me. When I reflected on the popular mind, I saw only "false consciousness" at work. To me, the enthusiasms of others were only distractions from the "real" agenda. I had no interest in what attracted the public, because I saw its interests principally as obstacles to understanding. I was waiting for its consciousness to connect with mine in the moment of revolutionary truth.

In the beginning of our editorial partnership, I challenged Peter on his judgments, proposing cover stories shaped to political purposes without reference to any other reality. In countering my suggestions, he often attacked me with such verbal savagery— implying that I was an imbecile, or worse—that I was wounded to the point where I was unable to answer. On one occasion I walked out of an editorial meeting, wondering if I was going to come back. People began to question whether we could maintain a partnership at this level of conflict, and waited for the final falling-out. But it never came. We were bound by some invisible cord that neither of us wanted to untie. Years later, when I asked him about these attacks, he said: "There was a disparity between your psychological getup and your mental powers that made you almost nerd-like. You didn't look people in the eye when you were talking to them. It was as though you had a kind of autism. I was attempting verbally what therapists do when they grab the arms of one of those autistic children to force it into the real world."

In connecting with the "real world," I soon became accustomed to following Peter's lead. When he committed himself to the idea that the revolution had arrived, I surrendered my better judgment and went along. I was so pleased that he had come into *my* (political) reality that I didn't want to spoil it by challenging his assumptions, even in an area I knew better. Two members of the *Ramparts* board were not so pliant, however, and resigned in protest.

Despite the excesses of Hayden's tract, printing it did not mean that we had given up the task we had set ourselves, of holding the Movement to higher standards. We still prided ourselves in opposing the tendencies to nihilistic violence and totalitarian politics that were becoming more and more dominant in the radical ranks. In March 1970, an explosion occurred in a New York townhouse, killing three members of the Weather Underground. It turned out that the explosion had been caused by a bomb the Weathermen were making in the building's basement. The tragedy inspired a self-critical "communique" by the Weather leaders about their "military error" in emphasizing violence to the exclusion of ordinary caution, if not common sense. I responded with an article called "Revolutionary Karma vs. Revolutionary Politics."

One of the victims of the explosion, Ted Gold, had previously come to Berkeley to recruit soldiers for the war against "Amerika." If Vietnamese were dying in their homes, Americans should not expect to have a sanctuary in theirs, Gold argued. It was time to bring the war home. Anyone who resisted this logic was a racist, hiding behind "white skin privilege." I listened to Gold's manic appeal from the audience, alongside Todd Gitlin (a former president of SDS), who understood the dangerous lunacy that had been released into the political air. I appealed to Todd, as someone with activist credentials, to challenge Gold and interject some reason into the moment. My lack of the same credentials, and my connection to *Ramparts*, denied me the credibility to do it myself. But Gitlin had no stomach for challenging his peers. Like others, he had long been intimidated into a state of silence by the rhetorical overkill of our political comrades, and the Weather faction in particular. If he spoke up now, he would be accused of moral cowardice, of "hiding behind white skin privilege," of selling out. Gitlin merely shrugged and said nothing.

Later, I reflected on the fact that Gold's fate was not unconnected to the rant he had delivered that evening. According to Weatherman's own postmortem: "At the end, [the townhouse victims] believed and acted as if only those who die are proven revolutionaries. Many people had been argued into doing something they did not believe in, many had not slept for days." In my article I pointed out that in their quest for authenticity, the Weathermen had lost all sight of the practical consequences of their actions. What was important to them was the will to be revolutionary, and therefore better than everyone else: "Revolution here has almost ceased to be a strategy for social change and has become instead a yoga of perfection." This attitude, I warned, would always lead to a perversion of values. "For the revolutionarily virtuous naturally assume the mantle of a priesthood, and the priesthood soon flaunts the old vices: self-righteousness, arrogance and privilege."

Weatherman's uncritical admiration for the Vietnamese Communists and other Third World radicals was widespread in the Movement, and increasingly alarming to me. In a series of articles on the purges that had begun in Communist China, I tried to restore some sense of the dangers of Leninist politics, and to revive the tragic memories of the revolutionary past. I commissioned Deutscher's widow, Tamara, to review Solzhenitsyn's just-published *Gulag Archipelago*, which had removed the veil from the Soviet nightmare once and for all. I had grown up in an environment where the Soviet Union was the focus of all progressive hopes and political efforts. My acute sense of our complicity in these crimes made it difficult for me to read more than a few pages of Solzhenitsyn's text at a single sitting. When the review appeared, we received a letter from Saul Landau, who had helped me to get my first book published and had recently made a pro-Castro propaganda film, *Fidel*. Landau was incensed that we had even given space to Solzhenitsyn. In the course of his denunciation, Landau said that the gulag survivor's "sensational" claims distracted attention from America's atrocities in the Third World.

It was a standard radical response. I answered with an article titled "Solzhenitsyn and the Radical Cause," which we published along with a second review of the book itself. I also wrote an editorial preface to the feature:

> We are devoting a significant portion of this issue of Ramparts to a discussion of the exiled Soviet writer Alexander Solzhenitsyn, and to a review of Solzhenitsyn's book The Gulag Archipelago by the Soviet Marxist and historian Roy Medvedev. We are doing so because we believe that the efforts of Solzhenitsyn, Medvedev and other Soviet "dissidents" to reveal and document the truth about the Stalin terror, and to challenge the system of political imprisonment and repression that remains as its legacy, is not a secondary issue, peripheral to the Left, as has often been suggested or assumed. Rather, this article makes the case that it is one of the most important struggles in the world today, and that supporting this struggle is one of the first and most pressing responsibilities of radicals and revolutionaries everywhere.

I was glad for the opportunity that *Ramparts* provided to make this kind of intervention, but I was less sanguine about its possible impact. Several memorable confrontations with Movement activists inspired my caution. On one occasion, I had written an article on the armed conflict between the Chinese and Russians over an island in the Ussuri River. The island had both Russian and Chinese names, reflecting the rival claims. One day the *Black Panther* paper arrived at *Ramparts'* offices with the headline: "We will never allow Soviet Revisionists to invade and occupy China's sacred territory—Chenpao Island." Because of my aversion to the Panthers' violent dogmatism, I had never set foot in any of their facilities. But now I hurried over to Panther headquarters on Shattuck Avenue, to confront the author. This turned out to be no Panther at all, but Bob Avakian, the prodigal son of a Berkeley judge, whose previous claim to notoriety was scaling a flagpole at an antiwar protest in order to tear down the Stars and Stripes. Avakian stared blankly at me while I rehearsed the long and tortured history of the conflict about which he had written, going back to the 1930s with Stalin's intervention in the Chinese revolution. I stressed the totalitarian character of both parties, and the danger to the American left of unthinkingly supporting either's claims. Avakian was unimpressed. It turned out he had copied his article, almost word for word, out of *Peking Review*, which provided all the information he cared to know. Later, he went on to found the Revolutionary Communist Party, and to become its chairman for life, meticulously reproducing the political style of his Maoist icons.

On another occasion, Scheer's ex-wife, Anne Weills, submitted a feminist review she had written of Visconti's film *The Damned.* Its images of the Holocaust, she wrote, had inspired her to reflect on the oppression of women. When I rejected the article, she came angrily into the office to protest. Explaining my decision, I suggested—as gently as the circumstance permitted—that her analogy between Hitler's final solution and men's attitudes toward women might be overdrawn. Instead of responding to the point, she defended her text on the grounds that "Women don't think in a linear way." "Susan Sontag," I replied, "seems to manage it quite well." This ended the discussion.

Incidents like this were beginning to give *Ramparts* a bad name again in the Left, particularly among those Peter dubbed its "myrmidons" (after Achilles' sycophantic followers in *Troilus and Cressida*). After rejecting another article, we were visited by a delegation of myrmidons from the North American Congress on Latin America, led by a sometime *Ramparts* researcher named Jon Frappier. NACLA was a research group supported by the National Council of Churches, with headquarters in Riverside Church in New York, and its "theology" was of the "liberation" school. The organization proudly described itself as an intelligence operation for revolutionary movements in Latin America.

We had given press credentials to NACLA regular Julie Niccamen, so that she could visit Cuba. We did it as a general service to the Left, but she took the assignment literally and returned with an article celebrating the virtues of the Castro regime. One of the episodes in her story was an account of how a "law against laziness" had been passed, with 3.5 million Cubans—half the population—participating in its drafting. We pointed out that if this were true and so many people were civically involved, the Cubans hardly needed such a law. To add salt to the argument, we recalled that "laziness" had been a form of rebellion among black slaves. Frappier and his NACLA delegation stared irritably at us as we presented this argument. Then, with all the solemnity of a tribunal, they stood up, while Frappier informed us that as "First World beneficiaries of imperialism and white skin privilege" we had no right to judge Third World revolutionaries. When he was finished, the group marched *en masse* out of the *Ramparts* office.

In the interval between the Cambodian moratorium of June 1970 and the May Day demonstration in Washington the following year, the political air went out of the Movement balloon. The 30,000 May Day demonstrators provided a pathetic contrast to the million who had protested the year before, and afterwards there were no more large demonstrations for the duration of the war. The reason was evident: Once the Nixon Administration made clear that it was going to "Vietnamize" the conflict and end the draft, it had removed the rationale for most people to protest.

When this fact registered on me, its effect was devastating. The driving force behind the massive anti-war movement on America's campuses had been the desire to avoid military service. Because of my early fatherhood, I had never been draft eligible, so had failed to realize how paramount a factor this prospect had been in motivating college students against the war. Other considerations may have swayed their opinions, but only this seemed to have prompted their actions. Now, only the most hard-core of political believers remained to protest. And they had changed, too. The revolutionary fantasy had finally eclipsed the earlier free spirits of the Movement. Now there were only Castro wannabes like the NACLA group, and others who had fallen prey to the totalitarian temptation, aspiring to become a domestic Vietcong. It was reminiscent of the condition my father had written about on his trip west in the Thirties: *I've had a feeling, riding on the buses, that I'm in a foreign land ...I'm afraid that most of us aren't really "patriotic," I mean at bottom deeply fond of the country and the people.* The wheel had come full circle.

One day a carton of books addressed to Scheer arrived at *Ramparts*. Inside were the collected works of North Korea's dictator, Kim Il Sung. We learned from Jan, who was a member of Scheer's new political "affinity group," that he intended to write an introduction for an American edition of Kim Il Sung's thought. Like other die-hards, Scheer had formed an urban guerrilla commune with Hayden and his ex-wife, Anne, which they called the Red Family. It was run on Maoist principles, and the walls of their headquarters on Bateman Street were draped with large portraits of the North Korean dictator and Ho Chi Minh, alongside Huey Newton and the Apache Geronimo. Shotguns were propped in the corners of the rooms. Political education for the communards consisted of readings from *The Black Panther* and Lin Piao's *On Peoples War*. Commune discussions focused on such questions as whether underwear should be shared, and if it was a bourgeois hang-up to close the bathroom door when using the toilet.

Scheer took advantage of the "criticism self-criticism" sessions to drive a wedge between his ex-wife and his rival. One weekend, Hayden returned from a court hearing in his Chicago conspiracy case to discover he had been charged with "bourgeois privatism" in his relationship with Anne. After a kangaroo court orchestrated by Scheer convicted him, Hayden was expelled. Fleeing Berkeley, he went to Los Angeles, where he met and married the actress Jane Fonda. Michael Lerner produced the only *bon mot* of his career to describe these revolutionary maneuvers, which he called "armed snuggle."

Six months earlier, Hayden had provided me with a summary moment of what I now recognized to be the end of the New Left. He appeared in my backyard with Scheer's three-year-old son, Christopher, on his shoulders, and bearing a beaten look of indeterminate origin. I was honored by the visit, which was rare—usually one had to go to Hayden for an audience. I still regarded him as the only New Left leader of any intellectual substance, and was curious to hear what he had come to say, now that the popular energies that had driven our struggle were gone. For a while we chatted reflectively about the bewildering decline of the Movement. He wanted to know what I thought could be done. I didn't see that much could. The Movement had self-destructed, and it would take a generation to put anything new together. In any case, I was not the activist-leader; it was more appropriate that he should tell me. He then revealed his plan. "I'm forming a new Communist Party," he said.

Hayden's expulsion from the Red Family distracted him from forming the new party, but in his exile in Los Angeles he soon resumed his political wars. In the summer of 1972, he paid a visit to the *Ramparts* offices, which we had moved to Berkeley. He told us he had been to Paris to meet with the National Liberation Front and representatives from Hanoi, and he wanted us to publish an article he intended to write on the military situation. It was called "The Prospects of the Vietnamese Offensive" and was a detailed account of the battlefront in Vietnam and the political situation in America. He dictated all 13,000 words of the article into a tape recorder in one sitting in the office, referring only to some notes he had brought with him. It was an impressive demonstration of his intellectual powers. The article concluded: "Vietnam, country of countless My Lais, will be liberated. May we speed the time."

I knew that Hayden's article was Communist war propaganda. Peace negotiations had begun in Paris, and the terms of any treaty would be critical to the war aims of both combatants. If the situation could be stabilized to preserve the regime in the South, the United States would have prevailed in the conflict. If the conditions facilitated a Communist "liberation," the other side would have won.

The Nixon Administration wanted a truce signed before the November election. It had launched a dramatic gambit to pressure the Communists into a stabilizing peace. After more than two decades of U.S. quarantine, Nixon recognized the Communist regime in China and made visits, accompanied by Secretary of State Henry Kissinger, to Moscow and Peking. They hoped to persuade the Communist rulers to pressure Hanoi into a settlement on unfavorable terms. Hanoi responded with its own strategy, which was to launch an offensive in South Vietnam to alter the facts on the ground. The task reserved for Hayden and other New Left radicals was to intensify the divisions in America, behind enemy lines.

I listened to Hayden's request with an anxious feeling, because there was a "gut check" in order whenever he asked for a political favor. Once he had summoned me to the Bateman Street house that he and Anne occupied across from Scheer. When I got there, he asked me if I would hide a Black Panther in the shack behind my house. It occurred to me that the Panther might be wanted for an actual crime.

But I ignored the thought for the same reason that everyone did: The Panthers were a vanguard under attack. Even more important was my desire to impress Hayden with the fact that I was not just an intellectual strategist, but also ready to put myself on the line.

The same consideration underlay my readiness to serve Hayden's purposes now. Because I had acquired a reputation for being critical of the Communists, I even emphasized the point. I told him that I admired the way he was willing to offer his pen in their service, because it would also serve the Vietnamese people. At the same time, I stressed my own task as one of remaining independent of *any* party line. Hayden eyed me with a cynical squint. I felt I had to warn him— since he was working directly with the Communists—that I was going to write an article in the same issue that would be critical of Hanoi's Communist allies in Moscow and Peking. By welcoming Nixon to their capitals, the Russians and Chinese were playing into his hands. Hayden refused to admit that there might be any conflict of interest between the Communist forces. Whether he actually believed this or was just playing the political role he had assigned himself as a spokesman for Hanoi, I didn't know and never found out.

My piece, much shorter than Hayden's, was titled "Nixon's Vietnam Strategy: How It Was Launched With the Aid of Brezhnev and Mao and How the Vietnamese Intend to Defeat It." The *Los Angeles Times* ran a long article on its editorial page attacking what I wrote, under the heading "Bloodthirsty New Left Wants the War to Continue." One *Times* reader wrote a letter to the editor, saying that the NBC reporter named David Horowitz should be fired for expressing such views.

Neither my piece nor Hayden's was the most explosive feature of the August 1972 issue *of Ramparts*, however. This honor belonged to an unsigned article by a man who called himself Winslow Peck. It was titled "U.S. Electronic Espionage: A Memoir" and, as we soon discovered, publishing it would violate a section of the Espionage Act of 1918.

The article had literally come over the transom of our Berkeley office. It was passed on to me as *Ramparts'* resident expert on national-security subjects. At first, I dismissed it as the work of a crank. The author claimed to know about top-secret military intelligence matters, and included capitalized words like COMINT, ELINT, RADINT, and SWAMP. I had no way of assessing these claims, and was inclined to discard the manuscript without further thought. But I gave it to Bob Fitch, who had once told me the Panthers were going to burn my house down, and who had replaced Jan Austin on our staff when she left to become a full-time member of the Red Family.

After reading the article, Fitch came back looking pale and frightened. It turned out that he was an ex-military man and had served as an intelligence operative in the 82nd Airborne Division during the Cuban Missile Crisis. As a result of his training, he recognized secret military codes in the text of the article—codes that he was under oath never to repeat. If we printed them, he said, we would all go to jail. Fitch had authenticated the document. Peter and I arranged a meeting with Peck at a local Berkeley cafe. We learned that he had been employed by a top-secret branch of intelligence called the National Security Agency, which encompassed 80 percent of U.S. intelligence but was unknown to the public at the time. Precisely how unknown was indicated by an anecdote Peck told us: He was present at a briefing session with Vice President Hubert Humphrey in 1967 when Humphrey "asked a couple of pretty dumb questions that showed he didn't have the foggiest notion of what NSA was and what it did."

Peck's most sensational claim was that the NSA had cracked the Soviet intelligence code. This meant that U.S. intelligence could read Soviet electronic communications at will:

> As far as the Soviet Union is concerned, we know the whereabouts at any given time of all its aircraft, exclusive of small private planes, and its naval forces, including its missile-firing submarines. We know where their submarines are, what every one of their VIPs is doing, and generally their capabilities and the disposition of all their forces.

Peck himself was stationed at a base in Turkey and had listened in on the last conversation between Soviet Premier Kosygin and a Soviet cosmonaut just before he burned up in space. Peck also claimed to have intercepted and read the message to the front, from Israeli headquarters in Tel Aviv, recalling General Moshe Dayan during the 1967 war.

I was struck by what I thought were the momentous ramifications of Peck's disclosures. If we knew where every Soviet missile and tank was, there could be no surprise attacks or false "missile gaps" based on erroneous estimates, such as had underwritten Kennedy's arms buildup in the Sixties. To print Peck's article would strike a blow against the war machine. It would promote peace on all sides. Or so I deluded myself in the emotion of the moment. In fact, as I realized after the deed was done and the article printed, what we had revealed was the most carefully guarded intelligence information of all: the knowledge that we had penetrated the Soviet code. Agents were killed when such secrets were at stake to prevent the other side from knowing what their own knew.

When I realized what we had done, I had second thoughts. There was no one-time breaking of a code; the other side could always respond by creating a new one. By revealing to the Soviets that their security had been breached, we had merely alerted them that they needed to repair it. Even if I had understood the real significance of publishing Peck's claims, I might have agreed to print his story, anyway. For me, the overriding justification was one that weighed heavily on all the political decisions I made: It was important that America should lose the war. I did not believe that an NLF victory would mean "rice roots" democracy, as Hayden had written, but I was convinced that America's loss would be Vietnam's gain. An American defeat would weaken oppression everywhere.

When Peter and I told Fitch that we were going to run Peck's article, he panicked. We would all be tried for treason and go to jail, or even worse, he whined. We brushed his fears aside, practically laughing in his face. Where was his revolutionary spine? Where was his commitment to the cause? When we refused to reconsider our decision, Fitch announced he was quitting the magazine. He was not about to go down in flames with us. We enjoyed seeing this rhetorical maximalist exposed as a coward, but his departure caused a lurch nonetheless. What if he was right? We were ironists enough to realize that our bravado was a way of keeping our own fears in line. Both of us had families. Were we ready to jeopardize their futures, even for a grand gesture like this? We began to sense that we might be out of our depths.

Taking a step back, we decided to defer a final decision until we could consult a lawyer. I thought of contacting the defense team for Daniel Ellsberg, the former Pentagon official who was then on trial in Los Angeles for leaking a classified report on American policy in Vietnam. We had just completed a *Ramparts* cover feature on his case. I put in a call to Los Angeles, and was soon talking to Harvard professor Charles Nesson, one of the nation's leading constitutional law experts and a member of the Ellsberg team. After I had outlined the situation, Nesson explained the law. Technically, he said, we would be violating the Espionage Act. But, he added, the act had been written in such a way that it applied to classified *papers* removed from government offices, or material *copied* from government files. The government was able to indict Ellsberg because he had reproduced actual papers. It was important for us, in insulating ourselves from possible prosecution, not to acknowledge that any papers existed. If we took his advice, Nesson suggested, we might get away with publishing the article. To make its case in a court of law, the government would have to establish that we had indeed damaged national security. To do so, it would be necessary to reveal more than the government might want the other side to know. In fact, the legal process would certainly force more information to light than the government would want *anybody* to know. On balance, there was a good chance that we would not be prosecuted. I had just been given advice by a famous constitutional law professor on how to commit treason and get away with it.

We published the article, and it became our first journalistic *coup*, receiving front-page coverage in the *New York Times*. But the *Times* story was disappointing to me because it did not even mention my notion that the NSA's technology made surprise attacks impossible. Instead, it focused on the more pertinent question of whether Peck's claim that American agents had broken the Soviet code was accurate. Experts were quoted by the *Times* to the effect that it was not. The account also revealed that the real name of the man we knew as Winslow Peck was Perry Fellwock, a fact that could only have been learned from intelligence sources. The press conference we held in the *Ramparts* offices, after the *Times* story appeared, was attended by an impressive media cohort. We decided that one particular reporter was the CIA "plant" because he kept asking us whether we had any written documents. But we held to the strategy that Nesson had devised, and said there were none. After the press conference was over, we spotted Fitch—who had been missing for weeks—having a cup of coffee with our suspect at a local cafe.

Thinking about these events, I have asked myself in retrospect whether there was any practical difference between my actions and those of radicals like Tom Hayden and Saul Landau. Landau had volunteered himself as an agent of the Castro regime, while Hayden self-consciously served the Communist rulers in Vietnam. When Hayden and Jane Fonda went to North Vietnam and urged American troops to defect, it made me as uncomfortable as had Schoenman's broadcasts over Radio Hanoi. Remembering my parents' experience, I had long before resolved that I would never commit myself to any regime or party that did not reflect my own political values. Yet war does not leave room for fine discriminations or intermediate stands. Looking back at what I actually did, my "critical independence" seems to me now a distinction without much of a practical difference. The same, moreover, can be said for all those antiwar demonstrators who might have been critical of Communism but were willing to march behind slogans that called for the withdrawal of American troops "now"—a policy that could only result in a Communist victory. They did not see Communism as a superior way of life as Hayden and Landau did. But, in regarding it as the lesser of two evils, they helped the enemy to win all the same.

A peace treaty was signed on January 27, 1973 on terms that proved favorable to a Communist victory. Nine months later, while the Communists were pressing their advantage in the South, I was invited to speak at a convocation of Robert Hutchins' Center for the Study of Democratic Institutions. Called "Pacem in Terris III," it was held in the grand ballroom of the Shoreham hotel in Washington, D.C. with a thousand people in attendance. On the program, I was sandwiched between the political scientist Ronald Steel and the Reverend Theodore Hesburgh, president of Notre Dame. Steel's presentation was an academic discourse on the changing concept of the national interest since World War II. The audience listened to his remarks politely, responding at the conclusion with equally polite applause. I stepped up to the microphone and began a peroration:

We are not yet disengaged from the most criminal war in our history,
a war against a technologically defenseless people which—let us not
mince words—ranks with the worst atrocities ever committed by one
portion of the human race against another.... One would have thought
that [this] gathering would be prepared to ask itself... whether this
[war] does not [have] its roots ... in the very character of the American
enterprise and ambition; whether Vietnam is not so much a betrayal
of the American tradition, as its fulfillment....

When I finished, the audience of comfortable, middle-class professionals rose to its feet and gave me a standing ovation. As the applause
subsided and the audience settled back in its seats, the next speaker,
Father Hesburgh, approached the microphone and began with these
words: "If I had ideas like that young man, I would jump off a bridge."
I had provoked the theologian to an un-Catholic thought, but the
audience's enthusiastic response to my diatribe indicated how close
America itself was to doing just that.

My speech illustrated the real importance of Vietnam to the
radical cause, which was not ultimately about Vietnam but about
our own antagonism to America, our desire for *revolution.* Vietnam
served to justify the desire; we needed the war and its violent images
to vindicate our destructive intentions. That was why the victory of
our "anti-war" movement seemed so hollow when it came. The peace
killed the very energies that gave our movement life. When it was
ratified, there was no dancing in the streets by massive crowds of
antiwar activists, no celebrations to match the protests that had made
the Communists' triumph possible. Long before, our revolution had
failed—and the marchers had all gone home.

GENERATIONS

I N 1971 WE SOLD OUR HOUSE IN THE BERKELEY HILLS AND BOUGHT a larger one in the flatlands to accommodate our growing family. Although it had two more bedrooms, it was only marginally more expensive than the one we had left. The move came just before the great real-estate boom of the Seventies, and the old house went for a slight loss. I had considered renting it out, but—after reflection—rejected the idea. I was steeped in the arguments of R. H. Tawney and other socialist writers who had condemned rental income as "parasitic," and could not imagine shouldering the moral burden of being a landlord. This proved a costly decision when the value of the property increased more than $100,000 during the next decade.

The new house was architecturally unattractive, with a stucco facade like the first. But inside it had a warm feeling created by dark wood beams and oak floors, an ambiance enhanced by the plants Elissa hung from the ceiling or placed on the built-in cabinets with leaded glass doors. A wood trellis sheltered the backyard patio with a ceiling of wisteria that bloomed in profuse lavender petals in the spring. The yard itself was deep and overgrown, and vines of ivy covered an old garage that was useless for any vehicle wider than a Model T. I had the shack converted into a serviceable room for use as an office, and it was there that I hid Hayden's Black Panther for a two-week spell.

Elissa had no liking for Hayden or any of the other political friends who, on occasion, came to our house. In part this was a reaction to the way they ignored her, revealing their contempt for her housewifely condition; but it also reflected her disliking for the harsh edge of politics itself. For me, the political combats were bracing, tapping as they did emotional memories of the dinner-table arguments with my father in Sunnyside. I was as bewildered by the negative impact they had on others as I was by my mother's distress long ago. In a gentler way, Elissa made me aware of how cutting an abstract argument could feel to others. As a result, I made an effort to be more sensitive in social situations, modulating my sharper judgments and selecting my targets to avoid unnecessary hurts.

Our social life revolved around schools, camps, and various family events, and our circle of friends was pretty well confined to couples with small children. Because we had begun our family early, the adults we knew tended to be older than ourselves and had already settled into mid-life sobriety. Careers and children raised significant obstacles to radical activity, so that these friends were usually not part of the political community I was involved in.

Without realizing it, I had developed two lives. There was something attractive in this, as though I was getting more than I should, but I also felt I was missing something. One of the children's elementary-school teachers, Jackie Dennis, was married to Gene Dennis Jr., the son of the late chairman of the Communist Party and my campmate at Wo-Chi-Ca. I felt an instant bond, and wanted to invite them to dinner, but Elissa dismissed the idea because they had no children, and therefore we had "nothing in common." Here, as elsewhere, I failed in the attempts I made to bring the radical community into the perimeter of our home life.

The sheer volume of activity involved in managing our household was sufficient to force us into the private circle of ourselves. For each child there were separate friends, interests, and activities—including music and dance lessons, Little League, Brownies, Y Indian Guides, and Blue Birds. Then there was school and its related functions: PTA meetings, teacher consultations, graduations, and holiday events. There were the animals that augmented and complicated life: cats that had to be taken to the vet for distemper shots, dogs that disappeared and had to be found, rabbits that escaped and had to be retrieved, ducks that had to be protected (by elaborately constructed pens) from marauding raccoons. The adult energies absorbed by all this were further increased when Elissa decided not to burden the children with chores around the house; six individuals were a formidable group to constantly move from one task or place to another. Once, in frustration, I calculated that our dinners required three hours to prepare, eat, and clean up after, a routine that put strains on the time available for other tasks. Yet, to contend with her on this was so emotionally draining, and so tore at the family fabric, pitting me against her and the children, that I eventually gave up in frustration.

On the other hand, I could understand her position. The actual hours spent during the dinner ritual were occasions to engage in talk that became an intimacy between us. They provided an opportunity for me to integrate my other (political) life with hers, and a time during which we compared notes on the children. In the give-and-take of these exchanges, the juices of our marriage were restored. There was something satisfying and indispensable in being able to resonate with her—to see the trials we endured, along with the achievements, appreciated by the other. To be *known*. We already were more familiar to each other than to the families we had left. We had entered new territories and created new life, an uncharted world which no one else shared, and the bond this forged between us had become as real and intense as any of flesh and blood.

When we were not attempting to restore order in the sibling war zone, dinners were also a time to enjoy the family we had created. And, since I was a compulsive theorist, to reflect on its significances. The four children we had spawned were all so different in character and disposition that they posed a challenge to my radical worldview. The belief that environment shaped human destinies, and that therefore human character could be molded in some fundamental way, was essential to all utopian schemes. You could not change the world if you could not change the people in it. But our children were already so different from each other—Jon and Anne so aggressive and sociable, Benjamin so shy and emotional, Sarah so gentle and accommodating—that it was hard to see how our parenting had anything to do with these results. Each of them seemed to have been distinct persons in embryo, even before they had emerged to breathe the air.

Observing my own children, I was compelled to acknowledge the potency of the human soul, the power of its DNA over any conscious efforts to create a progeny in one's own image. There was something irreducibly given in their characters which created an independence that you could not reach. There was something irreducible in human character itself that rebelled against efforts to direct it too completely. You could encourage children, set an example for them, provide them with opportunities and support. But you could not program them to a desired result.

This was not to deny the stamp of parentage altogether. Nor did it rule out the potency of filial attention and desire. It was difficult, but not impossible, to guide children to positive ends. But it was easier to lose them. And perhaps this was the ultimate meaning of the parental trust. We anxiously watched many of our children's friends fall to the destructive influences around them. Drugs were a conspicuous culprit. The permissive attitude toward marijuana that was widespread in our community took a particular toll. Harmless as it may have seemed to adults, its impact on adolescents was difficult to control. Many a youngster in our circle who "tripped out" on marijuana went on to harder drugs, or psychosis, and never came back. These tragedies caused us not only to redouble our attentions to our own children, but also to ingest humility, grateful that ours were not among the victims. The responsibility for other, more vulnerable lives separated us from our childless peers. Elissa was right on this: Having offspring did not in itself make you an adult, but not having them—as our generation seemed intent on proving—was an invitation to remain a child.

When I thought about my parental mission in terms of passing on the radical legacy, I had to confront another aspect of my children's independence. Coming after me, their experience of the world was irretrievably other than mine. The fact of generations created a gulf that ultimately could not be bridged. You could attempt to span the gap by filling in the memories. But there were limits to what words could transmit. You could tell your children what life had taught you. But to them it would always be just a story. You could not take your pain off the shelf and let them feel it. You could not provide them with the experience that made you *know*.

The very task that life had set for children, which was to discover a self apart, made them natural rebels and put you at odds with them. This was the case even when the resistance was passive and assumed the form of a refusal to let the lessons take. On one occasion, I tried to make an exemplary case for my son out of the funeral of George Jackson, a Panther whose indictment for murder had been made into an international cause by the Left. In one version of Jackson's political myth, he had stolen a $70 bicycle, and spent nine years in jail for the crime. He was then falsely accused of murdering a guard. Before a trial could be held, his younger brother, Jonathan, was killed in a desperate effort to free him. In the following year, Jackson attempted to break out of San Quentin by himself and was gunned down in the prison yard. The Left framed this story as a modern *Les Misérables,* an emblem of the way young black males were doomed to destruction by a racist society. In reality, Jackson's arrest came after a string of armed robberies; he boasted to others that he had killed the guard; and his lengthy sentence was the result of other crimes he had committed in prison.

The Jackson funeral was held in Oakland, and Angela Davis and Huey Newton were scheduled to speak. I saw the event as an opportunity to connect my son's experience with mine, a link with the Rosenberg vigil I had attended eighteen years before. But he declined the invitation. The Oakland A's were playing on TV, and he wanted to watch. I became more insistent. Finally, under my pressure he went along, but brought his transistor radio so he could follow the game during the speeches.

The incident made me feel I had failed as a father. Through some deficiency in my care, he had been incompletely formed and did not feel injustice in his heart, as I did. Or at least not in the way I did. The gap this revealed between our sensibilities made me fearful of losing him eventually. Yet the memory of my own youth made me reluctant to confront him. My father had been unable to separate himself from his judgments; he had made *his* standards and *his* justice the conditions of his love. Or so I felt. My father had left no room for me, and that very fact had driven a wedge between us.

This intuition did not make the conflicts with my son any easier, or the rejection I felt any less deep. I still might have reacted as my father had if not for Elissa's intervention pulling me back from the brink. Look at him, she said, and see how he loves you. And, because of the way I trusted her instincts, the advice proved sufficient.

I was still trying to connect with my father. My parents would come to visit us during the summers, and he and I would take long walks, and test the space between us. Actually, my mother often set up these occasions. I always had ambivalent feelings when she approached me on my father's behalf, because it was *she* I wanted to talk to—the more interesting of the two, the one I felt I could make contact with if only she would let me get that close. While my father regarded every political difference between us a sign that I was moving away from him, she had long ago seen beyond that. The family, she had decided, was more important than politics. Whereas he had a generally negative view of my political generation, she had a genuine enthusiasm for what we had accomplished. She had been at Martin Luther King's 1963 "March on Washington" and other demonstrations, including the 1967 antiwar protests at the Whitehall induction center in New York, where she was interviewed by a reporter for the *New York Post:* "I think the war is immoral," she told him. "We're a technically superior country laying waste to an underdeveloped one. We're using up our youth. I came here to support them."

I marveled at my mother. To stay abreast of the youth culture, she had taken herself to a rerun theater on 42nd Street to catch *The Buddy Holly Story,* and she kept the *Kama Sutra* and the *Joy of Sex* on the dresser in her bedroom. After finishing her library degree, she had enrolled in an extension course in photography and become an amateur reporter, making a visual record of the street artists who stole into the city trainyards at night and spray-painted graffiti on the subway cars. Her photograph, titled "Welcome to Hell," was eventually hung in the Museum of the City of New York. She got to know the artist who had assumed the name "Cain," a refugee from Communist Czechoslovakia who was later murdered.

And yet, when my mother would pull me aside from the family commotion on these visits to Berkeley, I would not get to talk to her as I wanted, to explore the place she had arrived at in her own life or find out how she viewed mine. She was always guarded, never dwelling on emotional issues, constantly steering the subject to the practical. When she took me aside now, it was to discuss the business of wrapping up her household, the last parental rite. She would give me a set of keys to the house on 44th Street, where they still lived, and tell me where she had put the life insurance and their wills, along with other details that might be useful to know. My father had labeled each key—"outside porch door," "inside front door upper lock," "inside front door lower lock"—as though I could not figure out these intricacies myself when the time came. I had an aversion to these lectures, and waited impatiently for her to conclude so we could move on to something else, but the opportunity never presented itself. When she had finished her points, she would say, "You should take a walk with Phil," and press the point until I realized I could not alter her agenda.

My father had been suffering for years with arthritis and was now walking with canes, after a hip replacement she had persuaded him to undertake. They were temporary prostheses until the post-op therapy was complete, but he seemed to regard them as permanent crosses he had to bear, cursing at intervals when he could not make his crippled legs bend to the still undiminished will. And he was full of complaints. The doctors had short-changed him; they had lied about the hips, which failed to work the way they had promised. His distrust was not merely because they made too much money, but because they made any money at all. They cared about profits, not him. There was nothing new in these indictments, and besides, he had lost me as a disciple years before. But I was intrigued by the extent of his suspicions. Looking at the nudes in a *Playboy* magazine, he said: "These women are fake." It occurred to me that his Marxism provided a consolation for the things that had eluded him in life. It also occurred to me that it was not the doctors who were the object of his wrath, but my mother, who had made the decision for him—because he could not stand up to her.

Over the years, my father's features had contracted into a permanent frown, but when he saw me after a long absence, his wintry depression would thaw into a smile. A cane in each hand, he would reach out to embrace his son in one of those bear hugs that caused me to wince, and I would look at him and imagine we were swimming toward each other again on Long Island. He took an interest in my children, especially when they responded readily to his overtures, and then he would show himself again a born teacher, instructing them the way I remembered. He was childlike himself, however, easily persuaded that he had been left out when attentions were not focused in his direction. When the moment of reunion had dissolved into the routines of the visit his saturnine expression returned. The two of us would then find an occasion to set out on our walks, during which I, invariably assuming the parental role, would welcome the challenge of injecting cheer into his gloom. "You want Cadillac legs," I chided, "but you've got a Model T." This would elicit an appreciative laugh—but with an edge as though I had somehow trapped him.

When I exhausted my side of the conversation, I would attempt to switch roles to see if I could get him to be the father again, but invariably came up short. While he enjoyed the attention I paid to him, he seemed unable to reciprocate. It was not that he was uncurious about my life: He asked first about Elissa and the children, for whom he had genuine affection, and then about my health. Yet his questions would stop there, as if he had reached a precarious edge and was fearful of going over. About my interior life—the life over which we had shared our deepest connections and our severest conflicts—he remained stubbornly mute.

These silences came naturally to my father. He had retreated so far into himself that he would sometimes get lost in internal regions I could not penetrate. At such times, he would lapse into solipsisms that were bizarre, albeit revealing. Once, when we were turning the corner to return to my house, he stopped in the middle of the side-walk. He had drifted off in a reverie, and now came up as if from the bottom of a deep well and asked, "Where were you between the ages of 6 and 16?" I stood there puzzled for a moment. Was this a statement of his own guilt? Yet it came as an accusation. How was I to answer? *I was there, Dad. Where were you?*

And yet I had no sense of deprivation because of his absences. It was his *presence* that posed the difficult questions: What did he think of me? What did I want from him? I had asked myself this so many times in frustration that I finally got an answer. I wanted a paternal blessing. I wanted him to acknowledge the distance his son had traveled. I wanted his acceptance of my political choices, because that was what mattered to him. Other things he could allow me: The family I had made, which was larger than he thought appropriate; the career I had achieved, which was more like the one he wanted but could not handle. These he could acknowledge in one way or another as accomplishments that impressed him. It was in the political realm that he could make no concessions.

When our discussions veered into the areas of our political disagreements, I was made to feel the spine of his being. It was as though we were back in the house on 44th Street, arguing over the *Times* again. Yet these new eruptions were quickly muted by my decision not to press them. I would raise the issue of Solzhenitsyn's new book, to see that he had not changed. But when the expected response came, I did not push him to the wall, as I once had. He was too weakened, too beaten, for that. When he dismissed Solzhenitsyn as a reactionary doing the Americans' work, I let it pass. Sometimes I would pare down my quest until it was a simple demand for respect. But even this proved impossible. He merely looked hurt, and pretended ignorance of what I wanted. At other times his comebacks could be sharp and insulting: "No one believes an idea like that," he snapped at one of my most cherished beliefs. It provoked me so much that I had to stop the conversation as we dug silently into the familiar trenches of our lifelong conflict.

What I wanted was my father's recognition that I, too, had won a few hard truths. That he could look on my writings as a worthy contribution to the cause we shared. I wanted a parental sign that would make me his son again, even though in some basic way, as we both understood, I had long ago left him.

We turn corners in our lives without realizing we have done so. One day, Peter Collier approached me at *Ramparts* and said, "Let's write a best-seller." I didn't hesitate before dismissing the idea: "You're nuts," I said. Nothing was more remote from my ambitions than the project he was proposing. Best-sellers belonged to a commercial world that Marxists had consigned to history's dustbin. It was no more than a crapshoot. If someone else beat you to the finish on a subject, your efforts were in vain, no matter how good a book you wrote. Why waste precious time on such a quest? And why *me?* I didn't have a clue as to what made the public respond to one product rather than another.

Peter's proposal was unattractive for another reason: I had already begun working on a book for Random House that was to be an expansion of a series of *Ramparts* articles I had written about the Carnegie, Rockefeller, and Ford foundations and their influence on American politics and culture. Once I began the writing, the conception had expanded and the scope of the book now included universities and, in fact, *all* organized intellectual activity. It didn't even occur to me that Random House might not want to publish such a dense academic treatise. I was driven by the idea that it *had* to be done. The new book would be a "sociohistory" beginning in the mid-nineteenth century with the creation of the modern university and the formation of a national ruling class. It would combine a narrative of institutional developments with an analysis showing how social ideas were shaped by class interests. I was going to call it *The Social Foundations of Knowledge.*

Peter's idea for a best-seller was to write a biography of the Rockefeller family modeled on *The Forsythe Saga,* which had recently been featured as the first television "miniseries" on PBS. It told the story of several generations of a single powerful family, spanning its rise and fall. Ours would be about a real family that was also America's most powerful dynasty. There was another factor inspiring the project. We had raised money for *Ramparts* from two daughters of the present Rockefeller patriarchs, Marion and Abby, who were in their thirties. Our book would be about the radical scions of the archetypal family of America's ruling class. Marion and Abby would provide us with inside sources.

I understood at least one reason why Peter was coming to me with this proposal. During the student strike at Columbia in 1968, I had written a memo about the Rockefeller influence on Columbia's trustees through Socony Mobil, one of the Standard Oil companies. The memo became famous around the *Ramparts* office because of its hortatory conclusion:

> Who subverted the ideal and made Columbia the pimp of criminal militarists and avaricious power? Socony Mobil. Who made the authentic academics at Columbia mere front men and fig leaves for state power? Socony Mobil.... It's time for a lube job.

I had also written about the Rockefeller fortune in the *Ramparts* series on foundations. It was this expertise that made some sense of the idea of the partnership he was proposing.

Nonetheless, I had no desire to write a biography, and no idea of what writing one would entail. On the other hand, Peter seemed eager for my help, and I didn't want to turn him down. He made it seem more my kind of project by suggesting that we would write it like *Moby Dick*, interspersing the biographical chapters with descriptions of the "whale"—the ruling class and its system. When I finally said yes, I was thinking that my contribution would be pretty much confined to these chapters. But Peter had in mind a more equal collaboration. My inability to visualize the exact nature of the enterprise we were undertaking, or to grasp what Peter expected of me, went unnoticed at the time, but was soon to create a rift between us.

Our plan was to go to New York, to auction the book on the basis of a proposal Peter had written and the verbal presentation we would make when we got there. The auction idea was suggested by my agent, Georges Borchardt, who was now representing us in our joint venture. Before leaving for New York, I went to see Marion Rockefeller, who lived in South Berkeley with her husband and two daughters in a brown shingle, furnished with student economy. A bespectacled woman with wispy blonde hair and soft features, she appeared at the door in a sari-like dress she had made herself, part of a life project she had undertaken to become independent of the Rockefeller millions. No sooner had we begun to talk than she disappeared into another room, returning with a piece of paper on which she had drawn a diagram of her family's empire. Concentric circles represented the layers of servants, advisers, and other employees who worked out of Room 5600 in Rockefeller Center, and whose job it was to insulate family members from the rude surfaces of ordinary existence. She had labeled the center of the diagram "The Disease." As she began describing it to me, I realized that even though she had given lots of money to causes like *Ramparts*, radical politics was hardly the force driving her. Whatever it was, it was more psychological than political—something that troubled her very soul.

Peter and I flew to New York, to present our proposal to six publishing houses. Our initial meeting was at Holt, Rinehart with

its editor-in-chief, Aaron Asher, who was famous for his generous advances to Philip Roth and other writers. He was particularly
impressed by our connections to sources who would make it possible
for us to tell the "inside story" of the Rockefellers for the first time.
After we left his office, he called Borchardt to make an offer: "Would
you laugh if I said $50,000?" It was more than I had paid for my house.

We pitched our proposal to two other publishers on that first day.
Afterwards, my anxiety reached a high enough level that I felt compelled to call Abby Rockefeller and check that she was on board. This
was not the first time I had talked to her; she had called me for advice
once, when Trotskyists tried to take over a feminist magazine she had
financed, *No More Fun and Games*. The magazine was published by
Cell 16, a militant group which trained its members in martial arts
and took a generally dim view of the male gender. Abby had written an
article titled "Sex: The Basis of Sexism," in which she argued that men
oppressed women in order to have them available for sex. Feminism,
in her view, was "not just a 'war between the sexes,' it was a war over
sex." In my conversation with her, it became apparent that she was
also a Marxist, and familiar with my work. This made me confident
that she would be willing to cooperate. I told her about our project,
and that we needed her as a source. As I expected, her response was
enthusiastic—but then she added: "You guys are the perfect people
to write a book about my family, but I'm not going to talk to you. It
would cause too much trouble for me."

It was what Peter liked to call an existential moment. We had
already identified Abby to Aaron Asher as one of our inside sources.
Should we tell him the truth now, and risk losing the $50,000? Were
we opening ourselves to lawsuits if we allowed the next three publishers to believe that we had Abby in tow? What should we do? Actually,
it was more a case of what Peter thought we should do. I had followed
him into a landscape which was foreign to me. Was a source like Abby
really crucial to the project? I didn't know. But Peter decided that she
was, and also that we should brazen it out. The deception made me
uncomfortable, but I consoled myself with the idea that eventually
I could persuade her to cooperate. Given her politics and her confidence in us, how could she refuse?

We went through the second day of interviews using the same presentation as the first, as though the phone call had never taken place. When it was over, there were just two bids from the six publishers we had met with, and Aaron Asher's was five times larger than the other.

In September 1973, my mother went alone to Bangkok to deliver a paper on specialist libraries at an international conference. After receiving her master's degree in library science, she had created a unique classification system for family-planning subjects which were adopted by most Planned Parenthood affiliates and also by family-planning libraries all over the world. Two years later, she was elected president of the Association for Population/Family Planning Libraries and Information Centers International, which she had helped to found. She charted her trip to Thailand from the west coast, leaving my father in Berkeley with us.

Before her departure, she expressed anxiety about him and the fact that he would be without her for the first time in nearly forty years. But her worry proved groundless. He took pleasure in the vacation, especially on the walks we went on to exercise his recovering hips. My attitude toward my parents had changed as I became a parent myself. I began to see them more as equals, to imagine them as children thrown into the world like the rest of us, without much in the way of maps to guide them. I started to look at their marriage with a certain detachment, too, curious about what kept them together. The tensions that surfaced between them puzzled me with their intensity. Where did they spring from? Their lives were relatively simple now, with none of the tugs of children at home, or the pressures of earning a living. Why weren't they enjoying themselves more?

Sensing my father's relief at not being under my mother's watchful eye, I stepped into the vacancy. I became collusive with him, drawing him out in an effort to locate the sources of his unfamiliar pleasure. I pressed him about his feelings, until a moment of revelation came that made me almost sorry that I had. He was still using the canes, and we were moving slowly through the neighborhood streets until we came to a stop at Live Oak Park, where we sat down on a retaining wall to rest. For some reason I asked him about the renovations they had recently undertaken on the 44th Street house. I knew of course that this was not the ordinary question it might seem. Although they thought of themselves as revolutionaries, they had achieved a stability in their environment that made it seem almost petrified. They had lived at the same address for twenty-four years, ever since we left the nearly identical house on Bliss Street when I was 10. Except for one chair that my mother had re-covered, nothing had changed—not even the paint color on the walls. They were still using the cheap flatware they had bought as part of a special offer to subscribers to the *Daily Compass*, which had been defunct since the early Fifties. Their toaster even had the yellowed and now brittle Scotch tape my father had used to fix the plastic handle when it broke twenty years before.

Against this background, the measures my mother had recently taken were radical. She had redone the bathroom, ripping out the sink and putting in new tiles. In their bedroom she had *faux* wood-paneling installed, which gave it a Sears catalogue look—an incitement to my father all by itself. I was curious to see how he was reacting to these changes, but I was unprepared for the violent emotions they provoked. When I brought the subject up, his body clenched as though stung and his face screwed into a grimace so tight that he could only spit his feelings out in fragments. "She's done it," he said. "The pain. The *torture.*"

I probed for something else behind his suffering. But there was nothing. In his mind, a few surface changes had turned his home into a chamber of horrors. I knew this was not about bathrooms and bedrooms. It was a metaphor for his life, and more particularly what he had allowed it to become. His passivity was infuriating. Why did such small things have such power over him? Why did he put up with what he could not stand? I asked these questions of myself, rather than of him. Why was he so helpless before the circumstances of his life?

The intensity with which I pressed this internal argument exposed my identification with his dilemmas. Without exactly realizing it was happening, I had begun to feel the walls of my own life closing in. Perhaps it was the approach of middle age: I would be 35 in a few months; I was no longer a young man with my future uncharted in front of me. Perhaps it was the collapse of the Movement. I had not been one of those who believed in the imminence of the revolution, but I could not escape the deflation that followed its defeats. We had been a vanguard, and now it was clear that none of our grandiose aspirations would be realized. The tide of history had run out, stranding us on ordinary shores.

Even as the historical hopes that lifted us so high proved empty, my private world came under increasing pressure. Peter and I were still editing *Ramparts,* and the responsibility for keeping it afloat fell principally on my shoulders. The biography we had begun required me to travel for the necessary interviews. Meanwhile, my book on the social foundations of knowledge was beginning to seem more ambitious than I would be able to handle, given the obligations I had undertaken. How was I even going to gather, no less master, the material—the history of so many institutions, the disciplines of knowledge they produced, and the sociological framework for analyzing them all?

I had begun to put together a new leadership team at the magazine, and to bring in new financial backers so that Peter and I could retire and devote full time to our biographical venture. But even as I did so, Peter and I began to have conflicts over the collaboration. When the project was several months old, he accused me of not doing my share. I had provided notes for a chapter he wanted written as a text. But I had no feel for the narrative mode. A biography was not a sociological analysis, which was almost all that I had written until then. What was I to put on the page? Perhaps if I had not been pressed for time, because of the book I was also writing on the sociology of knowledge, I would have been up to the task. But I could hardly explain to him why I was unwilling to put this project on hold. In contrast to the gamble at fame and fortune that he and I were collaborating on, this was about my *mission,* the life work I had undertaken as a Marxist intellectual. If we failed to write a best-seller about the Rockefellers, that would be a disappointment falling within the parameters of reasonable expectations. But if I failed to produce a significant contribution to Marxist theory, my sense of self was at stake.

About this time, I had a glimpse of how such a failure might feel. Hal Jacobs, a radical sociologist, stopped by my backyard office one day and saw the stacks of books I was studying: biographies of educational founders like Ezra Cornell and Stanley Hall, texts in the sociology of knowledge by Mannheim and Gramsci, long treatises on the academic professions. "What are these?" he asked. With cautious pride I set out for him the architecture of my ambition; here was somebody who could understand. Hal had the academic equipment to grasp the scope and implication of the undertaking. But when I finished my description, he said: "Why do you want to waste your time doing that? We already know the ruling class runs everything. We don't need you to tell us. What we need is a revolutionary plan."

I had already written two hundred heavily footnoted pages, and was expending what felt like my lifeblood on a book he was telling me even sympathetic radicals would not read. A few years earlier, such a thought would have had no impact. At that time, I burned with a sense of mission, and nothing could have stopped me. But, since then, I had written *The Free World Colossus* and *Empire and Revolution* and they had moved no mountains. Life was proving more complicated than I had bargained.

Yet there was no one I could turn to for counsel. The relationship with Peter, while helping to shake me out of my bubble, was proving unsettling in the process. I was becoming more aware of the world outside the revolutionary melodrama—outside myself. His displeasure at my performance on the biography fed my self-doubt. I had little support from him, and still did not understand what I could do to remedy the situation. When I turned to Elissa, I realized she couldn't provide much insight or help, either: She was too polarized against Peter to offer me good advice. The two had taken a strong dislike to each other from the moment I introduced them, and the project had made their rivalry even more intense. The trips I took to interview Rockefeller sources, although confined to three- or four-day intervals, also put significant strains on our bustling household, whose maintenance depended on me in many ways. As the pressures grew, I began to feel overwhelmed and not in control. Like my father.

I no longer expected advice from him, either. Once he had seemed to have the answers—the practical pointers I needed to help me along, the understanding of the larger world which he explained in crystalline Marxist categories. But that tutelage had not survived my youth. After I entered Columbia, he began to feel out of his depth with me. He would often complain, as a way of providing an explanation, that he had not kept up his reading. In terms of family and career, I had traveled so far from his point of departure that he had given up trying to offer me guidance. What I sought from him now was something different: I wanted to step into the next filial zone with him, to take the collusion that had developed between us in my mother's absence, and turn it into a friendship.

I was inspired by the idea that I would make us the subject of our talk, taking some drama we had enacted long ago and using it to meet him behind the scenery, so to speak. An episode from the past suggested itself as a text: a fourth-grade play about Mozart, in which I was given the role of the prodigy as a child. I had only begun piano lessons in the year before, and could just manage the simple minuet necessary for my performance. A student named Louis, who was already displaying virtuosity on the keyboard, was assigned the role of Mozart as a young man. One day, the school principal came to observe us at a rehearsal. Suddenly my teacher, a large and overbearing woman, called me to the stage to demonstrate my pianistic ability. I was pretty certain she didn't mean me, but I was too frightened to say anything. I was hoping that if I picked the most difficult piece I knew, perhaps no one would notice. Barely a few bars into it, however, I heard her shout, *"You're* not the one"—and as I shrank from the stage: *"Louis!* Get up there."

There was a second incident attached to this memory. It occurred after the play was over, when my family gathered in our backyard and I asked my father to photograph me in my Mozart costume. My mother had dressed me in ruffles and a blue satin jacket with knee breeches and white silk stockings. Readying myself for the camera, I tried to assume the serious look appropriate to a genius. As I struck the attitude, I realized my father was laughing at me. Raising his eye from the viewfinder with a mocking grin, he said, just before the shot, "What a *poseur!*" and snapped the shutter.

What linked these episodes was the feeling of being an impostor unmasked. There is an element of impersonation in any growth, an invisible line between the determination to be *like* the one we aspire to be and to *be* him. To this normal confusion there was added for me our romance as secret agents of the revolution, and the pretense— if only through silence—of being ordinary Americans to the publics we faced. It was a deception that had always made me uncomfortable. The charade was so ritualized it had developed into a form of self-consciousness, and then self-doubt. When I began to appear before actual audiences, the sense of not belonging was so strong that I felt as though my personality was split between the figure on stage and the voice behind it.

On one occasion I was debating the U.S. consul general in London before an antiwar gathering of several hundred people when I experienced something akin to psychic fission. I started to think about what I was saying—about the *fact* that I was saying it. Suddenly there was myself thinking and my voice speaking, until I could no longer maintain the two postures. In horror, I realized I could not remember what I had just said, or what I intended to say next, and was forced to stop until I recovered myself enough to start speaking again. After this episode, I learned to prepare for my role, and never to step outside it when speaking in public. Eventually I made peace with myself, in accepting my status as a public figure, and the problem disappeared.

I felt now the urge to talk about the conquest of these self-doubts with my father. By this admission, I hoped to put us on a more equal footing and provide an opportunity to heal old wounds. I began by saying to him, "When I was nine, I asked you to photograph me as Mozart, and you laughed at me." I could not resist also asking whether his reaction wasn't a little harsh. Perhaps this was a provocation. Instead of the sympathy I was searching for, a darkness enveloped his face, and he leaned forward on his canes. Looking me directly in the eye, he said: "I was jealous of you since the day you were born."

PART 5

PANTHERS

(1973–1974)

Let my people go

—Negro Spiritual

HUEY

ONE DAY I WAS SUMMONED TO THE *RAMPARTS* PHONE WITH THE message that a Frenchman was calling from Black Panther Party headquarters. It turned out to be Jean Genet, the famous writer who was touring the country on behalf of the Panthers, whose leadership was now either in hiding or in jail: Newton for shooting Officer Frey, Bobby Seale for allegedly ordering the death of a Party member; and Cleaver, who was in Algiers to escape prosecution for ambushing two policemen. The Left, of course, was proclaiming the innocence of all three, and portraying the legal proceedings against them a federal plot to destroy the militant leadership of the black community. "Nothing made the idea of revolution more vivid to the white left," as Todd Gitlin put it in his history of the Sixties, "than the Black Panther Party."

In America, Genet took up the Panther cause. He wrote an introduction to George Jackson's collection of letters from prison, *Soledad Brother,* and spoke at public rallies in his behalf. Like most French leftists, Genet's hatred for America was both extravagant and second-nature. According to Genet, America had kept Jackson in prison because it was afraid of its "Red Blacks," a term he invented for street gangsters who had discovered Marxism. The criminal as a kind of "primitive rebel" was an idea that Sartre had developed in his biography of Genet, who had been a petty thief himself. But Jackson was shrewder about leftist intellectuals than either of the Frenchmen were about black criminals. Jackson explained the connection between Marxist theory and the outlaw mentality when he told his white editor: "Marxism is my hustle."

In a series of public statements, Genet claimed that white Americans went to Vietnam "out of ignorance," while blacks like Jackson were sent to prison instead because of their "advanced" political understanding. With peculiar Gallic logic, Genet argued that Jackson could not, in fact, have murdered the prison guard, as accused, because he was engaged in far more dangerous activity: thinking and writing.

The purpose of Genet's call was to see if *Ramparts* could provide him with a translator, since the Panthers hadn't bothered to arrange one. After consulting with our receptionist, Judy, whose French was fluent, I offered them her services. Genet also said he was writing a book about the Panthers, and asked to spend some time discussing its contents with a group from the magazine. When we met him, he turned out to be a gray little man who introduced himself as a "vagabond" and carried an Alp-size chip on his shoulder This was accompanied by an expression more sour than my father's. We met with him over several days, even assembling at his bedside after he contracted a virus. During these sessions, he explained that the Marquis de Sade was "the greatest revolutionary who ever lived," and that America was the "absolute enemy" of humanity and progress. At some point in our discussions, I was transporting Genet from one destination to another, when a silence enveloped us. I flipped on my car radio, thinking it would make the situation more comfortable, but he immediately pounced on my gesture as an occasion for yet another lesson in New World degeneracy. "Americans are always playing the radio," he snapped. "When do they have time to think?"

Judy accompanied Genet and what turned out to be his Panther entourage to Los Angeles, where they stayed at the Beverly Hills home of Donald and Shirley Sutherland. When she returned, Judy told us she had been "raped" by Panther "Field Marshal" David Hilliard. I didn't know what to make of her accusation, since she seemed sorry for Hilliard, rather than angry at what he had done, and had no intention of pressing charges. Hilliard was about to go to jail for his role in the shoot-out involving Cleaver, and, according to Judy, had cajoled her into bed by suggesting that this was a sentence from which he might never return. She still seemed half ready to believe what he said.

When I pressed her further, she shifted the subject: "You should call Shirley Sutherland about raising money for *Ramparts*," she suggested.

Many months later I acted on her advice. Peter and I had taken a day trip to Newport Beach, to see a Litton executive whose son had been hanging around *Ramparts'* offices. It was the only time Peter and I had gone out of town to raise funds for the magazine. The executive received us cordially, but provided no help. Hoping to redeem a wasted trip, we called Sutherland, who said "You must talk to Bert Schneider," and gave us a number. I dropped another quarter in the slot and called Schneider. "I really want to talk to you guys," he said, "but I'm busy. Call me again."

I phoned Schneider every day for a month, but never got past his secretary, and he never returned the calls. When I had just about given up, he phoned to say he was coming to San Francisco and wanted to see us. He was a tall, angular man with aquamarine eyes, a face framed by long, blond curls, and a nose which was blunt at the end. There was a feminine flow about his movements, and his entire demeanor was one of constant seduction. He told us he had produced the Monkees, one of the most popular bands of the Sixties, and *Five Easy Pieces,* which starred Jack Nicholson and won an Academy Award.

When the introductions were over, Schneider revealed an agenda of his own: He wanted us to remove Eldridge Cleaver's name from the masthead. Cleaver was listed as our "International Editor," a title Scheer had given him after his flight. Cleaver was still in Algeria, and we had not been in contact with him since Scheer's own departure from the magazine, years earlier. Since then, the Panther world had been turned upside down. Newton had been released from jail on an appeal over a technicality, and George Jackson and his brother Jonathan had been killed in their desperate escape attempts. A split in the Party had developed following recriminations over these deaths, and Cleaver and Newton had emerged as bitter enemies on opposite sides of the conflict.

From the Cleaver faction came accusations that Newton was responsible for the botched escapes. He was accused of "setting up" Jackson and abandoning the "armed struggle." The conflict had already resulted in at least two violent deaths. While no one took credit for these fratricidal killings, and their details remained obscure to a Left which preferred not to know, the leadership battle raged on. Cleaver attacked Newton for living in a penthouse, sporting a "swagger stick," and referring to himself as the "Servant of the People" while snorting large quantities of cocaine. Many radicals believed Cleaver's charges, and regarded Newton as a sellout, although they continued to support the "Panther vanguard."

If Peter and I were also suspicious of Newton, we had no reason to support Cleaver. We regarded his appeal for armed revolution as extreme, but still had reason to resist Schneider's request. We were jealous of our independence, and did not want to appear to be making editorial decisions under pressure. Schneider accepted our scruple, and asked only that we meet with Newton before making a final judgment. As I drove him back to his San Francisco hotel, I found myself explaining our difficulties in keeping the magazine alive, and realized there was something in me that looked to him not just for help, but as a possible solution to responsibilities I found overwhelming. I also noticed that he didn't much care. When he sent us a check for only $5,000, I was disappointed but not surprised.

Peter and I decided that we would accept Schneider's offer to meet with Newton, who was back in court on the original charge of killing the officer. Schneider picked us up and escorted us to the penthouse apartment overlooking Lake Merritt in Oakland that he had rented for the Panther leader. On the way, he explained to us the rationale for the luxury quarters that Cleaver had so mercilessly attacked: Newton was surrounded by enemies—the Cleaver faction as well as the police. Attempts, or what appeared to be attempts (there was a vagueness in his account of these incidents, as there was when Newton described them to us later) had been made on his life. The penthouse was in a security building, and images of people entering appeared on a TV monitor in Newton's apartment. The argument was strengthened by the fact that Newton himself expressed unhappiness with the arrangement, which he presented as having been forced on him by his concerned supporters. This hardly fit the Cleaver picture of a leader driven by selfish impulse, a fact which Newton understood.

The scene inside the penthouse completed the seduction. Across the lake was the Oakland courthouse, where Newton's retrial had just begun. A telescope was focused, through one of the penthouse windows, on the "strip cell" in the county jail where a naked Newton had been forced to spend weeks in solitary confinement because he would not cooperate with his guards. But the most impressive artifact was Newton himself, now stripped to the waist, bearing the ripped biceps and bulky pecs he had built doing push-ups in his isolation cell. Along with these, Newton displayed a prominent scar from the bullet wound inflicted in his shoot-out with the officer that marked him as a warrior. The picture was completed by a disarmingly high-pitched voice, and a demeanor that appeared almost childlike in its openness—the very opposite of the badassed swagger that the Panthers had perfected, or the dictatorial posture that Cleaver had attacked.

After the introductions, and with obvious feelings of slight, Newton told us he had recently returned from China where he had been received by Premier Chou En-lai, but not Chairman Mao. My previous experience with Panther Maoism, when I had confronted Bob Avakian in the Party headquarters, prevented me from letting the subject pass without an opinion. China, I said, was a police state and no friend of the Vietnamese. Newton reacted by defending China as an embattled Third World nation, and the two of us became locked in an argument so intense that I was not sure, as he advanced to within a few inches of my face, that he was not going to hit me. But he seemed to enjoy the ideological combat, and I was encouraged to escalate my criticism, pointing it in his direction: "What kind of a revolutionary party is it," I challenged him, "that turns 180 degrees on a disagreement between two men?"

It was his answer that hooked me. "You're right," he said. "The Party is not a Black Student Union. The people in it are uneducated and from the streets. We're trying to do something difficult, which is to take these people from where they are and bring them to another place." Then he asked if I would assist him in this task, and also in making the Party more democratic, so that it could better serve the cause we shared. By respecting our differences, he had already treated me as an equal. Now he was telling me that we had agendas in common, and he was prepared to listen to my advice. I was ready to help.

When we left the apartment, Schneider was furious: "How could you attack him like that? The man's just come from trial." But I hardly heard him; I had found a political soul mate, and that was what mattered. Peter was less impressed. When Schneider had gone, he commented on Huey's seductive routine, the bared biceps, the way he grabbed an arm—almost like a laying-on of hands—to emphasize a point. I could see that Peter was not going to be part of my new mission, and made a mental note to recruit Kaldenbach instead.

Kaldenbach and I went on a tour of Panther facilities, to see what help we might offer. We visited the "George Jackson Free Clinic," where doctors friendly to the Party provided their services to Party members at no cost. But Audrea Jones, who ran the clinic, was sullen and hostile, and we left without accomplishing anything. At the *Black Panther* offices, we received similar treatment from its editor, Ericka Huggins, who kept us waiting for nearly an hour in a room that seemed like a dumping ground for discarded oak school desks. There must have been a dozen, all bare and apparently waiting to be moved. I settled as comfortably as I could into an oak chair, put my feet up on an empty desk, and tried to pacify Kaldenbach, who was becoming more irritated by the minute. His pique made me anxious: Ericka was one of the heroes of the Movement. Her husband, John, had been murdered—along with Al "Bunchy" Carter—on the UCLA campus, by members of Ron Karenga's organization. She had been one of the defendants in the New Haven trial. When she finally entered the room, a tall woman in a drab frock, she was stiff-lipped and uncommunicative, and studied us through cold, almost lifeless eyes. I explained to her that we had come prepared to share our expertise and help her paper build up its circulation and generate funds. But this offer failed to elicit the slightest interest.

Our only encouraging reception was at the Black Panther school, a brown-shingle house on 29th Street in East Oakland. Fifty children lived in the building, which was not large enough to accommodate them. On the second floor, their metal-frame bunk beds were stacked so closely in the rooms that there were no aisles between them. The principal, Brenda, was an elegant, light-skinned woman with an aristocratic mien accented by aviator shades and red snakeskin boots. One of the teachers, who was instructing a three-year-old to read, told me she had never graduated from high school. When I mentioned this to Brenda, she explained: "Everyone has something to teach someone."

The phrase stuck, and later I created an "Each One Teach One" club, to raise money for the school. At this initial meeting, I asked only if the Party could afford monthly payments on a clothes dryer, which I had noted the house lacked, and offered to co-sign a loan so they could buy one. When she replied that they could, I knew I had found my first project.

After making these rounds, I went to the penthouse to tell Huey what had happened. He already knew most of the details through reports he had received from the people I'd met. When I finished, he said he was surprised that Brenda had been receptive, because she was a "cultural nationalist" and distrusted whites. He added, "I also have a report on you from Ericka." Then he told me what she had said: *"Why do you send this racist dog to me, who puts his feet on my desk?"* Almost stuttering, I attempted to explain that whatever I had done to insult Ericka was inadvertent, that we had been kept waiting a long time, and that nobody appeared to be using the desks. But Huey cut me short. "That's *her* problem," he said.

Huey continued to make gestures like that, calculated to secure my loyalty. The most seductive were those in which he accepted my advice. Although he had said he wanted to make the Party a democracy, I noted that he was still referred to as the "Servant of the People," a title more suited to a cult figure. One day, when I called the penthouse number, an answering machine with a taped female voice responded, "The Servant is not in. Leave a message." I decided to speak to him about this. I told him the message was intimidating. If he was serious about encouraging people to speak up, he should change the tape. The next time I called the penthouse, the voice said, "Huey is not in. Please leave a message."

Successes like this prompted me to suggest other changes. The Party is an anachronism, I told him during one of our meetings. The idea of a "vanguard" was itself undemocratic, and the Leninist principle of centralism, which the Panthers observed, had proven historically catastrophic. Why have a "revolutionary party" at all, if the conditions for revolution don't exist? The Party should be dissolved, I advised him. He surprised me by agreeing. Perhaps his reaction was just a con; perhaps every concession he made to me was a con. I have no way of knowing. Whatever the case, he added that he could not dissolve the Party immediately because there were too many people in it who would fight such a move. Many had died or gone to jail to make the Party what it was. The rank and file would have to be persuaded before such a plan could be carried out.

Talking to Huey as a kind of equal, in this manner, emboldened me to raise yet another difficult issue. A strain of anti-Semitism had developed in the Party during the years he was in prison. Of course, the Panthers were not alone among black radicals in their attacks on Jews. In 1966, Stokely Carmichael and the leaders of SNCC had expelled whites from the civil-rights organization, accusing them of being a fifth column inside the movement. Since Jews were a near majority of the whites in these organizations, and had played a strategic role in organizing and funding the struggle, it was clear to everyone that they were the primary target of the assault. This was underscored by the support that Carmichael and the black left gave to the Arab states during their 1967 attack on Israel.

I had not paid much attention to these developments, in part because I was in England when they occurred, but also because Israel was so strong militarily—its forces had crushed the Arab armies in just six days—that I did not believe there was much danger to Jewish life, let alone survival, at the time. The subsequent Arab aggression during Yom Kippur, in October 1973, convinced me otherwise. In that war, Israel's survival was indeed threatened—and it became clear to me that the Arabs' hatred toward the Jews was implacable. Consequently, when the *Black Panther* ran an article during the conflict, attacking the "Zionist, racist 'state' of Israel," I felt the need to say something.

My views were shaped by my old teacher, Isaac Deutscher, who had collected his articles on the subject in a volume called *The Non-Jewish Jew*—a reference to Jewish "heretics" like Spinoza and Marx, who were "of Judaism but not in it," and whose outsider status had led to their revolutionary views. Deutscher's perspective on the Jewish state had its origins in his experience in Europe between the two world wars. Like other Marxists, he believed the nation-state was an anachronism, and that socialism would abolish all borders. During the Thirties, Zionists had urged Jews to flee to Palestine, while Deutscher and his fellow socialists agitated for a revolution that would end the nation-state, and thus solve the problem of anti-Semitism once and for all.

But the Holocaust caused Deutscher to have second thoughts about his anti-Zionism. "If, instead of arguing against Zionism in the 1920s and 1930s," he wrote, "I had urged European Jews to go to Palestine, I might have helped to save some of the lives that were later extinguished in Hitler's gas chambers." The Zionists had created Israel as a "raft state," and it had to be defended as such, until the time came when the international revolution, in which he (and I) still believed, would eliminate the need for such a refuge.

I presented this argument to Huey with some misgiving, not knowing how he would respond. Once again he surprised me by suggesting I write a position paper on the Middle East for the Party. He then published it as an official policy statement in the *Black Panther*:

Though the ultimate survival of Jews and Palestinians, as of all peoples, depends on the revolutionary overthrow of world imperialism and capitalism, we call upon Jews and Arabs in the Middle East to recognize the national rights of their opponents: upon the Government of Israel to recognize the claims of the Palestinian people for independent national institutions, as originally provided by the UN, and of the Arab states and the Palestinian liberation movement to recognize the existence of the State of Israel, as the national sovereignty of the Jewish people. This is the moral basis from which a political solution to the immediate crisis in the Middle East can be found.

Having Huey's ear made me feel politically powerful in a new way. I had no illusions about the Panthers' role as a revolutionary vanguard. I had become involved with them out of a sense of the exhaustion of the Movement, and with the idea of doing something of immediate benefit for people in the community. I was tired of pouring energy into grand abstractions like "the revolution," and longed to see my efforts lead to practical results. However; for a political intellectual like myself there was a seductive aspect to a partnership with Newton (even in so modest an enterprise) that was also grandiose. Until now, my theorizing had had little visible impact. *Empire and Revolution* I felt had resolved many of the problems that confronted the Left, but the Movement had pretty much ignored what I had written. My working relationship with Newton promised to increase whatever influence my ideas might have. If we were successful as a team, we would create a model that others might follow.

I had one initial setback. The Panthers had a restaurant and bar called Jimmy's Lamp Post, which was owned by a cousin of Huey's named Jimmy Ward. Huey was in the process of transferring ownership from Jimmy to the Party, he explained, because he had put $60,000 into it that had not been paid back, and he wanted Kaldenbach to go over the books. Shortly after I gave the task to Kaldenbach, Huey summoned me to the penthouse. He was visibly upset: Kaldenbach had deposited the account books on the Lamp Post doorstep early that morning, and was taking no calls. I apologized to Huey, and went looking for Kaldenbach, to find out what had happened. When I reached him, he told me that his wife, who was Mexican and hated the Panthers, had given him an ultimatum: "Quit working for the Panthers, or I'm leaving." From then on, I was on my own.

After the incident with Ericka, Huey assigned a Party member, whom I will call Charles, to work with me. He was a soft-spoken military veteran with a college education to whom I took an instant liking. He seemed to get along with me, but—as with everybody else I encountered in the Party—there was something withheld about him. It was as if he was always preselecting his words, fuzzing lines to make whatever he said less committal and less specific than a normal communication. This was especially true when I posed questions about the Party and how it operated. Sometimes, when he would hint at a Party problem that put obstacles in our way, I would say to him: "Tell me what it is and I'll take it to Huey." Charles would get a worried look and reply, "I don't think that would be a good idea." This puzzled me, but something told me that it would be better to let the issue pass.

I had begun to raise money for the Panther school. Huey had shown me a Baptist church that was for sale on East 14th Street in the heart of Oakland's ghetto. It had thirty-five classrooms, a full-service cafeteria, and an auditorium, and was set on a full city block of land. Huey said he was planning to raise the $165,000 necessary to buy it, but after showing me the facility, he made several trips across the country without doing so. I concluded that he was probably not going to. My thought was reinforced by an activist from New York named Marty Kenner, whom I had known since the early Sixties and who was working for the Party. When we discussed the school, Kenner said that he had often seen Huey entertain schemes like this which never came to fruition.

A balding man, younger than I but already owning a paunch, Kenner came from a familiar intellectual region of the Left. He had been involved in the Columbia "uprising" of 1968, and was an indispensable functionary for Huey. It was Kenner who organized the famous Leonard Bernstein party for the Panthers that Tom Wolfe satirized in *Radical Chic*. In an irony I had become used to on the left, where many "revolutionaries" were living off of trust funds from their wealthy parents, Kenner was also a Wall Street investor. He even knew the "King of the Street," Warren Buffet, and got him to call me with a contribution to *Ramparts*. I had no idea who Buffet was, and accepted the $500 gift as if it were hugely generous—ignorant of the fact that he had made billions in the market. Kenner put the Panthers in touch with the left-wing lawyer community in New York, and to manage their assets (mainly houses that Schneider had bought for them) created a company called Stronghold. When the conflict with Eldridge erupted, it was Kenner whom Huey dispatched to European governments in an effort to bar Cleaver's entry, should he attempt to leave Algeria.

Kenner provided me with intelligence about the Party, too. He had warned me that Elaine Brown, one of its rising stars, was "crazy," and even dangerous. After a disagreement, she had accused Kenner of being an agent, and threatened to kill him, before Huey intervened. I knew that Kenner's privileged position as Huey's emissary and adviser gave him an up-close view of the Party reality. The story he told me about Elaine suggested a familiarity with the uglier sides of this reality that was reassuring, since—despite what he knew—he remained an enthusiast. His stories lent substance to Huey's self-presentation as a leader struggling to educate his followers while keeping violence-prone defectors like Cleaver at bay.

It was not just Kenner who provided reassurance. Huey and the Panthers were still resonant symbols of black rebellion, while the reigning intellects of American culture had given Huey an *imprimatur* that was hard to dismiss. Erik Erikson, perhaps the most respected psychologist of the time, had recently invited Huey to coteach a seminar at Yale. They had just coauthored a book, based on the seminar, titled

In Search of Common Ground. The much-admired journalist Murray Kempton had reviewed Huey's autobiography, *Revolutionary Suicide,* on the front page of the *New York Times Book Review,* concluding: "We must hear [Huey] out because we suspect that he comes not as avenger but as healer. Here is the only visible American who has managed to arrive at a Platonic conception of himself...." Kempton also cited the Yale seminar, and compared Huey favorably to Martin Luther and Gandhi, two famous Erikson subjects. Kempton's own book, *The Briar Patch* (about the trial of the New York Panthers— the Party's most violent wing), was reviewed in the *Times* by another respected journalist, Garry Wills, who wrote: "Never, it would seem, have people threatened more and been guilty of less... And in the end there is a sense of the almost incredible ability of men to find dignity in resisting the viciousness of other men—like lifting a 500-pound weight with one hand while stooped under a 1,000-pound weight kept on one's back."

I now undertook to shoulder some of that weight, counting on Kenner, who had entered the inner sanctum of the Party, to help me share the burden of the school. But when I pressed him to move to the West Coast and take over the project, he backed off, saying he was burned out and needed to take care of his personal life. I realized that if I didn't raise the money and set up the school myself, it would not be done. As on so many other occasions in my life, this somehow proved compelling.

I went first to Bert Schneider, who gave me $12,000 to start. With the help of an attorney who had worked for the IRS and was now advising radical groups, I created a tax-exempt foundation, which I named the Educational Opportunities Corporation. Then I passed the hat to a Schneider friend, film director Bob Rafelson, who had won an Academy Award for *Five Easy Pieces.* Rafelson wore welder's glasses, and affected a tough-guy aloofness. When I asked him for money, he replied: "I know this is going for a bayonet school, David." I thought his sense of humor perverse, but he wrote a check for $10,000—adding, "The only reason I'm doing this is so I can tell the head of my kids' private school that I can't give *him* a contribution because I already gave it to the Panthers."

I also asked Marion Rockefeller for money, and took her to the penthouse. Huey was in a hostile mood, and rambled distractedly. "I searched for God in love," he told her at one point, "and had sex seven times in one day, but only skinned my penis." It was an excruciating hour. Afterwards, Marion said she didn't like Huey, but gave me $30,000 for the school, anyway. I eventually raised more than $100,000 and bought the property with a check written on the account of the Educational Opportunities Corporation. It was the largest check I had ever seen, let alone signed. At our meeting, the white Baptist minister who negotiated for the other side asked me for reassurance that the church would not be used for a violent organization like the Black Muslims. I assured him it wouldn't.

When we began the project, Huey promised me the school would not be a Party institution. Our plan, instead, was to make it a working model for Oakland's black population, which would eventually be turned over to the community. I devised a name for the new facility— the Oakland Community Learning Center—and sent Charles off to acquire the necessary permits. With Huey's support I also created a "planning committee" to run the school. Brenda, Charles, and several other Panthers whom Charles proposed for my team, were also appointed to the committee, which met weekly in the penthouse. Among those we recruited was Audrea Jones, the head of the George Jackson Free Clinic, who had been hostile when I first met her, but who turned out to be Charles's girlfriend and was happy now to be on board an important new project.

There were 150 youngsters in the school, almost all of them children of Party members. On his release from jail, Huey had dissolved all the Panther chapters, with the exception of Chicago's—whose leader, Bobby Rush, he did not seem able to control. He called the approximately 200 adult members to Oakland, where they then lived in the communal houses that had been bought by Schneider. Their children needed to be taken care of, so the adults could carry on their Party functions. This was the reason that the entrance age for the school was three, and the schedule went all day long.

I solicited educational expert Herbert Kohl for advice. Kohl helped us devise a curriculum, and made available a program he had developed (University Without Walls), which was able to credential some of the teachers. I also sought advice from a black music teacher in the Berkeley schools, and soon we had a performing jazz band with thirty children, their instruments paid for by the United Airlines Foundation. Imaginative arrangements made it possible for a student who could play only a few notes to be part of the shows. Huey refurbished the school's 400-seat auditorium, and we organized a two-night benefit at which Oscar Brown Jr. performed "The Signifying Monkey" and other tunes he had made popular, and raised several thousand dollars. I began thinking about other elements of the Learning Center that we could create, such as health-care clinics, child-care facilities, and adult education classes.

I was uncomfortable being a white person in so strategic a position, and from the beginning pressed Huey to help me recruit blacks with skills like mine, to replace me. I brought Troy Duster, a black radical sociologist, and several of his colleagues to see Huey. The meeting seemed to go well, but it didn't lead to any ongoing relationship. I took a high-school teacher and neighbor, Joel Clark, to the school, but he also remained aloof. I was relieved when Huey found a black bookkeeper to keep the accounts of the Educational Opportunities Corporation but soon was told she had been fired because her boyfriend was a policeman and had beaten her. To replace her, I hired Betty Van Patter, who had kept the books for us at *Ramparts,* and who was white.

Instead of being a signal to me to be cautious, our failure to recruit black professionals gave rise to feelings of superiority and annoyance. I viewed Troy Duster and his friends as middle-class blacks who, despite their radical politics, had turned their backs on their origins. My friend Joel Clark, who had come from humble circumstances in Louisiana, also seemed more intent on moving up the ladder of bourgeois respectability than working to bring others along with him. My attitude toward the derelictions of these two fit the political perspective that the New Left had developed toward Martin Luther King and other blacks who sought respectability in "white" society. If not exactly "Uncle Toms," they had allowed themselves to be co-opted— lured by the crumbs that the system offered to select members of oppressed groups, while the rest of the community was left behind to starve. Radical blacks like Malcolm X and Huey, on the other hand, had taken on the daunting task of rescuing not just individuals, but the community as a whole.

Even if my new project didn't enhance my standing among black intellectuals, it did increase my cachet in Hollywood. In Los Angeles, I would stay in Schneider's Benedict Canyon home, which had previously belonged to Dean Martin. Schneider lived with his girlfriend, Candice Bergen, the most exquisitely formed human being I had ever seen up close. Later, Bergen wrote an autobiography, *Knock on Wood,* in which she identified Schneider by a pseudonym, "Robin," and described his other side—controlling and infantile—as he heaved TV sets across the room when he didn't get his way. At Schneider's parties Huey and his bodyguard were always a showpiece, and the guests included such stars as Jack Nicholson, Jane Fonda, and Sondra Locke. One of these affairs turned out to be a laughing-gas party which brought out the puritan in me. The guests were supplied with plastic beach toys filled with helium. Producers and actors were rolling around on the floor of Schneider's living room, embracing giant dolphins and Goofy dolls and sucking from their spouts the gas which produced uncontrolled fits of giggling. Everyone else appeared to be having a good time, but I couldn't get past my fear of appearing ridiculous, and didn't participate.

Huey did not indulge, either. Not a party type, he was strangely out of touch with that culture, preferring classical music to soul, and never dancing. At this social gathering he preferred to engage in abstract discussions about the dialectical relationship between the One and the Many, and his concept of "revolutionary suicide." It was almost a minstrel show in reverse as he reveled in the spectacle he had constructed of a black ex-con, spinning late-night theories about Being and non-Being, like a Trappist monk. He pushed these discussions far into the night, until his interlocutors collapsed with weariness. His disquisitions regularly bored Bergen, which drove him to extremes of frustration. One evening I noticed her, clad in a diaphanous nightgown, nod off on the sofa while Huey became ever more anxious as she worked herself toward a state of unconsciousness.

When he had exhausted his other listeners, Huey would turn to me for his final companionship of the evening, and the two of us would talk into the early dawn. Courvoisier (which he called "Vas") in hand, he would sit with me on the terrace by Schneider's pool while everybody else slept, the lights of Los Angeles a flicker below. It would be mostly Huey's monologue, and largely confessional in theme. He regretted that he had left the Party to Eldridge's command; and told me how Eldridge, in adopting the foul language of street thugs, had driven the churchgoing community away from the Party; and revealed how his adventurism had led to the deaths of Bobby Hutton and others. He bemoaned the $5 million that he said the Party had raised from white liberals like Leonard Bernstein and then squandered on bail. As he said this, he stared into the night's vacancy as though calculating all he could have accomplished with the money that was gone.

The more personal elements of Huey's discourse focused on his shortcomings as a leader, and the threats he perceived to his hold on the Party. He was self-conscious about his high-pitched voice, and his weakness as a public speaker. He was bothered by the fact that the Cleaver faction still exerted a strong pull in the ranks among those who were impatient for action. He revealed feelings of jealousy over the popularity in the Party of his old street buddies, David Hilliard and Bobby Seale, whom he regarded as younger siblings but whose public adoration conferred on them a power he could not control. He was convinced that David and his brother June were plotting a *coup* against him, even though David was still in jail. June had been sent on a mission to kill him, he said, but had been unable to go through with it. He had expelled both of them, sending June back to his home in Alabama because of the loyalty he had exhibited, instead of dealing with him more harshly. He described the vote in the "Central Committee" that had ratified these decisions, and his ability to detect those who were secretly against him by whether they hesitated before raising their hands to vote. I could not separate what was real from what was paranoid in his discourse—but I was convinced that Hilliard and the others he expelled were the old gang elements of the Party whom I distrusted and wanted to see gone.

I stayed awake, during these sessions, on the adrenaline I pumped as a result of the confidences he shared and the trust he obviously placed in me. During one, he told me he had been up for three days and nights. I later realized that it was cocaine that fueled these marathons, but at the time, I was innocent of the drug and marveled at his stamina. After Kohl's meeting with Huey in the penthouse, he said to me, as we descended in the elevator, "He was sniffin'." Although Harvard-educated, Kohl habitually employed ghetto diction as a kind of revolutionary credential. I had no idea what he had said. "Huey was sniffin'," he repeated. "He was doin' coke." I didn't believe him—though I did remember Huey's disappearing into the bathroom frequently during the meeting, emerging with tissues to blow his nose. "He had a cold," I replied.

Back in Berkeley, Kohl repeated his comment about the coke to others, and Huey's network of spies reported it back to the penthouse. The network was, in some sense, the Left itself. In the political circles in which Kohl moved, the Panthers still were icons. Many were bound to disbelieve his story, as I did, and regard it as a smear of one of the Movement's heroes. The natural response would be to report the renegade and defend the vanguard. When Huey summoned me to the penthouse and told me, I was as embarrassed, because I had brought Kohl into his inner circle, as I had been about the Kaldenbach affair. He said he would no longer have anything to do with Kohl, but if I considered Kohl's contribution important to the school, I could continue to work with him. It was another vote of confidence.

One reason I had high hopes for the Learning Center was that Oakland had appointed an administrator named Marcus Foster as its first black superintendent of schools. If the Learning Center could teach inner-city children basic skills by utilizing the talents of ordinary community members, as we were already doing, it could become a model center for Oakland. Taking advantage of the Panthers' political reach, we could even mobilize forces in the educational establishment, the media, and the government, in order to replicate its programs nationally.

But on November 6, 1973, Marcus Foster was gunned down in a parking lot behind the Oakland school-district building. The killing was really an execution. Three figures armed with shotguns had stepped out of the darkness to release a hail of cyanide-tipped bullets at the unsuspecting administrator. On the following day, the press received a document identified as "Communique #1" from a group calling itself the Symbionese Liberation Army. The communique contained a "Warrant Order" for Foster's death. It cited an

Oakland school-board proposal for student identification cards designed to cut down the truancy, vandalism, and violence that had plagued the district:

> The vast Black, Chicano, Asian and conscious White Youth communities of the Oakland-Berkeley area understand that this newest extension of police surveillance is patterned after fascist Amerikan tactics of genocide murder and imprisonment practiced by Amerikan-financed puppet governments in Vietnam, the Philippines, Chile and South Africa.

The communiqué concluded with a phrase made popular by Eldridge Cleaver: "Death to the Fascist Insect That Preys Upon the Life of the People."

This military-style message was reminiscent of the "communiqués" that the Weather Underground had issued, declaring "war" on "Amerika." In fact, Bernadine Dohrn, who was still at large, issued a new communiqué offering the SLA moral support for its revolutionary struggle, as did a group calling itself the "Black Liberation Army" that was associated with the Cleaver faction.

A month later, the heiress Patty Hearst was kidnapped from her house in the South Campus area of Berkeley, and the SLA became national news. To ensure the continued safety of their "prisoner of war," the SLA ordered Hearst's father to provide $70 worth of food to all people with welfare cards, food-stamp cards, parole or probation papers, and jail- or release-slips. The final tab was about $4 million. By this time, the SLA's leader, General Field Marshall "Cinque," had been identified as an escaped black prisoner named Donald DeFreeze. The other members of the SLA were white radicals from the Berkeley area.

In response to these events I wrote an unsigned editorial for *Ramparts*, under the title "Terrorism and the Left."

In "executing" Marcus Foster and in making no effort to justify that execution by any doctrine of specific guilt, the SLA assumes the power of life and death over everyone.... It recognizes no authority except its own will, which it identifies with the will of the people in much the same manner that many psychopathic killers claim to be instructed by God. It has killed a defenseless individual whose guilt is not only not proved, but is mainly a fantasy of his executioners. It has committed a crime not only against the individual in question, but against the entire black, brown and Asian communities of Oakland.

My editorial was intended as an intervention in a debate that had developed within the Left. "Do we really believe every Vietnamese village chief cut down by the NLF deserved to die?" asked one New Left activist defending the SLA. "Have we such supreme faith in the Cuban government that we can state categorically its revolutionary firing squads were never aimed in the wrong direction?" I was relieved when Huey condemned the SLA, although I understood that his position was in part inspired by its sympathy for the Cleaver faction.

The episode made me realize that the Left had its own generational problem. The activists who had seized center stage in the revolutionary moment of 1968, and for whom the Weathermen were a radical archetype, were ten years younger than we were, the SLA members probably another five. They had a bigger appetite for violence than we did, and had never heard of the Khrushchev Report. Above all, they had no sense of the abyss over which every revolutionary act was suspended—the fratricide and nihilism ready to erupt from the breakdown of social order and the breakthrough to the other side.

After my editorial appeared, the SLA went on a criminal rampage, robbing banks, kidnapping individuals, and killing a pregnant woman in the course of one of their crimes. Finally, the core of the group (minus Hearst and two others) were trapped in a house in Los Angeles which was surrounded by the FBI and police. When the occupants refused to surrender, a gun battle ensued in which so many rounds were fired into the house that it went up in flames, killing those inside. This prompted pious complaints from radical attorney Leonard Weinglass, who had represented the Chicago conspiracy defendants and who now said that the SLA members had been denied their constitutional right to a trial. It also elicited a letter to *Ramparts* from Yippie leader Stew Albert, accusing my editorial of "giving a green light to the police to murder the SLA." Fearful of reprisals that the SLA might take on my family, I had not signed the editorial. Looking back, I realize that this was the first time in my life I had been afraid of the Left.

My name was not only absent from the editorial, it was missing (along with Peter's) from the *Ramparts* masthead. Once we had started the Rockefeller book, we decided to "retire" from the magazine. This was not a simple task, because there really was no one to replace us. David Kolodney could handle the editorial tasks, but he would be unable to raise the money necessary to sustain the publication. To solve this problem, I assembled a group consisting of Adam Hochschild, Richard Parker, and the writer Paul Jacobs to come on board. Hochschild was both a writer and the scion of a wealthy family, and Parker had the confidence of Stanley Sheinbaum, who could provide additional funding. Unfortunately, my plan didn't work, because the old staff and the new team quickly became embroiled in intractable personal conflicts. As a result, the new trio left the magazine, to found a competitive journal which they called *Mother Jones*. Afterward, as we had predicted, Kolodney was unable to raise money and two years later, (in 1975) *Ramparts* folded.

By the time we left *Ramparts*, Peter and I were well along in the Rockefeller project. I had interviewed nearly a dozen members of "the Cousins" generation, the most important of whom was Nelson's son Steven. Steven drew my attention to the family creed his grandfather, John D. Rockefeller Jr., had engraved in gold on the facade of Rockefeller Center: "I believe that every right implies a responsibility; every opportunity, an obligation; every possession, a duty." This creed obviously put a heavy burden on the bearers of the name, but they read it as having an even more portentous meaning. In the eyes of its members, the family had been given great wealth so that they could use it for the noble purpose of changing the world.

In an odd way, the Rockefellers thus had much in common with the Left, regarding themselves as social missionaries whose task was to uplift humanity. Theirs was a kind of inverted radicalism. They regarded themselves as an anointed vanguard, harassed by those who wanted them to give up the money rather than deploy it "to promote the well-being of mankind," which was the motto of their Foundation. But Steven Rockefeller told me he had reached a point where he no longer believed the family myth. Ceasing to think of Rockefellers as special (or even superior) beings, he had set about constructing for himself an ordinary life. Peter and I called this path "a separate peace." Steven's insight into the family ethos provided us with an organizing theme for our story, and gave me confidence that I could penetrate the family mysteries. The mentality of the social missionary was something I understood.

I had solved the Abby problem by arranging interviews in Cambridge, where she lived, and phoning her when I got there. "Since I'm already here," I said to her, "you surely won't refuse to meet me, even if we don't do an interview." She agreed, and we set a date for dinner. I arrived at her house before she did, and sat down on her front porch to wait. Soon, a broad-shouldered woman dressed in a red Lacoste T-shirt and jeans, with a boyish bob to her hair, bounded up the steps and greeted me. She told me later that she had worn the same T-shirt and jeans every day for a year, as a protest against women's clothing. As we entered the house, she led me under the stairwell. "Do you want to see my *clivus?*" she asked, as I found myself standing in a closet-size room looking into the hole of a toilet seat. This was, she explained, no ordinary toilet but a *clivus multrum,* a Swedish device she had invested in, which turned household refuse—including human wastes—into topsoil. With an ironic smile she told me that it was her "Rockefeller thing," because she saw it, "God help me," as a way to transform the world.

After the awkwardness of this encounter, things began to flow more smoothly. I enjoyed challenging her attempts to prevent me from exercising male prerogatives like opening doors, walking on the street side of the curb, and paying the restaurant bill. To gain a tactical advantage, I yielded on some points, but trumped her over the bill by asking how it would look if a writer doing a book on the Rockefellers allowed one to pay for his dinner. She had an active intellect and was a close observer of human psychologies, which prompted me to suggest that she might help us by providing insights into her family as "background." If later she decided to talk to us on the record, I said, I would allow her to see the text and edit her own remarks. She promised to think about it, but by then I had no doubt that she would.

During a second visit, I invited Abby to come to the West Coast. When she did, I took her to an event at the Panther school, where she was impressed enough to make a contribution. My friend Charles was disappointed that he had not met her. "Introduce me and maybe I'll marry her and become a millionaire," he said. For some reason, this provoked a memory of my father's instructions to me as a child on the evils of capitalism. He had told me that it was impossible for one person to spend a million dollars. It was his way of emphasizing the irrationality of a system that allowed people to accumulate such sums. As with many of the propositions my father instilled, I had never bothered to examine it. On impulse, I decided to test it. "You couldn't even spend a million dollars on yourself," I said. "Oh yes I could," Charles replied, disabusing me of the notion all at once. "To begin with, I'd buy me a Lear jet."

BETTY

T HE EVENT TO WHICH I TOOK ABBY WAS A SUNDAY-MORNING service at the Son of Man Temple, a secular church of Huey's invention housed in the auditorium of the Learning Center. Its "preachers" were the Party's public figures, Bobby Seale and Elaine Brown. Originally, I had asked Huey to keep the Party out of the facility. If we were eventually going to turn the Center over to the East Oakland community, it would not be helpful to make the Party a visible presence. My experiences with Ericka Huggins and Audrea Jones were sufficient to underscore the problems that this could cause in attracting outsiders. I did not want the Party's militant strutting and hectoring attitudes to drive people away. Still, it was clear that they couldn't be totally excluded. Occupying a full city block in the heart of the community, the Center was simply too impressive to deny them access. Huey's solution was to create an arena which Bobby, Elaine, and the others could consider theirs.

The Sunday-morning service was attractive enough. Elaine and Bobby were compelling orators, and they were backed by a choir that sang political songs in a gospel style. But the service allowed me to see how isolated the Party was. The larger East Oakland community was not present. The faces I saw—some eager and enthusiastic, others sullen and bored—were depressingly familiar. There were other signs that were disheartening as well. One day when I came into the auditorium, the band was rehearsing and Brenda was in tears. She did not tell me what was wrong, but I soon learned that she had been replaced by Ericka. I tried to find out why, but even Huey wouldn't give me a straight answer. It was another reminder of how much surrounding the Party remained secret. The rationale for the secrecy was of course the external enemy. But under *this* cloak *anything* could be hidden, the trivial as well as the important, the political as well as the personal (which turned out to be the case with Brenda's firing). There was no way to tell.

I had already concluded that Ericka was a disturbed individual. Along with Bobby Seale, she had been one of the defendants in the Panthers' New Haven trial accused of the torture-murder of a Party member named Alex Rackley. Ericka had been present—nobody disputed this—while Party members poured boiling water over Alex Rackley's chest. What kind of person could do that? One day I came into the school and saw her disciplining a nine-year-old girl in her office. She was instructing the girl to write, one thousand times, "I am privileged to be a student in the Oakland Community Learning Center because...." I began to wonder what I had created.

I had already had a confrontation with Ericka at a planning-committee meeting, over the $25,000 that was left from the money I had raised to buy the school. Ericka wanted to spend the remaining cash on new bunk beds and underwear for the children. I tried to explain to her that the money was capital and could be used to start a new program or finance a new building on the property. Capital was difficult to raise, while money for the items she was proposing would be relatively easy to collect if we made an appeal for that purpose. Ericka glared at me the entire time I was talking. When I was finished, she said: "The children *need* new beds and underwear." Huey sat mutely observing this exchange, making me even more uncomfortable as the unspoken text around the table grew louder and louder: *Who is this white boy telling us we can't spend* our *money on* our *children?* Nothing was actually decided at the meeting, but the beds and underwear were bought.

A session even more intense followed the Malcolm X Day celebration that the Party held at the Son of Man Temple. Huey did not attend the event, whose featured speakers were Elaine and Bobby. "This was an opportunity for us to bring in the whole black community," I said, after we had assembled around Huey's dining-room table. "Instead, one speaker after another got up and proclaimed 'The Black Panther

Party is the only true continuator of the legacy of Malcolm X.' What kind of leadership is that? It's just sectarianism. It's the same problem we have with the school. We're talking to ourselves." My remarks were greeted by a grudging silence. Huey said he would look into it.

After the meeting, Huey took me aside and said he wanted me to meet Elaine. Elaine was living at Mills College, to which he had sentenced her to a kind of Party exile because of a temper that was seldom under control. "I sent her there," he told me, "because I knew she would hate it." Elaine was the one Party member, he added, who could replace him if something happened, but she lacked the discipline to keep her temper in check, and could be needlessly cruel, and those factors worried him.

I met Elaine in her dorm room. She was a striking woman with fine bones, radiant coffee-colored skin, and a toothful smile. Both charming and voluble, she complained about her punishment even while praising Huey as a kind of demigod whose sentence, however onerous it might seem to her, would be seen in the order of things to be indisputably just. At some point in our conversation, she said that Ericka had informed her about the planning committee meeting: "Ericka said you complained that Malcolm X Day was too black."

This information was not transmitted hostilely, but as a confidence, a fact that made me feel the importance and power of my position. I knew Elaine was ingratiating herself with me because she believed I had Huey's confidence, and that the Center was the Party's showpiece. But I was still troubled by the fact that it remained a Party operation: For months I had been unable to affect the course that events were taking. And I was feeling more and more isolated from Huey, who was increasingly unavailable. I would leave messages asking for a meeting, but find myself unable to secure one. Finally, however, I had a positive response to one of my requests. I arrived at the penthouse in the middle of the afternoon and was ushered into Huey's bedroom, where he lay under the covers with a knit watch cap on his head, sweating as though sick. The sight was disconcerting, and made me feel guilty for pressing so hard for the interview. He apologized for being unavailable, and in a distracted way listened to my complaints. Then he assured me, in a gesture without conviction, that he would soon be taking care of things.

At about this time, I discovered that Huey had expelled Bobby Seale from the Party. The details, related to me by Kenner, were bizarre, involving a quarrel over a script that Huey was intent on making into a film. Bobby wanted to play a role Huey had reserved for himself, and compounded the offense by referring to "the Party we started." I was depressed by this development, but there was worse to come. On July 16, Huey was arrested after a scuffle with two policemen at the Fox, an Oakland nightclub. When I was able to talk to him about it, he dismissed the incident as yet another case of police harassment, a payback because he had beaten them in court. At about the same time, a small item in the papers reported that three men with shotguns had driven up to an "after hours" club in Oakland, and killed the doorman. A witness claimed that Huey was one of them.

What did I believe about these incidents? I wanted to believe that the reports were manufactured by the police. I *did* believe that. But I didn't really know the truth. For the first time in my relationship with Huey, I had a sinking sense of doubt. Maybe there *was* an inconceivably dark side to him. But the implications were unthinkable. It would mean taking the enemy's view. The press and the authorities, who were responsible for the reports, wanted to destroy the Panthers and the cause they stood for. To doubt the Panthers was to jeopardize the faith that the Left had placed in them. Even though the era of revolutionary enthusiasm was over, they had remained a symbolic vanguard, the embodiment of black America's revolt against white oppression and the incalculable odds every radical faced. All the hidden forces of American racism made them a target.

Six days after the Fox incident, Huey was arrested for shooting an eighteen-year-old prostitute named Kathleen Smith. The bullet lodged in her jaw, the trauma to her spinal column sending her into a coma. She was in the hospital for three months before dying. When her ordeal finally ended, Huey was charged with murder. But he failed to show for his arraignment, fleeing instead to Cuba, with Schneider's help. At a press conference, the Party's lawyer, Charles Garry, justified the flight, telling reporters that a contract had been taken on Huey's life by local gangsters, and the police would not protect him. There was a half-truth in this. Months before, Schneider had told me that Huey had received a call from Oakland police chief Charles Gain, warning him that there had been a meeting of pimps at a North Berkeley location, and that a $10,000 contract had been taken on his life. Schneider told me that Huey's response to the warning had been to press Gain for a permit to carry a concealed weapon. Schneider chuckled at Huey's *chutzpah* in making the demand. A more important aspect of the story was revealed to me much later: The pimps had taken out the contract on Huey's life because he was shaking them down.

I should have left then. But there was a strain of loyalty in me, an inability to let go of something I had committed myself to, that held me back. The Party and the school I had helped to create were facing their greatest trials since my arrival. It would have been easy for me to leave. At any time, I could have gone back to my "privileged" life and left the Panthers and the East Oakland ghetto behind. But the very ease of my potential exit made taking it impossible. As a white radical, I needed to prove that I was not just a fair-weather friend of blacks, that I would not run when things got tough.

Huey had left Elaine in charge, making me wonder whether he had known he was going to self-destruct months later, when he had asked me to see her. All the images of danger I had associated with her began to surface, particularly when I saw the worried look in Charles's eyes as he told me the news. Ironically, it was Charles who made certain that I would *not* leave—not just then. Elaine had summoned a group from the planning committee, along with Gwen Goodloe (who ran the Party's finances), to discuss her agendas for the Learning Center. I was heartened by her plans to clean and paint the school and make sure it conformed to the health codes. But when I arrived for the second meeting, she confronted me with anger blazing. Charles, Audrea, and the other members of the planning committee were gone. They had left without telling even their intimates in the Party. Elaine directed her anger at Charles, whom she accused of taking a Party car and reneging on a loan she had made to him.

The effect of Elaine's attack was to make me want to prove myself even more. Somehow, she was able to make me feel responsible for Charles, as though the fact that Huey had chosen him to work with me made his actions reflect on my character and political *bona fides*.

The following week, Gwen Goodloe left. This was almost a relief, because I'd had no connection with her in my work. But Elaine was beside herself. Huey had been driven out of the country, the Party was under attack, and—as she put it—the rats were leaving the ship. Now she had no one to run the Party finances, so she turned to me for advice.

After a little hesitation I suggested Betty Van Patter, who was taking care of the books for the school. I liked Betty, a good-looking woman with olive skin and high cheekbones, who, at forty-two, really belonged to another generation. (Her twenty-four-year-old daughter Tammy was sometimes employed by us at *Ramparts* on a part-time basis). But I had some misgivings about my suggestion. Betty seemed conservative, in a generic way which manifested itself in dress and manner different from ours—more "proper" and reserved. I had previously proposed her services to Huey, when Kaldenbach backed out of the Lamp Post project. But, after listening to my description, Huey had said she would not be right for the job. I mentioned this to Elaine, explaining that while Betty was able and politically willing, she could be "overly scrupulous." I recalled how she had complained when we put half the *Ramparts* staff on unemployment, a move she thought immoral. I was additionally puzzled by her harsh view of Kaldenbach and myself, since we were only trying to keep the magazine afloat. But I noted that she had neither quit nor caused us any other problem. Elaine hardly listened, and Betty was hired.

One of the things about Elaine that appealed to me was her grit in taking on an organization like the Panthers, which was dominated by males. In her new regimen, women appeared to be in control. She was constantly drawing attention to this achievement, and I agreed that it was something to be proud of. Yet I had also seen her brutalize female subordinates like her second-in-command—a bright but somber woman named Joan Kelley. By profession a computer programmer, Kelley was nevertheless sweeping and dusting Elaine's apartment one day when I was there. Suddenly, Elaine lit into her for missing some dust on a surface, and continued shouting at her as if she were a servant—or worse. It was the most humiliating episode I had witnessed around the Party, and showed the other side of Elaine's volatile spirit.

A display of temper that I found even more disturbing occurred during a phone call Elaine made in my presence to a public TV reporter named Bill Schechner. After being expelled from the Party, Bobby Seale had disappeared. Now he had contacted Schechner, who was going to interview him on the air. Elaine did not want Bobby airing his side of the story, and was letting Schechner know how she felt. "I will *kill* you, motherfucker," she shrieked into the phone, "if you put Bobby on your show." I was appalled that she would talk to *anyone*, let alone a reporter, like that. But I also discounted the threat as merely blowing off steam. (Schechner didn't, as he admitted later, and Seale did not appear.)

Countering these negative impressions was the way Elaine threw herself into the effort to make the Learning Center a success. Within weeks she had brought in the local community, as I had long wished, and organized a teen dance. Before Charles left, he told me the affair had attracted 500 neighborhood youngsters. But the next one ended in a shooting. "Deacon," a pintsized Party member whose real name was Bruce Washington and whose large teeth flashed when he smiled, was dead. His assailant, a sixteen-year-old from the neighborhood, lay wounded in the hospital. The incident crushed any hopes I still had that we would turn a corner and leave the Panther past behind. There seemed to be no end to the troubles the Party attracted. I called Elaine. When she started to blame the police and even the CIA for what had happened, I felt a door close inside.

Deacon's funeral was held in the auditorium of the Learning Center on a sun-drenched October morning. When I arrived at the school entrance, I encountered the face of the Party that Huey had successfully concealed from me. A group of men were milling on the sidewalk, scrutinizing the arrivals. The closest to me was one Darron Perkins, a fellow who appeared in Elaine's inner circle after Huey left. Like the others, he was wearing pinstripes, a white carnation in the buttonhole, a fedora tilted in Bogart fashion. He looked as though he had stepped out of a gangster film. I had seen Perkins before, but this time the image registered differently. I don't know whether it was seeing him with the others, or just the accumulation of incidents over recent months, but I had a sudden intuition: This is not style; this is *real*. When I went inside, the children and their parents were reassuringly assembled almost as though attending a normal Learning Center event. But in front of the stage, beside the open casket, was an honor guard of blue-shirted Panthers, berets aslant, shotguns held aloft, as in the old days before Huey went to jail. The juxtaposition—children and guns—was jarring, and caused me to shudder.

I felt as if at the bottom of an abyss. Tears streamed down my cheeks, and a strident voice sounded in my brain: *"David, what are you doing here?"* When I left the service, I knew I was never going back.

Over the next two months, the phone rang several times with calls from Elaine. She wanted to know why I had not "been around," and whether I was bailing out because the Party was under attack and things were hard now that Huey was gone, and whether I wasn't just afraid. I attempted to assure her that it was really because of the pressure of my work on the Rockefeller biography, now in its final stages, that I hadn't been around. Another factor was that my wife was going to nursing school and I had to take care of the children. During this time, I also received two calls from Betty Van Patter. In the first, she told me that Elaine was running for the Oakland City Council, and was going to make her the campaign manager. Betty was excited at the prospect. The second was toward the end of November, and she was upset. She needed to talk to Elaine, but was unable to reach her. Could I help? I told her I hadn't seen Elaine for more than a month, since the shooting at the school, and hadn't worked on any Party project since then.

I had warned Betty, at the time I offered her the job, that she should not do anything that made her uncomfortable. I didn't know of any illegal activities which the Party was engaged in, but the possibility was there, and I wanted her to understand that I wasn't asking her to undertake anything she wouldn't normally do. By telling her now that I was no longer involved and referring to the shooting, I was giving her as much of a warning as I felt I safely could. I did not have a good rapport with Betty. I felt her disapproval, but wasn't sure about its source. She was seven years older than I, and more conservative in dress and manner. Perhaps the problem between us was just a matter of style. Perhaps feminism caused her to see me in a harsh light. I just didn't feel I could risk more candor with her.

Moreover, there was nothing concrete that I felt I had to warn her about. I had left the Panther project because I was defeated and depressed. Perkins and the others were menacing to me now, but there was nothing new in their presence. The sense of menace was in my new intuition. I didn't really know what the Panthers were capable of. I had developed a healthy fear of Elaine, but Betty liked her. How could I share my fears, when I knew there was a chance that Betty would disbelieve me and repeat them to Elaine, and that Elaine would regard them as a betrayal? It was safer to leave it all unsaid.

On Tuesday, December 17, 1974, I received a phone call from Betty's daughter. Tammy was worried about her mother, who had gone out Friday night and had not been heard from since. She had called the office at the Educational Opportunities Corporation, but the woman who answered said Betty no longer worked there. Tammy wanted my help in getting information out of the Panthers that might help to locate her mother. A cloud of panic began to mushroom in my stomach. I told Tammy to go to the police, and called the Learning Center myself. Joan Kelley answered and said that Elaine wasn't in. I asked her what had happened to Betty, since she apparently wasn't working there anymore. Joan said that on Thursday (the day before she disappeared), Elaine and Betty had an argument. Elaine became furious and "fired" Betty.

When Elaine called back, I told her that Betty was missing, and asked if Elaine knew anything that would help us to find her. Elaine's response was irritated: She had more important things to think about than Betty Van Patter. She had a Party to run, and five Panthers in jail whom she "had to make bail for." I tried to engage her self-interest. "We *have* to find Betty. Her daughter's gone to the police. The publicity will be bad," I said. Her reply was sharp: "Are you accusing me of a crime, David?" I backed off. "No, Elaine. But she's a white woman and you're running for office, and the press will be all over this." Again my words had no impact. She began to talk about what a trial Betty was for her. How Betty demanded this and that, and didn't appreciate what Elaine had done for her, and how her behavior was bizarre. How Betty wouldn't come in to her office if there was a full moon, or called her at home to tell her a dream she had in which she was Rapunzel locked in a tower and unable to reach her. Soon Elaine had worked herself into a passion. "She went around sticking her nose into everything, asking everybody questions. She knew all our little secrets. *You* told me she could be trusted. Do you know who she worked for before she came to us? The firm has offices in Hong Kong and the Philippines. She was probably working for the CIA."

Then her ire turned toward me, just as I hooked my tape recorder into the phone: "Last time I saw you, David, was at Deacon's funeral and you were so upset, as though it was our fault that Deacon got killed. That's when I said I know what happened to David. When Deacon got killed, he got scared. I'm trying to make a press statement at 10 o'clock in the morning and you call here at nine and ask me about some goddamn missing woman. A hundred thousand motherfuckers have called here and asked about Betty. Do you think anyone called once to say how did Deacon get killed? Nobody cares about Deacon being dead. Now that wasn't nothin'. The dead guy's just a nigger. Betty's daughter is going to the police to investigate Betty being missing. This woman is *missing*, Deacon is *dead*. Did anybody investigate Deacon's death? The nigger gets killed, nobody says a word. Just one white woman leaves, I'm supposed to go do backflips about her."

After she had hung up, I called Schneider and told him what had happened. I said I had written a letter of resignation from the Learning Center board because I had not been consulted about Betty's firing. Schneider tried to calm me. He was concerned about the reaction my letter might trigger, and urged me not to send it. Later I learned from him that Elaine had flown to Los Angeles that same day and begun attacking me as soon as she got off the plane, saying I must be working for the CIA. He had defended me, assuring her that I was just distraught over Betty's disappearance. Later that week, I got a call from Elaine. "David," she said, "I'm your best friend. If you were to be run over by a car or something, I would be very upset, because people would say I did it."

I still didn't allow myself to think that Betty wasn't coming back. I kept hoping there was something we hadn't thought of, some explanation for her disappearance that would point in a direction other than the Panthers. A few days later, there was a knock at my door—a policeman wanted to talk to me. Since my parents were visiting from New York, I asked him if we could step out into the street. It was nighttime, and as we moved into the darkness we were joined by a second officer. They told me that Betty was probably dead, and believed the Panthers had killed her.

I answered, as best I could, the questions the officers put to me, but really didn't know anything specific that could help them with their case. When I returned to the house, my parents asked what had happened. I told them it concerned the Panthers, which seemed to be sufficient. Police inquiring about Panthers were to be expected. The progressive code of silence discouraged any further inquiry. It was better not to know. Protective of *them.* Yet, my mother seemed to suspect something more. I could see the cloud of worry in her eyes, but there was nothing I could say that would allay it.

I sensed that my life had changed, unalterably. *What would I do if the worst turned out to be true?* The great fear behind all my denial, I realized, was that I could not face this possibility. I could no longer sleep without being jolted into consciousness by unwanted thoughts. I had a pressure in my chest that I could not relieve, and a panic that was never absent, no matter the time of day. The events of the past week constantly churned in my mind as I tried to piece together the evidence I had been given, in order to make it come out all right.

Tammy had kept herself abreast of the police investigation. Her radical politics would not allow her to suspect the Panthers, but in talking to the police, she had learned details that pointed inexorably in their direction. Betty had last been seen at The Berkeley Square, a bar she frequented on University Avenue. Several customers remembered that a black man, whom she seemed to know, came in and handed her a note. Around 9:30 P.M. she left the bar by herself, and was not reported seen again. There were other details. Betty had taken no money or clothes with her from home, and she had left her birth-control pills behind—so it seemed clear that she had not intended to stay out, or take a trip. The police had contacted her small circle of friends, and none of them had seen her in more than a week. They had checked the motels and hotels up and down the state and elsewhere, and she hadn't been in any of them. The only encouraging sign was that she hadn't turned up in any morgue, either.

My distraught mind worked over these facts in the compulsive rhythms of a nightmare. The appearance of the black messenger with the note, whom Betty seemed to recognize, indicated that an organization was involved. What could it be, other than the Panthers? Elaine's reactions when I called her—her lack of interest in helping to find Betty, and her attacks on the missing woman and myself—were not the responses of an innocent person. I knew how the Party worked. I knew that if the Panthers were involved, it was Elaine who had given the order.

I decided to take a step I would never have considered before. I sought out the friendlier of the two officers, with the intention of telling him everything I knew. Perhaps there was still time to save Betty's life. In my radical cosmos, the police had always been the enemy. They were the guardians of the *status quo* and the persecutors of our vanguards. I was about to step over an invisible line that had never seemed possible to cross. There was also—I couldn't forget—real danger for me if Elaine were to find out about this move.

The meeting with the detective, whose name was Michael O'Keefe, turned out to be more an education for me than an occasion to provide information for him. I related what I considered the relevant facts about the Party. I told him that some of its individuals seemed to have been drawn by its political ideals, and to be law-abiding citizens. Others seemed to have gravitated to it because they had no real home. I called them "waifs," and thought of them as well-meaning, and probably incapable of harm. But there were some I had recently become acquainted with, like Perkins, who had an air of menace about them and who definitely were capable, I felt, of criminal acts. I told O'Keefe that I had witnessed Elaine make threats of violence against individuals, and that after my phone conversation with her I felt she could have killed Betty.

In exchange, I learned from O'Keefe how difficult it was for an individual to kidnap a victim, or even hold one for any length of time, and not be noticed. I learned how difficult it was to dispose of a body, which proved to be one of the greatest obstacles to a successful homicide. I learned that an organized gang in possession of "safe houses," and with members who did not need to interface with the outside world, was well equipped to accomplish such acts.

On January 17, 1975, a month after Betty disappeared, her corpse was found at the far end of San Francisco Bay. Her head had been caved in by a heavy instrument. The police estimated that she had been in the water for two weeks. Although the story was a front-page item in the Berkeley and Oakland papers, and despite the Left's belief that there was a repressive atmosphere surrounding the Panthers, little was made of it all. Nor did the fact that she had been employed by a Panther front increase press interest. No suspicions were raised about the Panthers, or any role they might have played, and there were no repercussions for Elaine's candidacy for the city council. The story disappeared the next day.

By now, I was in a state of internal free-fall. In my entire life I had never experienced a blacker night. I had no idea of how I was going to face the days to come. Betty's funeral was to take place at a little cemetery in Richmond, and I resolved to tell her daughter what I had come to believe. I arranged to pick Tammy up and drive her to the burial site. It was a small affair, attended by people from *Ramparts* and a few family members. Betty's aging mother was there with Betty's ex-husband and his new wife. Tammy's brother Ray, who was 23, played a guitar but seemed to want to be anywhere else than at his mother's graveside. Her youngest brother, Greg, who was 18, was also present. Unlike Tammy, he was not political, and had no sympathies for the Panthers. He had dropped out of school and become familiar with the Oakland streets, where Huey Newton had a different reputation than he had among white radicals. Greg had warned his mother that the Party was a dangerous gang, but she ignored the warnings, dismissing them as politically biased. Since Betty's disappearance, Greg had been telling anyone who would listen that the Panthers were responsible for his mother's death.

When Tammy got in my van, I braced myself to deliver the words I felt I had to say to her. My chest was aching, and my throat was so filled up with tears that I could hardly talk. "From everything I know," I finally said, "I think the Panthers killed your mother." For what seemed a long time, I couldn't raise my eyes or look in her direction.

But then I heard her say, "The Panthers are good people." When at last I did look, I could see that she didn't believe me.

PART 6

PRIVATE INVESTIGATIONS

(1975–1980)

The dream is over...

—JOHN LENNON

QUESTIONS

I N SLEEP, THE BODY RELAXES AND TAKES DOWN THE MIND'S DEFENSES, making the early hours of the morning the most dangerous. In the unguarded dream state, repressed memories and unbearable thoughts come streaming to the surface, flooding consciousness with unwanted truth. Every day in the spring after Betty's death, tears would well uncontrollably in my eyes and blades of pain spike at my chest, as morning approached, until I would bolt awake in a futile effort to escape the visions of my broken life.

Before the police retrieved Betty's corpse, I was able to rescue myself from the darkest of these thoughts by conjuring explanations of her disappearance that were benign. Perhaps she had been distressed after Elaine's abuse, and just run off (it didn't even occur to me how improbable this was). Perhaps she had taken a trip with a friend. But why, then, hadn't she brought along her birth-control pills or credit cards? Perhaps someone besides the Panthers had abducted her, and would soon be apprehended. In truth, in every synapse of my being I felt that the worst had already occurred. But I made these desperate efforts to deny that, continuing to construct a future in which either Betty would turn up safe, or (if not) the Panthers would be found blameless, so that I could go back to my former life.

These speculations had a perverse effect. As I rehearsed the facts again and again, I was forced to eliminate each of the possibilities, until I came face-to-face with the realization that Betty was dead, and it was the Panthers who had killed her. When her body finally turned up and the future was no longer unknown, I was forced to confront myself in a way I never had to before. Every escape route I could look to had closed; every act I had committed was irrevocable. Everything now appeared before me in a pitiless, unrelenting light.

In retrospect, I see that I did not have to look at myself, or the past, this way. I could have continued my denial. I could have said: "This event was avoidable, a contingent fact of my existence. It was no more related to who I am than if a car had hit me from behind." If I *had* taken such a view, my life might have gone on pretty much as before, the way the lives of other radicals did who knew about Betty's death. Or deaths like Betty's. But, for me, this was not a possibility. Something in me *wanted* to look. I needed to know.

Perhaps it was irony that impelled me. I had fallen into a trap that my entire political life had been an effort to avoid. The skepticism I had maintained toward political dogmas, and my reluctance to join political vanguards, had sprung from a single desire: I *wanted to escape my parents' fate.* Their political ideals had embarrassed them, making them complicit in others' crimes. I had resolved that I would not repeat their mistake. Now I was guilty myself.

I had to understand my relation to this deed, this murder of inno-cence, committed by my political comrades. Everything I had believed in and worked for, every effort to ally myself with what was virtuous and right, had ultimately led to my involvement with the Panthers, and the invitation to Betty to take the job that killed her. Others on the left may privately have held reservations about the Panthers. But no one on the left—*no one*—had dissociated themselves from the Panther cause. No one had publicly said: "These are criminals. These are dangerous people, and to be avoided." There was a reason for this reticence. It would have meant saying, "The police are right, and deserve our support. We have been wrong." Everyone who identified with the Left understood, for the record, that the Panthers were *of* us and *for* us. Because they had been made the symbol of the revolu-tion, they could not be condemned without negative consequences for everything we stood for and had said. If there was anything at all that I now had to understand about my political commitments and myself, it was how this had happened; how we—how I—had arrived at this point; the steps that had brought me to the brink of this abyss.

Before the police found Betty's corpse, the nightmare of my mornings had been absorbed in visions of a possible future that would bring me release. Now my mind was filled with images of a past that could not be reversed. What had I seen, yet somehow forgotten? What should I have noticed before that might have saved Betty, but did not?

As soon as I was able to focus my thoughts in this way, reading back from the event, images I had buried began to resurface. I recalled Charles's strangely evasive responses during the days when we worked on the Learning Center together. I remembered his words when I urged him to take a problem to Huey, convinced that the leader would provide a solution. "You don't know, David," Charles would say, a worried look darkening his brow. "You just don't know." Why had I ignored these warnings? Or the alarm sounded in Eldridge Cleaver's attacks? Did I think that just because Cleaver had his own agendas, he had made everything up?

Now I resurrected images of the shadowy figures I had noticed around Elaine, even before Deacon's funeral. I recalled the newspaper account I had seen and dismissed of Huey's drive-by shooting. I remembered the reactions of Troy Duster and the black intellectuals who accompanied him to the penthouse meeting, their friendliness and offers of support in Huey's living room, and their silence and distance after they had left. They *knew.* That was why there had been no follow-up. *It was too dangerous to get close.* When I told my neighbor Joel Clark what I suspected about Betty's death, he shrugged and recalled what Dick Gregory, the black comedian and activist, had said after meeting with Huey and Eldridge: "They're thugs." *He knew.* Anger welled inside me. Why hadn't Joel said anything before? Why hadn't Charles? Or Troy? Why hadn't they warned me? The answer was clear: They did not want to be accused of betraying the Left. But there was another factor as well: They saw that I was blind, and therefore dangerous to trust.

This principle of silence now ruled me, as well. Except for those closest, I could not tell anyone what had happened—especially my friends on the left. I suddenly realized that it was *they* who were the greatest danger to my safety. If I were to tell *any* of them what I thought—that the Panthers had killed Betty—I would have been disbelieved at first, and then suspect. Why would I even suggest such an idea unless I regarded the Panthers as enemies, or intended them harm? And not only them, but the cause as well. And why would I do that unless I had been infected by racism, or joined the other side? Even if I was willing to risk these charges, there were greater dangers involved in the accusation. What if they discussed it with someone else on the left, who then leaked it to the Panthers? Would Elaine make good on her threat?

While I was wrestling with these issues, Bert Schneider called and asked me to meet him in Big Sur. I had not talked to him since my attempt to resign from the Learning Center board. I guessed that his real reason for wanting me to come was to see how I was reacting to Betty's death. As a meeting place, he had chosen a resort called Ventana, which belonged to one of his friends.

I still looked to Schneider as a worldly figure who might know what to do in a situation like this. My first impulse—as though I had learned nothing from my experience—was to confide in him and tell him my suspicions. If he did not realize who the Panthers were, he might be in danger himself. But, driving down Highway 101 and fighting back the tears (which seemed to be always with me), I began to have doubts about showing him my real feelings. To do so might put me at risk. *He must have known.* He was too close to Huey, and had been too calm about what happened, not to. A more disturbing thought surfaced: What if he had known they were holding Betty before she was killed?

The Ventana resort was a cluster of pine bungalows nestled among the sloping cliffs of Big Sur, above the cloud level. I found myself sitting nervously, in my street clothes, by the outdoor pool. Schneider was in his bathing suit, reclining languidly on a deck chair in the sun. Deception had never come easily to me and, as our conversation began, I worried about my response, were he to ask me directly about Betty's death. But he seemed willing to leave the matter unaddressed, testing my reactions (or so I imagined) with questions that were indirect, as though he did not want me to be aware of his interest.

He asked me perfunctorily about the school, and lapsed into silence. Then, tilting his face to catch the sun at a new angle, he made an abrupt shift: "What do you think the prospects for revolution are now?" His manner was offhand and casual, but the question tapped my inner fears. Since Betty's death, I had not been able to think without bitterness about the cause that had animated my life. I did not want Schneider to see this mood, fearing it might indicate I was a danger to the Panthers—and to him.

I began responding to his question as vaguely as I could, reviewing the global conflict in a way that would conceal the extent of my despair. I worked off the theme that America was about to lose its war in Vietnam, a loss that would encourage other revolutions in the Third World. In saying this, I did not reveal to him the considerations I had begun to formulate—that, even if this scenario were to prove correct, those revolutions might be led by vanguards like the Panthers, from whom no good could come. Laying out these optimistic predictions, I was sure my voice betrayed me as it faltered and cracked when I couldn't summon the energy to make it sound normal.

But Schneider seemed not to notice. Midway through my little speech, I saw his eyes wander off into the middle distance, as if he had stopped listening. "What are you thinking about?" I asked. "I was wondering," he answered, "whether to go first into the sauna and then the hot tub and then the pool, or first into the pool and then the sauna and the hot tub."

Six months had elapsed, and I was still in the dark about most of the events that had derailed my life. The interview with Schneider had ended without resolving my questions. It also failed to provide new insight into the people with whom I had so imprudently entangled my fate. But the meeting had confirmed one critical fact that was beginning to overwhelm all others: *No one cared.* Even though I was suspicious of Schneider, I still hoped that he didn't know, and was still my ally. But his demeanor showed something else entirely. I was shocked that he wasn't interested in Betty's death, or the possibility that the Panthers might have killed her.

Until now, my political comrades had felt like family I could trust. We had all been recruited from the same tribe of sentiment, raging with common indignation over the injustices we perceived, and sharing visions of a retribution that would make things right.

Schneider was one of us. But a mother of three, who was also one of us, had been murdered by people we knew. And he didn't care.

Even before I went to see Schneider, I already had a powerful sense of how isolated I was in my fear and grief. Betty had worked for *Ramparts,* and her daughter Tamara was on the staff at *Mother Jones*—making them both familiar figures in the Bay Area left. The Panthers were an integral part of this community, drawing on its members for political and financial support alike. There were dozens, if not hundreds, of activists with direct links to the Party and its membership—including many with high public visibility, like Hayden and Scheer—who were aware of what had happened to Betty. Yet no one came forward. No one raised even a general question in public about the unsolved murder, or the Panthers' possible involvement in it, or asked why the investigation had been so perfunctory and inept.

This silence was more than unusual for people who normally felt compelled to protest injustices—even those that took place at the far ends of the earth. In the past, they hadn't hesitated to identify good and evil in regions they could hardly locate on a map. Or to express indignation in cases beset with the deepest ambiguities, if only the political symbolism was right. Newton's own case had been a prime example. A convicted felon with a history of violent crimes had built a paramilitary organization dedicated to opposing police. He had been quoted in the *New York Times* saying that he was prepared to kill cops if he thought that necessary. Shortly afterwards, an officer had been shot trying to arrest him. At his trial, the chief prosecution witness was a black bus driver who had pulled up to the crime scene, catching the perpetrator in his headlights as he fired the fatal shot. Yet the Left easily convinced itself that Newton was innocent—that the police had suborned the witness and framed the suspect. Radicals poured into the streets to demand Huey's release.

There were no protests for Betty. No one called for an investigation. Not a single article appeared in the left-wing press to suggest that there might be a connection between the Panthers and Betty's death. Nobody suggested that the authorities might try harder to discover who had killed their comrade. There was only silence. A political activist working for the Black Panther Party had been murdered, but because the suspects were the Panthers themselves, it didn't matter.

The incident had no usable political meaning, and was therefore best forgotten.

I spoke to some of my close friends who were concerned about me and seemed genuinely saddened by Betty's death. But their questions quickly showed that they were equally concerned about the Panthers, and even more about the political impact of what I might reveal. On their scales of right and wrong, the Panthers' "social contribution" far outweighed any individual's fate. If they were willing to consider the possibility of Panther guilt, they were just as certain that the crime had been provoked by government pressure. The *real* guilty party was the unjust System that had *forced* the Panthers to be who they were.

If even my friends reacted this way, who on the left wouldn't? More disturbing yet was how invisible Betty had become. No matter how hard I tried now to bring her to life, I could not make them see her enough to care. Perhaps the thought entered their minds that she was an "agent," as Elaine had charged, or for some other reason deserved her fate. The Panthers, on the other hand, were a vivid presence, their histories and persecutions all too familiar to them as social progressives. And because their sense of themselves was tied to the Panther cause, they felt that any blot on the Party would reflect badly on them, too.

I began to think about murder cases that were not even political. From the moment of an arrest, the focus of public attention was always on the accused—whether he was innocent, what circumstances had led to the crime, what suffering *he* had to endure because of the events. The accused remained always the central character of the drama—the one in the spotlight, constantly tugging at the spectators' emotions—while the victim was absent from the theater itself. Who even remembered Officer Frey, the 26-year-old cop that Newton had shot in the back? Or his widow and child? The three trials that Newton went through after the shooting were showcases of *his* life, *his* torments, *his* travails. Who could even name the prostitute he had killed? Like Betty, Kathleen Smith was invisible and forgotten. It was Huey who would always be center stage.

The one friend I confided in who shared my anguish was my partner, Peter. He had stood back when I became involved with the Panther projects, although he did give some money to a Christmas fund I created for the children. His view of Newton and Seale had grown sour even before the events. He would refer derisively to Seale as Newton's "Stepin Fetchit," which caused me an internal wince. He was resentful of the time I took from the Rockefeller book to devote to the Panther cause. Yet, in this crisis, he rallied to me like a brother.

Because I had been so close to the Panthers, any move I made to contact the police or the press would be regarded as a betrayal, and therefore dangerous to me. Understanding this, Peter agreed to see if he could get the press to take an interest in the case. He went to Marilyn Baker, a Pulitzer Prize-winning reporter who was the anchorwoman for KPIX-TV's local news. But Baker told him she wouldn't touch the story unless black reporters did so first, and they wouldn't. He went to the police, who told him: "You guys have been cutting our balls off for the last ten years. You destroy the police and then you expect them to solve the murders of your friends."

No one cared. The faith I had when I was ten years old was an illusion. There was *no* authority to appeal to, *no one* to bring justice and make things right. Betty and her children were finally and brutally alone.

At the end of June, I received a phone call from Carol Pasternak, my Sunnyside comrade in the Young Progressives. She had called to tell me that our friend Ellen Sparer had been raped and strangled by a black youth in her Englewood, New Jersey home. Coming after Betty's death, this information threw me into a new level of depression. I could think of nothing else for a long time.

I had last seen Ellen at her wedding, fifteen years before, when I was still a student at Columbia. Our friends were critical of the couple. They thought Ellen had married "down" because her groom, a schoolteacher, not only wasn't political, but also was the less powerful of the two. In the intervening years, Ellen had drawn close to—and perhaps even joined—the Communist Party. Yet I still felt a powerful affinity for her, which made her death even harder. Like me, she was driven by a missionary zeal, willing to cross boundaries and take chances that others would not. Ever since I had printed her poem about Willie McGee in the *SYP Reporter,* I felt a bond between us. This connection was strengthened by the fact that Ellen had at one time helped the Black Panthers—a move which had become a source of tension with her husband, who was particularly concerned for the safety of their three small children. After Ellen's murder, he told me that she had invited political activists and ex-prisoners to the house who seemed to have a potential for violence. These and other conflicts had led to the divorce, so that Ellen was alone in her home with her children when she was killed.

After moving to Englewood, an integrated community, Ellen had become a math teacher at the local high school. At the time of her death, she was praised by her superiors as an outstanding teacher whose dedication to her students, and especially the disadvantaged ones, was extraordinary. She told Carol that her talents would be "wasted teaching bright kids."

At the time of the murder, Carol gave a statement to the *New York Times* reporter who came to cover the case. She said that Ellen had left her house unlocked regularly until a rapist began plaguing women in the neighborhood, "and then we had to tell her to lock her door." Carol summed up her feelings for the *Times'* reporter with this remark: "That something so senseless and brutal should happen to Ellen is the ultimate irony, because it was the antithesis of everything in her life." Before Betty's death, I might have accepted this judgment or passed it over. But it was impossible for me to do so now.

A few months after the murder, I went to Englewood to see Carol and her husband, to share their grief and unburden my own. They introduced me to Ellen's boyfriend, a large and gentle black man named Mel. After I had returned to California, Carol sent me a letter about Ellen, in which she described their relationship:

January 19, 1976

Mel brought humor (which Ellen did lack, though she had a sense of fun) into Ellen's life, and although in some ways he also fit the pattern of lost souls that she helped, he gave her a great deal in return, unlike many of the others who just took. Mel is a bright, sensitive, complicated, funny guy—who also happens to have a dependent personality which Ellen zeroed in on and used to trap him—i.e., he could never fully commit himself, but neither could he leave that good food and good mothering. Ellen wanted to be mother to the world, mother to the revolution, and I think her strongest wish was to mother a black child. Some people said they felt Ellen's kids were sorry they weren't black—I don't know about that, but I do know that [Ellen's daughter] said Mel wouldn't marry Ellen because Ellen wasn't black.

Mel and I had dinner at a little Mexican restaurant in Manhattan, and I told him my story: how I had become involved with the Panthers and had not really known who they were; how this blindness had led to Betty's death. Although I had not seen Ellen for years, I told him, I felt a kinship with her—with her heedless determination to do good, her missionary impulse to rescue others, and her obliviousness to the gravitational pulls that worked against such heroics. Mel acknowledged the truth of my intuitions. He observed that Ellen never locked her front door, and thought she had left it open that night, although her daughter later said she herself had taken care to lock it. He told me he was regretful because he had spent the night in his own apartment in New York, to be ready for a dentist appointment the next morning. He had offered to leave his pet German Shepherd with her as a watchdog, but she had refused the offer saying that the dog scared the neighborhood kids who came to the door. He returned to the point more than once. Her refusal had been long-standing. She would not allow him to leave the Shepherd on nights when he was away, and would not reconsider her decision because of the neighborhood kids. On the night of the murder, she had refused for the last time. It was typical of her, he reiterated, to disregard the dangers that surrounded her.

I was obsessed with these details about Ellen. Since Betty's murder, there was no more important task, in my mind, than to establish the connection between who we were as radicals and what had happened to us. I told Carol how I both identified with Ellen, and knew in my bones that her death was linked to the view of the world we had taken in with our mother's milk. Carol was not persuaded. A psychiatric social worker by training, she was willing to entertain the idea, but as a radical she could not accept the connection. She expressed her thoughts in the letter she sent:

At first some of us thought we could tie Ellen's death in some way to the overall pattern of her life, and thus come up with something neat and tidy which would thus help us feel less helpless and despairing. It was not hard to imagine, because Ellen did take risks that most of us would never take (physical, like setting out on impossible bike trips, or canoe trips with an infant in the canoe, leaving the kids alone, having the two older ones—perhaps 8 & 9 years old—put the 2 year old on his bus to the day care center after she had already left for work, etc.) Or political risks—like revealing to the Queens College newspaper, in the middle of the student rebellion, that the chairman of the math department had made racist statements to her. That not only led to the guy's resignation shortly thereafter, it also ultimately led to the loss of her job—because once the Black and Puerto Rican Coalition came into power, they did not want any troublemakers around to disturb their comfortable sinecures!

It is also true that she befriended and succored all the sad, lonely, dependent souls with whom she came in contact—black and white, male and female. She was a sucker for a good sob story, and as I think I told you did end up losing over $1,000 by twice co-signing a loan for one of her [black] students. [The money, Carol told me, was for an abortion]. She also, I believe I mentioned, came close to losing her job when one of her outraged neighbors went to the principal to complain that Ellen had abetted her daughter's flight from home. The kid was indeed very disturbed and did have a rotten relationship with her mother, with which Ellen got caught up by way of fantasies of rescuing the kid. Rescue fantasies are pretty common, after all, but Ellen was an action person and didn't believe in just sitting around and fantasizing when there was work to be done.

Carol even went so far as to imagine that the murderer might be one of the many dependent objects of Ellen's efforts: "Most importantly, she made herself personally available to the kids at all times, opened her home to them, answered questions about the homework while stirring supper, etc. From my point of view this made it quite possible that some very crazy kid misinterpreted her intentions and killed her out of sheer craziness." But having come this far, Carol was unable to take the final step:

> However, and this gets to the point which I tried to start with, what we now know suggests that her killer was not connected to her in any personal way, but is an extremely brutal young man whose motives are robbery and rape, and he may have killed her simply because she was not able to produce any money. Ellen was usually broke, in debt. She used to keep her cash in Gorky's Mother (her favorite book—she read it to her kids), and apparently that book was not in its usual place when Mel finally got back into the bedroom after the police finished their investigation.

Nearly a year after the tragedy, the police apprehended Ellen's killer, who had raped and murdered other women, including a 60-year-old black schoolteacher he kidnapped in October. As it turned out, the killer, a 16-year-old who acted out of psychotic motives, was one of the disadvantaged youngsters Ellen had tried to help.

Carol had concluded that Ellen's radical outlook had nothing to do with her death. If it hadn't been for a series of circumstances beyond her control, she would have escaped the fate that befell her. My view was just the opposite: Given who she was and how she approached the world, I felt she was fortunate to have avoided her fate as long as she had. A similar idea about myself had entered my mind: Given what I had done and with whom I had become involved, I was lucky to be alive.

Our dispute was a reflection of the new way I was beginning to look at the world. It was the first sign of an attitude that would alter my perspective, change my politics, and separate me from the community of my childhood forever. When I had completed the change a decade later, Carol and I would clash again over our differing interpretations of Ellen's death, in a disagreement that would end our 40-year friendship.

It now seemed obvious to me that both Ellen and I were destined to some kind of grief. We hadn't understood the way in which our good intentions could be dangerous, either to us or to others. It was as if there was a flaw in our DNA that deprived us of sensors that would have provided warnings. Of course, we understood that we were taking risks. But they were risks we could predict (like persecution by our enemies, the defenders of injustice), which were ennobling and therefore welcome. There were also necessary risks which came from misunderstanding, because the help we brought was coming from the camp of privilege and the white-skinned oppressor. But we were sure that once our good intentions were understood by the objects of our mission, such dangers would vanish.

Thinking this way blinded us to signs that might have saved us. We thought of ourselves as self-effacing, but in fact we were arrogant. We regarded ourselves as better than others from our privileged caste who were unwilling to perform the deeds we did. That was why we didn't listen and couldn't see. Like all radicals, we were intoxicated by our own virtue.

Ellen's character appeared to me with greater clarity than I was yet able to achieve about myself. She was, as Carol had said, a rescuer. She mistook poor people, who lacked her intelligence and seemed in need of her help, for her children. They were mirror reflections of herself, deficient only in the political understanding and resources she could easily supply. The trouble they found themselves in was the result of their social condition, which was external to them. To her, these people were the *objects* of their histories, while she was the *subject* of hers. What she failed to appreciate was their power to be subjects, too—with desires and agendas of their own.

About a year after Betty's death, I received a call from my Panther friend Charles, who had left when Elaine took over. Charles did not want to talk on the phone, so I arranged to travel east to see him and the others who had left. I met with each, separately, in the different states to which they had relocated, and then talked to them afterwards on the phone at intervals of several months. Each time I made contact, I was looking for only a small piece of the puzzle. I knew I could not get the story whole, and understood their continuing caution in not being ready to provide it.

In my new career as a biographer, I had learned the techniques of getting information out of people who were reluctant to provide it. There were levels of knowledge you had to penetrate, and degrees of complicity you had to establish, before you could get access to facts that someone preferred to hide. Knowledge itself was a form of complicity. If you could acquire a single piece of information at the next level, often the subjects would conclude that you were familiar with other, similar facts. Consequently, they would consider themselves less guilty of a breach of confidence in talking about them. As a result, a new detail might slip inadvertently, providing you with the key to information at a deeper level—and so on. The very fact that I knew Elaine was capable of murder (and was willing to say so) dramatically changed the way in which those who knew better than I, and had previously withheld their knowledge, were willing to talk to me.

Charles's group of exiles had left out of fear of both Elaine and—as I would soon learn—the Squad, which Elaine controlled. They could not reveal their fear to me before they left, because they could not trust me to believe it and protect them. But Betty's death had changed that. I had entered the circle of their reality, and could be told truths about the Party that I could not have been told (and would not have believed) before. Although even now they were cautious enough to hold back a great deal, I still was able to pick up a piece of information in one place and use it to elicit a different piece somewhere else, until I had enough to put together a reasonable picture of the whole.

Inside the Party, Huey had created the group of enforcers he called the Squad. It included Perkins, Big Bob, "Deacon" (the man killed at the Learning Center dance), and others I was familiar with, like Larry Henson and Flores Forbes. Big Bob had been recruited to the Party in Boston, where he came under the aegis of Audrea Jones, the chapter's leader. It was Audrea who told me that Boston was one of the more political Panther chapters. When the Party first gained national attention, she said, some chapters were rapidly formed just a short time after activists posted signs saying "Off the Pig." "Brothers" came right in off the street to join. When he stepped in to sign up, Bob told Audrea: "I'm so big, there's nothing I can *do* but be a criminal." She put him to work writing leaflets. However, after Newton was released from jail, and had dissolved the chapters and summoned the members to Oakland, he watched Big Bob step off a plane and noted his dimensions. Immediately, Newton took Big Bob aside, outfitted him in pinstripes, and assigned him to the Squad.

The Squad was Newton's personal gang. He used it to intimidate Party members, who were subject to beatings with bullwhips and chains for disciplinary infractions. It was also available for his personal vendettas and criminal ventures, accompanying him on the drive-by shootings at the "after hours" clubs. Squad members often acted out of their own sadistic impulses as well, so that no one was safe from their terror. When one of them was inadvertently insulted by the vice president of the Black Students Union at Grove Street College, the Squad retaliated by executing the offender. The murder was never prosecuted. After Betty's death, Big Bob confided to one of the exiles that, in the three years he had been in Oakland, the Squad had killed a dozen people. Betty, he said, was one of them.

The Panther exiles also knew that Newton had killed Officer Frey and Kathleen Smith. He had used a little silver pistol, concealed in his shirt, for the Smith murder. After shooting Smith, he stopped briefly on the Bay Bridge, to drop the pistol into the water. He then was driven to the Zen Center in Marin, whose guru, Roshi Baker, gave him refuge. From there, he went to Schneider's house in Beverly Hills. Later on, a film director who had been present at Schneider's described the scene to me: "Huey was sitting on Bert's couch, shoving drugs up his nose and sniveling: 'Get me more coke. I want some pussy.' He whined that it was the first time he had killed someone for reasons that were 'non-political'—which was typical Huey bullshit."

I also learned, later on, why Brenda was in tears when I last saw her at the Learning Center. In a gesture to revolutionary theory, the Party frowned on marriages. *All* the women in the Party were to be available for Newton's pleasure. He had merely to summon any of them—which he did, sometimes several at a time. Brenda had been secretly married to Newton's bodyguard, and when she found herself in Newton's bed, she told him about her marriage. Newton wanted her to tell her husband about their affair, because he felt it would be dangerous for his bodyguard to discover the relationship behind his back. When Brenda refused, Newton arranged to have her husband summoned to the penthouse when he and Brenda were in bed. The discovery wrecked the marriage, and ended her husband's career as Newton's bodyguard, as well as her own at the school.

Another disturbing revelation concerned the school benefit night, starring Oscar Brown Jr. Afterward, a group had been invited to the penthouse, to snort cocaine. When a dealer was summoned to replenish the supply, Newton gave him $3,000 in cash—the entire proceeds of the benefit. Brown was distressed by this transaction and began to protest, but was silenced when Newton grabbed him by the throat and threatened to throw him off the balcony to the street, twenty-five floors below.

I was also told that at the time Newton came out of jail and began making speeches about putting away the gun and serving the people, he was announcing privately to his inner circle—which included my informant—that he intended to control everything illegal in Oakland. That was what the shootings at the "after hours" clubs were about, and why the pimps had taken out a contract on his life.

Who *was* this man I had served at such great cost? I began to rethink every thought I had ever had about him. It occurred to me that the word "bad," used by the Panthers as a term of praise, was something more than merely a colorful slang for "good," as I had assumed. It also meant *bad*—as in having the balls to do what is truly evil. Like murder.

All along, Newton had provided me with clues to his dark side, but I had ignored them. I recalled an evening at the penthouse, where I had asked for a private meeting to tell him my concerns about the school. When I had said my piece, he went over to the quadraphonic stereo that Schneider had given him, and turned up the volume. It was a self-dramatizing gesture to indicate that he was about to tell me something he didn't want the FBI to hear, since he was sure they had bugged the room. When the music was loud enough, he launched into an analysis of *Dillinger*, a recent film about the famous gangster. He called my attention to a scene in which a kid asks Dillinger for his autograph, and then one in which Dillinger looks across the Mexican border to certain freedom—but instead turns around and goes back to his doom. Escape, Newton observed, would have meant obscurity, giving up the important life he had created for himself. And then he drew the parallel to himself: "When I was young, I wanted to be a revolutionary or a bank robber," he said. "If I can't be a revolutionary, I'll be a robber."

Not yet understanding, I protested that we could raise the necessary money for the Learning Center legally. Oakland had a new black superintendent of schools, and public attitudes then current would support an effort to do something to educate the inner city. I was certain we could raise significant money from government sources. (My intuition would soon prove correct when Elaine began securing city and state grants for the Learning Center.) But Newton wasn't interested in what I was saying. He *wanted* to be a criminal. He had a constituency on the streets, which he had never left, whose respect he craved as much as he did ours, and which he could achieve only by excelling as a gangster—only if he proved himself *bad.*

Previously I had looked on Huey as a victim of circumstance, destined by fate for a criminal life but able, by force of intellect, to transmute his rage into political rebellion. It was a triumph of consciousness over social destiny. Radical politics brought him again into collision with the law, but this time—in the Left's Hegelian formula—with socially constructive potential. Now I saw that every step of his criminal way was an act of will. *Being* did not determine consciousness; there were always *choices.* He had made his circumstance, even as it had made him. His brother Melvin, raised in the same household, had become a college professor. His revolutionary alter ego, George Jackson, had been a criminal since the age of twelve, but Jackson's father had been a hardworking postman all his life. It wasn't about race or class. It was about who they were as individuals, and how they defined themselves in their own right.

My reflections did not stop with the Panthers. I understood better now who they were, yet was puzzled by the way they seemed to operate with impunity. This was a reality that was a far cry from the image of the persecuted vanguard we had created (and were able to establish widely in the press). Law enforcement seemed unable to stop them, and at times was even paralyzed in its efforts to do so. If one thought about it without ideological blinders, the authorities we accused of harassing them were surprisingly forbearing, and on occasion even showed exceptional consideration. Although Newton had murdered an Oakland policeman, the chief of the Oakland force had warned him when his life was in jeopardy, even though the danger was created by his own criminal acts. And this was not the only instance I knew of. During Bobby Seale's campaign for mayor, one of his bodyguards, jittery from lack of sleep, in the early morning hours had inadvertently shot and killed a crippled newsboy. This presented the authorities and the press alike an opportunity to destroy the campaign and do the Panthers serious damage. But the bodyguard was arrested and prosecuted quietly, while Seale went on with his mayoral quest—which included regular denunciations of the "fascist" power structure and its brutal repression of Panthers like him.

While I was pondering these ironies, the police made a raid on the 29th Street house that had been the original site of the school. They found more than a thousand weapons, including M-15 and M-16 semi-automatic rifles, Thompson submachine guns, M-60 fully automatic machine guns, and even M-79 grenade launchers. Charles Garry, the Party lawyer, called a press conference to claim that 29th Street was a "dormitory" for teachers at the Learning Center, and that the police had planted the weapons as part of their ongoing political repression of the Panthers. Garry's strategy was successful (the press was more than ready to believe him), and no one was prosecuted. The house may well have been a dormitory, but it was also (as Elaine herself boasted nearly twenty years later, in her autobiography) a Panther arsenal, just as the police had claimed. (Elaine even catalogued the weapons, her list corresponding to what the police had actually said at the time.) Meanwhile, Elaine was appearing on college campuses with other leftists, making speeches about American fascism and denouncing the FBI's "cointelpro" program to infiltrate and neutralize the Panthers solely because of their political beliefs.

If there was such a program, where were its agents? Why hadn't they saved Betty? Why hadn't they prosecuted Elaine, or the Squad? Where was the press, the supposed "tool" of the power structure? Why hadn't they turned the glare of publicity on this radical stronghold and its dirty secrets? I couldn't answer these questions and they wouldn't go away. In the absence of a serious investigation, and in the silence that surrounded Betty's murder, Elaine was able to complete her campaign for city council and win 40 percent of the Oakland vote. A year later, the electoral machine she put together from the Party apparatus was made available to Lionel Wilson, and provided the margin by which he was elected Oakland's first black mayor, as the press and the authorities continued their silence.

I later learned that jurisdictional disputes were part of the reason the police were prevented from conducting an adequate investigation of Betty's death. The victim had lived in Berkeley, but her body washed ashore in Foster City, across the Bay. Oakland, where the Panthers operated, was not even involved in the case. This confusion hampered the investigative effort. The high level of scrutiny the police could expect from a liberal press, the threat of legal suits from radical lawyers, and the charges of persecution that would accompany any serious probe, completed the constraints. Years later, I joined a downtown athletic club, where one of my workout buddies turned out to be the former head of homicide for Oakland. "Why didn't you guys ever nail Huey Newton?" I asked him. "Oh," he said. "We never wanted to get a call from that side of town, because you guys and your lawyers would be all over us." The cops were just working stiffs with jobs to protect. There were no Ko-jacks, and there was no repressive state.

In creating a protective shield around the Panthers, we had repeated a figure of the progressive past. Trotsky had described the Communist parties of the world as frontier guards for the Soviet Union. Their function was to explain away Stalin's crimes, put obstacles in the path of those who resisted his policies, and discredit witnesses who testified against him. The New Left had formed a similar frontier guard around the Panthers and their crimes.

An episode involving Bobby Seale now illustrated the wide latitude the Panthers enjoyed because of the protection their supporters provided. After being beaten by Newton and threatened by Elaine, the former chairman of the Black Panther Party had disappeared. In 1975, in democratic America, one of the most prominent figures in the political culture simply vanished. And no one publicly noticed that he was gone, or cared: not the press, not his political supporters in the white left, not his former followers. It turned out that Seale was in hiding, in fear for his life. A year and a half after Seale's disappearance, Charles told me that Seale had fled because of Elaine's threats, and no one knew where he was—not even his mother. Seale was easily the most public and popular of the Panther leaders, personally known to most of the prominent figures on the left, including his codefendants in the Chicago conspiracy case—Dave Dellinger, Tom Hayden, Jerry Rubin, and Abbie Hoffman—and their lawyer, William Kunstler. In all the time he was missing, not one of these champions of the persecuted and oppressed raised his voice to ask where Bobby Seale was, and thus provide him with protection. None of them was willing to do so, because Seale's persecutors were the Panthers themselves.

The entire episode seemed such an unlikely occurrence that fifteen years later I began to wonder that it had happened at all. Then, in the course of doing research for a piece I was writing, I came across a 1976 article about Eldridge Cleaver in *Rolling Stone*, called "Revolution on Ice." The article mentioned in passing that Bobby Seale had disappeared, and noted that his family had not heard from him and was "concerned." What the article did not say was that many people knew *why* he was missing, but their lips were sealed.

The silence that enveloped Seale's disappearance resurrected the feelings I had after Betty's death: the loneliness that closed around a person identified as an "enemy of the people"; the immoral core of the community of the Left; its lack of conscience when the victims were among those it had politically damned. Lenin had called his opponents "insects" that the revolution must exterminate. If you were merely a peasant and got in the way of the revolution, your life was flattened into a single abstraction, as in "The achievement of socialism requires the liquidation of the *kulak.*" The particular individual with distinctive features simply disappeared. Stalin's innovation was to make these condemned souls "unpersons" even before their deaths. Even heroes of the revolution were not immune. You could be as famous as Trotsky, and it would count for nothing when the revolution turned against you. Not only would Stalin kill you to the applause of the people, but it would be as if you had never existed. Your achievements would be removed from the historical record, and even your image would be erased from the photographic memory of the time. When socialist justice was complete, there would be nothing left of you at all.

For a while, Bobby Seale became an unperson in America. Among all those who had once considered him a hero and friend nobody cared. Or they were too terrified to care. This was how Itzhak Feffer had disappeared—forgotten and abandoned by his friends. Of course it was still America, the Panthers did not control the state, and (in the end) Bobby Seale survived. But what if the Panthers, or radicals like them, eventually *did* succeed?

Thinking about this caused me to reflect on the difference between our adversaries and us. There was plenty of injustice in the system we opposed. But it had created procedures and institutions designed to redress grievances, correct injustices, and put checks on the power of government. In rejecting our radical agendas, our opponents had always stressed the importance of "process" and following rules, even when the issues seemed obvious. As radicals, we were impatient with order and had contempt for process. We wanted "direct rule" and "people's justice," unconstrained by such legalisms and the hierarchies they required. We had no use for law that pretended to be neutral between persons and classes, that failed to recognize *historical* grievances or the way rules were shaped by social forces. We did not believe in bourgeois legality and objective standards. The revolutionary *will* embodied justice and truth. We were going to eliminate "checks and balances" and let the *people* decide.

As a result, we had no justice. There were no means to redress the crimes committed by the Panthers or other tribunes of the people—in America or anywhere else. There was no institutional recourse, and no moral standard, to which we were committed. And there was no rationale to create them. This contempt for order, for objective values, for moralities that transcended particular interests, separated us from our enemies, and made their justice superior to ours—even when they were wrong. The Smith Act decisions that had sent Communist leaders to jail during the McCarthy era had been reversed by the courts a short time later. The Rosenbergs had received no such reprieve, but at least the system had allowed their cause to be heard. As a result of this respect for individuals and rights, the prosecutions of the McCarthy era had become the object of a national soul-searching and many judicial and political reversals. The truth—whatever it was—eventually had a chance to breathe.

Socialist justice provided no such opportunity, and no such reprieve. It had been forty years since Stalin's purges. The victims were dead, their memories erased. They were unpersons without public defenders, expunged even from the consciousness of the living. Those who knew the truth had to keep their silence, even as I had to keep mine. If we actually succeeded in making a revolution in America, and if the Panthers or similar radical vanguards prevailed, how would our fate be different from theirs? Our injustice, albeit mercifully smaller in scale, was as brutal and final as Stalin's. As progressives we had *no* law to govern us, other than that of the gang.

After Betty's murder, I ceased to be politically active. I couldn't even think about politics apart from these events. In my heart, I knew that it would not be possible for me to work for a cause again until I had resolved the issues of her death. As New Leftists, we felt ourselves immunized from crimes that the Left had committed in the past, both by acknowledging that they had occurred and by resolving to change the attitudes that had caused them. But we had changed the attitudes, and now the crimes were being repeated. I began to ask myself whether there was something in Marxism, or in the socialist idea itself, that was the root of the problem.

I was not alone in raising this question now. The Polish philosopher Leszek Kolakowski had been an intellectual leader of the New Left until his defection to the West in 1968, after the Soviet invasion of Czechoslovakia. Five years later, Kolakowski organized a conference at Oxford, which asked: "Is There Anything Wrong With the Socialist Idea?" In a paper delivered to the conference, he suggested that there was: The goals which socialists had historically pursued contained the seeds of the socialist nightmare.

The ideal of human unity was one. The end of "self-alienation" was really the core of the socialist hope. Socialists believed that private property divided human beings, making some rich and some poor, some oppressors and others oppressed. Private property was the root cause of social conflict. Socialists proposed to abolish property and unite people in the socialist state. But the abolition of property was really the abolition of private association and civil society, and of the bourgeois rights they underpinned. Socialist unity could only be achieved as a totalitarian solution.

Kolakowski then turned to the goal of equality, and showed that it led to a similar impasse. Even if one assumed all human beings to be equal by nature (a dubious proposition), historical circumstance had made them unequal. After the revolution, these historical inequalities would have to be redressed. But the class of people that decided who would be made equal, and at what rate, would—by the very fact of that power—become a new ruling caste. The quest for equality would create a new inequality. There was no exit from the cycle of human fate.

Along with Kolakowski's questions came others. I had been reading *Political Messianism*, by J. L. Talmon, which described nationalism and socialism as secular religions that lacked a doctrine of original sin. After reading Talmon's account, I began to wish that I had inherited such a concept. The idea of original sin—that we are born flawed, that the capacity for evil is lodged within us (no matter how our consciousness may be raised)—would have instilled in me a necessary caution about individuals like Huey Newton, and movements like ours. There were people who had a *will* to evil that no amount of political enlightenment could overcome. Nor could any movement (no less humanity) hope to purge itself of the potential for evil that lurked in us all.

Solzhenitsyn had formulated this insight in the following way: "The line separating good and evil passes not through states, nor between classes, nor between political parties, but right through every human heart—and through all human hearts." But if this was true, what could socialist liberation mean? If evil was a choice that *any* individual could make, then human beings would always pose a danger to each other, and there could be no "withering away of the state." There would *always* be a need for law above individuals, for police to enforce the law, and for prisons to contain those who broke it. We could *never* dispense with the apparatus of repression, even after socialist justice had been instituted. But if this was true, how could we dispense with "bourgeois" law, the best system of rules and institutions yet devised to protect individuals from the predations of their government and each other? If we really cared about liberty and justice, we would have to give up our superior status as revolutionary opponents of "bourgeois" order, and enter the universe of its morality and thought.

Bourgeois morality was not all that we would have to accept. If there was indeed an element in human nature that could not be reshaped by socialist ideas, then not only was the rule of law necessary, but the rule of the market as well. As radicals, we had decried the absence of a social plan, and what Marx called the "fetishism of commodities"—the fact that in capitalist economies "things were in the saddle" and the market ruled, instead of man. But if human beings were corrupt in their nature, they would corrupt the plan as well. How could there be a social plan *not* driven by ego and self-serving desire? Better to be governed by markets that were impersonal, by neutral rules that were *not* subject to human will.

The unraveling continued. If it was necessary to "seize power" and "smash the state," the individuals who rose to the fore in revolutions were likely to be fanatics with an aptitude for violence. The readiness of Lenin and Stalin to be ruthless and brutal—to do what was "necessary"—had caused others to follow them, and the rest to get out of their way. My own political experience confirmed the rule. In volatile situations, the momentum was always seized by those most certain in their conviction, least impressed by ambiguity, and most ready to take risks or manipulate facts to achieve their objectives. When you went into combat, it was only natural to put your trust in warriors who were prepared to be ruthless and brutal. But these characteristics of the revolutionary vanguard were *not* the traits of good rulers, in whom judiciousness, moral scruple, and caution would be obvious virtues. Yet how could the conquerors be persuaded to step down?

I wrestled with these questions for a long time, unable to find satisfactory answers and equally unable to pursue them to their logical conclusion. To give up the socialist idea was still unthinkable. It had been the standard by which I judged right and wrong, the principle that had created my communities and friendships and shaped my actions. The pursuit of the ideal had made me what I was, until I had no conception of myself without it. When I thought of leaving the socialist movement, the feeling was the same as leaving my own life.

But I could not drop the issue, either. I began to discuss my questions with friends and in informal groups, and even arranged to conduct a class at a radical institute, on the topic "Is Socialism A Viable Idea?" This formulation was the closest I was ready to come to the precipice in front of me. I hoped the announcement would attract peers who could persuade me that my intuitions were wrong. But the only participants who showed up were new to the Left. When I confronted friends, they evaded the issue—responding instead to its dangerous subtext, which I was trying so hard to suppress: *"If you are asking such questions, David, you must be planning to leave us."* Michael Lerner, who came to recruit me into a vanguard he was calling the New American Movement, summed up their reactions with characteristic crudeness. "Even to raise such questions," he said to me, "is counter-revolutionary." Like a person being pushed unwillingly out a door, I protested passionately against these charges. My intentions were constructive, I argued; there was no reason to conclude that the questions I was raising were unanswerable. But over time my reassurances to myself grew less and less convincing.

The attempts to involve others in my quest came to an end, finally, when I was invited by a sociologist friend, William Kornhauser, to attend a seminar on "Marxism and Post-Marxism" at UC Berkeley. The seminar was held under the auspices of the Institute for Social Relations, which was headed by Troy Duster, the black sociologist whom I had taken to see Newton. I looked forward to the group because it was made up of veterans of the movement who would be knowledgeable about the issues I wanted to discuss. Among them were Robert Blauner (who had written books on alienation and race), a former SNCC activist, Hardy Frye, Todd Gitlin, Jeff Lustig, Victoria Bonnell, and David Wellman. Wellman's father had been one of the Communist leaders prosecuted under the Smith Act in the Fifties. I was the only one attending the seminar who was not on a university faculty.

Once the sessions got underway, however, it became apparent that the others present had different agendas than mine. They divided themselves into Marxists and "structuralists." The latter were Marxists who thought that the practical failures of socialist revolutions had made Marx's analysis untenable, and who sought to rescue the Marxist agenda by sophisticating its radical theory. But I wanted to question radical theory itself, and specifically its destructive attack on "bourgeois" culture and institutions in the absence of any practical idea of what to do when the destruction was accomplished. To "annihilate" bourgeois society in the name of an abstract ideal seemed to me intellectually empty and politically irresponsible. To carry on a radical critique of the existing order without any practical idea of what would replace it was nihilism.

When I attempted to raise these questions, I encountered a wall of resistance. Instead of a response, there was only an awkward shuffling into the next subject. I began to feel permanently "out of order," an intruder into someone else's conversation. My own thinking, at the time, had been shaped by a book I was reading, *The Ordeal of Civility*, by John Murray Cuddihy, which had won a National Book Award. In Cuddihy's view, the theories of Marx and Freud were strategies for dealing with their predicament as members of a despised social group. European Jews had been given rights and were admitted to civil society only after the French Revolution. But they had been denied full acceptance through a kind of "institutional racism," a code of civility that continued to put them in their place. It was Cuddihy's thesis that the revolutionary ideas of Marx and Freud were attempts to deconstruct these civil orders, and replace them with a universal one in which they would finally be granted the acceptance they craved. Thus Freud claimed to show that bourgeois civility was a mask for sexual repression, while Marx argued that it mystified economic exploitation. Each had a vision of liberation—science for Freud, socialism for Marx— that would provide a universal solvent in which the significance of ethnic identities disappeared.

Earlier in my life I would have thought Cuddihy's idea merely peculiar. But the events of the past year had made me acutely conscious of my own ethnicity. In the aftermath of Betty's and Ellen's deaths, I thought about how vulnerable we were because we were white; how this had made it difficult for me, for example, to plead Betty's cause. For the first time in my life, I had felt isolated and made helpless by my race.

I thought of how we had extended ourselves to bring justice to others *because* they were black. How for myself and Ellen this had begun when we were still adolescents, and yet how little this care seemed to be reciprocated. I thought of how Troy Duster had known the Panthers were dangerous, but had done nothing to warn me. Nor could I have reasonably expected him to do anything to help me after Betty was killed. In all my efforts on behalf of black people, I had never thought to ask: Would my black comrades extend themselves to gain justice for *me?*

I began to review events of the past to which I had paid little attention before, like the expulsion of the Jews from the civil-rights movement in 1966. Jews had funded the movement, devised its legal strategies, and provided support for its efforts in the media and in the universities—and wherever else they had power. More than *half* the freedom riders who had gone to the southern states were Jews, although Jews constituted only 3 percent of the population. It was an unprecedented show of solidarity from one people to another. Jews had put their resources and lives on the line to support the black struggle for civil rights, and indeed two of their sons—Schwerner and Goodman—had been murdered for their efforts. But, even while these tragic events were still fresh, the black leaders of the movement had unceremoniously expelled the Jews from their ranks. When Israel was attacked in 1967 by a coalition of Arab states calling for its annihilation, the same black leaders threw their support to the Arab aggressors, denouncing Zionism (the Jewish liberation movement) as racism. Rarely had a betrayal of one people by another been as total or as swift. Yet radical Jews like myself had continued our dedication to the black movement for civil rights—to *their* struggle and *their* cause. What was it that made us so willing to support those who would treat us like this, who would not support *us* in return? Why did we think it was all right—even noble—to operate according to standards so different from those that governed others?

Just two months before Betty's disappearance, I had written a cover story for *Ramparts,* "The Passion of the Jews," in which I defended the denial engaged in by progressives like myself. It opened with an encounter that posed the same question. A Jewish doctor had asked me: *"Do you have any Christian friends whom you could trust with your life?"* I was appalled by the question, by his implication that there could be none. It was such a "plummet into tribal depths," I wrote, that I did not want to confront it. Comfortable and safe as he was in America, this doctor could not forget the fate of Germany's Jews, who had also felt comfortable and safe before being turned in by their Christian friends. In my answer, I attempted to place his anxiety in the frame of the revolution I still believed in and which I still believed would provide a solution. By rejecting their own societies, radicals had entered a stateless diaspora, like the Jews before the creation of Israel. Having no state to defend them, they identified with those who were powerless and oppressed. Out of this identification, a new community was forming—a "community of faith in the revolutionary future which would rescue us all from this dilemma:

> The revolutionary belongs to a community of faith that extends beyond the classes and the nations and reaches across the boundaries that divide and oppress. Within every national group it forms the basis of a new human community and a new human identity. Today the revolutionary is isolated, obstructed by the divisions that form the cultural and political legacy of the past; the revolutionary is of the nations, but not in them. For the revolutionary's eye is on the future. Today there is Black and Jew, American and Russian, Israeli and Arab. But within each nation—Russia, America, Israel, Egypt—there are the aliens, the persecuted, the unassimilated, the "Jews" who know the heart of the stranger and who struggle for human freedom. Today they are separated; tomorrow they will be joined.

Betty's death killed this fantasy in me. There was no revolutionary community. There would be no redemptive future. *There is no one to save us from who we are.*

One day Troy Duster interrupted our seminar to talk about Harry Edwards, a black sociologist who had recently been denied his tenure at the university. Edwards was a former athlete and well-known activist who had led the protests at the 1968 Olympics, where black medalists raised clenched fists, during the playing of the national anthem after their victories, instead of saluting the American flag. He was denied tenure when a slim departmental majority decided that his publications, which were about the sociology of sports, did not merit an appointment. Edwards had denounced the decision as "racist." Now he was considering a new twist in the strategy to save his job. "Harry has been approached by the Russians," Troy announced. "They want to bring his case to the UN, as a human-rights violation. What do you think?"

When it came to human rights, the UN was not a friend of the Jews. In the Middle East conflict, the General Assembly had censured

Israel many times, but not the Arab states who had declared war on Israel. It had recently given a standing ovation to the African dictator and cannibal Idi Amin, who had massacred tens of thousands of his countrymen, and had voted to condemn Zionism as "racism." It had turned a blind eye toward the Russian police state, where the Brezhnev regime was accelerating the persecution of Jewish dissidents like Andrei Sakharov and Natan Sharansky amidst growing fear as to where the attacks would lead. Jews had only one powerful ally in the UN—the new administration of Jimmy Carter, which had proclaimed a policy of defending "human rights" and which had put pressure on the Kremlin to halt its repression of Soviet Jews. This was why the Russians had approached Edwards: to neutralize Western protests over the persecution of Soviet Jews.

I was outraged that Edwards would even consider cooperating with the Russians in this situation. Vicki Bonnell, whose husband was a Soviet dissident (and Jewish), described the severity of the repression in Russia, and argued that making Edwards' case parallel would be inappropriate, and would compromise their struggle. Others agreed that the move would be misinterpreted, and was therefore unwise. Later, I thought about how respectfully everybody had treated the proposal, and how the terms of the discussion had been confined to "dissidents," skirting the issue of the Jews. What if the roles were reversed? What if blacks in the Soviet Union were being denied basic civil rights, and thrown into psychiatric institutions as a punishment for dissent? What if a Jew had proposed compromising *their* cause? The response would have been immediate and direct. The two blacks in the room—Troy Duster and Hardy Frye—would have said: "If you don't support us there, we're not going to support you here." And that would have been that. Black radicals had a clear sense of their ethnicity and the threat they faced, even if we did not.

The issue came to a head when Robert Blauner presented a paper to the seminar. Blauner argued that Marxist theory had overlooked the most powerful forces in the modern world—nationalism and racism— because Marx had come from a relatively "homogeneous" society. Our task was to correct those deficiencies in his theory. When Blauner finished, I spoke. Far from being part of a homogeneous society, I said, Marx belonged to a despised minority that had only recently won its civil rights. He was descended from a long line of famous rabbis, but his own father had given up the family religion in order to retain his government post. Marx had written a notorious essay ("On the Jewish Question") identifying capitalist exploitation with Judaism. He had built his entire theoretical edifice on a concept—class—which was pointedly free of ethnic and national characteristics, in order to formulate the idea of socialism as a community liberated from these distinctions. Socialism would "solve" the Jewish question by eliminating Judaism, along with all other ethnic and national identities. What we had to ask ourselves—and here I paused for effect—was whether Marx wasn't a self-hating Jew, and whether socialism was anything more than a wish to be included.

"*B-u-l-l-shit*" boomed the voice next to me. It was Jeff Lustig: "We've heard this all before, and I find it boring," he said. When he finished, I spoke again: "I'm glad that Jeff has settled these questions," I said, "but just out of curiosity I'd like to hear how the other Marxists in the room identify themselves *ethnically.*" I knew, of course, that they were all Jews, and that not one would demean himself to acknowledge that fact. As the words left my mouth, and as if to prove my point, David Wellman began a tirade at the end of the table, his face turning apoplectic red: "I'm sick and tired of Horowitz's questions," he sputtered—"his interrogations, his attempts to obstruct this seminar with questions that don't interest anyone else."

When Wellman finished, I offered to leave. I didn't want to interfere with the seminar's work, I said, and if everyone felt as he did, I would go. Vicki Bonnell, Kornhauser, and one or two others spoke up for me. The rest, including Gitlin (whom I had known since my days at the Russell Foundation), sat there sullen and silent. When it was over, no one except Wellman had said that I should leave. But at the next session, only three others besides myself showed up. The seminar never met after that. When I discussed this strange conclusion to an intellectual enterprise with Kornhauser, he pointed out that Troy Duster's institute, which had sponsored the seminar, was financed by a foundation grant that had been given to Wellman. It was his "Marxist" explanation as to why the others had joined the boycott. He also told me that Wellman was only half-Jewish, and had become visibly upset at a gathering two weeks before, when someone had referred to him as a Jew and he had denied that he was.

Shortly afterward, Harry Edwards was given his tenure when the chancellor of the university overruled the sociology department. For a faculty body to be overruled by an administrator on a matter of tenure was an unprecedented infringement of a jealously guarded prerogative. It was said that the Soviets had directly intervened with the Carter Administration, on behalf of Edwards, and that President Carter himself had called the chancellor. There were no protests over this blatant political intrusion and violation of academic freedom. Professor Edwards subsequently became a national figure as an adviser to the major sports leagues, and a spokesman on issues of racism. At Berkeley he caused a commotion in the Jewish community—but nowhere else—by assigning exams on the Jewish high holy days, and refusing to allow Jewish students, absent for religious reasons, to take makeup exams at another time.

The seminar had provided an answer of sorts to my questions. If these issues could not be discussed in a left-wing institute, in a university setting, where *could* they be discussed? How could the Left be reformed if it didn't have the courage to confront itself? How could it propose to change the world if it was unwilling to ask whether its ideas were valid? How could it transform the world if it couldn't transform itself?

The seminar also provoked a new question: Why was the socialist dream so hard to look at? Freud had suggested an answer. In *Civilization and Its Discontents,* he had analyzed the expectations of socialists—that the world would be governed by justice and love—as an adult fairy tale. Socialism was a wish for the comforting fantasies of childhood to come true. I had an additional thought: The revolutionary was a creator, just like God. Socialism was not only a childish wish, but a wish for childhood itself: security; warmth; the feeling of being at the center of the world.

One evening shortly after the seminar collapsed, I went to Moe's Books on Telegraph Avenue, to browse. As a writer, I always had a difficult time in bookstores, and especially Moe's, which was an entire building, four stories high, and contained books in every conceivable category of knowledge. Like the revolutionary, every writer creates his own universe. Even if he is not the subject of the work, the writer's eye is still the center of its world. In every artistic creation there is the same impulse, as in childhood, to be the center of attention. Visiting Moe's, I would sometimes get a headache just trying to take in the multiplicity of works and put them into some order in my mind. There were so many titles competing for others' attention, so many competing with mine.

That evening, my difficulties were unusually intense. I envisioned not only the universe of authors, but the universe of audiences as well. Audiences that did not know the others existed, or care. There were entire worlds of readers who devoured nothing but mysteries, or romances, or works on the occult, or science fiction—all of which were as foreign to me as the worlds of sociology and political economy were to them. Whole tiers of Moe's were occupied with these disparate universes, sufficient in themselves to exclude awareness of others. While I was thinking these thoughts, I had a sudden shock of recognition. Although my own books were confined to a tiny portion of a single shelf in this vast array of human learning, I had always found security in the belief that a hierarchy ordered it. I visualized a pyramid whose apex was Marxism, which was my life's work and which provided the key to all other knowledge. Marxism was the theory that would change *everyone's* world. And put mine at the center. But in that very moment a previously unthinkable possibility also entered my head: The Marxist idea, to which I had devoted my entire intellectual life and work, was false.

All around me, the room went black. In the engulfing dark, the pyramid flattened and a desert appeared in its place, cold and infinite, and myself an invisible speck within it. *I am one of them,* I thought. *I am going to die and disappear like everyone else.* For the first time in my conscious life I was looking at myself in my human nakedness, without the support of revolutionary hopes, without the faith in a revolutionary future—without the sense of self-importance conferred by the role I would play in remaking the world. For the first time in my life I confronted myself as I really was in the endless march of human coming and going. *I was nothing.*

DIVORCE

M Y FATHER HAD ASKED ELISSA, JUST BEFORE OUR WEDDING, whether she thought I was "going to come down slowly, or all at once." This time the old man had got it right. The only question was how far I would fall. Even before Betty's death, I knew I had entered a zone of trouble. No matter how great the energy with which I attacked my environment, life no longer seemed to give back what I needed. Dissatisfaction increased with effort, a residue at the edge of all my endeavors. Unable to identify the source of the malaise, I was powerless to combat it. With a relentless logic, the routines of my existence had come to seem like a trap. It was as though I had pushed my limits as far as they would go, and now they were pushing back.

I had been faithful for the fifteen years of my marriage, but while working on the biography with Peter, I had a brief affair with Abby Rockefeller. This might have passed with no repercussions if guilt had not driven me to disclose the breach, and with no further incident if I hadn't continued the relationship at a distance. Abby's wealth made it possible for us to communicate via daily phone calls, and to these Elissa seemed to acquiesce. Her passivity allowed me to persuade myself that they all were merely part of an innocent business routine. This illusion was encouraged by the fact that the conversations focused on the biography in progress, or on political matters, and not on any romance between us. Abby would argue, for example, that arrogance shaped the charitable impulses of the Rockefeller family, and was the true source of the guilt her generation felt. On a tape of our conversations I kept, she said: "What they don't want to get down to is the explicit statement of their sense of superiority. And so instead of actually rooting that out, or finding what merit there is in it, they use guilt as a shield to secure it." I disagreed. The guilt, in my view, followed from the injustice of their wealth. But Abby was not easily dissuaded. "The reason I think the superiority is primary," she responded, "is because they are so willing to express the guilt, to acknowledge it. When I see someone so willing to express guilt, then I conclude that it is an easy cover for other things."

I was intrigued by her analysis. As a Marxist, I was not used to thinking in psychological terms—a fact which made the biographical task that Peter had set for us even more difficult. I thus welcomed the help Abby provided in gaining insights into her family's inner life. Equally refreshing was her own Marxism, which was a relatively pure faith. Although she was close to me in age, she had come into the Left later, and didn't share my uneasiness about the radical foundations. If she was unable to persuade me from my own doubts, the force of her conviction was nonetheless bracing. It generated in me an energy of renewal I seemed no longer able to summon for myself.

I was relieved when the sexual aspect of our affair ended almost as swiftly as it had begun. But she was not so reconciled to this Platonic distance. From time to time, she would press me about my commitment to my marriage. I resisted these advances gently, but also firmly. I did not want to leave my family. I loved Elissa, and could not imagine a life without her. Still, I continued to need whatever fuel it was that Abby was providing, and was blind to the jealous fires our conversations lit.

In December 1974, as the Rockefeller manuscript neared its completion, Abby decided to visit Berkeley. I tried to dissuade her, fearing what her presence might provoke, but failed. She did not represent the only threat closing in, however. My clandestine relationship had also aroused Peter's suspicions and concerns. Months earlier, in a move to protect our project, he had extracted a promise from me that I would not show Abby our text before it was published. But that was merely charade on my part, since, to induce her to cooperate, I had already promised Abby I would do exactly that. It was a replication of my dilemma with Elissa—I could not keep the trust of both.

Now Abby and I were sitting across from each other at dinner in the Berkeley marina, and she was telling me she wanted everything that we had written about her excised from our book. Despite all that had transpired between us, and all that she had told me about her family (tape recorder running), she wanted to preserve her original position, and innocence. She conceded that what we had written about her was accurate—but this didn't alter her resolve. There was no way I could accede to her request. I had kept my end of the bargain: Peter and I had rendered her fairly and truly. We had even protected members of her family from revelations she made to us that would have been unnecessarily hurtful if published. Once she agreed to talk, it never occurred to me that if we made these concessions she would be unreasonable. To remove her from the book would hardly be fair to the family members she had talked about in her interviews who had no such privilege. And how could I face Peter with her demand? I had gone behind his back to keep my trust with her. How could I ask him to jeopardize nearly three years of effort to honor a promise that was a betrayal of *him?* I told her I could not. "You prefer the truth of your book," she said bitterly, "to the truth of me."

The next day she flew back to Cambridge. Before leaving, she called Peter and told him she had read the text, thus exposing my breach of faith, and she wanted to see the chapter about her removed. Before Peter had time to react, however, Elissa's jealousy erupted. We sat facing each other in our living room, I blind with tears, she staring coldly toward me. Not even the original revelation of the affair had produced in her such a black passion. I had confessed because I could not stand the separation that its secret had created. Now the knowledge of it—irrevocable, irremediable—had erected a wall between us. Her eyes, which were dead to me now, had once been the safest place I knew. For nineteen years we had been one flesh. Now I was cast into outer darkness, uncertain I would ever get back. My brain swelled against my skull like a tumor about to explode. But nothing I said, no forgiveness begged, could move her to relent.

These torments were interrupted by the telephone. When I answered, it was Betty's daughter, Tamara. It was the call telling me that Betty was missing.

The miseries that now closed on my life like the jaws of a vise contained a single blessing: For weeks on end I was entirely numb. In the space, daily routines reasserted themselves and a desperate calm settled over our household. Elissa and I did not even dare to brush up against the wound that had opened between us, because too much was at stake. Perhaps if we did nothing, was our unspoken thought, we might recover some measure of what we had lost.

It was my partnership with Peter that suffered the first break. He didn't raise the issue of my betrayal, but he hadn't forgotten it, either. As the architect of our biographical project, he had taken charge of the final revisions of the manuscript, and had cut two hundred pages from the text, to make it more readable. Among the sections he had decided to cut were those on the "whale"—the chapters that would explain the workings of the System. I had not abandoned my Marxism yet, and in my mind removing these sections also removed any self-respecting rationale I had for my collaboration. It was another blow to my increasingly precarious sense of self.

As I went over Peter's changes, I sank deeper into my gloom. I began drinking over my work, which I had never done. In reviewing the changes he made, I scribbled in the margins angry comments I lacked the strength to confront him with directly. Beside a passage he had cut over my objections, I inserted: "I love the way you make these decisions." When I sent him the manuscript, he called me up to vent his rage. He was furious that I had exposed our conflicts to the woman who was typing the final version. The words "self-righteous" and "narcissistic" stood out in the bill of his indictment. But I hardly noticed the particulars of the tirade. What I remember clearly is the warm pleasure of the feeling, like a ribbon of blood coursing from under the skin, as the words cut into me. I deserved this punishment. I *desired* it.

When the editing phase was over, Peter said: "This book is so boring, no one will want to read it." But our agent Georges Borchardt was enthusiastic, and our editor Marian Wood wrote back to us ecstatically: "It reads like a Greek tragedy." It was adopted as a main selection of the Book-of-the-Month Club, which meant that a minimum of 150,000 copies were presold. Before it was even published, we knew it was going to be a best-seller.

I felt strangely detached from this good fortune. Money and fame were not going to put my life together again. Our success could not even heal the wound between Peter and me. The incident with Abby was only a final straw; ever since Peter and I had begun our collaboration on *Ramparts*, there had been tension between us. It was not unlike the conflict with my father: I never seemed able to satisfy him. I also noticed that whenever the tension surfaced, it was Peter who dominated the exchange. Despite my best efforts, I was never able to locate the source of his displeasure, or to dismiss his grievances out of hand. If they seemed unfair, they never appeared unjust. His complaint that I was self-righteous and self-serving, if true, was cause enough. But it did not square with my view of myself. I thought of myself as just the opposite. I had undertaken the book as a favor to him, and a service to the cause (which he had diminished by his cuts). *Everything I did was a mission to others.* This attitude was so deeply embedded in my sense of self that it never occurred to me that it might be the very source of the problem.

Earlier, even if I had been aware of it, there was no possibility that I could alter so basic a disposition. But, as a result of Betty's death and the break in my marriage, I had entered a zone of personal free-fall, and the spectrum of possibility had changed. For the first time in my adult life, I could not be proud of what I was doing. As a consequence, the defenses that had become instinctive to me were suddenly disarmed. I still felt misunderstood by Peter, and injured by his attacks. But I no longer had the conviction of my own virtue.

After *The Rockefellers* was published, Peter became more and more remote, until a moment came when I realized that if I didn't call him, there would be no communication between us at all. Then one day I decided I wouldn't call him until I understood the source of our conflicts, and could meet him on more equal ground. It would be two years before we would speak again.

About this time, my parents came to Berkeley for a visit. My father and I took up our walks, and I resumed the ritual of my efforts to make the connection with him that continued to elude me. In our phone conversations he had expressed dissatisfaction with my writing projects. I had abandoned the book on the sociology of knowledge, but under prodding from my publisher had undertaken an assignment to write a book about America for the bicentennial. By describing America's beginnings, I would attempt to explain its ends, to show that character was a destiny, for nations as well as for individuals. Its working title was *Promised Land*. My father took a negative view of this book, as he had of the others. He did not think I should waste my time writing family biographies or historical studies. I should write a book, he said, about the "economic crisis." By this he meant the "final crisis" of capitalism—a Marxist chimera in which I no longer believed.

The critical reception of *The Rockefellers* had been extraordinary, including a glowing review on the cover of the Sunday book section of the *New York Times*. Even though my father hated the *Times*, he read the paper with a religious devotion. The most vivid memory I have is of him sitting at the dining-room table, coffee cup in hand, poring over its pages. But when I showed him the *Times* notice a week in advance, he brushed it aside and began to lecture me on the futility of my effort. The Rockefellers were boring people, he said, and nobody would want to read about them. I knew he meant himself. "You should write a book about the American revolution," he went on as my jaw tightened. "I *am* writing a book about it," I said. He did not mean, he said, the historical event, but the one that was coming. The one he had waited for, ever since he was a young man in his prime, fifty years before. "There *is* no revolution coming," I replied angrily, and left.

Unhappiness settled over my life like an arctic snow. Nowhere I looked provided me comfort. In the privacy of my grief, I focused on the past. I seemed to gravitate toward the center of my disorder, taking morbid pleasure in becoming my own prosecutor, testing to see how darkly I could depict myself and what I had done. I had come to the end of everything I had ever worked for in my life, and I had no idea how to disentangle myself from my fate.

The misery that now engulfed me would have been harder to give in to, had my children not grown to ages of independence which took them out of the house. Jon, the oldest, was almost a senior in high school, while Anne had already entered the first grade. Elissa had returned to school to earn a degree in nursing, and had started her first job. Everyone was out during the daylight hours, leaving a cavernous space in which I was left to myself. I would begin the work day by going to my desk and struggling with the manuscript of *Promised Land*. But by now the depression was so deep, and the paralysis so extensive, that I could only summon the mental energy to labor for an hour in the morning before my personal darkness set in. After that, all alone in the house with everyone gone, I would collapse on the sofa and plumb my sorrows, sinking into their murky, bottomless depths, weeping in silence, until one by one the family came home.

I had been betrayed by my community, and embarrassed by myself. I had helped to destroy an innocent life, and—who knew?—maybe others. My marriage, the rock on which I had built my family and my happiness, was split to its core, and I didn't know if it could ever be made whole again. My defeats were so overwhelming that I felt powerless to affect them. I could not alter what had happened. I could not bear to look at what I had done. I was utterly and helplessly alone.

While Elissa was waiting for a hospital position to open up, she had taken a job in a nursing home. The work was hard and low-paid, and the practices in the home were so below standard that she began to be afraid her license might be in jeopardy if she stayed. I pleaded with her to quit, and take time off that we could spend together— hoping that I could draw energy from her to rekindle the life force that had flickered out. Perhaps my desperation frightened her. Until then, I had been the provider, the worldly half of our couple. As best I could, I had shouldered my share of household chores, ferrying the children to their appointments, taking on the emotional load with her. Even in my disorder, I still managed to put up a front for them, acting the father in their presence, maintaining my self-control. But she saw the truth and felt the collapse. In her eyes our marriage was first of all a joint partnership in creating a family. I had defaulted on my side of the contract, and it unnerved her. For as long as I had known her, she had never spent a day in bed, no matter how severe her illness. I saw in her eyes that the weakness I manifested was alien and unworthy And I had betrayed her.

She said no to my proposal. She said she felt she would "disappear." I was hurt and resentful. I had taken care of her, of the family, of *Ramparts*, of the Panthers—of everyone—for so long. Now I was in trouble deeper than I had ever known, and there was no one to take care of me.

It was two years since Betty's death, and I was still in a state of mourning for the life I had lost. I began to wonder whether there was something in me of my father's depressive nature—whether I would ever feel normal again. It was in this state that I went to pick up our youngest child at Oxford elementary school and bumped into Jackie Dennis, the wife of Gene Dennis Jr., whose father had been head of the Communist Party. It was a bright spring day, but my chest was aching and I had to fight back my tears. The embarrassment of my distress caused me to notice how radiant and happy Jackie looked. Her hair was piled in opulent curls, and her complexion was an earth color that made her smile warm and inviting. "What are you doing with yourself these days?" I asked, hoping she would provide a clue to the source of such health. "I'm into psychic phenomena," was the unexpected answer. Almost reflexively, I thought: *Another one off the deep end.* But the desire to know her secret persisted. "What do you *do?*" I asked. "I'm a psychic healer," she responded. I heard myself cry out: "*Heal me.*"

I arranged for a session, but didn't tell Elissa. It would have been difficult to admit on its own terms, but I also felt a pulse in my interest that I knew was dangerous. The appointment was in her home in a cottage in North Oakland. She was estranged from her husband, and lived alone. On the way over, I felt a curious mixture of anxiety and expectation. On the one hand, I was fearful that my skepticism might betray me and embarrass us both. On the other, I had an improbable hope that I might stumble on some magical release from my unbearable state.

I sat on a wooden chair in her kitchen and closed my eyes, taking deep breaths from my diaphragm, as she instructed. I was being "grounded" and "centered." I was to imagine that my feet were growing roots, and to feel the flow of the earth's energy moving up my legs. I was to picture a shaft of light extending like a tail from the base of my spine, reaching down to the center of the globe. I tried not to feel silly, but rather to give myself over to the fairy tale—and to the fairy godmother whose honey voice was ministering to my damaged soul.

When the exercise was over, I lay down on her living room carpet and for an hour submitted as she moved her hands over me without touching my flesh, rocking silently with closed eyes. This was to "clear" my "aura," a field of energy that was supposed to envelop me. I felt the surface of my body fur with emotion, as though such a field did indeed exist. Afterwards, we talked and I felt safe enough to open my wounds. She listened with an attitude that was sympathetic and accepting. The solace she offered was enhanced for me by her political credentials: She had met her husband at the University of Wisconsin, one of the places where our crusade had begun, and she still shared the ethos of the movement we had created. I trusted her enough to tell her about the Panthers, and I felt in her care a small but needed portion of the absolution I craved.

About the psychic realm she introduced me to, I suspended disbelief. I was too thirsty for the elixir she offered to do otherwise. Entering, if only imaginatively, a world in which history and politics were left behind was healing in itself. And why, in any case, should I feel metaphysically superior? I had schooled myself in Hegel and Marx, and where had they led me? I had worshipped the gods of reason, and they had delivered me into the company of killers.

Like a desert wanderer to an oasis well, I returned to these sessions regularly. But each time I dipped into the healing waters, the dangerous undercurrent grew stronger. Finally, I plunged into the stream itself and let the passions surface. This was a far more threatening affair than the one with Abby. In my present state, I lacked even the inner restraint I had before. Why should I deny myself, when others did not? What would justify such sacrifice? There was no bottom to the despair that engulfed me, and no apparent limit to what I would do to be free of it. Nor were my actions driven strictly by the need to escape from pain. Alongside the thirst for health, there was a parallel desire to increase adversity, to punish myself even more.

In the perverse environment I had entered, I discovered strange new satisfactions. Jackie had declared her feminist ideals. It made me curious to see how she would react to the advances of a married man. At first she protested her concern for my wife, and then her guilt when the concern proved empty. I enjoyed watching her betray her principles. Here was company. Here was behavior in accord with my new appreciation of human possibility. Was there a rule to be broken? I wanted to break it myself.

If I had been able to give myself completely to this newfound cynicism, I would have spent less time mired in the swamp of emotional torments that now followed. But I quickly discovered that I could not sever myself so easily from the person I had been. I could not even *think* of leaving my family. *What would I do without them?* I still loved Elissa. I still wanted to be the good husband and father, though I was neither. I couldn't let go of my past that was dead, but I couldn't breathe life into it, either. I wanted to split myself in two, letting one half continue with what was left of the old life, and sending the other on to see if it could make a new one. But the more I struggled with these dilemmas, the tighter the knots became. I had created my own prison, and it had no exit.

In this predicament I began to realize just how insular my existence had been. How little I had really tested myself before making the choices that had shaped my life. How scarce the occasions I had taken to find out how other people made theirs. I had been too busy recruiting them to my important agendas. Intimacy had not broadened these horizons. I had married a woman who was herself averse to experience. But in her this attitude was not, as for me, the product of abstract thinking, and was not going to change. There were worse things, in her view, than a sheltered life. Who was I to argue? Her stubborn consistency had provided a strong foundation for the family we created. I was grateful for this.

The disorder of my life—which I understood to be a disorder of my self—allowed me to see inside for the first time. I had stepped so far outside bounds that were familiar that I began asking questions I had never thought to ask: *Why am I doing this? What do I want? What do I need?* As the life I had so carefully and purposefully constructed disintegrated before my eyes, I realized that I really didn't know

The chaos I found myself in had shifted my perspective: It was no longer the world I had to change, but myself. I was still protected from the judgment of others by the secrecy with which I conducted my affair with Jackie. But the image of myself was clear enough to *me*.

It was dishonorable and humiliating. It made me want to avert my own eyes.

And yet the very sense of failure, of bottomless defeat, proved ultimately a grace. For the first time in my life, I could not address others from a moral high ground. I was no longer busily bringing them the good news. It was I who needed help. For the first time in my life, I wanted to *listen*.

As I shuttled between my two lives, I was finding it harder to keep the necessary deceptions consistent, or the pressures from both in check. My double life was proving untenable, and it was impossible to get clarity. I had no peace. But it was only when I tried to end the affair, and return to my marriage, that I realized how dire the situation had become.

I had persuaded Elissa to go for a romantic weekend to Crater Lake in Oregon. It was the first time we had been away alone together since our marriage, nineteen years before. We stayed on the rim of the crater, which was eerily beautiful, the lake set deep in the cavity below. But the trip failed to provide the emotional reunion I had hoped for. There were moments when everything went well and I could feel the flow of passion and understanding that had bonded us for so long. But there were others that went poorly, where the current short-circuited. "You're thinking of *her*," she said when I drifted for a moment—sparking my anger and revealing that it might be impossible to repair a broken trust.

On the highway back, I was stopped for speeding. I had recently been accumulating violations. Not long after the episode in Moe's bookstore, I had bought a white 260Z with a houndstooth racing stripe. The Z was used, and cost less than our family Datsun, but it was a significant departure from normal. Long and sleek, with two bucket seats, it was impractical for a family man, and inexplicable for me. For fifteen years I had driven nothing but a VW bus, and station wagons suitable for family purposes. I had never owned a sports car. I would not have previously considered any vehicle that was without utilitarian value. The Z felt obscene—but I wanted the power. The feeling was liberating, an act of defiance. Selfish. It was in your face to everything I had been.

The trip back to Berkeley took seven hours, and we returned home after dark, weary from the road. The younger children were packing their things for summer camp. A flashlight and a comb were missing from the provisions, and I went out to buy them, my destination a convenience store 10 minutes away. Instead of returning directly, however, I decided to pass by a house where Jackie and I had once trysted. There would be nothing there but memory and the chance to savor its passion, but I could not resist. Taking a small and unfamiliar side street, I braked at a stop sign, my head buzzing with exhaustion and my thoughts wandering into the maze of emotional confusion I had so deviously constructed for myself. In my distraction, I did not notice the way the street in front of me became suddenly illumined, as though from a giant beam. I did not see the tracks. I released the brake and pressed the accelerator. A split second elapsed; then a wall of steel, 20 feet high came rushing across my hood from the right.

When the engine appeared, I flipped the steering wheel left in an automatic reflex, drawing parallel to the tracks—but the right side of my car was caught by the behemoth, dragged along and crumpled like a paper cup. It was like being in a film of my own death. The train carried the Z across the road, and then dropped it when the car wheels hit the curb on the other side. A dozen railroad cars passed the crossing before the train was able to screech to a stop. Jumping from their cab, the trainmen hurried to help me, and found me dazed and in a mild state of shock. But, at the same time, a crystalline clarity had formed in my head about my present state: I was now a danger to everyone around me, especially myself.

The unhappiness I was causing Elissa was now greater than I could bear. I was no longer able to deceive myself into believing that things would get better. I had agreed to "work" on the marriage, but in the sessions with a counselor I saw that what I really wanted was that our marriage—my life—would be different. All the torment of the recent past—the emotional confrontations that were not resolved, the wounds that would not heal—impressed on me the inertial forces ranged against this possibility. *People don't change.* Elissa had thrown the axiom at me many times, in frustration, when I pressed these issues in the past. She was almost Protestant in her stoicism—her reconciliation to the fact that life was going to be a trial, and that grownups should be prepared to endure it. My entire being rebelled at the idea. I wanted more. I wanted *her* to want more. Now I found myself resigned to the truth in what she had said: We were who we were. Neither she, nor the terms of our life together, were going to change.

The free-fall continued, and I went to therapy alone—a humbling experience for a man who always prided himself on having the answers. "Do people change?" I asked the therapist during a session. "Only if they get in enough pain," was the response. "And not always then."

I was in enough pain. I wanted out. But I still couldn't confront what that meant. How could I face my children? How could I leave Elissa? For months, I tortured myself with the impossible alternatives, miserable at the prospect of staying or leaving. In the midst of this paralysis, a picture of my father appeared to me, as he was in his life. I had come to loathe this image. I hated the self-pity he allowed himself, the sniping at my mother as though she was his keeper. It was not that his complaints were groundless. But I saw how assiduously he knit the filaments of his own web. How he made himself depend on her, and then resented the dependence; how he denied himself, and then blamed her for what he missed. *If you want it, go for it!* I sometimes wanted to shout at him. But I knew it was futile. Like *his* father, he was unable to become the master of his own life. I was not going to be like that. I would not grow old griping, as he did, at an ungenerous world, a prisoner in my own body. Whatever it took, whatever the price, I was going to be free of this legacy. I would not live out my years blaming my wife, and being penitent like a child afterwards—like him.

Before making my decision, I turned to friends for advice. I was concerned how others would judge me if I left. It was a last-ditch hope that someone would dissuade me. But when I sought them out, no one so much as put up an argument. In the two decades since Elissa and I had met as teenagers, the environment of marriage had changed along with everything else. All around us marriages were dissolving, without communal regret. The nuclear family was under attack— the patriarchal cornerstone of the Old Order. Half the parents in my youngest's third-grade class were already divorced. The only friend who actually advised against it said: "Wait until the children are older," and then whimsically: "Marriage is a sentence." Nothing could have incited me more.

In September 1978 I moved out. Before departing, I sat down with my children to explain to them what was happening. The youngest, Anne, was only nine years old. What could I tell them? I was destroying their home and breaking their innocent hearts. I could hardly explain it to myself. My lips formed words that were totally inadequate while my own heart cracked. I was not leaving them, I promised. I would stay nearby. I would be there for them when they needed me. It was a promise I would live up to. But it could not make up for the one I had broken.

My mother's response to these unhappy events was as supportive as she knew how to be in circumstances where nothing really could be done. I heard the concern in her voice, and was grateful for it. My father's reaction was terse and to the point: "You've poisoned the family well," he said.

There is no need to go further, reader. For me, twenty years have not buried this pain.

I had chosen an inopportune time for my departure: The remainder of the monies I had received for my share of the Rockefeller book had run out. I still had financial responsibilities for the four children, although Elissa was now working and could share the burden. But with Peter gone, there was no certainty that I could secure an income from writing. I still lacked a feel for the popular culture. I had never thought of myself as someone with an exceptional talent. I was a Marxist first, and a writer only because I had a truth I wanted to tell. Now that truth was bankrupt, and with it every expertise I could claim to possess. In desperation, I began to write a novel based loosely on my experience, hoping that I could turn personal disaster into an asset. I named my central character Brownstein, which was my mother's family name, but also Trotsky's—*Bronstein.* When the revolution turned sour, the chief rabbi of Moscow had come up with a saying: "The Trotskys make the revolution and the Bronsteins pay the bills." I felt like both: Trotsky *and* Bronstein.

A few months into my new life, I went to New York to discuss the 150 pages I had written with Alice Mayhew, my editor at Simon & Schuster. Alice had been my editor for *Empire and Revolution,* and the abandoned book on the sociology of knowledge. I was hoping she would give me a new contract and an advance. The corner I had backed myself into was so recessed that I didn't even provide myself with an alternative if she said no. But when we met in her office, she said, "You're good at what you do. Why do you want to do something at which you're just ordinary?" The reality was that I had no aptitude for fiction. I was uncomfortable making things up. Philosophically, I accepted the idea that fictions could provide another path to the truth. But psychologically I was blocked. In attempting to deal with my own experience, every invention felt to me like a lie.

It is not difficult to understand why I had these feelings. The movement to which I had devoted myself was built on a lie: that there was a redemptive future within our grasp. Millions had been sacrificed to it, and were being sacrificed still. The lie had killed Betty, and protected her killers. If the Panthers had not been "progressives," shielded by the faith, the authorities would have been able to bring them to justice. The chasm between the reality I knew and the fiction to which my political community was still devoted had not gone away, and seemed to be growing still.

Since Betty's death three years earlier, I had watched as Elaine Brown and the Panthers became ever more powerful in local politics, until their influence reached to the governor of the state. In a painful irony added to my cumulative woes, the public base of this success was the Learning Center I had created. Elected officials and local businessmen were taken on tours of the school, and came away converted. By 1977, the Learning Center was the beneficiary of hundreds of thousands of dollars in grants from local and federal agencies. The vision I had outlined to Newton that evening in the penthouse had been carried out by Elaine.

Elaine had run for the city council with the endorsement of the local congressman, Ron Dellums, and all of organized labor, and won 44 percent of the vote—despite the fact that she was under investigation for Betty's murder. In the following year, her political ally, Jerry Brown, became governor and appointed a trusted Panther lawyer, J. Anthony Kline, to be his Legal Affairs Secretary. This meant that Kline oversaw all judicial appointments in the state. Another

Party lawyer, Fred Hiestand, also became a gubernatorial adviser. Years later, a high-ranking Party member described this moment in Panther history to a journalist: "The [authorities] knew all about our clandestine activities. We had politicians, judges, police, respected businessmen in our pockets. There were members of the police force who would call us up and tell us when someone in the department was going to move on us." It was a line out of *The Godfather*, which was Newton's favorite book.

In the 1976 election, a Party protégé named Lionel Wilson became Oakland's first black mayor, with the help of the Panther machine. Elaine had deployed her new connections in Sacramento in order to give the campaign its winning issue. Working with the governor's office, she was able to secure the completion of an artery into downtown Oakland previously blocked by environmental groups. With the governor's help, she was appointed to the Oakland Economic Development Council, a coalition of downtown business interests that would oversee the project. In her autobiography, Elaine describes her meeting with the chairman of the council, who was also head of the Clorox Corporation, Oakland's largest business. The price of her cooperation, she told him, was control of the construction jobs involved in the project. She warned: "I've got the ability to take down this entire city if you and I fail to see this thing to completion. I mean the City Center, the port, and all twenty-two stories of the Clorox Building." She had the muscle to make her threat plausible: Under her leadership, the Squad was continuing its campaign to control the Oakland underworld through a series of drive-by shootings and murders.

I had to watch helplessly the progress of a monster I had helped to create. Then, in the spring of 1977, an opportunity presented itself to do something about it. I ran into Kate Coleman, a journalist who had written articles for *Ramparts,* at a Telegraph Avenue hangout called the "Med." Kate sat down at my table and began talking about Elaine. She had been assigned by a commercial magazine to do a profile of the Panther leader, and wanted to share Elaine's impressive exploits with me.

It was a moment I had dreaded. A year before, I had breached my code of security, and the results had not been reassuring. I had tried to warn two young activists against participating in a radical collective called the "Food Conspiracy," which distributed food wholesale and had become a million-dollar operation. I was concerned because the collective provided jobs for convicts who were eligible for parole. This was the way Eldridge Cleaver had come to work at *Ramparts*. I tried to convey to them what I had learned, and to warn them about the dangers they were inviting. But I could see by their reaction that this only made them think I had been contaminated by racist ideas. I felt both endangered and unclean. A year later there was a shooting in the collective that left several people dead, as the ex-cons vied to get control of the assets. When I met the young activists again, they told me they would have been present the night of the killings, if not for a fortuitous circumstance that kept them away.

I tried mentally to calculate the risks I was taking, not only for myself but for my family, if I decided to talk to Kate. She was a friend, but she was also a Movement person. I waited until we had gone out in the street, where I thought nobody could overhear us, and told her my story. She listened carefully, and seemed sympathetic. When we parted, I had an ache in my stomach from having exposed myself to dangers I couldn't assess. But I also had the hope that something positive might result.

While Kate was writing her article, Huey Newton returned to face the charges against him. Elaine had maintained daily phone contact with Newton in Cuba, and had visited him there as well. Their discussions had convinced him that Elaine's political connections reached deep enough into the Democratic Party and the California judicial system to give him an odds-on chance of beating his raps. His return revived my feelings of gloom. The nightmare was going to continue.

When Newton landed, he told reporters that the charges he faced were part of a government frame-up involving the FBI, the CIA, and the Oakland police. He announced that the Party's lawyers had filed a $100 million lawsuit against the FBI for launching counterintelligence efforts to destroy it. He was praised as a returning hero by local political leaders, and invited to the state capital to receive an award for the work of the Learning Center. The award was to be presented by Assemblyman Tom Bates, who was married to Berkeley's radical mayor. Newton appeared at the ceremony in Sacramento two hours late as described in a scene Elaine recorded in her autobiography:

> Huey and Big Bob finally arrived, disheveled and unseemly. I realized then that Huey had returned to cocaine. [Of course, Elaine knew that he had never stopped.] He and Ericka and I stood on the capitol steps in the late afternoon. Bates handed him our official proclamation certificate. Huey's body shivered. His eyes bulged, and he could hardly accept the parchment for wiping his nose and sniffing.

Newton's trial for the murder of Kathleen Smith came up in October. On the morning of the preliminary hearing, Newton sent a hit team to kill the chief prosecution witness, a prostitute named Crystal Gray. A gun battle ensued, in which one of the assassins, a Squad member named Louis Johnson, was killed instead, while another, Flores Forbes, was wounded. Forbes fled the scene, stopping off to pick up a Panther named Nelson Malloy, who drove him to Nevada. Fearing that Malloy might reveal the Panthers' role, Newton sent his gunmen after them. They caught up with the pair in the Las Vegas desert, shot Malloy twice in the back, and then buried him by the roadside under a pile of rocks. But Malloy wasn't dead, and his moans attracted the attention of passing tourists, who dug him out of his shallow grave. He told police what had happened, and was sent back home on a stretcher, paralyzed for life.

The affair made headlines, and tore the public veil from the Panther reality, unraveling the web of political influence that Elaine had spun. Mayor Wilson and other dignitaries removed themselves from the Learning Center board. Then, while the events were still fresh news, Elaine herself disappeared. Like Bobby Seale, she had fallen out of favor with Newton—who expelled her, and beat her so severely that she had to be hospitalized.

Six months later, Kate's story appeared in the July 10, 1978 issue of *New Times* magazine. It told the story of Betty's murder, and described the circumstances that made the Panthers suspects. The article began with a graphic account of a rape Newton had committed after returning from Cuba. The victim, black and the mother of three, was forced into Newton's car by Big Bob, and sexually assaulted at gunpoint for hours. The psychological trauma was so great from the assault that she had to be hospitalized. After notifying police and telling them her story, however, she was afraid to file charges because Newton had taken her address, and threatened to kill her children if she made trouble for him. Kate's story, written with *Chronicle* reporter Paul Avery, was called "The Party's Over: How Huey Newton Created a Street Gang at the Center of the Black Panther Party." It laid out their criminal record publicly for the first time. The most important information I had given Kate was about the existence of the Squad. She and Avery had conducted their own extensive investigation, using court records, police reports, and interviews with members of Oakland's black community to fill in the story.

When the article appeared, Kate went into hiding and Newton held a press conference to denounce her. He was flanked by Bert Schneider and Michael Kennedy (his latest attorney, who had made his reputation defending drug dealers and the Weather Underground). Accompanying them was a troop of youngsters from the Learning Center, carrying signs that said: "Kate, Why Do You Want To Take Food From Our Mouths?"

When the trial for killing Kathleen Smith was finally held, Newton was acquitted. In the course of his long criminal career, he had become an expert at manipulating his audiences. In court he had his lawyers select whites for his juries, because whites were most likely to be impressed by his myth—his self-taught literacy out of Plato's *Republic,* his rise from the ghetto, his persecution by racist police. Whites were not likely to be aware of his street reputation as a thug. The witnesses against him in the Smith case were black prostitutes and pimps, whom it was easy to discredit. By contrast, Huey was a famous figure who had authored books, and could summon impressive character witnesses to vouch for him and testify that he was targeted by police for his political views. In the Smith case he was able to get help from progressive allies like Donald Freed, a screenwriter who maintained under oath that Newton was with him, working on his doctoral thesis, the night Smith was killed.

It was disconcerting to see a man I knew to be guilty of murder go free. But even more unsettling was the response of my comrades in the face of these events. Kate's bombshell was followed by deafening silence. No radical leader proposed any second thoughts about a gang they had anointed as their revolutionary vanguard. Nor did any radical critics. This silence of the Left would endure throughout the life of the generation. When Todd Gitlin came to write his history of the Sixties a decade later, there was no mention of either Betty Van Patter or the Panther Squad. In a private letter to me, after I called him to account, he wrote: "I don't doubt [the Panthers'] vicious, murderous record, nor do I attribute it to the depredations of the FBI...." But his public writings remained a different story. His chapter on the Panthers was unchanged in the revised edition of his book that appeared in 1992. It was titled "The Bogey of Race," indicating to the reader that the Panther threat was an invention of the police and other establishment racists. "The Panthers' 'nitty-gritty' audacity, matched against the patent brutality of the police, could make their gun-toting 'self-defense' look excusable, even alluring," Gitlin wrote by way of excusing himself and other white radicals who supported them. "The Panthers were streetwise, disciplined, fearless, Marxist-Leninist, revolutionary, and, most miraculously of all...they welcomed white allies," was the way he summed up their appeal.

The only concrete allusions Gitlin allowed himself, in his book, to the Party's darker side were two footnotes. In one, he dutifully reported Eldridge Cleaver's admission that the Panthers had ambushed a police car after Martin Luther King's death, but simultaneously undermined the testimony by describing Cleaver as someone who was "now reincarnated as a born-again Christian and a follower of Reverend Sun Myung Moon." In the other, he dismissed an investigative *New Yorker* article, which documented both the Panthers' assaults on police and their criminal activities, saying that its author, Edward J. Epstein, "tended to take Panther accounts at their worst while taking self-serving police accounts at face value." Twenty years after the fact, Gitlin still presented the Panthers as victims: "The provocative Panthers often played innocent, but no fair-minded observer could deny that they were being shot down." It was the party line. In his autobiography, Tom Hayden summarized the close of the Panther chapter in the history of the New Left with a single sentence: "The Black Panthers were disintegrated by a combination of internal rivalries and costly police and legal pressures."

An academic literature would also appear about the Panther era. These footnoted tomes, equally disingenuous and disdainful of the facts, would establish the Panther myth for a new generation. Because of the Panthers' militance in behalf of the oppressed (or so the radical myth maintained), they were victims of an official "genocide." Typical among these tendentious texts was Kenneth O'Reilly's *Racial Matters: The FBI's Secret File on Black America*. O'Reilly's chapter on the Party and its battles with the law was titled "The Only Good Panther" (i.e., is a dead Panther). In other words, the Panthers were victims of repression.

I was disturbed by the failure of Hayden, Gitlin, and others like them, to come forward with the truth. They knew, or had access to, pieces of the story that still remained hidden. They could provide credibility to what Kate had written. More importantly, they could set an example for the Left by initiating its long-overdue confrontation with what it had done. Perhaps by such candor they could prevent a new generation from repeating our mistakes. But none of them did.

Thinking about their silence, I was struck by how it contrasted with that of our political opponents when confronted with their own misdeeds. Once the government became convinced that its "cointel-pro" program targeting black militants had been abused, the program was discontinued. Under the pressure of criticism, moreover, J. Edgar Hoover's image was completely transformed. Long an American hero, he quickly became a figure almost universally reviled. As in its Vietnam operation, official America had shown itself capable of looking at its own deeds, and changing course. The democratic system made this possible. But the Left lacked any similar mechanism of social conscience. In our generation—the generation that mattered—there would be no second thoughts about the support it had given to a criminal gang it had mistaken for a moral vanguard.

Equally important, there would be no second thoughts about the myth it had created of a government repression. If the government had been as malign and intrusive as the Left maintained, how had the Panthers been able to operate at all? How had they committed murder and gotten away with it? This idea of government evil was even more important to the self-image of the Left than was the preservation of the Panther legend. The specter of the oppressor was what kept the

Left's innocence intact and fed its indignation. *The government had set out to destroy black militants from racist motives.* This was the myth that radicals had to keep alive to justify their cause. The truth was closer to the opposite: The destroyers and racists were the militants themselves.

The oath of silence that buried this reality was not exclusive to progressives. It was an atavism common to other communities and tribes. I had even encountered it in my research on the Rockefellers. Nelson's son Steven had told me:

> *The family is something you dare not violate. It incarnates itself in certain figures toward whom you must act in a reverent, respectful fashion, the way people act when they go to church.... Worshipping God, well, it's worshipping the family. It's the same. The family is a holy thing: you dare not transgress against its principles, standards, ideals, and so on. The result of all this is that a lot goes unsaid.*

It was an accurate description of the Left I knew.

Under the pressure of these realities, I began to develop a political dyspepsia. When talking about the Left, I would find myself speaking in ways that provoked strong reactions. I seemed to relish the anger that came back at me.

But on one occasion my provocations failed to produce the expected result. I had dropped in on my friend Ezra Hendon, a Movement lawyer who had defended "Los Siete de La Raza," seven Chicano youths accused of murdering a policeman. We had written about the case in *Ramparts,* presenting it as yet another aggression of the power structure against the oppressed. The seven youths were acquitted. Later, it turned out that they were in fact criminals, and subsequently were convicted of other murders and crimes.

In the aftermath of Newton's release, I had begun thinking about cases like this. Following George Jackson's death, the two remaining "Soledad Brothers" were freed and then also came to bad ends. John Cluchette committed another murder, and was sent back to prison. Fleeta Drumgo was arrested for beating and raping his girlfriend, and then executed for a drug burn before he could be brought to trial. Ignoring these facts, Angela Davis, who had been George Jackson's lover and an administrator of his defense fund, spoke at Drumgo's funeral and eulogized him as a "communist martyr." Davis herself had been a fugitive in the Seventies, attempting to flee prosecution for supplying guns to Jonathan Jackson for the hostage-taking that had caused several deaths, including his own. After months of flight, Davis was caught and put on trial. Few people in the Left believed that she was innocent, but the jury acquitted her. This did not prevent her from touring the capitals of Communist dictatorships to receive political awards, while condemning American justice as racist and a sham.

I was in a mood to provoke Ezra and get a dose of indignation in return. "You know," I said, "except for the Rosenbergs, I can't think of a single case since the beginning of the Cold War in which radicals were tried for a crime, where they were not only guilty but also acquitted." After saying this, I sat back and waited for his attack. Instead, he answered: "You know, I've read all the books on the Rosenberg case, and thought about it a lot, and I'm not convinced they were innocent." I was speechless. My own faith in the Rosenbergs' innocence had never wavered. They had proclaimed their innocence to their children and the world. How could they have lied? The thought itself was repellent.

That same summer, James Weinstein—an old friend—came through Berkeley and paid me a visit. Ten years older than I, Jimmy had been in the Communist Party when the Rosenbergs were arrested. At the beginning of the Sixties he had founded *Studies on the Left,* and now he was launching a new socialist weekly, based in Chicago, which he was going to call *In These Times.* He wanted my name, as one of its sponsors, for his masthead. Since Betty's death, I had not engaged in any political cause, but I had still not left the community of the Left, or even faced that prospect. I regarded Jimmy as one of the more sensible radical intellects, and told myself I would be sponsoring a more enlightened attitude in movement ranks. Disillusioned as I was, I gave him my name.

Then I told Jimmy about my conversation with Ezra, and waited for *his* indignant response. But my expectations were confounded again. Instead of reacting negatively, he told me that he, himself, had been called to the Rosenberg grand jury when he was a student at

Cornell. He explained that just before the Rosenbergs were arrested, his roommate and Party cell leader, Max, had borrowed his car without explanation, and driven it all over the state. When Max returned the car, he asked Jimmy to drive his companion, a man named Julius, to New York. Two weeks later, the Rosenbergs were indicted. Jimmy thought that Julius Rosenberg was indeed involved in spying, but on industrial rather than military targets.

Shortly after Jimmy's departure, another summer visitor appeared. It was Ron Radosh, whom I hadn't seen since my years in London. Ron was an old friend of Jimmy's and had been an editor of *Studies on the Left*. He was now a professional historian and the author of several respected works. I told Radosh about the two conversations. When he was a youngster, Radosh had been a member of the Rosenberg Defense Committee and, after their execution, had joined the Committee to Re-Open the Rosenberg Case. Although Ron and Jimmy were old friends, Jimmy had never mentioned to Radosh his connection with the case. After our conversation, Radosh went back to New York and began work on what became *The Rosenberg File*, which he coauthored with Joyce Milton, and which was published in 1983. Based on a massive search of FBI files secured under the Freedom of Information Act, and interviews with principals, the book was received as the definitive work on the subject. The authors concluded that Julius Rosenberg had organized an atomic spy ring and provided valuable information to the Russians. Jimmy's story provided confirmation of a key witness's testimony revealing Julius' guilt.

From their review of the FBI files, Radosh and his coauthor concluded that the government had insufficient evidence to link Ethel to her husband's crimes. They uncovered government memos that suggested she was prosecuted to "break" Julius, and condemned this as a perversion of justice. But when the book appeared, the Left was still outraged. Radosh was not yet a disillusioned radical like myself. He continued to believe in the socialist future. He still had faith in the Left. Ever since he was thirteen years old and joined the Labor Youth League, Radosh had devoted his talents to the radical cause. But, in coming reluctantly to the conclusion that Julius Rosenberg was guilty, he had committed an unpardonable sin. His oldest friends now shunned him. *The Nation*, and other radical magazines he had

written for, condemned him. At meetings of the American Historical Association, progressive historians turned their backs on him. His
neighbors crossed the street when he approached. The New Left had
come and gone, and nothing had changed. It was just like in the days
of the Khrushchev Report.

The Left could not look inward and it could not look back. At this
late date, who would not consider it a reasonable supposition that
the Rosenbergs might have committed the crime? (I myself did not
share Radosh's belief in Ethel's innocence.) The Rosenbergs had been
dead for twenty-five years. An entire era had passed. Outside the Communist Party, there was no one on the left who did not understand
that the Soviet Union was a police state, or that the Party, to which
the Rosenbergs belonged, was a conspiratorial network that carried
out Kremlin orders. Why such passion over the suggestion that they
might have been spies? Why the frantic denial? Why did questioning
the Rosenbergs' innocence make the questioners pariahs and, eventually, outcasts? I felt I knew the answer: The Rosenbergs were not
just individuals. They were totems of the radical tribe, martyrs to its
cause. Their innocence was an article of the radical faith. In it, we
knew ourselves: that *our* justice was superior to our opponents.' This
sense of righteousness confirmed our belief that we had been chosen
for the mission of social redemption.

That same summer, there were reports of a bloodbath in Indochina.
The Khmer Rouge had swept through Cambodia, leaving a killing
field in their wake. From Vietnam itself had come reports of a hundred
thousand summary executions, a million and a half refugees, and
more than a million people imprisoned in "re-education camps" and
gulags in the South. These events produced a shock of recognition in
some quarters of the Left. Joan Baez took out a full-page ad in the *New
York Times* for an "Appeal to the Conscience of North Vietnam." She
enlisted a number of former "anti-war" activists to sign her call to the
Communists to show more humanity in their treatment of their opponents. As soon as her statement appeared, however, Baez was attacked
by Tom Hayden and Jane Fonda as a tool of the CIA. A counter-
ad was organized by Cora Weiss, who had traveled to Hanoi and

collaborated with the regime in its torture of American POWs. The Weiss ad praised the Communists for their moderation in administering the peace.

The significance of this conflict derived from the role that the Left itself had played in the tragedies. In 1973, Nixon and Kissinger negotiated a peace treaty that was designed to keep the South Vietnamese regime in place and remove America's military presence. I knew that the outcome was not going to be the "liberation" we had promised. However, with American forces out of the picture, I saw no compelling reason to remain politically in the fray.

But Hayden and others like him did. After the anti-draft movement disintegrated in 1970, Hayden and Fonda organized an "Indochina Peace Campaign" to cut off remaining American support for the regimes in Cambodia and South Vietnam. For the next few years, the Campaign worked tirelessly to ensure the victory of the North Vietnamese Communists and the Khmer Rouge. Accompanied by a camera team, Hayden and Fonda traveled first to Hanoi and then to the "liberated" zones in South Vietnam, to make a propaganda film. Called *Introduction to the Enemy,* it attempted to persuade viewers that the Communists were going to create a new society in the South. Equality and justice awaited its inhabitants if only America would cut off support for the Saigon regime.

Assisted by radical legislators like Ron Dellums and Bella Abzug, Hayden set up a caucus in the Capitol, where he lectured congressional staffers on the need to end American aid. He directed his attention to Cambodia as well, lobbying for an accommodation with the Khmer Rouge guerillas. Nixon's resignation over Watergate provided all the leverage Hayden and his activists needed. The Democrats won the midterm elections, bringing to Washington a new group of legislators determined to undermine the settlement that Nixon and Kissinger had achieved. The aid was cut, the Saigon regime fell, and the Khmer Rouge marched into the Cambodian capital. In the two years that followed, more Indochinese were killed by the victorious Communists than had been killed on both sides in all thirteen years of the anti-Communist war.

It was the bloodbath that our opponents had predicted. But for the Left there would be no contrition and no look back. Baez's appeal proved the farthest it was possible for them to go, which was not very far at all. The appeal did not begin to suggest that "anti-war" activists needed to reassess the role they had played in making these tragedies inevitable. Ironically, it was Hayden who eventually came closest to such self-recognition: "What continues to batter my sense of morality and judgment," he wrote in *Reunion*, "is that I could not even imagine that the worst stereotype of revolutionary madness was becoming a reality...Pol Pot and the Khmer Rouge became the Stalins and Hitlers of my lifetime, killing hundreds of thousands of people for being 'educated' or 'urban,' for attracting the paranoid attention of a secret police who saw conspiracies behind every failure of the grand plan to be achieved. Most Western estimates settle on 1.5 million killed...." But, having acknowledged these facts and his confusion over them, he could go no farther. The terrible result, which he had worked so hard to make possible, failed to prompt a reassessment of the policies he had opposed: "None of this persuades me that Nixon and Kissinger were right...."

I had been having my own thoughts about the end of the war, attempting to place it in historical context as a way of judging what had happened. As a student at Columbia, I had read Euripides' tragedy *The Trojan Women*, which was inspired by his countrymen's conquest of the small island of Melos. Euripides intended his play to arouse the moral sense of his fellow Athenians about the war they had conducted and the suffering they had inflicted. When the Athenians saw Euripides' play, they wept for the people of Melos. In the eyes of my professor, Moses Hadas, this show of conscience was a tribute to Athenian civilization. How much greater, I thought, was the civilized response of America's democracy to the tragedy in Vietnam. I could not think of another historical instance where a nation had retreated from a field of battle it had dominated because the conscience of its people had been touched. And yet, America had withdrawn for precisely that reason. The Left believed that American policy was controlled by giant corporations, and that the war was being prosecuted for imperial interests which they would not relinquish. But the Left had been proven wrong. American democracy was *not* the "sham" we said it was. The Left itself had provided the spark that turned American hearts against the war. And when the American people turned against the war, there was no greater power that could make it continue.

This realization had a profound impact on my political outlook. In a democracy, where the people are sovereign, what justification can there be for self-styled "revolutionaries" like ourselves? In rejecting the democratic process, we had rejected the people, setting ourselves over them in judgment as though we were superior beings. Even more powerful in affecting my outlook was the failure of others on the left to notice what the success of our "anti-war" efforts had revealed. The withdrawal of America from a war that we said it could never retreat from made no impression at all. The rhetorical attacks on "American imperialism" and its "corporate ruling class" continued. In December 1979, Soviet armies crossed an international border beyond the Iron Curtain for the first time since the end of World War II, invading Afghanistan. President Carter proposed reinstituting the draft in an attempt to dissuade the invader. The Left responded by launching a *new* "anti-war" movement, this one directed not against the Soviet aggressor but the Carter White House. A "Stop the Draft" rally was staged in Berkeley, the symbolic crucible of the New Left revolution. It was addressed by Angela Davis and Congressman Dellums, both of whom denounced the "evil" in Washington, just as in the old days. As though nothing had happened.

Three weeks prior to the invasion of Afghanistan, I wrote an article for *The Nation* which proved to be my farewell to the Left. I had begun it the previous summer, after dining with E. L. Doctorow—who was giving a seminar in Berkeley. In *The Book of Daniel*, Doctorow had cited *The Free World Colossus*, and was interested in meeting me. I was flattered by his attention and, during our conversation, expressed some of my doubts about the Left. He appeared interested in the concerns I raised. "Why don't you write about them for *The Nation?*" he asked. I told him I was skeptical that *The Nation* would print them. But I knew he was on its editorial board, and decided to give it a try. I titled my article "Left Illusions," and *The Nation's* editors printed it in their December 8, 1979 issue. When I received the magazine, I saw that they had changed the title to "A Radical's Disenchantment," a subtle difference but significant to me. It was as though they knew something I did not: that I had already crossed a point of no return.

The article began with a statement of my current position: "Not long after the end of the Vietnam War, I found myself unable to maintain any longer the necessary belief in the Marxist promise. Along with many other veterans of the 1960s struggles, I ceased to be politically active." I followed this with a self-protective caveat, pointing out that we had not sought to join the conservative forces of the status quo: "Instead, politics itself became suspect. We turned inward." I explained that the inward turn was not narcissistic, but came from a sense that our failures could not be attributed simply to historical circumstance. We, too, were responsible for what had happened. It was the inability of others on the left to accept this responsibility that I felt was the root of the problem. "Antonio Gramsci once described the revolutionary temperament as a pessimism of the intellect and an optimism of the will," I noted. For the veterans of my radical generation, the balance toward pessimism had been tipped "when we sustained what seemed like irreparable injury to our sense of historical possibility:

> It was not...so much the feeling that the Left would not be able to change society; it was rather the sense that, in crucial ways, the Left could not change itself.

Despite the uniform disasters of socialist revolutions, the socialist goal remained unexamined and unquestioned. Even worse, the Left's responses to these catastrophes were shaped by a system of double standards. "The Left's indignation seems exclusively reserved for outrages that confirm the Marxist diagnosis of capitalist society. Thus, there is protest against murder and repression in Nicaragua but not Cambodia, Chile but not Tibet...Israel but not Libya or Iraq." Worse, still, the Left had accepted no responsibility for the part that its own ideas and actions had played in the revolutionary disasters. "Unpalatable results (e.g., the outcome of the Revolution in Russia) are regarded as 'irrelevant'—and dismissed—as though the Left in America and elsewhere played no role in them, and as though they had no impact on the world that the Left set out to change."

Equally important (and parallel to) these failures was the Left's inability to reassess the nature of the society it wanted to destroy. To illustrate this, I took an example from the writings of Noam Chomsky, who was at the time its most admired intellect. Chomsky had described the press in America as "the mirror image of [the press in] the Soviet Union, where all the people who write in *Pravda* represent the position which they call 'socialism'...." Chomsky applied this observation to the American media's reportage of the Vietnam War: "It is notable that despite the extensive and well-known record of Government lies during the period of the Vietnam War, the press, with fair consistency, remained remarkably obedient, and quite willing to accept the Government's assumptions, framework of thinking, and interpretation of what was happening."

It was a perfect example of how little leftists like Chomsky had learned from their experience. The reality, I pointed out, was just the opposite:

> *Not only did the American press provide much of the documentation on which the anti-war movement's indictment of the American war effort was based—including the My Lai atrocities—but in defiance of its Government and at the risk of prosecution for espionage and treason, it published the classified documents known as the Pentagon Papers, which provided a good deal of the tangible record of official lies to which Chomsky refers.*

I concluded the article with the questions I had been asking myself: "Can the Left take a really hard look at itself—the consequences of its failures, the credibility of its critiques, the viability of its goals? Can it begin to shed the arrogant cloak of self-righteousness that elevates it above its own history and makes it impervious to the lessons of experience?"

I already knew the answers, although I wasn't ready yet to draw the appropriate conclusions. Even at this late date, I was still hoping somebody would appear to convince me I was wrong.

REQUIEM

U NTIL NOW, I HAD BEEN GUIDED BY A VISION OF THE FUTURE IN which an unjust world would finally be put right. It was the prism through which I judged the reality around me, and whose spectrum provided the justifications for everything I did. Although its God was only history, this vision gave my existence its meaning, and myself a reason for action. It was the focus on the world to come that had produced the autistic effect that Peter found so frustrating, the impression that I was not only a Marxist but a Martian as well. Like all radicals, I lived in some fundamental way in a castle in the air. Now I had hit the ground hard, and had no idea of how to get up or go on.

I was, in fact, like a person who was already dead. Nothing outside of my own distress interested me, and I had no desire to do anything except find release. In this desolate space, I was kept on track only by the necessity of earning a living to support my children. It was my one connection: I couldn't fail them and live with myself. My chaos notwithstanding, I continued to work on my book, *Promised Land.* Even in this effort, though, my plans were frustrated. When it was finished, the publisher changed the title to *The First Frontier,* and when it was released it was a flop that brought me no income.

Meanwhile, the Rockefeller monies had run out. In an attempt to earn some cash, I called my friend Bob Rafelson, the Hollywood director who had contributed to the Panther school, and he arranged an interview for me with Richard Gere, who was just then becoming known. I sold the interview to *Penthouse,* but Gere's agents killed it when they read the text in galleys. He had described Hollywood as an "evil town," and they thought the remark might injure his career. I also interviewed Daniel Ellsberg, the man who had leaked the Pentagon Papers and who had become a close friend. But Ellsberg could never make up his mind to complete the sessions and, after weeks of work, I had to settle for a "kill fee" which was only a small fraction of what I had expected. Because of my depressed state of mind, I couldn't come up with a subject that I wanted to write about and could sell to an editor. Then, in January 1980, a suicide on the other side of the world changed everything.

Fay Stender had been the attorney for Huey Newton and then George Jackson, and had founded the radical prison movement. She had been living for a year in self-imposed exile in Hong Kong, after being shot by a member of Jackson's prison gang and paralyzed from the waist down. The far end of the world was the only place she could feel safe from further retribution. But freedom from her enemies on the left had not restored either her spirits or her health. She had sent farewell notes to her children and friends, and then taken her own life. When it was announced that a funeral service would be held for her in San Francisco, I decided to go. It was the first funeral I had attended since Betty's, five years before.

I had met Fay in person only once, in the early Seventies, when I was raising money for *Ramparts*. Later, I developed an affinity for her which was based on my sense that we were linked by a common fate. Like myself, Fay had been a missionary to the black revolutionary cause. She had secured Newton's freedom on a technical point after the murder of Officer Frey, and had made George Jackson an international legend by editing his letters into a book, and getting them published. Then, a series of events had taken place that were still obscure to me. Jackson had demanded that she aid him in his prison escape by smuggling in a gun, but Fay had refused, and so had been severed from his defense team. The radical members of her Prison Law Project had broken with her over this "stab in the back," and had formed the Prison Law Collective, to promote the militant cause. After Fay's removal from the team, someone (possibly Steven Bingham, a member of the collective who fled the country and was later acquitted of the charge) slipped Jackson the gun he wanted. After taking and murdering several hostages, Jackson himself was killed in his attempt to escape.

Nine years later, Edward Brooks, a member of Jackson's prison gang, appeared at Fay's door in Berkeley. Brooks made her sign a statement, at gunpoint, saying that she had "betrayed George Jackson and the prison movement, when they needed me most." Then he had shot her five times at point-blank range, in the pattern of a crucifix, shattering her hands and piercing her spine. Fay recovered enough to be taken in a wheelchair, disguised for her protection, to the trial of her would-be assassin. It was her last hurrah as the center of a courtroom drama. She appeared as both victim of the crime and chief witness for the prosecution—the first time she had been on the government side of a case in her entire professional life.

My only other contact with Fay was a phone call I had made to her shortly after Betty's death. It was in response to a book review she had written in the *San Francisco Chronicle*. The book was *Who Killed George Jackson?* by an English writer named Jo Durden-Smith. As a New Left activist, Durden-Smith was attracted to the Jackson legend, and had come to California after Jackson's death to establish that he had been set up by prison authorities and murdered. In the course of his research, Durden-Smith had been forced to drop his simple assumptions. He learned that the Panthers had been training an army in the Santa Cruz Mountains in order to free Jackson from his jail. They had been assisted, and supplied with weapons and explosives, by student and faculty radicals at Stanford University. A killing ground had been discovered at their training site, littered with the charred bones of comrades they had murdered for stepping out of line. Interviews with Soledad and San Quentin inmates revealed to him that Jackson was a prison gangster who ran dope and gambling operations, and was feared by other inmates for his ruthlessness. He had once knifed a man for reneging on a $10 bet, and had boasted to his fellow prisoners that he had indeed killed the Soledad guard, as accused. By the end of the research, Durden-Smith had become disillusioned with the corruption of the radical cause and, fearful for his own life, had fled California for good.

Fay hid Jackson's dark side from the public by excising from the pages of his manuscript the passages that revealed it. She didn't realize that, in doing this, she was also denying the reality to herself. This became clear to her only after she refused Jackson's request for the gun, and found his followers' hatred turned on her. In Fay's review of *Who Killed George Jackson?* I was struck by a single sentence: "His work is essential reading for those seeking to understand the relationship of prisons to black revolution and radical movements in the Sixties and early Seventies." When I read this, I knew I had to call her. I had only the vaguest intimations of the trouble that had taken place five years earlier around the Jackson Defense Committee and the Prison Law Project. I didn't know the parties personally, and had not heard any details of the internal conflicts. Like the Panther events with which I was familiar, they remained opaque to anyone not directly involved, shrouded in rumor and conflicting speculation. But when I read Fay's review, I thought: *I am not alone.*

When she answered the phone, I groped for words. I felt the need to be cautious—to allude, rather than speak directly, to what I knew. I used the revelations in the new book as a code in referring to my own Panther experiences. Her voice was reserved but sympathetic. She said: "Everything that is in this book that I know about from my own experience is true." This encouraged me to ask if I could meet with her, but she refused. "I will not talk about this," she said. "But I will tell you one thing: I don't defend prisoners anymore." It was all I needed to know. The prison movement that Fay founded was built on the common radical premise that outlaws were rebels, that "There are no criminals, only political prisoners." To Fay, prisoners were the wretched of the earth, more sinned against than sinning. No one who believed this could come to the conclusion she had expressed on the phone, unless she had been through an experience like mine.

The funeral service was held at the Sinai Memorial Chapel in San Francisco. More than 300 people from the Bay Area's progressive community attended. I noticed immediately that there were only a handful of blacks. The dead woman had devoted herself to the cause of black prisoners and their struggle against racism. She had taken their cause into the halls of government, and had presented it to the public at large. In her professional life she had defended hundreds of black prisoners. But blacks had not come to her funeral to pay her a last respect. It occurred to me that the black community might have a different view of these criminals than did white radicals like Fay.

The memorial proceedings were unsettling. Speaker after speaker went up to the platform to remember Fay—lawyers who worked with her, comrades who had served with her, friends who loved her. They were political activists who would normally have made a political symbolism out of the most trivial occurrence. Yet, on the occasion of Fay's funeral, they had nothing to say about the sequence of events that had ended her life. One after the other, they rose to praise her in abstract terms as a woman who had dedicated herself to the cause of social justice. They lauded her lifelong service to the powerless and the persecuted. But not one of them could bring themselves to confront the terrible ironies that had brought them all together. She had been killed by a black ex-prisoner who, in justifying his awful act, had invoked the memory of George Jackson—the most resonant symbol of Fay's radical life and of her dedication to the cause of the oppressed. No one present referred to this irony. No one mentioned Fay's expulsion from the Jackson defense team, or the fact that she had stopped representing prisoners. No one reflected on what these events might mean to them, or to her. The truth was too threatening to the cause in which they still believed. So they suppressed it. In her last years, Fay herself had chosen to preserve the silence surrounding the events that had altered—and then ended—her life. Leaving the funeral, I knew I had to break that silence.

Among the mourners at Fay's memorial, I noticed a slim and ascetic-looking woman standing against a side wall of the chapel, sobbing uncontrollably. It was Eve Pell, a journalist who had written for *Ramparts.* She was also a socialite from an aristocratic family in Rhode Island, and a cousin of its Senator Claiborne Pell, who had been recruited by Fay to the George Jackson Defense Committee from the board of the San Francisco museum. I knew that Eve and Fay had been estranged for almost a decade. Their friendship had ended during the bitter split in the Prison Law Collective, over Jackson's fatal escape attempt from San Quentin. Though I was vague on the details of the dispute, I knew it was related to the conflict over "armed struggle" that had also driven a wedge between Cleaver and Newton. It was this conflict that had produced the charge of "betrayal," which eventually led to the shooting. Eve had been one of the radicals at odds with Fay, and had not spoken to her during the eight years that had elapsed since Jackson's death. It was this history that caused me to notice the force of her grief. When the service was over, I went up to her and said I was thinking about writing Fay's story, and would like to interview her.

A few days later, we met for lunch at Ivy's, a restaurant on Hayes Street, behind the San Francisco Opera. Eve acknowledged some of her feelings about Fay, and I told her about Betty, and of my experience with the Panthers. Then she began to tell me about Jackson—how she had gone to see him in prison, and how he had made an impression by taking her seriously. "When I went to see him, it was the first time I had ever been in a prison. I thought: This man is not going to like me. This man is going to say, 'Go back to your dumb little life and don't bother us revolutionaries.' Well, that didn't happen."

Having won Eve's loyalty, Jackson took her into his confidence, to make her complicit in his outlaw schemes. On subsequent occasions, he boasted to her that he had killed twelve men in prison. (A warden I interviewed later claimed that Jackson had inflated the number.) Another time, Jackson told her he had a plan to poison the water system of Chicago, where he had grown up. This was one of the items that Fay had edited out of *Soledad Brother*, to make her client more palatable as a political hero. "He was charming and he was a homicidal maniac," Eve explained to me, adding: "That's off the record." The homicides Jackson claimed to have committed were not for attribution, either. Several times during our talk, Eve begged me to protect her. She made me turn off the tape recorder each time she came to a fact she thought might be considered a betrayal by the prison gang that had sent Brooks to hunt down Fay.

I had found the soul mate I was looking for. Eve and I wept over our common misfortunes and shattered dreams, and felt bonded in our present fears. She was afraid that she would be regarded as a traitor for having spoken about the Jackson events, just as I feared the consequences were I to write anything too specific about Newton and the Panthers. I assured her I would protect her, just as I was confident she would protect me.

One point Eve made was confirmed by others in the Prison Law Project I interviewed, and became a central theme of our story: Fay had crossed the line that separated her professionally from her clients. She had become emotionally, and then sexually, involved with Jackson. She was not content to remain just his lawyer, but had become his lover and political comrade. Following her lead, the other women members of the Prison Law Project had become similarly involved with the prisoners they defended. It was this crossing of the line that had led to Jackson's feelings of betrayal, with the consequences that were fatal. "For us," Eve told me, "it was an intense emotional identification with [these prisoners] as heroes, as lovers, as comrades... [Fay] had led us into involvement with the prisoners on a personal and political level, and then held back."

I interviewed Fay's family and her friends and colleagues, including the radicals who had denounced her, and even the wardens who had observed her prison affair with Jackson. Many of these conversations were therapeutic for me. I discovered political activists other than myself who had arrived at a sense of the reality that was distinct from our myths. I was curious to see how they dealt with their awareness.

I interviewed Doron Weinberg, a former law partner of Fay and a member of the National Lawyers Guild, the Communist front organization my mother had worked for in the Fifties. The Guild had continued as an organization of the hard-core left in the legal profession. It was Fay's professional community and base. The Guild lawyers were distraught when they first learned of the shooting. When Fay's black assailant was arrested, they suspended their lifelong mental attitudes and showed sympathy for the police and the prosecution. Weinberg recalled sitting among a group of radical attorneys when the news came:

> Everyone in the room had to grapple with the same questions: Oh my God, is this guy going to get out on a technicality? Is some civil liberties lawyer going to come along and get him off?

My interviews with Weinberg and the other lawyers who knew Fay took place in an atmosphere of fear, and even terror. The police had discovered in Brooks' possession a list of others besides Fay who were targeted for execution. The Guild lawyers were convinced that Fay herself had been marked for death by a member of their own small political community, a Chicana paralegal who had worked for Fay at the Prison Law Project. A short, plain-looking woman with a sullen expression, she was a personal friend of Brooks and was providing him with legal assistance. She was also close to a San Quentin maximum-security prisoner named Yogi Pinell, who was the reputed head of the Black Guerilla Family, Jackson's prison gang. Pinell was one of the "San Quentin Six" who had been part of the Jackson escape attempt, and whom Fay had refused to defend. The paralegal, who worked on the "San Quentin Six" defense team, visited Pinell regularly in prison. Police sources believed that it was Pinell who had ordered the hit on Fay.

I went to see the paralegal in her Berkeley home. She sat on a straight-back chair, tightly wound, barely able to keep her anger against what she referred to as "the white legal left" in check:

> I was just seething at the way the white left reacted to Brooks' arrest. It was racist. They had never taken this attitude when someone was shot in the past. They had said Third World people can't get fair treatment from the police and the courts. And yet, when one of their own was shot, they immediately cooperated with the cops and used the same system they said could never treat people of color fairly.

I was shaken by the force of her utterance. But when I attempted to interject some mollifying words, it only made things worse. "People are afraid," I suggested, "because they don't know why Fay was killed." (Neither of us noticed that we had transposed the final deed from Fay to the gunman.) Clenching her jaw and looking straight into my eyes, she hissed: "People know why Fay Stender was killed. She was killed because she was corrupt." As she spat out her words, I had the impulse to run. Here was someone who could easily have killed Fay herself. At the first reasonable moment, I excused myself and left. When I returned home, I went out and bought a gun. It was a 38 Ruger, the first weapon I had ever owned.

Now I not only *understood* the fear I had seen reflected in the faces of the Guild lawyers—I *felt* it. But I had little sympathy for their continuing silence. Like me, they had helped to create the universe in which such a terror could rule their lives. But I also saw that they had no second thoughts. They wanted to isolate Fay's tragedy as an individual case. Because she was a friend, they were willing to forget the "social dimensions" of the situation, which they were forever emphasizing on other occasions. Nor did Brooks' action cause them to rethink their view of criminals as a class of the oppressed. They remained politically myopic in the way Fay herself had been. An ex-prisoner named John Irwin, who had observed Fay's prison activities up close, told me in one of my interviews: "I don't think Fay ever understood the commitment to criminality that many of the persons she dealt with had. Fay really had a strong belief that prisoners were going to be in the vanguard of the social revolution."

The Guild lawyers wanted Fay's story told, hoping that the publicity would help to protect them. But they wanted me to do the telling. The dark areas they were willing to be interviewed about were "not for attribution." Yet their public testimony would have been far more effective than mine, because they were still active in the Left, while I had already been on the sidelines for nearly five years. I was at least as vulnerable to reprisal as they were, because Huey Newton and his Squad were still close by, and aspects of the story affected him directly. I was angry at their silence—but I was determined to go on. I felt, more than ever, the truth had to be known.

As I confronted the task before me, I thought more and more about my missing writing partner. Shortly before the end of my marriage, I had made a phone call to Peter. It was the first time we had spoken in nearly two years. I missed him as a friend, but the call was not only an impulse to repair the broken cords of our relationship. It was also a quest for health. I needed a sign that there had been gain from the losses, that I had learned something from my defeats. In one of the painful confrontations that punctuated the last months of my marriage, Elissa had said "There's no use talking to you; you're always right." It was the same charge Peter had made: self-righteous, self-absorbed. I had lost them both, the two people I was closest to. How could I dismiss their judgment? I had been taken down, and humbled, and forced to look at myself from the outside. Now I was about to test what I saw.

My grievance against Peter was that he erased me when he excised the passages I had thought were my contribution to our book. *But why, then, had he wanted me as a partner at all?* At the time we stopped speaking, I had no answer. But in the solitude I had constructed for myself, the question came up again, and I remembered something he had said when he was pressing me to interview the Rockefeller cousins: *This will make the book.* At the time, I had no idea what he meant. Now I began to ask myself why this might be so. The difficulty I had in understanding him resulted from the Marxist convictions I had now jettisoned. Before, I had never really embraced the biographical enterprise. In my view, the narrative we constructed, and the psychological portraits we drew, were so much window dressing for the important message about the System—the message that Peter had excised. The Marxist paradigm had provided the measure of everything's worth, including my own.

Now I began to look at the book, and the work I had done on it, without this Marxist filter. Our portrait of the Cousins' generation had been drawn from my interviews. They had revealed the ethos of the family, which framed the narrative as a whole. Others had interviewed the Rockefellers before, but had not come up with the story we had. Through the whole process, Peter and I had talked our way through each character and episode, playing devil's advocate to the other's take. The portrait that emerged was one that neither of us would have come up with alone. For the first time, I began to appreciate what I had contributed, and this allowed me to acknowledge why I had been so insecure. I was intimidated and overwhelmed by Peter's talent. He was the better writer. He had shaped the narrative and defined its prose. When the book appeared, I had accepted the critical applause but felt it undeserved. I knew I could not write such a book without him. But I realized now, and was able to accept, that *he* would not have been able to write the book without *me.* Reviewing our battles over the text, I saw that Peter had no intention of erasing me. I always knew that I needed Peter, but it had taken me until now to see that he needed me.

Our first phone conversation was stilted and didn't last long, but we set a date for lunch the following week. Driving to see him in my white Z, I braced myself for the witty ridicule that the new vehicle would invite. But, as I drew up to his house, I spotted a black Mercedes coupe in his driveway. On our separate paths, we had moved in similar directions. His Mercedes was a 1957 model, which, it occurred to me, was typical of Peter. He had bought a "classic" to mask the baser instincts behind the purchase.

Over lunch, we caught up on our respective lives. A decade earlier, Peter had married Mary Giachino, a handsome, elegant woman with whom he had three children, all several years younger than mine. Like me, he had suffered financially from our failure to follow up our success with the Rockefeller book, and was planning to give up his Oakland home and move to the California gold country. He had written a novel, *Downriver,* about a child of the Sixties who had given himself to history, which had failed him, and then returned home, to try to heal family and self. It was a powerful, beautifully written story which had been published during a newspaper strike, depriving him of the success he deserved. Peter protected himself against such disappointments by lowering his expectations. We were opposites in this: I always expected more than I was likely to get. He was also typically critical of his accomplishments. "We're mediocre," he said after we had gone on for awhile. I had the impulse to hit him, the remark made me so mad. "But," he continued, "we're good together as biographers. We should do it again."

I thought of the article I was writing about Fay—how much better it would be if he were involved. And then I thought of the risk I was taking—that he might overwhelm me again. For an instant, the idea made me hesitate. Then I asked him if he would write the story with me.

I gave Peter my draft, and he suggested more interviews: Fay's live-in lover, and Fay's estranged husband and children. When these were completed, Peter rewrote my draft and we went over it once more. The style was the one he had designed for *The Rockefellers.* The narrative voice was authoritative and sympathetic. We attempted to "inhabit" Fay, as a novelist would his central character, entering her world and seeing what she was able to make of what she had been given.

After her conflict with Jackson and the Prison Law Collective radicals, Fay had become a feminist, involving herself in women's legal issues. She had left her husband (who also was a radical lawyer) and become a lesbian. On the night she was shot, she and her lover were in the house together. I interviewed Fay's lover over the phone, since she was too frightened to meet me in person, or to tell me her real name. When we finished the article, we showed a draft to her. She felt the portrait was so accurate and sympathetic that she gave us, to include in our story, the last note Fay had written to her.

In the article's final paragraphs, we attempted to sum up our views of Fay as "a radical Every person," which was Peter's imaginative trope on the hero of *Pilgrim's Progress*. In the summary, we drew on an interview I did with Ezra Hendon, who had been Fay's law partner and ally:

> Her funeral marked the end of an era in my life, and I think the end of an era, period. Her conviction that you could be committed to a political goal, work for it, and be brilliant in its service—in a clean way—that's over for me. I don't know about the others, but I can't have that belief anymore.

We ended our text with this final comment:

> As he said the words, Hendon's eyes rimmed with tears. Like others who missed Fay, he was mourning not merely for a lost friend, but for a lost cause as well.

We called our article "Requiem for a Radical," and it appeared in the March 1981 issue of *New West* magazine. It was the first time I had been able to write about the reality that had so impacted my life. Even this oblique telling was not without risk, though, because at certain points we had to deal with the criminal side of the Panthers themselves. A less threatening but more important concern was the reaction of the Left. I was aware of what happened to bad-news messengers who tried to tell their story. Throughout the history of the revolution in Russia, anarchists, Trotskyists, and generations of Soviet refugees had tried—often at great personal risk—to convey to their socialist comrades the horrors they had seen. For their courage they were stigmatized as "renegades," marginalized, and banished from the faith. Their reports were painted as lies, and their suffering was discounted. They were anathematized as enemies of the poor, of socialism, and of human progress itself. They were made unpersons in their own communities. In being so tainted, their mouths were sealed as effectively as if they had actually been killed.

In the issue of *New West* that followed our article on Fay, a "letter to the editor" appeared. It was written by Eve Pell:

> When J. Edgar Hoover wanted to discredit the civil rights movement, he spread rumors that Dr. Martin Luther King, Jr. had affairs with white women. Horowitz and Collier have used the same technique against the prison movement. Just as readers are titillated to think of Dr. King carousing, so are they titillated to think of white women trysting with blacks behind bars, and thus they are distracted from the atrocities of racism and prison brutality....
>
> In their obsession with the naiveté of some prison activists, Collier and Horowitz play into the right-wing mentality, which is now so powerful in the United States and which Fay abhorred. It would be tragedy compounded if a requiem for Fay Stender furthers the inhumanity she fought so persistently in her too-short life.

J. Edgar Hoover. Right-wing mentality. The inhumanity Fay had fought. It was a classic attack, turning us into the enemy. In writing our story, we had protected not only Eve, but our other radical sources who lived in fear of reprisal. As a result, we were now the sole bearers of the bad news, the only authorities—besides the police and other "enemies of the people"—for the claims we made about the criminal reality that clashed with the radical myth. We had devoted our lives to the Movement but, as with others before us, this would hardly matter to the flock of the faithful. Our motives were already being tainted and our commitments put in question.

Eve was not content with this smear alone. As the outgoing president of a progressive association of 5,000 Bay Area journalists called Media Alliance, she expanded her letter into a feature for its paper. In it she identified the article of faith that we had violated. The task of progressive journalists, she argued, was to serve the objectives of the political struggle. "David Horowitz has impressive Left credentials," she went on in her attack, "so when he wanted to interview me

about my part in the prison movement of the early 70s, I agreed....
But the information I gave (and others gave) got twisted against the
prison movement, against Fay, and against us, and used to construct
an image I find profoundly wrong."

Eve then repeated her comparison of J. Edgar Hoover to us. She
noted that "The Reagan Administration is tearing down social programs which help the poor" and that the government was getting
ready for a "new McCarthyism," and concluded that it was "a politically opportune time to trash the Left." She added: "I heard that
New West paid twice the usual fee for the Stender story." (It was a
particularly hypocritical tack. She, herself, had just returned from
a three-month pleasure trip around the world.) In her conclusion,
Eve warned: "People who were and are active in progressive political
groups must beware of what we write and whom we talk to, for the
consequences can be extremely serious."

One passage in Eve's attack struck a special nerve: "Instead of
writing about his own role with the Panthers and Huey Newton,
which Horowitz says troubles him now, he writes about Fay Stender,
who cannot defend herself...." Thus, while posing as the champion
of a woman she had once attacked as a traitor, Eve had exposed me
to the forces who had killed Fay for betraying them. She had broken
our trust, publicly marking me as a danger to the Left, who was bad-
mouthing the Panthers. I decided to reciprocate and blow her cover.
It was the only way we could preserve the credibility of our story—to
let others know that it was Eve herself, not J. Edgar Hoover, who had
provided the testimony that Jackson and his cohorts were murderers
and psychopaths.

The editor of the paper, which was called *MediaFile*, allowed us to
reply. We answered Eve's attack point by point, inserting the quotes
from our tapes that refuted her present claims. Then we got to the
central issue between us:

> Eve's ill-advised and intemperate attack on us raises...the thorny ques-
> tions of journalism and personal commitment. Eve offers one vision of
> what it is to be a "radical" and a "progressive" journalist. Not only are
> her criteria implicit in her letter, but also in her life. For she knew the
> story of what happened to the prison movement and sat on it for all

these years. Perhaps she had no obligation to speak up, but she cannot make silence into a virtue and then synthesize an outrage when others like us do what she should have in the first place. In fact, we asked why she hadn't spoken up previously, when we interviewed her. The answer she gave—and this is a direct quote—is this: "Because I was afraid of being called a counter-revolutionary, and I was afraid for my life." Afraid for her life, in other words, because of the very elements in the prison movement she implies in her letter we are attempting to discredit.

Two years earlier, Eve had written a profile of George Jackson for the *San Francisco Chronicle* in which she had presented him as a folk hero, a figure of the same myth that Fay had created and that had killed her. Eve had suppressed all of the truth that she knew and subsequently told us, and that we had now surfaced. "Someone who distinguishes between privately held and publicly espoused truths," we declared in our reply, "who suppresses facts in the interest of a 'higher morality,' is not a journalist but a propagandist."

Our response stung Eve into renewed silence, even as other progressives rallied to her side. Foremost among them was Jessica Mitford, who had sponsored events for the Panthers, and written a best-seller about scams in the funeral industry, *The American Way of Death*. The Mitfords were an aristocratic English family that had gained notoriety when Jessica joined the Communist Party, and her sister Unity became a lover of Goebbels and a Nazi. During the Chicago Conspiracy Trial, Jessica held a benefit for the Panthers at her Berkeley house, which ended in a melee when David Hilliard struck Hayden on the jaw for his failure to support Bobby Seale. Now she was circulating a letter among her political friends which decried our "appalling" and "atrocious" article, confiding: "I deeply wish it had never been written." At a public debate staged by Media Alliance to air the controversy, she repeated Eve's warning, which was—after all—a standard operating principle of the Left: The responsibility of progressive journalists was to suppress facts that hurt the progressive cause, and to print only those truths that served it.

Meanwhile, Eve attempted to get the Media Alliance board to fire *MediaFile's* editor for publishing our reply. When this move failed, she and two vice presidents resigned (one of them subsequently becoming editor of *Mother Jones*). They were joined by the organization's most famous member, former *Washington Post* reporter and Pulitzer Prize winner, Ben Bagdikian, a media critic and journalism professor at Berkeley. Bagdikian refused to accept a Media Alliance "Gadfly" award, in protest over the publication of our remarks. Three years after the affair, Eve published her own book, which she titled without irony: *The Big Chill: How the Reagan Administration, Corporate America, and Religious Conservatives Are Subverting Free Speech and the Public's Right to Know.*

By holding our own, Peter and I had won a pyrrhic victory. It was the attacks on us, and the name-calling, that had the lasting effect. Over the next fifteen years, not a single article or book appeared telling the Fay Stender story or dealing with the reality of the Soledad and San Quentin events. (Todd Gitlin's history of the Sixties is remarkably innocent of these episodes and what they reveal, though Todd himself was well aware of what we had written.) Shortly after the controversy, I bumped into Bob Scheer's ex-wife, Anne, in front of the Co-op, a supermarket where Berkeley progressives shopped. I greeted her warmly and asked how she was doing. Instead of responding, she looked me in the eye and said: "You know, David, people really hate you."

All during the controversy, I wondered to myself what Huey Newton might be thinking. In our story about Fay, we had kept his portrait vague in order to provide me some protection. But the impression we gave of the Panthers was certainly negative, and Eve had revealed that more unflattering tales could follow. Was I in danger? Would Newton react by sending his thugs? I felt a little bolder about taking the risks in the article, because I no longer had my family living with me. But I was still uneasy. The assassination attempt on the prosecution witness had damaged Newton, but not destroyed him. Without declaring any change in his agendas, he had allowed his criminal persona to surface in public, dressing in a white pimp suit and slouch hat, and always taking along his huge bodyguard, Big Bob. Occasional incidents made the press, as when Newton discharged a gun in a barroom incident. And many of his political connections remained. The Learning Center received a $600,000 grant from California's superintendent of education, Wilson Riles, whose son worked for the Party. Newton used the education grant to support the Squad in their version of gangster style.

Newton couldn't leave his intellectual audience alone, either. With the help of the historian Page Smith, he had enrolled in a Ph.D. program at the University of California at Santa Cruz. The program, called the "History of Consciousness," had been designed by Smith, as he told me in an interview, "to prove that the Ph.D. degree is a fraud." Angela Davis would later become a professor in the same program. By a combination of intimidation and deception, Newton was able to fulfill the lax requirements and receive a Ph.D. himself He suborned political supporters to write his papers, and menaced professors who objected. His thesis was titled "War Against the Panthers: A Study of Repression in America." Several thousand people showed up to observe his oral exam, which had to be rescheduled to a more private setting. He was made a Doctor of Philosophy in June 1980, one month after Fay committed suicide.

I decided that the anxiety I had developed over the article would be lessened if I knew how Newton was taking it. So I called Bert Schneider, whom I had not seen in years, and he invited me to come to his estate in Benedict Canyon. When I arrived, he was dressed in a bathrobe and greeted me with an icy stare. The room was thick with tension as he told me I had endangered his life. When I asked how, it turned out he was referring to a passage in which we had written about Jackson's death. In it, we had discussed the theories that had developed around the abortive escape attempt. One theory, from Jackson's prison gang, accused Newton of sabotaging the escape plan and setting Jackson up in order to be rid of a rival. Coincidentally, Schneider had been mentioned in Durden-Smith's book as being involved in Newton's maneuverings at the time. It was interesting to see how frantic Schneider was about his own skin. But what really got my attention was a remark he let drop: "Huey isn't as angry at you as I am." I told him I would like to see Huey, and he said he would arrange it.

Our meeting took place at a restaurant called Norman's on the Berkeley-Oakland border. When I arrived, Newton was already there, sunk into one of the vinyl divans, his eyes liverish and his skin pallid, drunker than I had ever seen him. He was friendly, but my caution and his inebriation made our conversation desultory. He didn't seem to be interested in the story, whose issues I didn't press. When the lunch was over, he asked me to drive him back to the two-story house in the Oakland hills that Schneider had bought for him. His alcoholic stupor made him seem harmless enough, but I wondered on the way whether this was just one more reckless move on my part—and whether I would ever come back.

The decor of Newton's new home was reminiscent of the penthouse—piled carpets, leather couches, and glass-topped end tables. Only the African decorative masks mounted on the beige walls provided a new touch. We sat across from one another and continued the conversation we had started at lunch, which now took a bizarre turn as Newton described to me a project he was working on to produce *Porgy and Bess* as a musical set in contemporary Harlem. He wanted Stevie Wonder and Mick Jagger to play Porgy and Sportin' Life. As he told me this, he got up and walked over to a cabinet, from which he pulled a glossy black folder. The pages from it that he handed me turned out to be a treatment he had prepared in Braille for the blind singer. I pretended to be impressed, and asked whether Stevie Wonder had agreed to do the part. A dark look came into Newton's eyes as he explained that "people" around the singer had badmouthed him and killed the deal. As he said this, his face contorted in an alcoholic grimace that was truly demonic. I had the urge to flee.

Just as suddenly, however, Newton's face relaxed, and he fell into a distant silence. Then he looked directly at me and said: "Elaine killed Betty." After a pause, he added a caveat whose cynicism and bravado were familiar: "But if you write that, I'll deny it." As soon as I could, I took my leave. Afterwards, the moment played itself over in my mind. Until then, I had thought Elaine was solely responsible for Betty's death, and that Huey was somehow uninformed about the decision. But the way he had fingered Elaine—a display of disloyalty out of character—made me suspect that it was *he* who had given the order.

In my conversations with Charles and the other Panthers who had fled when Elaine took over, I had expressed curiosity as to how she was able to control the thugs around her. They told me it was Newton who was really in control. He and Elaine were in daily phone contact, and, as long as the Squad thought he might return, he would remain in charge. As soon as I got home from my lunch with Newton, I phoned Charles and told him what I now suspected. He confirmed my intuition. He had learned from others that Newton had been involved in the discussions over Betty's fate. It had taken a week for them to determine what to do with her, and it was Newton who made the decision to kill her. "He was crazy," Charles said. "There was no reason for it."

It was as though I had to learn things from the beginning again. Setting up a house in middle age was not a prospect I had ever thought about. I had never lived alone, having moved out of my parents' home on my marriage day, twenty years earlier. In the spring of 1980, I moved into a one-bedroom brown shingle on the north end of Shattuck Avenue, at the foot of the Berkeley Hills. It was light and airy, and had a small garden in the back. During the days, the loneliness was almost physical in its intensity. My chest was electric with the anxiety I felt from the absence of my family, and the thought of a future without them. At night the feeling was desperate. I could not have felt more desolate if I had been transported to another planet. There was nothing either familiar or comforting. By this time, however, I had almost become inured to suffering. I had learned to go through the pain, putting one foot in front of the other until I came to another side. Gradually, I began to find oxygen in the new atmosphere, and to accept my solitary state. I discovered that taking care of my house, and even the simple act of cooking, could provide a sense of comfort. The solitude itself was interesting. I began to enjoy the control I had over my days and pleasures.

My fortieth birthday was an object lesson in this new regimen of self-reliance. As the date approached, I worried about the feeling of loss that its recurrent mirror promised, and the self-pity it might engender. I weighed alternative plans. Should I get on a plane, lifting myself out of time and place, in an attempt to escape the occasion altogether? In the end, I decided to throw myself a party, inviting everyone I knew. I had always been a collector of people, and when I gathered my friends for the occasion, the diversity of the collection became apparent. There were my old political comrades, who still managed to be friendly despite my recent deviations; and some of the parents whom Elissa and I had socialized with; and the New Age psychics and "bodyworkers" I had come to know through Jackie; and even a contingent from the Hollywood set that I had met through Schneider. The house grew animated as people discovered each other and explored their different worlds. In the middle of the festivity, one of my old Movement friends came up to me and asked, in a quizzical voice, "David, what are all these touchy-feely types doing here?" The event was an anodyne for my distress.

My new residence was only a few blocks from the home I had left, and I tried to keep the family from being torn even further apart by making dinner for my children three times a week, and keeping abreast of their activities and school work as best I could. Their anger sometimes made the schedule difficult to maintain, and often one or the other—particularly the youngest—would find an excuse not to come. The divorce seemed to have had a markedly different impact on each, the oldest two apparently least affected. Perhaps they buried their pain deep enough to make it hard to detect.

Jon had gone off to college in Los Angeles; Sarah, who was now sixteen, was the family conciliator, trying to make the best of the unhappy situation. Ben had moved toward manhood. Vulnerable and timid when he was a child, he had signed up for football, bulking himself out to play on the offensive line. I admired his physical courage, and also the way he assumed the chores around the household, helping Elissa out. My concern focused on Anne, who was now eleven. I had undermined my own authority, and could not provide the structure of support she would need in her adolescent passage. My father was right on this, too: Marriage is about families. I was reassured by the knowledge that they were always in good hands with their mother. I was grateful that, despite her anger, the children never became an issue between us.

Peter and I had followed our article on Fay with a series of crime stories. The editor of *New West,* William Broyles, thought "Requiem for a Radical" was a model of what the magazine should publish, and had put us on retainer. The first story we wrote, "Getting Away With Murder," was about the juvenile justice system in California. The Youth Authority, which administered the system, was the embodiment of enlightened liberalism and its ideas about how to treat society's "lost children." By the time we began our investigation, these ideas had developed to the point where they were so out of touch with reality that thousands of young murderers were being sentenced to three years in the Youth Authority and then released back to the streets, their records wiped clean. My first interview was with the mother of a twelve-year-old girl who had been sodomized and then strangled with a bicycle chain. Her killer was a thirteen-year-old who was released three years later into the same area, and was dating other girls even while the authorities concealed his criminal record because he was a juvenile.

Next, we wrote the history of a black gang in South-central Los Angeles. I spent many days "hanging out" with the members of the Santa Fe Crips in Compton, which was like a war zone where youngsters who crossed the wrong street into "enemy territory" could lose their lives. There had been 45 members of the gang, and a third of them had died violently before they were twenty years old. It was true that the area was poor, but these gang-bangers were only a small minority of the population they terrorized; other youngsters attended school, graduated, and went on to lead productive lives. When I interviewed the mother of a black youngster who had been murdered in a gang incident, her only complaint was that there hadn't been enough police to protect her son.

The interviews brought me into contact with other people who were dealing with grief and loss, while their stories were about tragedy that went beyond social and economic conditions. There were many poor people, but criminals were always a small percentage of the population willing to prey on others. Crime was a human activity that the Left couldn't understand: It didn't square with the hope for an earthly redemption. But the most therapeutic effect for me was seeing how the world was full of people who had borne traumas even greater than mine, who got no justice, and would get none, and yet somehow managed to go on. Going on, I had discovered for myself, was a matter of putting one foot in front of the other, and of finding interest in other lives along the way.

My parents came out in the summer, as they usually did, and I showed them my new house. It was filled with a morning light, and summarized my sense that I had turned a corner. I had survived my trials, and was beginning to pick myself off the floor and come back. I didn't know what I was going to do, but I knew I had to take the bad that had happened to me, and make it work for good—first for myself, and then for others in danger of falling into the same black hole. When my parents and I had completed our little tour of the house, I asked my father what he thought. He paused for a moment, and said: "You lead a charmed life."

PART 7

COMING HOME
(1980–1992)

I've seen the future; brother: It is murder

—Leonard Cohen

SECOND THOUGHTS

O NE OF THE PROJECTS WITH WHICH PETER AND I RENEWED OUR
partnership was a biography of the Kennedy family. The publisher had come up with the idea, and at first we regarded it
with some skepticism. It was true that the Kennedys had achieved a
kind of American royalty and as biographical subjects were worthy
successors to the Rockefellers. But so many books had already been
written on the Kennedy family that we didn't think there was a new
story to tell. On the other hand, Simon & Schuster was offering us a
large advance and an opportunity we did not want to turn down.

Once we began, however, we found the task even more difficult than anticipated. Simon & Schuster had already signed a book
on the Kennedys which was three years in the works. The author
was Doris Kearns Goodwin, who had written a best-selling biography of Lyndon Johnson. A Kennedy confidante, she was also writing
speeches for Teddy's then-current presidential campaign while advising his estranged wife, Joan, on how to put a public face of concord on
their broken marriage. If we didn't beat Doris to publication, however,
there was no chance that ours would be a best-seller—or even earn
back its advance.

Shortly after we became aware of this prospect, I received a midnight phone call from Doris's husband, Richard Goodwin, who had
been one of JFK's presidential advisers. Goodwin suggested that we
agree not to complete our book until Doris published hers. He was
writing a play about Galileo, he said, and this arrangement would
make all our lives simpler. If we couldn't agree, he added, "I'll have to

put aside my work, which I don't want to do, and finish her book for her." I thought this threat ludicrous but not untypical of Goodwin and noted that it was 3 A.M. eastern time. I said I would have to talk to Peter, but never called back.

It was clear that the Kennedys presented a more difficult puzzle than did the Rockefellers. We could count on Kearns Goodwin to block our access to the Kennedy circle as well as to the most important archival source, the Joseph P. Kennedy Papers, which had been donated to the Presidential Library in Boston. The Kennedy Library was a federally funded archive, but was effectively controlled by the Senator, who promptly shut us off. Nor was this the only door he closed. The family's political reach extended to all regions of the country, as well as to key institutions of the culture. People had been accumulating political debts to them through three generations, while others waited on their promised return to the White House and the centers of power. Fear of their reprisal was a common concern, particularly the threat of being cut off from their patronage and friendship.

When I interviewed "Red" Fay, a wartime buddy of JFK, a former undersecretary of the Navy, and a wealthy businessman in his own right, he told me how he had been banished from the circle of Kennedy acquaintances. A memoir he had published—*The Pleasure of His Company*—had incurred the wrath of the president's widow. Fay had cut 90,000 words from his manuscript in order to please Jackie, but had refused to suppress the book entirely, as she demanded. Years later, she read it for the first time and told him she regretted her *diktat* and thought it was the best memoir anybody had written about Jack. Like many other individuals we approached for interviews, Fay said he would talk to us only if we were able to get a "green light" from Steve Smith, the Senator's brother-in-law who ran the family operation from the offices of Joseph P. Kennedy Enterprises. Smith played a cat-and-mouse game with us, since he knew the Rockefeller book gave us the credentials to be noticed. He allowed us to interview Fay and a few others who were relatively remote from the present center of family power, but withheld his *imprimatur* when we got close to a significant source.

We decided that our best chance was to approach the family through the younger generation, as we had the Rockefellers (particularly its maverick elements). From our preliminary inquiries, we knew there was such a group led by Bobby Kennedy Jr., the third child of the Attorney General. I located him via a phone book in Charlottesville, Virginia, where he was attending law school. Without agreeing to be interviewed, he invited me to visit Hickory Hill, the Kennedy home in McLean. A white clapboard structure that had been the headquarters of a Civil War general, the house was set on rolling green lawns, where the famous touch-football games had taken place more than a decade before. The interior was warm and inviting, but also like a mausoleum, with every surface a stand for pictures of the famous clan and its celebrated martyrs.

At this time, the tarnishing of the Kennedy legend had been proceeding for several years. Revelations that JFK, while president, had affairs with Marilyn Monroe and also the mistress of a mafia chieftain, and that Robert Kennedy had attempted to employ mobsters in a White House plot to assassinate Castro, had dimmed the family aura. They had also implanted in its members an attitude of suspicion toward reporters. In attempting to induce Bobby to cooperate, my first tack was to refer him to our treatment of the Rockefellers. We had viewed the Rockefeller family through its third generation, a model we intended to replicate. Our approach was to ask how a family identity came to be established, and how subsequent generations handled the dilemma that the legacy posed. In short, how one pursued an individual destiny within the universe of a family myth.

The prospect of being in some way at the center of his family's epic intrigued Bobby, but failed to persuade him. It occurred to me, then, that my own story might draw him in—my life as a radical, and my involvement with the Panthers. This was not so different from the approach I had made to Abby and the other Rockefeller cousins even before Betty's death, but now there was an element of "waving the bloody shirt." It made me uncomfortable to watch myself turn my personal nightmare and Betty's murder into a story for Bobby's consumption. Still, it was a connection to his own family tragedies and a bond between us, and I could not really pretend I was someone else.

At first, I thought it was the Panthers' radical politics that piqued Bobby's interest, but I soon realized it was their outlaw behavior. Bobby's imagination was fired by the secrets whose exposure had begun to taint the family legend—the women, the mafia intrigues, the illicit drugs in the White House. It was the element of risk, the idea of getting away with things that mere mortals who were not Kennedy's couldn't, that excited him.

After our talk, Bobby invited me to come up to Cambridge, to which he was headed the next day. When I arrived, he was surrounded by an entourage of younger siblings and hangers-on. We chatted, and then one of Bobby's brothers entered the room. Without interrupting the conversation, Bobby laid out a line of cocaine and offered it to him. After his brother had snorted the line, Bobby said: "Oh, by the way, this is David Horowitz. He's writing a book on our family." This was typical Kennedy humor. His brother froze and went white, but Bobby knew there was little risk in the prank because of a deal we had made at our first meeting. In seeking Bobby's cooperation on the book, I knew I would have to confront the family drug problem. His brother David and his cousin Chris Lawford were in treatment for heroin addiction, and stories had appeared in the press about them. The deal I offered was not to write anything about illegal drug consumption that had not already appeared in the press. Sometime into my research, however, I uncovered a fact that was not publicly known: Bobby was a heroin addict as well.

One of the more arresting aspects of the Kennedy story for me was the insight it provided into the psychology of the Left. Jack Kennedy had been a conservative Democrat and a Cold War hard-liner. His brother Bobby was politically even farther right, having served as counsel to the McCarthy Committee and as the White House hawk on Vietnam. After JFK's assassination, however, Bobby had moved politically left. He had become a cautious dissenter from the war in Asia, and taken up the causes of minorities and the poor after Bobby's own assassination, the third brother, Teddy, emerged as a political figure to the left of both his siblings. It seemed apparent to me that personal guilt was driving this process. Bobby felt responsible for his brother's death, thinking that it was *his* enemies who were behind the assassination. Perhaps he had second thoughts about his involvement with the mafia in the plans to kill Castro after the same instrument was apparently turned on his brother. Whatever the case, it was clear that the worse Bobby Kennedy felt about himself, the more radical his politics became.

This was even more obvious in Teddy. As the spoiled youngest of the Kennedy clan, he was too unserious and personally dissolute to rise to the expectations that people had put on him. As a young man he had been caught cheating at Harvard, and ever since hadn't really felt worthy of the Kennedy mantle. When his brothers were martyred, elevating them to the status of political saints, he instantly became the leading presidential contender among Democrats, even though he was only thirty-five. The burden of expectation was so great that he veered to the edge of a nervous breakdown. His alcoholism was out of control, and his recklessness led to the death of Mary Jo Kopechne in the famous accident at Chappaquiddick. The drowning ended his presidential prospects, and added yet another taint to the family legend. In attempting to exculpate himself afterwards on TV, Teddy invoked the image of his martyred brothers and the "curse" on the Kennedy name—implying that they were targeted for destruction *because* they were good. The claim was rejected by the public as a thinly veiled attempt to evade his own responsibility.

But, like Bobby before him, Teddy had stumbled upon the only redemptive power that radical ideas actually possessed. After the accident, his personal dissipation continued, but he refashioned his public persona into that of spokesman for the voiceless, and champion of the "oppressed." The more unworthy he appeared to himself, the nobler was the face he presented to his constituents. He became the leader of the Democratic Party left. Higher wages for workers, school buses for integration, and universal health care became hallmark causes with which he associated his name. The subtext was obvious: No *matter how bad my actions may seem, my heart is in the right place.* It was the *mantra* of the Left—and its moral calculus as well. I once asked Leslie Harris, the head of the ACLU task force on women, how feminists could continue their support of a man who was such a prominent abuser of women himself. "We know that," she said, "but he's down for the political agenda."

The Kennedy story was difficult to research, and the money we received as an advance was not enough to keep us going for the three and a half years it took to write. To supplement our incomes, we turned to other stories. Some we wrote because even though we had retired from the political struggle we couldn't really get it out of our system. We referred to these articles as our "night moves," after the Gene Hackman *film noir* in which the hero pursues a mystery that deepens and widens until it engulfs him. After the raw hate directed at us over the Fay Stender article, and because the Left was omnipresent in the literary culture, we worried sometimes that this underside would catch up with us and undermine our new careers.

For *Rolling Stone*, we wrote Do It, a history of the Weather Underground. Initially, we hoped that the Weathermen (the last leaders of SDS) would provide a holograph of the Sixties. I interviewed thirty of their members, including half the Weather Bureau, their leadership group. But we found them, as individuals, to be little more than political delinquents with only the shallowest understanding of themselves or what they had done. Their attitude was reflected in an interview I conducted with Billy Ayers, the son of a utilities executive and the husband of the group's leader, Bernadine Dohrn. I met him at a nursery school in Manhattan, where he was a teacher. He was wearing bib overalls, and his blond curls rolled to his shoulders. After recounting to me his life as a political terrorist and celebrity, Ayers summed up the arc of his career in an epigram: "Guilty as hell, free as a bird—America is a great country."

I also interviewed Mark Rudd, who had led the "uprising" at Columbia in 1968 and been purged from the Underground after the townhouse explosion. I found him in Albuquerque, where he was teaching at a technical college. A large, affable man, Rudd alone among the leaders I interviewed had a basic honesty about himself and was feeling genuine remorse for the wasted and destructive years he had spent in the Weather army. He told me that the tragedy in which the three activists had died was caused by a bomb they were preparing for a service-club dance at Fort Dix. This was the first information about their planned target that anyone had revealed, and it produced a shock of recognition in Peter and me. The three bombers were SDS veterans; their intended target—young people at a dance—showed just how malevolent the Movement had become. Chastened by the loss of their comrades when the plot misfired, the Weather leadership later confined its targets to such symbolic venues as the U.S. Capitol building, where Bernadine and Kathy Boudin—who had narrowly escaped the townhouse explosion—planted a bomb in a ladies room.

Rudd also helped us to piece together the bizarre final acts of the Underground, which had initiated a series of purges in its ranks, complete with confessions and recantings—a farcical replay of the revolutionary past. The purist remnant that conducted the purges subsequently joined elements of the Black Liberation Army, to form the May 19 Communist Organization—celebrating a date which marked the birthdays of Malcolm X and Ho Chi Minh. The goal of these revolutionaries was to create a "New Afrika" in America's southern states, through a campaign of guerilla war. To finance this war, the group held up a Brinks armored car in Nyack, New Jersey. This led to a gun battle in which three policemen were killed, including the only black officer on the Nyack police force. The perpetrators—Kathy Boudin among them—were given 20-year sentences, ending their political careers.

Experienced as I was in the Left, I found it difficult to understand the mentality behind such acts. It was the fourth year of the liberal Carter Administration; the Vietnam War was over; Andrew Young, a black Sixties radical, was America's ambassador to the United Nations; Selma, Atlanta, and many of the other citadels of the segregated South had black mayors and police chiefs; and the entire South had undergone a political and cultural revolution as dramatic as any modern society had ever achieved. What could justify or inspire such extreme strategies of rebellion? Why declare war on "Amerika" now?

I had been given insight into the psychology behind such malignant politics in the previous year. Bernadine Dohrn had surfaced after nearly a decade underground, and was being interviewed from jail on the Phil Donahue show. I was watching the proceedings with my friend Jim Mellen, and it was his reactions that provided my instruction. Jim was a handsome, square-jawed man with a subdued affect, as if nursing some subtle grievance toward life. Married twice, he had become a close friend and confidant after my own divorce. I soon learned that he had two children from his first marriage whom he had abandoned—not seeing them since infancy—twenty years before. There was no way I could understand such self-induced separation from one's own flesh.

Jim's career was a case study in the opportunities that America offered. His father was an alcoholic who had left the family; his mother had worked as a soda-fountain clerk to support them. Jim was bright enough to earn a Ph.D. and win a Fulbright scholarship to Tanzania as an agricultural expert. On his return to America in the late Sixties, he decided to drop his academic career for the revolution. He marched with the Weathermen in their "Days of Rage" in Chicago, trashing downtown businesses to protest "Amerikan" racism and the "imperialist" war. He became the group's "theoretician," writing their famous declaration of race war: "You Don't Need a Weatherman to Know Which Way the Wind Blows." In this war, America's white radicals were going to act as a fifth column, to help the darker races conquer America and divide its ill-gotten spoils. It was the same war that the May 19 Communist Organization was seeking to instigate with its failed robbery attempt.

Jim got off the revolutionary train during a famous "War Council" held in Flint, Michigan, when Bernadine Dohrn praised Charles Manson and spread her fingers in the infamous "fork salute." "Dig it!" she cried to the assembled warriors. "First they killed those pigs, then they ate dinner in the same room with them. They even shoved a fork into a victim's stomach. Wild!" It was not the nasty rhetoric, but her call to actually begin the war he had advocated, that caused Jim to quit. Later, he tormented himself with the idea that he was a coward and could not stomach the risks his own ideas invited.

Because of Jim's Weatherman politics, the academic career he had begun was blocked. During the next decade, the rise of radicals in the university would prove this a temporary situation (even Billy Ayers would eventually become a professor of child education at Northwestern). But, for the moment, Jim was faced with the problem of finding a new profession. At first, he made solar heaters for hot tubs, then became a carpenter, a contractor, and finally a developer. By the time we sat down to watch the Donahue show, he had mortgaged the two-story house he had bought with his carpentry earnings, to finance the construction of a group of condominiums he had designed and built. With the profits he bought a small plane, and was already preparing to enter a new career by going to law school at night.

Given his humble origins and the outlaw status he had earned as a radical, Jim had demonstrated how rich in opportunities and how politically tolerant the system he had declared war on actually was. Yet somehow this revelation, and even his own success, failed to satisfy the radical hungers that gnawed his soul. On the TV screen, Bernadine was justifying her life as a political terrorist by attacking "Amerikan injustice" in the most lurid terms, picturing the country as a vast concentration camp for minorities and the poor, while denouncing its repressive state. It was as though the year was 1969 and she was still issuing war communiqués from Weather headquarters underground. What disturbed me, however, was not her rantings (which I expected), but the fact that Jim was hanging on her every word, and shouting comments of encouragement at the tube. "Jim," I said, incredulous, "you're still with her! If she went out and bombed the Capitol tomorrow, you'd probably say 'right on.'" He smiled at me with a look of utter self-satisfaction: "Nothing would delight me more."

For days afterwards, I couldn't stop thinking about Jim's reaction. Whatever rage was roiling inside him came from psychological layers so deep that he himself had lost contact with them. As in Bernadine's case, the bitterness he felt had little to do with anything that could have been inspired by the world outside. What worthwhile objective could bombing the U.S. Capitol conceivably serve? What intelligible "statement" could such an act possibly make? Had not Americans—*ordinary* Americans—recently demonstrated, and in the most dramatic way possible, their ability to alter the course of their history in the halls of that very Capitol by overthrowing the segregationist system and ending a war they no longer wanted to fight? What other government that anyone could point to had *ever* offered more than that?

The nihilism that Jim's reaction betrayed was hardly unique. Not too long afterwards, Peter and I encountered the documentary filmmaker Emile DeAntonio at Elaine's, an "in" New York restaurant. DeAntonio had made several celebrated political features, including *Point of Order*, which was about the career of Joe McCarthy, and *Milhous*, a savage portrayal of the Nixon era. When Bernadine and the Weathermen were still fugitives, DeAntonio had also made a documentary portraying them as American heroes. "Why did you like the

Weathermen?" I asked. Without hesitation, he said: "Because they were brainless and violent."

In our ongoing discussions, Peter had always maintained that the element of malice played a larger role in the motives of the Left than I had been willing to accept. I resisted his judgment because I could not readily locate such negative passions in myself. But now I was having second thoughts. If the Left was primarily motivated by the desire to "make the world better," why was it so indifferent to the consequences of its efforts? What else could explain its lack of concern about the deeds of its liberators in Indochina, or its Panther vanguard at home? Its disinterest in whether socialism *worked* or not? The more I thought about the moral posturing of the Left, the more I saw that its genius lay not in reforms but in framing indictments. Resentment and retribution were the radical passions. In *The Eighteenth Brumaire*, Marx had invoked a dictum of Goethe's devil: "Everything that exists deserves to perish." It was the progressive *credo*. To the Left, neither honored traditions nor present institutions reflected human nature or desire; the past was only a dead weight to be removed from their path. When the Left called for "liberation," what it really wanted was to erase the human slate and begin again in the year zero of creation. Marxism was indeed a form of idolatry, as Berdyaev had written, and the Creator/Destroyer that the Left worshipped was itself.

A "liberation" in America now allowed us a closer look at the consequences of this radical idolatry. In the spring of 1983, there were attacks on the Reagan Administration over its policy toward AIDS. Although only 1,500 cases had been diagnosed, the rate of infection was at epidemic levels, and doubling every six months. As part of our second-thoughts process, Peter and I had developed an aversive reflex to apocalyptic complaints from the Left. Activists were now accusing federal officials of withholding funds from the fight against AIDS, and thus "murdering" gay men. The extravagance of the charge reminded us of the verbal attacks on LBJ over Vietnam: "Hey, hey, LBJ many kids did you kill today?" Taking a leaf from the Sixties' protests, gay radicals had staged a "die-in" in front of the federal Health and Human Services building in Washington. One demonstrator donned a mask of Reagan and a black robe, and carried a sign that read "AIDS

Is Genocide." It was the kind of hyperbolic assault we had reveled in at *Ramparts* during the Vietnam War. But, recently, we had begun to think about the injustice of the charges against LBJ, especially after reading how wounded he felt by them. How many babies had the *Left* killed through the actions of the groups it had supported, the Vietcong and the Khmer Rouge?

Such thoughts changed our assessment of radical grievance. In regard to AIDS, the very posture of blame seemed suspect, almost like an avoidance of adult responsibilities. Federal bureaucracies notoriously did not move swiftly—if they moved at all—to address such problems. AIDS was still an obscure disease, and the $26 million already being spent seemed substantial. The head of the Public Health Service had declared AIDS a "number one priority." Ignoring these efforts, the demonstrators addressed the president as if he were a Great White Father with solutions to their problems, which he withheld at whim. Yet, if anyone possessed a solution to the problem, it was the community at risk. Although the virus that caused AIDS had not yet been isolated, the medical consensus was already clear: AIDS was a sexually transmitted disease which promiscuous behavior had turned into an epidemic. The first cohort of AIDS sufferers had an average of more than a thousand sexual contacts a year *per individual,* about a hundred times more than the average heterosexual male who was single. It was this aggressive promiscuity that explained the velocity with which the disease was traveling through the gay community.

Radical politics was one of the sources of the promiscuity. The gay movement had been launched during the high tide of the sexual revolution, and had defined its liberation as freedom from the chains of "sexual repression." For heterosexuals, the sexual revolution had ended in the Seventies with the spread of the herpes virus. Herpes was not deadly, like AIDS, but its symptoms were severe enough to persuade the nonideological public to come to terms with the hygiene problem created by promiscuous sex. Public sex clubs were closed, and sexual mores in general became more conservative. But there was no parallel sobering of perspectives in the gay revolution. For gay radicals, promiscuous sex was too integral to the idea of *liberation* to be surrendered even to hygienic concerns. In the homosexual community, venereal epidemics were already proliferating that were far more serious than herpes. But just before the outbreak of AIDS, Edmund White, the author of *The Joy of Gay Sex*, told an audience: "Gay men should wear their sexually transmitted diseases like red badges of courage in a war against a sex-negative society." A young gay activist named Michael Callen, who later founded People With AIDS, was in the audience and thought: "Every time I get the clap, I'm striking a blow for the sexual revolution."

By the late Seventies, a series of contagions were raging through gay communities, including rectal gonorrhea, syphilis, CMV, and Hepatitis B. Several of the epidemics were linked to cancer and to immune-system disorders, and were so extensive that the services they required were costing taxpayers more than a million dollars a day. Yet public-health officials refused to intervene with preventive measures. When I interviewed Don Francis, a top official at the Centers for Disease Control, he explained the rationale of this policy: "We didn't want to be interfering with an alternative lifestyle." It was an indication of how successful the gay revolutionaries had been in establishing their liberated zones. As the epidemics proliferated, the gay sex clubs and "bathhouses," which were publicly licensed, remained stubbornly open and continued to do a booming trade.

Even after the outbreak of AIDS, the sex clubs continued their business as usual. When a group of gay doctors encountered their own AIDS patients cavorting in a bathhouse, they reported the incident to the *San Francisco Chronicle*, hoping to shock the community and public-health officials into action. But the result of their efforts was only that they themselves were attacked by militants as victims of "gay homophobia," and silenced. Meanwhile, activists continued to blame Reagan and the lack of federal funds for the rising tide of illness and death, and to "demand" that the medical establishment produce a cure.

Peter and I decided to look into the story. The epidemic was still almost entirely confined to the gay communities in three cities— New York, Los Angeles, and San Francisco. The latter had the largest number of cases, and its Castro district was the base of the most populous and politically developed gay community in the nation. The political clout of San Francisco's gays was so great, in fact, that no mayor could be elected without their support. We decided to focus on the city as an emblematic case. As was my practice, I began the research by contacting other journalists who were covering the story. The most important of these was Randy Shilts, a *San Francisco Chronicle* reporter who had been assigned to the paper's "gay beat." I called Shilts and asked him to lunch.

He turned out to be a voluble, engaging man with a gossipy interest in everything that went on in the gay world. He had written *The Mayor of Castro Street,* a biography of San Francisco's first elected gay official, Harvey Milk, which also chronicled the rise of gay politics and the formation of the Castro community. I could not have found a more authoritative guide. Shilts was of our own. work and his respect for it was evident. As he filled me in on the AIDS situation, it became immediately apparent that our instincts had been right. Moreover, the political aspects of the story were more significant and troubling than we had imagined.

Shilts described an atmosphere of political intimidation in the gay community so thick that people were afraid to speak out. The doctors who had tried in vain to warn the public about the dangers of the bathhouses were only the tip of the iceberg. Studies conducted by university researchers showed that 1 of every 333 gay men in the Castro district already had the disease. "If one guy has sex with ten guys in a night, and some do," Shilts said to me, "the risk becomes one in thirty-three for this guy." If he does this regularly, he added (and "plenty did"), the prospect of getting AIDS was a dead certainty. According to Shilts, it was the gay leaders themselves who suppressed the research findings, along with the fact—now generally accepted by medical officials—that AIDS was a sexually transmitted disease.

This was difficult to believe, but when I checked Shilts's story, it turned out to be true. The Stonewall Gay Democratic Club, one of the political powers in the community, had summarized the politically correct view prevailing among activists in a slogan: "Sex doesn't cause AIDS—a virus does." The activists were afraid that identifying the disease with promiscuous sex and also with gay sex—95 percent of the cases in San Francisco were among homosexual males—would stigmatize the "gay life-style" and create a political backlash. The political clout of the activists was powerful enough to prevent information about the sexual transmission of AIDS from being disseminated by health officials to those at risk. Not a single piece of informational literature was available in the city's VD clinics explaining the sexual nature of the disease, the fact that it was a bloodborne virus carried by semen, and that passive anal sex was the source of almost all transmissions. The pamphlets on AIDS referred to the origins of the disease as obscure, and prescribed precautions like added sleep and more exercise.

A key figure in shaping San Francisco's AIDS policy whom I interviewed at Shilts's suggestion was the coordinator of all city health programs impacting homosexuals. This was a black lesbian named Pat Norman, who was not a medical professional but a political activist obviously over her head in dealing with health issues. Her official title was Director of the Office of Lesbian and Gay Health in the city's health department. A few months earlier, the Coordinating Committee of Gay and Lesbian Services, which she chaired, had blasted proposals to screen blood donors at the city's blood banks after several hemophiliacs had become infected. The committee denounced such screening as "reminiscent of miscegenation blood laws that divided black blood from white" and "similar in concept to the World War II rounding up of Japanese-Americans in the western half of the country to minimize the possibility of espionage." As soon as I referred to the absence of public information about the sexual transmission of AIDS, Norman grew evasive and hostile, and the interview was terminated.

On Shilts's advice, I also went to an AIDS workshop organized by San Francisco and attended by its mayor, Dianne Feinstein, and key AIDS researchers, including Paul Volberding and Marcus Conant. The doctors were in clear agreement that AIDS was a bloodborne virus, similar to Hepatitis B, and was transmitted from semen to the bloodstream, most likely through ruptures in the membranes during anal sex. The key to AIDS prevention was in not exchanging "bodily fluids" during sexual acts, and particularly those that might cause bleeding. The really bad news at the workshop)—and on this the scientists were unanimous—was that the nature of the virus was such that "No matter how much money was spent on research, there would not be a vaccine for five to ten years, and there might never be a cure." Attendees were reminded that, after decades of research, there was *still* no cure for polio, or even the common cold. The only feasible way to stem the tide of the epidemic was through public-health measures. This meant warning the homosexual community of the dangers it faced, and attempting to change its sexual behavior. But it was clear that this could not be accomplished if political considerations were going to control the information and prevent it from being disseminated among those at risk.

Near the end of our first lunch meeting, Shilts had said to me, "David, if you want to understand gay sex, it's boys without girls." There was no more central institution to illustrate this fact than the bathhouses, which were described to me by an activist as "symbols of gay liberation." Nationally, the baths were a $100 million industry. Studies had shown that nearly 70 percent of the gay population frequented them, and that the average bathhouse patron had nearly three sexual contacts on any given night, and a 33 percent chance of walking out with a venereal disease. With some trepidation, I told Peter I would go and see for myself.

The Liberty Baths were located in a nondescript three-story brick building, and had the look of a sexual YMCA. There were showers and a sauna, lockers, a TV room, and gay men in towels, wandering the halls. There were also private rooms, and stalls which Shilts told me were called "glory holes" after the openings that were cut waist-high for anonymous sex. As I tried to make out the gropings in the "orgy room," I was struck by the fact that nobody talked to anybody, and that it was dark—so dark, in fact, that in some areas you couldn't see a hand in front of you. It would be hard to design a more perfect petri dish for culturing and spreading sexual diseases.

The bathhouses had already become a source of bitter conflict among gay leaders. I interviewed one of them, Bill Kraus, who, like Shilts himself, was later to die of AIDS. Kraus was president of the Harvey Milk Gay Democratic Club, and was convinced that the bathhouses were a threat to the community's health. Privately, he believed they should be closed, but he knew this was politically impossible, and was afraid to say so publicly. His immediate concern was that the city post warnings in the bathhouses about the sexual transmission of AIDS. This was a matter of urgency, because the annual Gay Pride Parade was scheduled for June, only a month away. At that time, tens of thousands of unsuspecting gays from all over the country would descend on San Francisco to immerse themselves in its deadly culture of liberation and disease. At a meeting of the bathhouse owners and gay leaders, Kraus's proposal was rejected, and he himself was subjected to brutal personal attack. He was called a "sexual fascist," a "traitor to the community," and someone who wanted to "stifle sexuality." As one activist explained the radicals' logic to me: "You have a situation where institutions [the bathhouses] that have fought against sexual repression are being attacked under the guise of medical strategy."

Kraus was nervous about talking to me, and wanted to approve every quote before I included it in our article. But he was also grateful that we were writing the story, because the intimidation in the gay community was so great that it was impossible for dissenters to speak out. In talking to Kraus and others like him, I was reminded of my childhood experiences during the McCarthy era. There was the same fear of damaged reputation, political isolation, the loss of friends, and banishment from the community. It was these fears that had caused Shilts to give us a story that was properly his own.

At Shilts's suggestion, I also interviewed a lesbian nurse named Catherine Cusic, who was an official of the Harvey Milk Club and a care provider for AIDS patients. She had watched gay lovers die in each other's arms, and had comforted the families who came to pay their sons a last goodbye. Her testimony was chilling: "There are leaders in this community," she said, "who don't want people to know the truth. Their attitude is that it is bad for business, bad for the gay image. Hundreds, perhaps thousands, are going to die because of this attitude. This whole thing borders on the homicidal."

The attitude of gay leaders was crucial because San Francisco's director of public health, Dr. Mervyn Silverman, adopted the attitude that he could not implement any health policy on AIDS that was not preapproved by them. In my view, this was an abdication of his responsibility as a doctor and health official, but he adamantly defended the position. He would not even publicly challenge the politically shaped view that there was still uncertainty about the sexual nature of AIDS transmission. "If you take the attitude that there is still uncertainty about the way AIDS is contracted", I asked him, "how can you be so absolute in your public assurances that there is no risk of casual transmission?" The impossibility of casual transmission to heterosexuals (through saliva, for example) had been heavily emphasized in statements about AIDS by health officials who wanted to reassure the public because of the large number of gay-run restaurants and other business establishments in San Francisco. "Oh," Silverman replied without hesitation. "Gays are especially susceptible in ways that heterosexuals are not. The average gay male already has a depressed immune system." "You *know* that?" I asked, incredulous. He then proceeded to explain to me how T-cells were measured, how Hepatitis B depressed the immune system, and how the other massive sexually transmitted epidemics that officials such as he had allowed to run free in the gay community had produced a vulnerability of gay males to infection.

I was stunned by these admissions. Here was a community at grave risk from a sexual epidemic, and the chief public-health official—fully cognizant of the dangers—was refusing to close the bathhouses and other sexual gymnasia, or to post warnings in them, or even to tell the gay community and the public at large about the nature of the threat they faced. Silverman eventually left the public-health department to become the head of the national AIDS Foundation, appearing at gala benefits on the arm of celebrities like Elizabeth Taylor, collecting millions of charitable dollars to provide care for the terminally ill victims his policies had helped to create.

The article we wrote appeared as the cover story in the July 1983 issue of *California* magazine under the title *Whitewash.* The cover line read: "While the number of AIDS victims doubles every six months, gay leaders in California have obscured vital information about how the deadly disease is spread, endangering thousands of lives. ..." Pickets appeared at the magazine's headquarters to protest its "homophobic" contents, and there were denunciations from Pat Norman and other gay leaders. Following these cues, *Newsweek* dismissed our article as "sensationalism," and no one in the media did a follow-up to the story. It was not until four years later, when Shilts himself described these events in his history of the epidemic, *And the Band Played On,* that the political dimensions of the AIDS story became more widely known.

Later another young writer, Michael Fumento, was inspired by our reporting to begin an investigation of the politics of the epidemic. It eventually was published as *The Myth of Heterosexual AIDS*.

As a result of our article, I was invited on numerous talk shows, to debate gay activists. In my presentations, I was careful to acknowledge the concerns of the gay community. I wanted to reach the unsuspecting young men who were in the path of the epidemic. I knew that if they perceived me as hostile to their interests, they would not listen to what I had to say. On one of the shows, I appeared with Randy Stallings, head of the Alice B. Toklas Club, which was the third of San Francisco's powerful gay Democratic Party organizations. I began by deploring the treatment of homosexual Americans, reminding the listening audience that only recently it was still a crime to practice homosexuality, and that the epidemic was a human tragedy. "If you are gay," I said, "and have not been in a monogamous relationship for ten years [the presumed latency of the virus] you might be incubating a fatal disease." Stallings pounced on me. "You see, you *see!* He said *monogamous.* That's his prejudice, his homophobia coming out." I was not about to be intimidated. "We're not discussing philosophy," I said. "This is a matter of life and death." But Stallings persisted. He denied that the disease was sexually transmitted and that the city health officials were being derelict in not posting warnings. And he regarded any proposal to close the bathhouses as an attack on gays. It was a response typical of the political activists I debated on the issue.

After the article was published, Catherine Cusic invited me to appear with her in a public debate with Stallings at the Stonewall Democratic Club. When I arrived for the event, a hundred gay men had assembled in a meeting room at the Dover Club, but there was no Catherine Cusic. She had come under such heavy attack for the remarks quoted in our article that she had decided it would be prudent not to show. The debate began reasonably enough, and there was no heckling when I spoke. Again, I was careful to make clear that homosexuality was not an issue for me. I understood and sympathized with the fact that they were a persecuted community, and supported their claims to equal rights and respect. But public-health procedures and traditional morals could not be viewed merely as "heterosexist" instruments whose purpose was to oppress gays. Despite the attempt of the gay leadership to deny it, the fact remained that AIDS *was* a sexually transmitted disease, and promiscuity was dangerous—especially for gay males. Traditional public-health measures for combating epidemics should be deployed against *this* one. I could remember when public swimming pools were closed during the polio epidemic, thirty years before. Now the bathhouses were crucibles for spreading AIDS, and should be closed, too. It was not a political issue, but an issue of health. You could not require public-health policy to conform to political prejudices without serious consequences. The hour was late. Soon the disease would spread too widely for these measures to stop it. The time had come to discard the ideological responses that had dominated the debate for some practical common sense.

During the question period, the audience's mood began to turn ugly. "I feel compelled to denounce you," one man said as he stood up, his voice pinched into a whine. Then he rehearsed his personal pain as a homosexual, and the persecution he felt from people like me. Others joined the attack. Suddenly I had become a symbol rather than a person—an object of passion and fear. Nothing I said was being heard. Voices began to call out epithets like "Nazi" and "homophobe," stoking the general hysteria until one man cried out "I'd like to kill you."

Not one person spoke in my defense—not even to suggest that I might be owed some courtesy as a guest outnumbered a hundred to one. There was only the collective rage vented in my direction. The air had become so heated that when the meeting was finally declared over and people began milling toward the speakers' table, I braced myself for a physical assault. But no violence came. Instead, I was approached by a slight man with gray hair who addressed me in a near whisper: "What you are saying is right. Don't stop."

It was Larry Littlejohn, San Francisco's first gay sheriff. In the Sixties, Littlejohn had been president of SIR, the first homosexual civil-rights group. He said nothing more to me that evening, but later, inspired by our article, he waged a personal campaign to put a measure on the San Francisco ballot that would close the bathhouses. By threatening to collect the necessary signatures, he forced gay leaders—who did not want a public referendum on the issue—to compromise. By this time, the HIV virus had been isolated, and the sexual transmission of the disease was accepted. The gay leadership agreed to allow monitoring of the bathhouses to prevent "unsafe" sex. But this turned out to be an ineffectual measure at best. By then, the number of AIDS cases had almost tripled and spread to other regions of the country. After the compromise was struck, the *Bay Area Reporter*—the paper of record in the Castro community—published a "traitors" list denouncing those who had attempted to "kill" the gay liberation movement by forcing the bathhouses to close. Bill Kraus and Randy Shilts were prominent names on the list, which was headed by Larry Littlejohn, "traitor *extraordinaire.*"

When the traitors list appeared, I contacted Littlejohn and went to see him. I was curious about his history in the struggle for gay rights, and why he had been willing to make such a lonely and courageous stand. The story he told recalled for me the transformation of the civil-rights movement in the Sixties, when King's integrationist message was replaced by the radical separatism of Malcolm X and the proponents of Black Power. Like King, Littlejohn and his fellow activists originally intended to seek integration into the larger American culture, demanding the rights and respect accorded to everyone else. But in the late Sixties this idea had been supplanted by the radical concept of "liberation." Now the goal was no longer inclusion, but a liberated zone in which "gay power" and the gay "life-style" would prevail over "heterosexist" order. "Straight" morals and institutions, including—it turned out—public-health procedures, were rejected in favor of the revolutionary culture. Littlejohn came to believe that it was precisely this culture and the attitudes it encompassed, from publicly encouraged promiscuity to politically controlled health policy, that were destroying his community.

In 1987, four years after our article appeared, a gay march on Washington was organized, reprising King's famous demonstration in 1963. The march, 200,000 strong, continued gay leaders' denial that AIDS was a problem within the community, and featured slogans like "Reagan No, Sodomy Yes," as though Ronald Reagan was responsible for AIDS, and anal sex had not been identified as the principal means of its transmission.

For the first time in our lives, Peter and I found ourselves on the "conservative" side of a political argument. The path that had led us to this destination did not seem especially "political." The rules of personal hygiene were hardly the imposition of an oppressive caste, as radicals claimed. On the other hand, taking responsibility for what happened to oneself seemed a pretty basic ethical principle. It was something we had tried to impress on our children and to accept as a discipline ourselves. Ronald Reagan was obviously not to blame for the epidemic. Yet our refusal to point a finger at Reagan was regarded by the political left as an attempt to "blame the victims," and put us—whether we liked it or not—in the conservative camp.

The politics of the AIDS crisis reinforced many conclusions we had already come to. As Peter and I grew older, the moral traditions we had scorned as leftists had begun to seem less arbitrary, more inevitable. We began to see them less as the social constructs of a ruling elite, and more as imperfect lessons from experience preserved as conventional wisdom. Monogamy was not a blind prejudice, as I had learned to my own cost and as Randy Stallings had claimed. It was more like prudence, a rule of behavior that had been learned through centuries of human experiment, anguish, and misadventure. To spend a life blaming others—"society"—for what happened to oneself was to deprive oneself of the power to learn from experience, and to alter one's fate.

Once again I saw how the Left regarded people as objects of history, rather than as subjects who made the events happen. If people had free will, if you respected their willingness to do evil as well as good (to themselves as well as to others), then tragedies were inevitable. There was no "revolution" of attitudes or institutions that could overcome the forces of this nature. Through the deaths of Betty and Ellen, through the pain of my divorce, I had acquired a certain philosophical fatalism. I understood that the human tragedy I was now witnessing had already accumulated a specific gravity—that human will, fear, prejudice, and suspicion had already acquired such density that they would overwhelm all attempts to avert it.

The doctors at the San Francisco workshop on AIDS I attended had been in agreement on one crucial fact: *No matter how much money was spent on research, there was not going to be a vaccine for five to ten years, and there might never be a cure.* This would be the case even if the virus were to be isolated, as they expected it would be (and was) within the next six months. At the time of the workshop, the epidemic was still confined to three communities, and to a relatively small number of victims—chiefly gay men. In the absence of a medical antidote, the only way to contain the epidemic was through dramatic public-health measures designed to change the behaviors of the affected and to separate them from those at risk.

Yet it was equally clear that this would *not* be the path followed. The bathhouses and sex clubs were *not* going to be closed, lest the radical life-style be marked with a stigma. Though gays and (to a growing extent) intravenous-drug users were the principal groups affected and at risk, there were *not* going to be any measures focused specially on them. Instead, government health propaganda would describe AIDS as "an equal-opportunity virus," and enormous resources would be squandered in efforts to persuade the non-drug-using heterosexual population that it, too, was at risk—that its *own* epidemic was about to explode. For political reasons, there would be no systematic testing or reporting, or contact tracing of infected parties—standard health measures in stemming contagions in the past. As a result, it would be impossible to determine where the epidemic was spreading next, or to warn those in its path (specifically, the black and Hispanic populations, which were the next to be infected). The *only* campaign that would be politically acceptable to gay activists and their allies—thus to the public health authorities—was "education." But, as had already been made clear, even *this* campaign would be shaped to political ends. Instead of targeting those specifically at risk, all groups would receive *equal* warnings. Promiscuous anal sex accounted for more than 95 percent of the cases that were sexually transmitted, but those three words would never appear in sequence in the education materials that government agencies and private AIDS groups distributed, or in the press.

As I reviewed the inexorable spread of the epidemic, and the efforts of the gay left to control, weaken, and obstruct the measures to combat it, I could extrapolate the numbers who were going to die. By doubling the 4,000 existing cases every six months for the next 10 years, I was able to calculate (accurately) that by 1994 there would be almost 200,000 people—mostly gay men, mostly in the bloom of youth—who were going to die for an idea of liberation. And there was nothing that I or anyone else could do to stop it.

When I surveyed the political forces arrayed on the AIDS issue, the ironies were poignant and made me wonder where Peter and I were going to end up. The political left saw itself as the protector of the gay community, and was seen that way by gays themselves. As a result, the Left and its allies were the only political voices the gay community trusted. In cities where the virus was raging, Democrats controlled the administrative agencies and allowed public-health policies to be shaped by the gay left. About the time we did our story, gay leaders at a National AIDS Forum in Denver declared: "We oppose any legislative attempts to restrict sexual activities or to close private clubs or bathhouses.... We should never forget that we live in a homophobic society, or that homophobia is the major threat to our health." This attitude sealed the fate of the gay communities still free of the virus. With less than 2,000 cases nationwide, drastic measures—the declaration of a health emergency in the affected areas; the closing of the bathhouses; testing among those at risk; contact tracing to warn those in the infection's path—might have stemmed the tide of the epidemic and eventually saved tens of thousands of lives. Yet, gay leaders (supported by liberal Democrats in government) remained adamantly opposed to these measures because of the perceived "homophobic" threat from their enemies on the right.

This Right was actually divided into three groups, of which two were not especially hostile to homosexuals. There were those who did believe that AIDS was God's curse for immoral behavior. But there were many more who merely objected to the "in-your-face" aggressiveness of the gay left, and who, like Reagan, were uncomfortable about making sexual issues the focus of a public debate. There were others, finally, who endorsed the health policies that were being jettisoned by the Left, but were intimidated from making public statements, and rendered ineffectual by the Left's attacks. To challenge even self-appointed spokesmen for a community in which large numbers of young men were dying was to invite political lightning to strike. With liberals and radicals invoking images of the Holocaust in describing the epidemic, and identifying their opponents as "homo-phobes"—in effect, the Nazis of the historical analogy—there were understandably few conservative spokesmen who were willing to take a stand on the public-health issue.

Peter and I had no sympathy for the attacks from the far Right aimed at homosexuality itself. Yet we saw how the attitudes of the Left posed a threat to the very people they claimed to defend. Any attempt (such as our article) to challenge these attitudes invited a ven-omous attack. Not for the first time in our political lives did we find ourselves in a lonely space.

The AIDS epidemic was not the only political battlefront on which the alliance between liberal Democrats and political radicals caused us to line up on the conservative side. In 1980—three years before our article appeared—I had voted for the Democratic candidate for president, Jimmy Carter. It was the first time I had voted for either party since 1964, and in fact it had been my intention not to vote at all. But at the last minute, as friends pressured me to vote against Reagan, I thought of the guilt I would feel if he won by a narrow margin, and hurried off to the polls to cast my ballot against him.

This memory was now embarrassing to me. As Reagan's Admin-istration progressed, my response seemed in fact almost hysterical, and no less embarrassing because it was widely shared by my Berke-ley peers. The fact that I had voted so reluctantly made me a clinical observer of the events that followed. While the very name "Reagan" continued to be an anathema in my old political communities, as though he was the devil incarnate, I noticed that the policies that defined his rule hardly differed from those of the John F. Kennedy who had once tempted us: In domestic affairs, a capital-gains tax cut, and in foreign policy a hard line toward the Communist enemy. At one point, Reagan even proposed a radical measure: withhold taxes on interest and dividends. This was a blow directed at the income of the rich, yet when I went to my Berkeley cooperative savings and loan—an island of socialism—cards were provided so that customers could write to their congressmen to protest Reagan's assault on their income. It was apparent to me that, as result of his anti-Commu-nism, Reagan had become a totem for the Left, inspiring emotions so irrational that there was *nothing* he could do that they would consider correct.

It was Reagan's anti-Communism, in fact, that had begun to attract me. A Carter policy I had approved of was his decision, in 1979, to let the Sandinistas take power in Nicaragua without American intervention. I had viewed the events out of the corner of an eye, so to speak, without paying much attention to the details. I was still in a state of withdrawal from the political arena, suspicious of my reactions and cautious not to let my politics become a mere reflex of personal bitterness or grief. Thus, I suspended judgments I might normally have been tempted to make. In terms of the events in Nicaragua, I was pleased that the era of America's "imperial" interventions seemed to be over. I did not look closely at the Sandinistas, to see who they were.

When I did look, during the election campaign of 1984, I discovered them to be Marxist protégés of Castro who had announced their intention to turn Nicaragua into another Cuba. My political career had come full circle. On campuses across the country, a new radical generation was already forming "solidarity committees" to support the Sandinista regime. This time, I could not plead ignorance of what was going to happen if radicals had their way. In the twenty years of Castro's rule, Cuba had been transformed into a totalitarian state, its economy ruined by socialist plans, its jails filled with political dissenters. Cuba's gross national product now was less than it had been when Castro took power, a monument to the bankruptcy of the radical promise. Nor was the tragedy of Cuba unique. Every socialist state created by Marxists had been transformed into an economic sinkhole and a national prison. There were no exceptions. The policy debate in America was shaping up the way it had thirty years earlier. But this time the nation's shift to the left had created far more domestic sympathy for the Sandinistas than Fidel Castro ever enjoyed.

About this time, a book appeared revealing that I had played a small but significant role in shaping these sympathies. Like Castro twenty years earlier, the Sandinistas were able to seize power by concealing their Marxist agendas and leading a coalition of democrats against the Somoza regime. The United States had been a partner in the coalition, withdrawing its support from Somoza and precipitating his fall. But, once in power, the Sandinistas expelled the democrats from the ruling group and began implementing their Marxist design. Confronted with this *coup,* Washington decided not to intervene to oppose them. The point man on this decision was a White House official named Robert Pastor, who was head of the National Security Council staff for Latin America. Pastor was later interviewed by Richard A. Melanson, a professor of political science, who questioned him about the intellectual influences that had affected his recommendation not to intervene. Pastor told Melanson: "Horowitz's *Free World Colossus* had a dramatic impact on me and taught me the truth of the radical critique of the Cold War mentality.

The battle lines were clearly drawn. The Republican president, Ronald Reagan, had thrown U.S. support behind the opponents of the Communist regime. Civil war had broken out in Nicaragua, and the Administration was providing military and economic support to the *contra* forces, a band of peasant guerrillas whose land had been expropriated by the Sandinista regime. Reagan had stayed the course of Cold War containment that Truman had initiated against the Communist empire. Calling the Soviet Union an "evil empire," he had reaffirmed the policy of supporting peoples threatened by Communist tyranny. The policy had become increasingly muddled during the years of the Carter White House, when the President sometimes spoke as if American power and its abuses were the world's principal problems. When Reagan later condemned Soviet oppression in moral terms, he was attacked by a liberal chorus as endangering international peace, which underscored the perils of the current political moment.

Although Democrats were divided, the majority of the party was seeking to cut off aid to the *contra* guerrillas, just as they had in the case of the anti-Communists in Cambodia and Vietnam. On the party's left wing were pro-Sandinista radicals like Ron Dellums, who headed a key military committee in Congress. A Democratic victory in November would weaken the opposition to Castro, to the Sandinistas, and to the Soviet Empire, which had established a beachhead now on the American landmass itself.

On Election Day 1984, I walked into the voting booth and, without hesitation, punched the line marked "Ronald Reagan."

I had begun a new life in other ways, as well. Early in the year my son, Jon, had asked me if I would like to live with him in Los Angeles, where he had just graduated from UCLA. He had been sharing an apartment in West Hollywood with a rock band he had created, having inherited the musical talent from my mother's side of the family. Two of its members were setting up separate households, and Jon was getting ready to move to a smaller space. His offer came at a propitious moment and was too tempting to resist. The divorce had torn at the cords that connected me to my children, and I urgently wanted them to heal. I tried to imagine how it must feel to them to see their parents separate and their father move outside the family home. But I couldn't. Nor could I ever really gauge the dimensions of the wound, or calibrate the degrees of its repair It was not something one could discuss directly or hasten by words. One could only live through the pain, and hope that some day it would end.

The uncertainty produced an anxious feeling that was never far from the surface. I stayed close to my children, and involved myself in their efforts to establish first identifies and then lives for themselves, tried to be their guide and help. But the physical distance between us gave them an independence they had lacked when their house was mine, as well as a power to reject me—or so I imagined—that was fearful for me. Now my son had called to invite me to live with him. It was an offer to uproot myself and move far from the place where I had spent almost twenty-five years. But it felt to me like an invitation to come home.

Before accepting, I considered the other children. My second, Sarah, was already a junior at San Francisco State College, and Ben would be entering my alma mater, Columbia, in the fall. Only Anne remained at home, and she was already 16, a sophomore at Berkeley High. I decided they were well on their way to independent lives, and I could risk the move. Only one other question remained. I wanted to know if Elissa had really closed the door to the past.

We had been separated for five years, but the emptiness that the breakup of our marriage had left in me had never been filled. The family was now grown and increasingly scattered—one of those necessary losses that life itself engenders. I had shortened my enjoyment of this household, but it would have come anyway in time. The same could not be said for the companionship that Elissa and I had shared, and I missed. I had lost my best, my closest friend. In the five years of our separation, I had dated several women in an attempt to "move on" in my emotional life. But starting in the middle years was not the same as stepping into the boat of an unknown future, as Elissa and I had done so long ago. And yet, I realized, there was a wishful element to these regrets. When I turned back to look, having come so far in establishing a life on my own, I was forced to recognize how she and I were difficult halves to match. The lives we had chosen in our separate spheres revealed hardly a point of intersection, or a path that was common to both.

Her anger had seemed to soften, as the years went by, until we were able to confer over the children almost as comfortably as we had before the separation. But the condition of this peace had been my acceptance of its limits. We would resume the partnership in raising our children; we would not test the feeling that had been betrayed.

It was not in my nature to let this mystery alone, so I went to see her, to ask if she would consider spending time with me. Perhaps we could become a couple again. Her answer was no. She said it with the familiar firmness that had made her the guiding keel of our life together, but also with a great gentleness, and a missed beat—as though to signal that she was flattered by the offer, even though any sensible person could see that it just wouldn't work.

Jon and I moved into a one-bedroom condominium behind the Sunset "strip." He took the living room, rolling out the futon we had bought for a bed, while I set up my desk and computer in the bedroom. I had never lived in an apartment before, and enjoyed the sense of focus it provided. My days were organized for work. Peter and I had concluded the Kennedy book and just signed a new contract for a biography of the Fords. This dynasty was Peter's idea, but I was excited about it anyway because it would give me a chance to get up close to an industry and a company that were as much identified with industrial America as any I could think of I would have a last chance to look at my discarded Marxist ideas through an exacting prism of reality.

In the last stages of the Kennedy project, there was a recurrence of the kind of crisis that had confronted me when we were writing The *Rockefellers*. A key element in getting the story had been my ability to win the confidence of Bobby. Now my loyalties were again being put to the test. Early on, I had discovered his heroin addiction, and was being pressed by Peter to include it in our text. But I had promised Bobby I would not print such information if it had not already appeared. I was not ready to go through another trial like the one I had been through with Abby—yet there seemed no way to avoid it.

Bobby was now an assistant district attorney in New York, appointed by Teddy's friend Robert Morgenthau. So many people I interviewed knew of Bobby's heroin problem that it was difficult to imagine that Teddy, at least, was unaware of its existence when he recommended him for the job. But I had learned that such arrangements were never out of the question where Kennedys were concerned. In one of my last interviews, I had the surreal experience of sitting on a park bench in Manhattan with an Esquire editor, a Harvard roommate of Bobby's, who knew of the addiction, yet was talking to me as though it were perfectly natural about Bobby's plans to run for Congress in the next election. These facts added up to what I had come to think of as a group psychosis surrounding the Kennedys. At the center of the psychosis was the idea that had been so useful and at the same time so destructive to the family throughout its career: A Kennedy could get away with *anything*.

Fortunately, Bobby himself provided a solution to my dilemma. Just as Peter and I were coming to the end of the manuscript, Bobby had a drug episode on an airplane flight, and was discovered by the crew clutching his heroin apparatus in one of the plane's lavatories. The story made front-page headlines across the country, and relieved me of my problem. Shortly thereafter, Bobby's brother David died of an overdose. Before his death, David had called from Hazelton, a drug-rehabilitation center in Minnesota, to ask me for advice. He was distressed at the attention the family had paid to Bobby's plight, which contrasted with the way they had ostracized him when his own addiction made headlines. He had spent a year and a half in California without a single family member visiting. But when Bobby was in his trouble, they had all made a pilgrimage to his hospital bed, led by their mother.

The pain in David's voice when he related this was evident. I reminded him that he was marked as the family scapegoat, the one they would always point to as the Kennedy who had "dragged the family name in the mud." I urged him to make a separate peace with them and remove himself from the circle of their scorn. He could go back to California and make a new life for himself. But David could not break free. When Rose Kennedy became ill, a few weeks after our conversation, Teddy put out a call to the family to come to her side. David, who had been released from Hazelton, went directly to his grandmother's house in Palm Beach. A few days later, he was thrown off the estate because he was drunk—and shortly after that he was dead.

The sordid publicity generated a public interest in the Kennedys that was even greater than usual. Teddy's press secretary, Bob Shrum, issued a public statement suggesting that *we* were responsible for David's death, because of the distress that an advance excerpt of the book had caused him. But, fortunately for us, the press wasn't buying this excuse. Moreover, Doris Kearns Goodwin had not completed her own book, and the way was paved for ours to become another best-seller. The *New York Times* reviewer, Christopher Lehmann-Haupt, called *The Kennedys* "a hypnotically fascinating narrative," while the *Detroit* News called it "the best nonfiction book of the year." It was another Book-of-the-Month Club main selection, and went immediately to number one on the *New York Times* best-seller list. The paperback rights were sold to Warner Books for $750,000, with my half amounting to a bounty beyond anything I had ever imagined possible.

The possession of so much money worried me. I had reengaged the energies of a life, but I knew that the path out of my depression had begun with the necessity of earning a living. It was this that had forced me back into the world, and the residues of depression had not yet left my system. I was still suspended over a terrifying emptiness, fearful that without such pressure I might fall again into endless black space. This fear prompted me to decide to invest my share of the advance in a Tudor house located in the Fern Dell area of Griffith

Park. Fern Dell was a shaded glen at the opening to the park, traversed by a stream which was separated from the house by a private drive. In back of the house was a wooded hill, and on the front lawn there was a redwood easily a hundred feet tall. The purchase, along with the renovation I would undertake, would make me cash-poor. I hoped the pressure of earning the monthly mortgage to keep it would prevent me from falling back into my personal slough of despond.

In the spring and summer of 1984, while I was on tour for the Kennedy book and beginning my interviews for the Ford epic, I had the house renovated. I put in hand-tiled bathrooms, and a large kitchen with terra cotta tiles and a brick fireplace. The kitchen opened through French doors onto a natural black-bottom pool. The pool was landscaped with granite boulders and waterfalls, and a garden whose trees and moss hung over the edges. On the day the work was completed—October 30, 1984, nine months after I had moved to Los Angeles—I was married again.

M y new wife was a tall, statuesque Angeleno named Sam Moorman, but known to friends as the Countess Crespi because of her previous marriage to an Italian nobleman. Our wedding was attended by two hundred people who assembled for an informal wedding ceremony under the towering redwood on my front lawn. My son's band, *Candy*, played over a sound system set up on the roof of my garage. The guests (who were valet-parked, according to Hollywood ritual) included the director Oliver Stone, the actor Ed Begley Jr., a star from *Dynasty*, and other celebrities—all friends of my new wife, who was assistant to Brian *Grazer*, the producer of Tom Hanks' big hit, *Splash*. When one of my old friends commented on the discordance of the event with my prior self, I explained it as wanting to be "Godfather for a day." I had in mind the weddings that opened Coppola's epics. It was the desire, once again, to experience what life had to offer—not to miss out on anything I once would have denied myself because of the Spartan precepts of my discarded faith.

It was also one of the many efforts I had made to try on a new skin that didn't fit. One of my first thoughts on becoming single, seven years before, had been that possibilities were now open-ended: I could have any life I wanted. But my efforts to prove this often only demonstrated how deep the lines of character ran. I entertained the idea of romancing many women, and marrying only for financial security. Bitterness informed the idea; if you were going to find yourself alone anyway after twenty years, why not? But I discovered I couldn't change my attitudes toward love or money so surgically. It was impossible to remain detached from the feelings of others (a necessary talent for such ambitions). Soon I was drawn into familiar orbits by the gravitational pulls of self. My new wife had departed her Count penniless and without an estate, and she had an endearing seven-year-old daughter named Chloe. In many ways, I was still a nester—a family man missing what I had lost.

The courtship was a whirlwind affair. And, almost from the beginning of the marriage, I realized it was a mistake. Why had I gone through with it, and in such haste? Perhaps it was panic that set in when Elissa said her final no. Perhaps it was a more general anxiety to fill the hollows that still threatened me. Perhaps it was just a matter of not looking where I chose to leap. The courtship had lasted only a matter of weeks under circumstances—new fame and new wealth—that were bound to produce giddiness and unsober judgment. A few months into the marriage, I found myself living with a woman who had little sense of who I was, and no inkling of how to find out. Dwelling under the same roof with another human being without emotional intimacy was not my idea of marriage, and the proximity only made the feelings of loneliness more intense. Once again I was discovering that it was easier to tear apart a life than to put it back together. Less than a year after the ceremony, we separated for good.

Because there had been little substance to the marriage, there was little pain for me in the divorce, except for missing Chloe. But when the separation was established, I quickly discovered that other things had changed. For the first time in my life, I was a person with material assets that others coveted. Even though my ex-wife was "creative vice president" for a major producer, she retained a lawyer, claimed that I had made a million dollars during the months that we were married, and sued me for a property settlement. I had to hire an attorney to defend myself, although her case was eventually judged groundless, and thrown out of court.

Discussing the episode with my daughter Sarah, I remarked that a warning sign I should have heeded was Sam's attitude toward her own past. She had pulled up roots and reinvented herself. What she found unpleasant she simply erased—like her real name, which was not Sam, but Sharon. Having no identification with her past, it was not surprising that she would have so little connection to me. Having dispensed this wisdom, however, I failed to pay proper respect to it when the next occasion presented itself.

In the spring of 1985, I received a call from Walt Harrington, an editor at the *Washington Post.* He wanted my help for a piece he was writing about Congressman Joe Kennedy, Robert's oldest son. After he had picked my brain for leads, he asked me what Peter and I were up to. For some reason I replied, "You won't believe this, but we just voted for Ronald Reagan." *"That,"* he said, "is a good story. Would you guys like to write it for us?"

We realized at once that this assignment was going to be a big step. Until now, our political changes were a private affair. We had been able to pick the issues over which to reveal our views and define their parameters. But this occasion would be different. Ronald Reagan was a polarizing figure, and revealing that we had voted for him would be interpreted as embracing the whole spectrum of conservative views. It would be an announcement of our apostasy from the faith.

In truth, neither of us had systematically thought our way to a conservative position. Our attitude was more a rejection of the postures we had taken in the past that had proven so empty and destructive. "Casting our ballots for Reagan," as we put it in the article, was:

> A way of saying goodbye to all that—to the self-aggrandizing romance with corrupt Third Worldism; to the casual indulgence of Soviet totalitarianism; to the hypocritical and self-dramatizing anti-Americanism which is the New Left's bequest to mainstream politics.

We had chosen a title—"Goodbye to All That"—which accurately reflected our mood. But the *Post* editors changed it to "Lefties for Reagan," highlighting its incendiary quality and also its weakness. We could not, in only 3,000 words, justify both the dramatic turn we seemed to be taking, and also the specific vote we had cast for Reagan.

Despite this, we agreed to do the article for the same reason that we had cast our votes in the first place. Though we were not prepared to defend every aspect of the Reagan program, we did not regard that as necessary, either. There were defining issues which we were on board for, the most critical being the Cold War. In embracing the Left, the Democrats had become politically compromised on policies that affected its prosecution. One was their support for a nuclear freeze that would consolidate Moscow's strategic advantage in Europe. Another was their opposition to aid for the anti-Sandinista forces in Nicaragua. Reagan was a hardliner against the Communists, and so were we. If voting for him was going to be unpopular with our friends, so be it.

It was ironic that we should "come out" explosively like this. Our gravitation to the right had been timorous at first. We egged each other on, cognizant of the antipathy and loathing in store for us if we took the next step. On one occasion, I admitted to Peter that I had taken out a subscription to *Commentary*, "just to see what they were saying." His response was one of incredulity, but he began reading the publication as well. Peter had already experienced at least one political conversion, and observed that *this* one would be very different. Becoming a leftist was "like falling off a log," he observed, but the political forest was fraught with perils for conservatives. Especially for people such as we who inhabited the literary culture. *Here be dragons.* Every step to the right we took would create enemies among the liberal cognoscenti who ran the publishing houses, and the press, and the literary prize committees, and were in a position to shape our professional destinies.

What inspired us to disregard these dangers was the prospect of our former comrades busily resurrecting the discredited faith. There they were in Nicaragua, helping the new Fidels. Here they were, marching to disarm the West. They had even launched an "anti-war" movement against America's efforts to halt the Soviet invasion of Afghanistan. Like the Bourbons, they had learned nothing and forgotten nothing. It was all happening again, and we couldn't let the moment pass without joining the fight.

After our article appeared, I began to make speeches on political issues which forced me to define further where I stood. At a meeting in Washington to commemorate the tenth anniversary of the fall of Saigon, I spoke about "My Vietnam Lessons." In explaining my new perspective, I said: "My values have not changed, but my sense of what makes them possible has." I made the same point even more forcefully in a speech a year later to two hundred Berkeley radicals at a pro-Sandinista conclave to which I was invited as a token conservative:

> Twenty-five years ago, as one of the founders of the New Left, I was an organizer of the first political demonstrations on this Berkeley campus—and indeed on any campus—to protest our government's anti-Communist policies in Cuba and Vietnam. Tonight I come before you as a man I used to tell myself I would never be: a supporter of President Reagan, a committed opponent of Communist rule in Nicaragua.
>
> I make no apologies for my present position. It was what I thought was the humanity of the Marxist idea that made me what I was then; it is the inhumanity of what I have seen to be the Marxist reality that has made me what I am now. If my former comrades who support the Sandinista cause were to pause for a moment and then plunge their busy political minds into the human legacies of their activist pasts, they would instantly drown in an ocean of blood.

The rhetoric was heated, but by the time I reentered the political battle, I had made a decision to speak in the voice of the New Left—outraged, aggressive, morally certain. I would frame indictments as we had framed them, but from the other side. I wanted equity for those who had defended democracy against the Communist threat. I wanted justice for the victims of *our* crusades. I wanted my former comrades to be put on the receiving end of accusations like those they had made against everyone else. I wanted them to see how it felt. Evidently, it did not feel good. When I reached the point in my speech where I said "It is no accident that the greatest atrocities of the Twentieth Century have been committed by Marxist radicals in power," my words were shouted down and the microphone was cut off.

The speech was reprinted in *Commentary,* inviting the first significant personal attack on me in print. A leftist named Paul Berman had written an article in the *Village Voice* whose headline was tinged with the odor of an *auto-da-fé.* It was called "Intellectual Life and the Renegade Horowitz," and appeared in the August 1986 issue. Berman began by acknowledging that the individual who had appeared in Berkeley, supporting the policies of Ronald Reagan, was indeed one of the founders of the New Left "and the author of some of its best thumbed pages."

> *Other writers of the New Left figured larger in the awareness of the general public; but no one in those days figured larger among the leftists themselves. Horowitz was neither old and German, like Marcuse, nor a scientist and professor, like Chomsky, nor any kind of outsider or stranger to the student ranks. He was a Berkeley radical like any number of other people. He organized demonstrations. He helped put out* Ramparts *magazine.*

But that was the end of the article's commitment to any fair-minded presentation of my career. Berman was an extreme critic of American policy—which, according to him, was based on "the assumption that Americans have the right to arrange massacres of distant peasantries." Yet he also managed to pose as a defender of nuanced intellect against hot-blooded fanatics like myself. He set up his attack with a dubious reference to anarchists during Spain's civil war who, according to him, "used to board sleeping cars early in the evening, and alight at dawn, announcing that Jesus had come unto them, and had spoken, and long live fascism!" The rest of the article identified me with these zealots:

> *You might suppose that Horowitz today would enjoy going through his old books, sifting the superb from the absurd, ... doing what he could to maintain the continuity of discussion, trying to keep his old readers up to date. But Horowitz is in the American vein. He doesn't correct; he converts. What he denounced before, he announces today.... For David Horowitz has climbed into the sleeping car. And in the morning he has alighted, and viva the forces of Suicida and Commander Bermudez and the brave Somozista soldiers of democracy! Such is the life of the mind in our...American culture.*

Lenin said that the object of a political argument was not to win a debate but to wipe one's opponent from the face of the earth. Berman's caricature exemplified the principle. Since he had read my speech in *Commentary*, he knew that I had indeed maintained the "continuity of discussion," and had not simply "announced" what I "denounced" before. I viewed the Sandinistas' victory through the prism of the Cuban Revolution—a history I rehearsed at length in my speech. It could be read as a sermon in fact, on a theme articulated by the Czech writer Milan Kundera, which was cited in the text: *The struggle of man against power is the struggle of memory against forgetting.* This idea—as anyone familiar with what Peter and I had written in the last several years would know—had also become the theme of our political lives.

As far as Berman was concerned, the years since Betty's death that I had spent reexamining my political commitments might just as well not have taken place. His misrepresentation would become the refrain of every attack that followed: Our second thoughts were a religious conversion, therefore irrational and dangerous. Berman's agenda was to wipe us—and anything we had learned—from the progressive mind.

I had never heard of the Suicida mentioned in Berman's article, having not really followed the events in Nicaragua until they became an issue in the presidential campaign. He was, it turned out, a psychopathic *contra* officer whom the *contra* commanders themselves had executed because of the atrocities he committed. Of course, there was no atrocity the Sandinistas could commit (and they had committed many) that would cause them to execute *Sandinista* officers, or Berman to reexamine *his* allegiances. Individual crimes, in any case, were not the issue, but only a pretext for both sides to claim political advantage. The real issue was the order that would prevail when the war ended. For Berman, it was an order that would establish "social justice," ushering in a brave new world of progressive values. I had given up this illusion, whose destructive consequences the Twentieth Century had made all too evident. For me, the issue was less grandiose: to establish a framework in which the rule of law might prevail more often than not. The socialist order instituted by the Sandinistas had never produced the justice that radicals had promised, or the civil liberties I now more modestly desired. But the opponents of social-ism—and sometimes even its fascist opponents—*had*.

In this regard, the career of Franco—whom Berman's anarchists allegedly went off to join—had become a morbid fascination of mine. After World War II, there was no more hated name on the left than Franco's. The Spanish Civil War had remained one of the proudest moments in progressive memory, an event that confirmed they had been warriors in the "good fight" on the side of human freedom. But after defeating the Communists, Franco had established a social order in Spain that launched an economic "miracle" and made a peaceful transition to democracy possible. Shortly after his death in 1976, uni-versal suffrage and democratic institutions were restored in a peaceful and orderly transition. Meanwhile, the East European countries and Cuba—whose Francos had been defeated in civil wars which the Left had won—remained Communist police states (and economic disaster zones) where "independent socialists" like Berman filled the people's jails. This was no justification of Franco's fascism, but it did put the Left's utopias in perspective.

I wrote a response to Berman in the *Voice,* titled "Better Ron, Than Red." It explained why I was no longer a radical. For the first time, I told the story of Betty's murder, although I refrained—out of caution—from mentioning Elaine Brown or Huey Newton by name. "Although the Panther vanguard was isolated and small," I wrote, "its leaders were able to rob and kill without incurring the penalty of law. They were able to do so, because the Left made the Panthers a law unto themselves. The same way the Left had made Stalin a law unto himself. The same way the Left makes Fidel Castro and the Sandinista *comandantes* laws unto themselves." I concluded by explaining once more the continuity of my second thoughts:

> *The lesson I had learned from my pain turned out to be modest and simple: the best intentions can lead to the worst ends. I had believed in the Left because of the good it had promised; I had learned to judge it by the evil it had done.*

When the *Voice* article appeared, I received a letter from Betty's daughter. I had not seen Tamara for nearly seven years after her mother's funeral. I knew through mutual friends that she did not believe the Panthers had killed her mother, and even after Kate Coleman's article appeared in 1978 only allowed herself to think that they "could have." Given the guilt I felt for Betty's death, I did not know how to deal with this situation, and decided not to seek Tamara out. Shortly after Kate's article, Tamara attempted to join a Maoist sect called the Democratic Workers Party, which had been founded by a well known feminist professor. The party application required a lengthy personal statement in which Tamara noted there was a possibility that the Panthers had killed her mother. This was brought up at a "criticism-self-criticism" session for new Party members, and was linked to a personality trait her interrogators found objectionable: "You're just acting that way because the Panthers killed your mother," they scolded her.

Betty's murder itself was of no concern to the comrades. One of them, a New Left activist named Jon Frappier, had led the NACLA delegation that once marched into our *Ramparts* office to protest our views on Cuba. "There's been enough bad stuff about the Panthers," Frappier warned, "and it should not be capitalized on." Another activist told her: "The killing of your mother was an error and the Party member who committed it should be reprimanded." Tamara left the Democratic Workers Party and wrote herself a memo, which she called "The Politics of My Mother's Murder":

> The question that bothered me for years also kept me from facing my Mother's murder: how could an ideology that is supposed to change things for the better in the world result in the denial of murder to the point of condoning it as an "error."

In 1982, a mutual friend had arranged a meeting between us. It took place in a restaurant near the Kaiser Center in Oakland, where Tamara worked as a secretary. By then, she had begun to come to grips with her mother's murder, and wanted to know every detail I could provide her, including what I had learned from my last interview with Huey Newton. She was planning to hire Hal Lipsett, a private detective who had served many radical defense teams, including Newton's, in order to investigate Betty's death. Because of the work he had done for the Panthers and other radical groups, Lipsett's contacts in the

Left were extensive. Tamara hoped he might lay to rest the questions that were haunting her. I encouraged her to see Lipsett, and chipped in for the fund she was raising from friends to pay his $5,000 fee. I also agreed to see him at his Pacific Heights townhouse for an interview during the investigation.

In 1984, Lipsett reported his findings to Tamara: "You should have no doubt that your mother's death was Panther related. They did it." But he also warned her of the danger she faced if she publicly accused the Panthers: "I cannot guarantee your safety, because Newton is still alive."

At the time of our meeting, Tamara asked me to contact her before I wrote anything relating to her mother's death. I had forgotten this promise when I sat down to reply to Berman's attack. The letter I received from her asked me why I had not kept my word, and questioned things I had written in the article. She was particularly concerned about a passage in which I said the Panthers had "sexually tormented" Betty before they killed her. I had heard this from my Panther contacts in the east, I told her, and apologized for my dereliction in not informing her beforehand. I had written the passage in my anger at the Panthers and the Left, without thinking of the impact it might have on Betty's children—who still loved her, and were still in pain.

Four months before these events, my father died. He was 82 years old, and had been ill for a long time. For even longer, he had been disappearing steadily from this life. He had lost so much blood during a third operation to repair his hips that the trauma to his brain was like a stroke. Less and less coherent, he eventually was unable to complete sentences, and then only to utter a single word before lapsing into frustrated silence. After a previous operation, when he was still able to talk, I had gone back to New York to visit him in a hospital in Flushing. There had been a great softening in him over the years as though he had given up the struggle he had been losing since he was a youngster on the Lower East Side. He would often surprise me by becoming philosophical and accepting, when I expected him to be resentful and bitter. In these moods, he would have insights into himself which I had not thought him capable of. We sat on his hospital bed one evening, looking out through the window into the lit darkness over Queens, and talked with the intimacy we had developed in the years since I had become a father and he my needy son. Suddenly, in one of those inapposite moves that were so familiar, he turned to me with a calmness as if administering a benediction and said: "You know it's not death I'm afraid of. It's life"

He had stopped eating, as though determined he had had enough. When he went into a state of extreme dehydration, my mother took him to the hospital. But when they forced tubes down his throat to give him nourishment, she relented and took him back home to die. I returned to Sunnyside for the funeral. Crossing Skillman Avenue, I stopped to look at the leaded windows and mock parapets of Saint Teresa's Church. The little building was no longer a house of worship, having been replaced by a larger and more modem structure across the street. A placard on the exterior explained its new function as a bingo and social hall. Other than that, it was exactly as I remembered it forty years before, when I would pass each morning on my way to school.

The very familiarity provided me with a measure of other things that had changed. As a youngster, I saw the little church through my father's eyes, a small fortress of reaction, the symbol of everything we wanted to replace. But looking at it again, on the way to my father's last passage, I thought of the barren neighborhoods in South Central, where I had researched my gang stories, and the confused, drug-infested environment of Berkeley, where my own children had grown up. How fortunate were the youngsters of this place, I thought, to have a refuge where they were wanted, and might be shielded from harm's way. I thought about a line from the film *We All Loved Each Other So Much*, which recounted four decades in the lives of a group of Italian radicals. Toward the end, one of them, now settled into middle age, turns to his comrade and reflects: "We tried to change the world, but the world changed us."

My sister Ruth arrived before me, to spend the final days with him. It was only the second or third time I had seen her in the last twenty years. In the early Seventies, she had moved to a remote area in Canada. She had built herself a cabin in the harsh but beautiful countryside, married a wood sculptor named Ian Sherman, and had a son, Robin. Our relations were uneasy, the product of so much physical distance and the psychological wrenchings of the journeys we had taken. It was another bond I had with Peter, who had a sister, too, who had moved from the family circle to a part of the California wild.

My sister had ordered a simple, unfinished coffin and instructed the undertakers that, except for the embalming required by law, they should leave the body in its natural state, as it was at the moment of death. My mother wanted the burial to be taken care of by the Shea Funeral Home on Skillman Avenue. It, too, had not changed. Perhaps that was the reason my mother chose such an inappropriate institution: It was familiar, a piece of the life that was now gone. My father hated the Shea Funeral Home, even as he hated the office of the Veterans of Foreign Wars in the storefront next door, where he imagined the Sheas and their friends plotting against him. It was as though my mother had chosen to bury him in the enemy camp to mark his final defeat. In the years that had passed, the little progressive community of Sunnyside had all but disappeared—some dying, others just moving on. *Their* church, unlike Saint Teresa's, was only a church of ideas, and had disappeared with them. They had left no traces of themselves that my mother could turn to for comfort.

My father's gravesite was in a cemetery called Beth Moses, on Long Island, 50 miles away. My parents had bought a plot there, in a section reserved for members of the International Workers Order, a Party front of the Thirties that was now defunct. Before the three of us left for the cemetery with my father's coffin, we gathered in the Shea Funeral Home for a final viewing of the body. An open casket was a Christian tradition, and the only previous service I had attended with such a ritual was Deacon's funeral at the Panther school. For a long time I sat on a straight-back chair in a comer of the bare parlor, about five yards distant from the pine box my sister had ordered. Two or three of my parents' friends, who had remained in the neighborhood, came by to pay their respects. I watched them pass in front of the box and glance in, as my mother and sister already had when we entered.

I waited in my corner, immobile. It was not the prospect of death that frightened me. It was my father. I did not know what to expect when I looked into the casket. I did not want to be repulsed by the sight of his corpse, adding a final injury to our uneasy filial bond. Instead, I wanted to make this an appropriate farewell, one that I would not regret. I wanted to forgive him and to feel his spirit forgive me. I wanted nothing but love between us. *My father.* I wanted to feel the closeness of our swims in Hampton Bays, the companionship of our bicycle rides together, and the instructional walks we took through the Sunnyside Gardens. I wanted to remember the comfort and clarity his convictions provided, and the warm press of his muscularity against my youthful flesh. I wanted to know him again as I had known him and loved him—despite our conflicts, despite his inability to let go of whatever it was that was holding him from me and preventing him from just letting me be his son.

Finally I ended the war within me, and got up. Slowly I walked over to the casket, and looked. Inside was a stranger. His hair, still almost black despite his years, was shoulder-length, and he had a full beard, like a *rebbe.* In life, my father was always clean-shaven, and had kept his hair trimmed and slicked back. Now, his face was drawn inward by death, and his false teeth had been removed, which stretched the skin taut, exaggerating the Semitic bend in his nose and creating an Oriental squint of the eyes. In his little pine-box coffin, my father looked like one of those *shtetl Jews* in the old rotogravures, a *Yid* from the world he had tried all his life to escape.

For a long time I looked at the stranger in the coffin, trying to see my father in him but failing. I wanted to embrace him. To heal every wound. To *make* him my father again. When I felt only love, I leaned over—tears watering my lungs—to place a last kiss on my father's corpse. But as I bent down and pressed my lips to his forehead, the touch was cold, repellent. It was like a final rebuff, even though I knew it was only death that was rejecting me.

DESTRUCTIVE GENERATION

URING THAT SAME SPRING, PETER'S MOTHER DIED. SHE WAS younger than my father, and had concealed her cancer from everyone until she was left with only a month to live. Her strategy had a grim *karma* to it: The son she left behind was her truest disciple, jealously guarding the private spheres of his existence and shouldering his load without complaint. His mother had taken the strong course he would have taken himself, wishing not to burden her children with trials she considered her own. But Peter was a man of deep and passionate connections, who would have wanted to share this last travail with her, and now could not.

Our private ordeals slowed the progress of our work on the Ford biography, which proved costly. Once again we were in a competition to finish first or risk writing a book that would not earn its advance. Our rival had a six-month lead on us, and our task was further complicated by the respect we had won by our earlier efforts. Where once we had enjoyed the advantage of not being taken seriously, our challenge now was viewed as a formidable threat. Our rival's publisher sent an editor to Detroit, to help him finish his book, and the pressure on us led to sixteen-hour days and seven-day weeks, exertions that eventually broke my health, leaving me with chronic fatigue syndrome that took several years to recover from.

Despite its ruinous pace, I enjoyed the Ford research. Like most radicals, I had written critically in the past about America's multinational corporations on the basis of no actual experience with them. But now I had a license to explore a major American industry, from its factory floors to its executive suites. Ford was far more open about its operations than the Kennedy camp had been about theirs. Its corporate archives were accessible, allowing me to examine company records, and even the minutes of executive committee meetings. I interviewed the men who designed the cars and engineered them, the financial executives, the marketing directors, and the Ford family itself. I was impressed by the complexity of the corporate process, and even more unexpectedly by the fierce competitiveness of the industry (even before the import invasion, when it was controlled by the "Big Three"). Like most intellectuals, I had been schooled by John Kenneth Galbraith and other academic socialists who asserted, without real evidence, that manufacturers controlled consumer wants. It was eye-opening to speak to the men who were forced to gamble $100 million on machine tools for a new line of cars before the first unit was sold, and then wait to see if their product was a Mustang and success, or an Edsel that would end their careers. Almost to a man, the executives I interviewed had entered the company from modest origins, and by grit and intelligence clawed their way to the top, retiring as millionaires. They weren't all Horatio Algers, but they too showed the kind of opportunity that America offered.

For me, a compelling aspect of the story was that its central figure was a middle-aged man who had gone through a mid-life crisis to reinvent himself. Henry Ford II had taken the reins of the near-bankrupt company as a youth, and restored it to its place as a world-class corporation. But he had been born to responsibilities and expectations that left him without a self-defining space. The corporate role had been thrust on him, and was not a task obviously suited to his personality. Like many men he had developed a secret life to satisfy his inner longings, but in his middle years he had embarked on an odyssey to bring the two worlds together. It would prove a more daunting task than simply walking away from the life he had lived.

Henry divorced his first wife, and married his mistress, Cristina. But Cristina wed turned out to be different from Cristina wooed. The earthy simplicity that had attracted Henry, who was seeking escape from the complexities of his life, disappeared when she became his wife. She abandoned her simple tastes and pressed him to become even more immersed in the world from which he was trying to find relief. As his second marriage soured, Henry fell in love with Kathy DuRoss, a former auto-show model and sometime companion to wealthy men, whose candor and humor provided relief from the pretensions he found suffocating. In my favorite scene in our book, Henry confronted Cristina and told her that Kathy offered him what Cristina no longer did—companionship, sensuality, and domesticity. "You can't marry her," Cristina screamed at him, "she's a whore."

> *But Henry, who felt that he knew for the first time in his life what he really wanted, came back with a comment that rocked her: "Yeah, she's a whore. And a call girl. And a street-walker. And whatever else you want to call her. She's fucked everybody in Detroit. Seven guys an hour. But you know what? She fits me!"*

It was a romanticism with which I could identify. I was drawn to the rebel in Henry, the devil-may-care attitude in someone who had achievements to his credit and understood responsibilities as well. I identified with his denial of self to serve a cause, and the conflicts he faced in trying to square the circle of obligation and desire.

This time we lost the race to finish our book first. When *The Fords: An American Epic* appeared in the fall of 1987, our rival was already on the best-seller lists. In the daily *New York Times*, Christopher Lehmann-Haupt called ours "an irresistible epic" and our "best book" while the *Los Angeles Times* praised us as America's "premier chroniclers of dynastic tragedy." But the *New York Times Book Review*, which had become increasingly political, gave *The Fords* to a hostile critic and bumped us from our pride of place on its cover to page 19. It felt to us like one more price we were being forced to pay for our second thoughts. *The Fords* never made the best-seller lists, and though 70,000 hardback copies were sold, it didn't earn back its advance, and we didn't receive a dime for our efforts after it was published.

Henry Ford's declaration of independence had struck a resonant chord in what I realized was still my radical soul. Months after my second marriage, I began an affair with a woman who was seventeen years younger and who fit needs in me that had never been satisfied. She was an attractive blonde with an affectionate nature, and her name, Shay Marlowe, had a romantic aura that seemed particularly apt. Her person radiated a lightness that I found irresistible and seductive, not least because of the air of danger that never seemed far away. She was an artist with a whimsical talent that she brought into the center of our lives, turning modest occasions into festivities and adventures. Her favorite holiday inevitably was Halloween, and once she had moved into my house, it became an event anticipated by all my friends. She would do up the rooms in cobweb beards and coffins, creating a haunting ambiance, and then inspire in her person an infectious levity at the party itself. On the first of these occasions, she had appeared so disguised that I couldn't recognize her. Dressed in men's clothes, she had tinted her hair and put on a red beard, and glasses so thick that they made her look cockeyed. Even after she revealed herself, the character was so vivid that when she tried to kiss me with the disguise back in place, I burst out laughing, unable to complete the act. She flitted, nymph-like, from one object to the next, pollinating our environments with her high spirits. It was a tonic to the heaviness of being I had inherited from my father, and I often felt a surge of happiness at the thought that she had come into my life.

Under the surface, however, lay darker humors. Angers would sometimes boil from unknown depths, and old wounds open without warning. She had grown up in a dysfunctional household in the San Fernando Valley, the daughter of a telephone employee who had changed his Hungarian surname, Kanchar, to Marlowe. Chuck Marlowe was a brutish man who referred to his wife, Ruth, as a "broad," and instructed his daughter: "Keep your waistline thin and your mouth shut and you'll attract the boys." His two sons received the male prerogatives—automobiles, lessons, respect—denied to her, but they were also treated as unworthy competitors. The oldest was so psychologically beaten by middle age that he had become homeless shortly after Shay and I met, while the younger was a brooding follower of religious cults who was a janitor at the local school. The mother colluded in the abuse with an expression of blank tolerance for whatever her husband did.

While commiserating with Shay over her youthful trials, I felt fortunate to be their beneficiary. They provided me a chance to show her the affection and concern she had missed, and also seemed to inspire her exuberant determination that life around her would be generous and fun. At times, however, she would reveal a desperate unhappiness at the deficits she had incurred. She had a frenzied desire to win the lottery or be a "famous artist," futures so unrealistic that they almost seemed forms of revenge she longed to take on her family. When I passed new information to her, feeding her hunger for knowledge, or provided her with canvases and paints, she would sometimes burst into tears over the handicaps she had suffered from a childhood without instruction. She was fiercely jealous of my children, all of whom were now in college, or graduated, and who had been given such attentions when they were young. Her only instruction seemed to be the lyrics of the Sixties, and especially the songs of Bob Dylan, whose works she had put to memory like religious texts.

I tried to resist playing Pygmalion to her Galatea. I did not want such power, and my life seemed to be a lesson in the dangers of remaking humanity. But her passionate desire to fill up the black holes in her past made me want to help her, and touched me in ways deeper than I knew. About two years after we met, and a year after she had moved in, she wrote me an affectionate note:

David,

I was thinking of all the things in life I'm smarter about because of you [here, she punctuated the sentence with a little heart]:

Thai restaurants have great tea.
White males need better public relations.
In this world, second thoughts are best.
Anyone who is any good at composing music dies of syphilis.
Pachelbel had only one hit.
Jewish men make the best lovers.
You can be too skinny.
Intellectuals like to be around those who are not...just for fun.
Things you've told me, that I can't swallow:
Bob Dylan beats his wife.
Things I would change about you:
Your singleness!

With love and bites on your ass,

Shay

I was determined to be cautious. I waited almost a year before acceding to her desire to move in with me, saying yes in December 1986.

Shortly after Shay came to live with me, I called my mother, who was still in New York, to tell her I was coming to get her after my father's death, I had tried to move her to California, where I could watch over her. But she had resisted, and I could not bring myself to compel her She had lived in the 44th Street house for 37 years, and was terrified to leave. My son Benjamin was entering Columbia as a freshman, and I thought that if he lived with her the situation might be acceptable for a while. But nine months after my father's death, she had a stroke which affected her memory and her ability to cope with life's simple routines. When a laborer she had hired to paint the house began emptying her bank account, I knew I would have to get her and bring her back.

I put my mother in the third bedroom of the Fern Dell house—I had turned the second into an art studio for Shay. The room was warm and sunny, and looked out over the waterfalls and garden. My mother had lost her short-term memory, and wouldn't know how to return to the house if she walked a few blocks away. I took walks with her daily in the Dell. We enjoyed these moments, even though the conversations were repetitive and basic, because of her disability, and the life we had shared was lost. She never really adjusted to her new environment. "When am I going home?" she would ask. The question distressed me. I wanted her to be satisfied by what I had done for her.

She could no longer even recognize my father's name. They had been married for 52 years, and now it was all blank. I suspected there was more to it than mere physical disability. While my father no longer existed for her, she could still remember who my sister was, and that she lived in Nova Scotia, which was "a long way." She remembered her own house at 39-07 44th Street, and her "six neighbors," who she insisted would look after her if I let her go home.

Why had she forgotten my father? Perhaps she wanted to block the pain. At the very end, he had grown so crazy that he had made it impossible for her to leave him unattended, driving away the nurses she had hired to free her for a few hours, and then, just as irrationally, locking her out of the house, forcing her to get the police to let her in.

Once he had even tried to strangle her I was fearful for her safety, and had begged her to put him in a nursing home, but she had refused. I had watched her deteriorate psychologically in a kind of lockstep with him. But she would not leave him, even though it meant sealing her own fate. *"He will pull you down with him!"* I had warned her once, recognizing the absurdly oedipal nature of my plaint. But she was firm in her resolve. She was ready to marry him again, even though he was mute and maniacal, and—I was convinced—would destroy her. The ravages of age had made their passion strange, but I had to recognize that in the caricature was a romantic truth: People choose their fate. I had to learn my own lesson (why was it so difficult?) and stop trying to improve everyone else's life.

If my mother had forgotten most of the past, she still remembered pieces of childhood and its fantasies. These were so vivid, or perhaps the reality so faded, that she could not distinguish one from the other. She remembered that she had lived on Maple Street in New Haven, and that her grandfather had made ritual wine in the cellar, and that Mr. Penny, who lived across the street, used to greet her on her way to school. But she also remembered that she had been a dancer, and had performed at Carnegie Hall. My mother did love to dance. In our family albums there was a photograph of her, taken when she was thirteen years old, in a tutu with a rose in her hair. When I was a youngster, she took us to the ballet, and also to see the Moiseyev troupe. She even conducted a folk-dancing class at P.S. 150 in the evenings. But my father did not dance, so otherwise she never got to indulge her passion.

The stroke seemed to release her from her inhibitions. She now introduced herself, to people Shay and I invited to the house, as "Bianca Horowitz," exorcising her lifelong dissatisfaction with the plainness of her name and adding a touch of the romance she longed for. Shay entered her fantasy, plucking the white hairs from her chin, making her up with powder and lipstick, and taking her to a neighborhood dance spot called Reuben's. It was a place my father would never have set foot in; the sheer frivolity would have dissuaded him. But the male clientele at Reuben's were obliging, and with a few innocent steps across the dance floor, my mother was given a taste of the life she had given up to marry.

For Shay, this adoptive relationship seemed to provide a connection she had missed in her own family. But I was worried by the level of her devotion. She spent entire days entertaining my mother, as if they were two young girls together. I was fearful that this attention would eventually drain her. My mother was lost in her second childhood, greedy for Shay's time and jealous if she attempted to focus her attention elsewhere. But I couldn't get Shay to pace herself. "You can shut everything out when you're focusing on your work," she said to me, "but I can't." Her attitude was troubling because I saw that her own restless hungers were not satisfied. My mother was also jealous in a more disquieting way, forgetting almost that I was her son. She would spy on us, as though Shay were her rival, and then become depressed at our happiness together. "I'm down," she would announce when she was feeling neglected, as though challenging me to find a way out of her depression. I did not want to place her in a home, yet I felt I had to do something. I could see trouble in Shay's eyes, but she still couldn't extricate herself from her guardianship.

There was an apocalyptic element, I had begun to realize, to the way Shay approached decisions in her life. If she was going to be an artist, it would be world fame or failure. There was no middle ground. She was in her early thirties, but her past was a blur of disconnected experience. She had made her life into a *potlatch*, throwing everything out as she went along. She had brought a brass bed, her only worldly property, into our household, but not a single friend from her past to share our present. After nearly three years, she seemed as volatile as when she arrived.

One day Shay disappeared, returning only the next morning with no coherent explanation of where she had been. I interpreted this as a flight from the situation with my mother, for whom I moved swiftly to find a new place to live. I located an Alzheimer's day-care program, and then a living situation at the Beverly Sinai Towers, where one of the elderly people in the program was staying. She did unexpectedly well in the new surroundings. There were music and poetry sessions, along with children's games, in the Alzheimer's group. She was with people with whom she felt companionate and equal. The group even gave her occasions to dance before an audience of her peers. An elderly Alzheimer's patient named Boris would sit down at the piano and play a tune he remembered, and my mother would dance in choreographed steps as if on stage. I visited her often, and felt relief in the knowledge that her final years would be relatively tranquil and—the term she herself used to describe her state—"copacetic." The new living arrangement allowed Shay and me to develop our intimacy without distractions.

Shay's behavior continued to trouble me, but I knew from the pain that her mysterious absence had caused that my heart was already hers, and I would have to rely on the hope that things would change.

In October 1987, Peter and I received a call from the State Department asking us to go to Nicaragua, where the political situation had taken a dramatic turn. The diplomatic pressure from Washington, and the military successes of the contras, had persuaded the Sandinista government to lift its press ban and prepare for elections. It was a critical opening that could unleash the popular feeling against the Sandinistas and decide the fate of the regime. The State Department wanted us to speak to the opposition groups and "share our expertise as ex-New Leftists on how to stir up trouble for those in power."

It was an off-the-wall idea, intriguing enough for us to accept but not without a certain ambivalence. We had come to appreciate how tolerant the American government had been in the Sixties when faced with protest. Of course, activists had denounced—and were still denouncing—government "repression." But one would be hard put to find much repression in America's response to the political revolts of the previous decades. Hardly a radical had spent more than a night in jail, despite widespread acts of sedition and mayhem. The situation in Nicaragua was quite different. There, radicals were in power and employing police-state methods. We had no desire to incite Nicaraguans to undertake risks we were not in a position to assess, or were not about to take ourselves. Whenever we spoke in Nicaragua, we resolved to preface our remarks with these cautions.

If the Ford book allowed me to take a close look at American capitalism, the trip to Nicaragua took me to the front line of America's Cold War. Putting on my Marxist lenses one more time, I was curious to see how the world's chief imperialist power was confronting its revolutionary threat. The experience was illuminating. Although the political battle was at a critical point when we arrived, Washington's embassy in Managua was short six officers, and there was no ambassador. Only the consul general had any prior experience in a Communist country. When I discussed the base that the Soviets were building with our military attaché, a young man in his twenties, he actually apologized for being unqualified for the responsibility that had been placed on his shoulders. Once again, the reality had failed to live up to the radical myth.

Meanwhile, the Sandinistas and their Communist sponsors had powerful allies in Congress back home. Ron Dellums, a pro-Castro leftist, had allowed his Capitol office to be used as an organizing center for "solidarity" committees instigated by Cuban agents; George Crockett, the head of the subcommittee overseeing all Latin-American policy, was a lifetime traveler in the Communist left. I recalled the early days of the Cold War, when Vito Marcantonio, a Communist sympathizer and hero of my youth, had cast the only congressional vote opposing American aid to South Korea. Now, the congressional left was able to muster a majority of Democrats to cut off aid to the anti-Communist contras.

At the Hotel Intercontinental in Managua, we bumped into Paul Berman, who had attacked me in the *Village Voice*. I invited him to lunch at the hotel restaurant. Berman was a thin man with black hair, and a pinched look as if nursing some impenetrable grievance. He was obviously uneasy about accepting my invitation, but I pressed him until he agreed. Later, Peter asked me why I would want to be nice to someone who had treated me so maliciously. It was a good question, and I didn't have a persuasive answer. Berman had written an article in *Mother Jones* about the Sandinistas which contained some critical observations and had come under attack by other leftists. I knew that to deviate, even mildly, on this issue took courage, and I persuaded myself that Berman might be in some kind of ideological transition. Given our own rethinking and the abuse we had taken for it, I thought it would be wrong for us to be inflexible.

The discussion at lunch soon disabused me of the notion that Berman had learned anything from his observations in country. From his own account, he spent his time searching out Sandinista allies like himself, who were critical of some of their excesses but not of their socialist goals. We soon found ourselves arguing whether the Sandinistas were ruining Nicaragua's economy, or whether—despite their heavy-handed methods—they were pioneering "an alternative route to modernization," which was his contention. "How can you still believe that Marxists are progressive?" I almost roared. "Marxists are reactionaries. Marxism is bankrupt. Socialist radicals have wrecked every economic system they've ever run, including Cuba's, which is actually the model for these revolutionary clowns!" Suddenly, I realized how loud my voice had become and how many heads in the restaurant had turned in our direction, Sandinista agents' no doubt among them. Not for the last time during our stay in Nicaragua was I grateful that Washington knew we were there. Finally, out of sheer frustration, I said in full throat: "For the sake of the poorest peasant in this Godforsaken country, I can't wait for the contras to march into this town and liberate it from these fucking Sandinistas." With that, Peter and I stood up, invited Berman to come with us to the offices of La Prensa, and left.

Perhaps Berman would have learned something if he had come along. It was a historic moment—the ceremony to mark the reopening of La Prensa, which the Sandinista censorship had closed. Its editor, Violeta Chamorro, was an elegant woman who would soon be the new president of Nicaragua, elected on the popular tide that drove the Sandinistas from power. When the moment came for her to turn the switch and restart the presses, the crowd joined hands and, tears running down their cheeks sang the Nicaraguan national anthem. Here as everywhere we went, all the factions of the political spectrum that wanted to see democracy returned to Nicaragua supported the contras. They did so because they understood, as Berman did not that the only future Nicaragua could look forward to under Sandinista rule was the dire poverty and gulag existence of every other Communist state. Like other American socialists who flocked to Nicaragua, Berman was finally uninterested in the democratic revolution that was taking place all around him.

Returning to the States, we headed for Washington, where we had organized a conference with the help of a conservative named Jim Denton, the head of the National Forum Foundation. Denton had called us after the *Washington Post* story broke, and offered us support. We responded because he seemed to have no agenda other than to provide us with a platform for what we wanted to do. Jim was a former naval officer and the son of Senator Jeremiah Denton, who had been a prisoner of war for seven years in North Vietnam. The elder Denton had been abused by his Communist captors, who pulled out his fingernails and then displayed him for the television cameras to show that he was well-treated. But Denton had outfoxed them, blinking his eyes in Morse code to telegraph the word "torture," alerting the world for the first time to the plight of the POWs. When Jim introduced us to his father, we apologized for our role and for our comrades, like Fonda and Hayden, who had abetted his tormentors, denouncing him on his release as a liar and pawn of America's war machine. As with other POWs and veterans we met, like Senator John McCain, Denton was gracious to us—and more than ready to forgive.

We called our conclave the Second Thoughts Conference and designed it as a response to the attacks on us for our apostasy. We had already developed an appreciation for the skill with which the Left identified defectors and set out to destroy them. We were struck by the difference between the treatment "renegades" like us received, and those who traveled in the other direction. In the Sixties, the writer Garry Wills had been a protégé of William F. Buckley, and the fair-haired boy of the intellectual Right. Unlike us, he had defected to the Left in the middle of the battle. Yet, there had been no campaign to impugn his character or blacken his name. When Wills was referred to in articles by the Right, there were no epithets like "dupe" or even "leftist" attached to flag him for innocent readers. By contrast, we never appeared now in liberal or Left publications without some tag appended to identify us as renegades and turncoats, and to question our intellectual and moral credentials, or sometimes even our sanity.

To counter these attacks, we decided to assemble a group of former radicals who would recount their experiences and draw appropriate lessons. Our criterion of selection was that they had reached a point where they were anti-Communist and opposed the Sandinista dictatorship. The group included several former Sandinistas who had joined the *contra* cause. It also included the former president of the Saigon Students Association, who had collaborated with the National

Liberation Front, only to be jailed as a dissident by the Front after its victory. We hoped that the broadness of the spectrum would make the Left's effort to defame us more difficult. On the weekend of October 17, we gathered 25 ex-radicals and 200 spectators at the Grand Hyatt in Washington, D.C.

Opposition to the Sandinistas was an important litmus of second thoughts because of the Left's genius for reinventing itself. Since the demise of Stalinism, it had become relatively easy to criticize and distance oneself from past revolutions without risking apostasy. The litmus of radical commitment was to know who the enemy was, and take appropriate sides in any *current* battle. For the Left, an anti-America position on every Cold War front was the true test of faith. This was the case with the war for Nicaragua.

Besides these requirements, we did not prescribe any political program for our participants to endorse. Our friend Ron Radosh was a good example. He still described himself as a "democratic socialist" and had voted against Reagan, and for Walter Mondale, in 1984. We invited other Democrats, like David Ifshin, who had been president of the National Students Association and was the general counsel of the Mondale campaign. One of our speakers, Jeffrey Herf, declared that he was a "feminist" while others were self-styled "social democrats" and liberals. Julius Lester, a black civil-rights radical who had once written a book called *Look Out Whitey, Black Power's Gon' Get Your Mamma*, had arrived at a politics outside the parties. In a keynote speech to our conference, Lester recalled the New Haven trial of Ericka Huggins, Bobby Seale, and five other Black Panthers for the torture-murder of Alex Rackley:

> Three Party members admitted their active participation in the torture and murder of Rackley. Yet, black and white radicals were demonstrating on the New Haven Green, and many articles were published in the radical press demanding that the New Haven Seven be freed. The rationale? It was impossible for blacks to receive justice in America. White sycophancy toward the Black Movement had set a new standard for madness.

Our evening program was hosted by the humorist P. J. O'Rourke and featured a distinguished panel which included Hilton Kramer and the intellectual leaders of the previous "second thoughts" generation—Irving Kristol, William Phillips, Norman Podhoretz, and Nathan Glazer. Marty Peretz, who had been a funder of *Ramparts* and now edited *The New Republic*, was the moderator. While Peretz qualified as a second-thoughter under our rules, he still regarded himself as a man of the Left, and was generally regarded that way by others. In his introductory remarks, he revealed that he had received a considerable amount of "abusive mail" urging him not to participate in our event: "'How dare you,' was the drift of these letters, 'appear in such... retrograde company?'" Peretz then turned to the small contingent of radical journalists who had showed up to cover the event:

> *Lest the...representatives of the media who thought this might be an important or interesting enough event to cover get it wrong—as if one can actually pre-empt deliberate error by stating the facts in advance—it's important to point out that not only was there amazing diversity earlier in the day ... but that in general this is not a gathering of people on the Right.*

He might have saved his breath. All of the reporters in attendance—Alexander Cockburn and Christopher Hitchens of *The Nation*, Eric Alterman of *Mother Jones*, Todd Gitlin of *Tikkun*, and Sidney Blumenthal of the *Washington Post*—were leftists and experienced practitioners of deliberate error in the service of the radical cause. They formed a kind of journalistic firing squad, presenting us as "renegades" and "McCarthyites" who had defected to the Right, and had done so out of the most venal motives. Our long years of dedication to the causes of the Left earned us no respect and were, for them, no occasion for sober reflection. Our testimonies were dismissed, out of hand, as "sinister" and absurd, and our claims were ignored. In a typical evasion, Gitlin caricatured us as penitents confessing our "thought crimes," as though it was the political Right that was a quasi-religious cult and had staged the infamous purges of the past; as if our indictment of the Left was not about actual deeds. Cockburn even floated the suggestion that we were government agents who rode around Nicaragua in fancy embassy limousines. Their attacks were a left-wing ritual that had not changed since the time of Lenin. They were designed to label us toxic, ensuring that no one who considered himself progressive and might be affected by our second thoughts would bother to read them.

Blumenthal's account appeared as a front-page feature in the Style Section of the *Washington Post,* where a screaming four-inch headline proclaimed "THUNDER ON THE NEW RIGHT" over a picture of Peter and me. The headline perverted our purpose, which was not to establish a future agenda, but to reflect on what we had done. We were described as Don Quixote and Sancho Panza, knights-errant in pursuit of illusory foes, and the tone throughout was one of ridicule in a portrait that strayed far from the facts. We had mistaken Blumenthal for a legitimate reporter because of his connection to the *Post,* and granted him an interview. But the interview was only a pretext to gather phrases he could use to discredit us. In our discussion, Blumenthal never asked me a personal question, but in his text he explained:

> When Horowitz abandoned radicalism, he also left his wife and three children, escaping into conservatism and Beverly Hills. "When I was a Marxist, I was puritanical," he said. "Then I got loose."

There was hardly a detail in these sentences that was accurate. I had four children, not three; years separated my divorce from my political change of heart; I didn't "escape" into conservatism; I never lived in Beverly Hills; and the phrase about getting "loose" was pure invention. The groundless insinuation that I had abandoned my children, spread across the pages of the *Washington Post,* was particularly painful. But there was no way to call the words back.

Blumenthal had a well-deserved reputation for malicious personal attacks, and his ready substitution of windmills for the Soviet Empire revealed the political animus that motivated his assault. For Blumenthal there were no police states forming in Central America, no Soviet missiles poised at America's heartland, and there had been no Marxist bloodbath in Southeast Asia. Nor was there a dedicated radical fifth column busily undermining America's defenses. How America approached the Communist threat in this fourth decade of the Cold War was of no consequence to leftists like Blumenthal, who did not believe there *was* such a threat. There was only the duo of Collier and Horowitz, trapped in "a curious warp in time."

If there had been other reports in the press to balance these caricatures, I might have felt better. But, outside the conservative journals, there were none. In the central forums of the literary culture, our opponents had carried the day. Instead of the die-hards of the pro-Communist left being put on the defensive, as we had hoped, it was we who had to justify ourselves and repair our reputations. The experience reinforced my sense that there was no longer a political center. The Kennedy liberals who had carried the anti-Communist standard against us in the Sixties—and from whom we should have had support—had been overwhelmed by the tide from the Left.

Some, like the figures featured on our evening panel, had been carried by this tide to the right. In his memoir *Breaking Ranks,* Norman Podhoretz had explained the process. He recounted how, for years, he had fought a losing battle to retain the word "liberal" as a self-description after his own "second thoughts." Eventually, the sheer weight of the cultural left—now calling *themselves* liberals—forced him to accept the label "neoconservative." This was a term coined, in fact, by the socialist Michael Harrington, who understood the advantage that radicals like him would gain by pushing critics like Podhoretz to the right, and being perceived themselves as the political center.

Liberals less critical of the Left than Podhoretz were able to retain their identification by joining it in a "popular front." This coalition opposed the *contras* in Nicaragua, supported a softer policy toward the Soviet camp, and combated opponents of the Left like Podhoretz and us. The effect of this internal Cold War realignment had far-reaching consequences. While our Marxist enemies accused us of "selling out," we found ourselves pariahs in the literary culture, the very arena in which we had achieved our success. *The Rockefellers* had been nominated for a National Book Award; but we could expect no such honors again. Although we were best-selling authors, there were no longer friendly pages for our writings in its influential liberal journals—the *New York Times,* the *Atlantic, Harper's,* the *New Yorker,* the *New York Review of Books,* and (now that we had shown what our apostasy meant) the *Washington Post.* These were reserved for our literary executioners—Gitlin, Hitchens, Blumenthal, and their friends.

We should have found a home in Marty Peretz's New *Republic*, which took a strong anti-Communist stand under his leadership and supported the *contras*. But the magazine had a dual personality because of Marty's decision to give key positions to men of the Left, who declared war on us when we published a manifesto of our second thoughts. It was called *Destructive Generation*, and was composed of the articles we had written on Fay Stender and Weatherman, and new pieces focusing on the radical record. In a chapter called "The Fifth Column Left," we rehearsed our former comrades' complicity with the Communist bloc; in another, "Radical Innocence, Radical Guilt," we challenged their unwillingness to take responsibility for their deeds. The final section of the book consisted of self-portraits, including a joint account of our trip to Nicaragua, and the conference on second thoughts.

My autobiographical segment was written in the form of a "Letter to a Political Friend" who had refused to attend my father's memorial service because I had supported, as she put it, "the vile policies of Ronald Reagan." In the book I disguised her identity, but it was in fact my childhood friend Carol Pasternak. In leaving the Left, Carol said I had lost "the compassion and humanism which motivated our parents to make their original choice." But this original choice, I pointed out, was Communism, and her evasion in referring to it so obliquely was typical of our community of the Left. "Our parents were idolaters in the church of a mass murderer named Joseph Stalin," I corrected her. What motivated them was not compassion, as she claimed, but "the totalitarian idea." This was the idea that the world could be transformed into a human paradise—without poverty, inequality, or communal conflict. It was a vision so noble and a future so desirable as to justify any conceivable crime, and already had. As Vietnam and other revolutionary disasters had shown, the Left was unconcerned with the destructive consequences of its "compassionate" deeds. The only possible conclusion to draw in these circumstances was that the Left was ultimately motivated "not by altruism and love but nihilism and hate."

This brief autobiographical letter was the most difficult piece of writing I had ever completed. It took me seven tortured months to write its twenty pages, to face again the wasted years, the misplaced passions, the tragic results and—behind each second thought I put down—the bottomless hatred for "the renegade Horowitz" of the community that had been mine since birth and that was accusing me now from the lips of one of my oldest friends. In those pages I went over once again the bloody history of progressive politics, the revelations of the Khrushchev Report, the massacres in Indochina, the personal nightmares of the Panther experience and of Ellen Sparer's death.

The last now caused me added grief. When *Destructive Generation* appeared, I received an angry letter from Carol charging that I had abused Ellen's memory for my own political agendas. She even mobilized Ellen's children to hire a lawyer in an attempt to block the distribution of the book and remove the passages about Ellen from the text. It was not enough that I had lost my friend of forty years over our political differences. She did not want me to express my own view of what had happened to us.

Destructive Generation was the first (and for nearly a decade the only) critical book to appear about the radicalism of the Sixties. Tom Hayden, Todd Gitlin, and a dozen other left-wing authors had already written accounts of the era which—despite superficial gestures of candor—contained no real second thoughts. Their texts remembered the Movement as brave and innocent in its intentions, driven to whatever malevolent acts had been committed in fits of "madness" by the evil they all had so heroically opposed. Mark Rudd had summed up their attitude when he explained, on the anniversary of the Columbia takeover, "The Vietnam War drove us crazy." Peter and I dismissed this for what it was—a "devil made me do it" theory of history. For Gitlin, Hayden, and the others, the Left could do no wrong of its own volition. Whatever its faults and "errors," its progressive heart was always in the right place. *Destructive Generation* was a direct challenge to this adolescent posture. It was a call to our peers to grow up, finally, and undertake an accounting of what they had done. But it was just this reckoning that proved impossible. "One of the strongest holds the Sixties had on our generation," we explained in our introduction, "was its promise of eternal youth, a state of being that would never require a balance sheet of one's prior acts."

Just before publication, I had a taste of what the book's reception was going to be like when I was invited to appear on Lewis Lapham's public television show, *Book Notes*. Lapham was the editor of *Harper's* and a dour aristocrat with a leftist outlook. When I arrived at the studio I discovered that he had invited his friend Christopher Hitchens to be a "commentator" on the book. Hitchens had described the proceedings of our Second Thoughts Conference in *The Nation* as "sinister," and we had paid back the compliment by portraying him in our book as an Englishman who had "traded his green card for a gold card," coming to America to take advantage of its bounties while making a career of trashing the institutions that provided them. In normal circumstances, Hitchens' personal interest in our text would have disqualified him for the role that Lapham assigned him. But, for the Left, this was political warfare; professional norms did not apply.

I had met Hitchens in London, and he had visited me in Berkeley, when I was editing *Ramparts*. "Where's the working class?" he asked, poking his feral head into my office. The question struck me oddly even then. "Go ask the Trotskyists," I replied, "they would know if anyone did." As a Trotskysant himself, Hitchens had few illusions about the utopias that the Left had built, but—like Tom Hayden and Jim Mellen—he was driven by internal demons that could not be pacified. This inner rage fueled his animus against the country that had treated him so well, and prompted him to compose a recent article which provided a rationale for Shi'ite terrorists at war with the West. (Later, he even wrote a book attacking Mother Teresa, if only because everyone else regarded her as a saint.) Sitting across from me at Lapham's right, Hitchens looked like a badger, his mood black and his head, with hooded eyes that scowled in my direction, sunk deep into his neck cavity. As soon as we began the proceedings, his bile spilled onto every surface, souring the entire mood of the show, which reached its nadir when I mentioned the passage in which I had written about my father's funeral. "Who cares about his pathetic family?" Hitchens snapped.

When it was over, I returned to the green room, where the author David Rieff was waiting in ambush. Hitchens had apparently alerted him to my presence, and they had come to the studio together. As soon became apparent, Rieff was incensed by the final chapter of *Destructive Generation*, in which we had described an incident at the Miami Book Fair involving him and his mother, the writer Susan Sontag. We had gone up to Sontag after a talk she gave, and told her how we admired the way she had stood up at a leftist meeting in New York's Town Hall some years before and blurted out the truth. "Communism," she had said, "is fascism with a human face." But we also confronted her about her political retreat since then, and the fact that she had allowed her euphoric 1969 account of Communist Vietnam to be reprinted without explanation or regret. She replied that she was "not political' and that we "pushed everything to extremes."

A young woman dressed in black who had been hovering around Sontag even before we appeared hissed, "You guys are really pissing a lot of people off." At this point, David Rieff stepped in and said, "Susan has to go now." As mother and son walked off, arm in arm, we realized she was right—we did push things to extremes. But the judgment on us was also a judgment on her and others who understood the political stakes but didn't push things far enough.

It was this little tale that upset Rieff, who was wearing an elegant tan suit and, at more than six feet, towered over me. Still smarting from Hitchens' blow, I did not immediately connect Rieff's presence to him, or even to myself. I extended my hand and greeted him with a smile before I saw his agitated state. Letting my hand hang in the air, Rieff made a sarcasm about the Nicaraguan *contras*, whom he opposed, and about the portrait we had drawn of him in our text. "I guess we did get you," I conceded, and was about to continue when I felt a wind cross the top of my head. It was Rieff spitting at me as he turned on his heels and stormed out.

Hitchens was a soldier in the radical army we had targeted, and Rieff could be excused as an irate son. But, shortly afterwards, two damaging salvos were launched at us from an unexpected quarter. The first was a review by Rick Hertzberg, managing editor of *The New Republic* and a former White House speechwriter for President Carter. As Marty Peretz's editor, Hertzberg should have been sympathetic to our case. But his article, appearing in the *Washington Monthly*, was more malicious and deceitful than anything even *The Nation* worthies had devised.

It began inauspiciously, calling itself "A Tale of Two Hippies," which title bore no relation to anything we had ever said or been. To Hertzberg, who exceeded even Hitchens in his capacity as a hater, no epithet he could attach to us was undeserved. We were "traitors, liars and fools" before we had our second thoughts, and self-righteous authors of "witless polemics" after: "They once apologized for Communist atrocities; now they apologize for anti-Communist atrocities," he wrote, without offering a single instance of where we had done either.

We had provided Hertzberg with his bludgeon via a literary device we used to make our *mea culpa* inclusive. Knowing that ours was going to be a lonely voice, we had employed the editorial "we" to include those whose silence about the past was unbroken. Thus, we acknowledged excesses of the Left in which we had *not* participated, along with those in which we had. As writers, we had recorded so much of what we actually did and believed—including our campaign, within the Left, to oppose its totalitarian tendencies—that we felt there was little chance of anyone misconstruing the stances we had actually taken. But Hertzberg simply ignored the facts in order to seize on our inclusive "we" and use it against us, making us guilty for *all* the excesses the Left had committed, and then making us guilty alone. Although our book was presented as a *mea culpa,* and we had even been attacked by his friends for making a public "confession" of our sins, he accused us of adopting "a strategy for avoiding personal responsibility." We had done this, he said, by pretending that our "clique of Berkeley radicals" was somehow "the Left," instead of a bizarre fringe of the real thing. The real thing, according to Hertzberg—the Left to which he and Hitchens belonged—was actually innocent of all that. It was Peter and I, and our Berkeley faction, who had done everything that needed to be condemned. Hertzberg even accused us of murdering Betty:

> During their radical years Horowitz and Collier, according to Horowitz and Collier, were guilty of treason. They were motivated "not by altruism and love but nihilism and hate"—specifically, hatred

for their country, their parents, themselves, God, and all humanity ...
Finally, they were guilty of being accessories to murder before and after
the fact—not only the faraway murders of nameless Vietnamese and
Cambodians after the Communist victory they ardently supported
but also, and more chillingly, the murders of Bay Area neighbors and
co-workers killed by members of the Black Panther Party....

You had to appreciate the brazenness of the assault. We had lost
friends and reputation to attempt an accounting that others refused
to make. Now our accounting was being used by those who wanted to
forget *their* past to prosecute *us.*

Hertzberg did not think the damage he had inflicted was sufficient,
so he invited Paul Berman to continue the attack in the pages of
The New Republic, where Berman elaborated his idea of the clique that
could be assigned all the bad acts the Sixties had committed. Ignoring what he had written in the *Voice* about my seminal influence on
New Leftists like *him,* Berman now argued that Peter and I belonged
to a "criminal-intellectual" subculture which was outside the radical
mainstream.

Outlaw leftism tended to be inarticulate, anti-intellectual, without
ideological spokesmen (except in a marginal way, the Yippie writers,
who spoke in a loopy language that was more of a joke than anything
else). But in the San Francisco Bay Area—perhaps the existence of
a magazine like Ramparts was not unhelpful—an authentic crimi-
nal-intellectual left-wing culture did spring up.

Since Panther gangsterism, in Berman's newly contrived version,
flourished only in this San Francisco subculture, the Left as a whole
had nothing to apologize for. Peter and I could only blame ourselves.

This was denial on a prodigious scale. Left-wing criminality was
hardly a provincial problem or a minority subculture. It was the New
York chapter of the Panthers that had broken with Huey Newton
and his Bay Area organization because the West Coast's Party wasn't
criminal or violent *enough.* The same New Yorkers spawned the Black
Liberation Army, which ambushed and killed several policemen in
the 1970s, while fellow New Yorker and former SDSer Kathy Boudin

and her May 19 Communist comrades held up a Brinks armored car and killed three officers in Nyack on the Hudson. It was Hayden, Dellinger, Kunstler, and other well-known national leaders of the Left who had closed down Yale University to defend the torturers and murderers of Alex Rackley. It was the *New York Review of Books* that printed, on its front page, instructions for making Molotov cocktails, so that revolutionary aspirants would know how to do it. Midwesterners from Chicago and Ann Arbor transformed SDS into the Weather Underground, America's first terrorist cult, and it was another Midwesterner, Tom Hayden (probably the most representative New Leftist of all), who advocated guerrilla warfare in American cities, and toured the country on behalf of the "Panther vanguard" *after* the Rackley murder.

Far from being peripheral, a criminal-intellectual outlook was central to the vision of Sixties radicalism, articulated in the writings of its most-read authors (Sartre, Debray, and Fanon), and in the speeches of Malcolm X. It was, in fact, a core tradition of the radicalism that went back through Sorel, Bakunin, and Lenin to the Jacobins, the "conspiracy of the equals," and Gracchus Babeuf—in short, to the very origins of the modem Left.

Berman's *faux* innocence extended even to his own political faction, the "democratic socialists" grouped around the magazine *Dissent*, which had published the seminal manifesto of New Left nihilism, Norman Mailer's "The White Negro." In it, Mailer celebrated the criminal psychopath as the archetypal "rebel without a cause," the revolutionary *avant la lettre*:

> The psychopath murders ... out of the necessity to purge his violence, for if he cannot empty his hatred then he cannot love ... It can be suggested of course that it takes little courage for two strong eighteen-year-old hoodlums ... to beat in the brains of a candy-store keeper.... Still, courage of a sort is necessary, for one murders not only a weak fifty-year-old man but an institution as well, one violates private property, one enters into a new relation with the police... .

This was the precise sentiment that inspired Tom Hayden when he talked about getting heads cracked in order to make revolutionaries; SDS leaders when they promoted drugs in order to make outlaws and then radicals of middle-class youth; Bernadine Dohrn when she elevated the Manson murders to radical myth; and the New Left generally when it embraced the Panthers and mobilized "peace" movements whose slogan was "Bring the War Home." In New Left thinking, criminals were only "primitive rebels"; we were the real thing.

When Berman's attack moved to the personal, he also ignored what Peter and I had actually said and done—facts he could have checked by means of a couple of phone calls. Instead, Berman preferred to frame his indictment from a close reading of the two memoirs we included in our book. Several factors made these texts fertile ground for an attorney without scruples. Since Elaine Brown and Huey Newton were still active, I had kept my own memoir veiled, avoiding details and never mentioning the principals by name. Peter, who had not had contact with the Panthers except for the initial meeting with Newton, pitched his memoir in more impressionistic terms. His use of the pronoun "we" was often directed generally at the Left. It was these gaps, along with an occasional imprecision in language or faulty memory, that Berman exploited. Peter wrote:

> There had been rumors on the left for a long time that the Panthers had used the Santa Cruz Mountains as a sort of killing grounds, where they got rid of members who had been accused, in councils of pandemonium, of being "police agents." We not only ignored these rumors; we said that it was good for a vanguard organization to purge its ranks of informers.

Berman interpreted this without ambiguity: "Collier and Horowitz, in short, approved of Panther murders...."

Actually, the Santa Cruz murders were unknown to us at the time. We didn't learn about the killing grounds there until after Betty's death, when we read about them in Jo Durden-Smith's book *Who Killed George Jackson?* Nor did we have any specific knowledge of killings associated with the Panthers that wasn't available to Berman and everyone else through the press—provided one believed what one read in the press. It was Betty's murder that made us believe.

What Berman did not want to acknowledge was the general readiness of the entire Left to exonerate the Panthers when they committed crimes. But that was precisely what the protests against the

New Haven trial—led by the president of Yale—were about. Saving the Panther vanguard was more important than achieving justice for Alex Rackley. The issue in court was not whether the Panthers actually *had* a policy of torturing and executing informers. They did. But no one on the left protested this. The complicity went far beyond the matter of Party informers. Who (besides Staughton Lynd) among the Left and its supporters had raised a moral objection to the Panthers' chief slogan, "Off the Pig"—an incitement to *murder* police officers? Did Berman, or any other leftist, even *care* whether Huey Newton had actually shot Officer Frey in the back, or whether George Jackson had thrown the hapless guard, John Mills, from the third tier of Soledad prison? Who even thought of the other police officers whom the Panthers murdered—including a mixed team of white and black cops who were heroes in the poor community they patrolled in New York?

It was interesting just how little concern there was for such crimes by people who considered themselves "society's conscience." But I understood why this was so. It was the same reason that prompted Berman to discredit our attempt to own up to what all of us had done: Once the Panthers committed the crimes, the truth was a threat to the progressive cause. The radical author of *Who Killed George Jackson?* experienced just this revelation while investigating the Soledad events: "Finding out that [George] Jackson was indeed a killer completely cut away the underpinnings of what I took to be my moral purpose. For what was truth, if Jackson's innocence was untrue, but a bogus label for whatever it was you wanted to believe? What was reality but a one-sided answer to the larger question of whose side you were on?"

Whose side were you on? That was the real issue between Berman, Hertzberg and us. Our willingness to have second thoughts about the police who had been murdered, and about the Vietnamese and Cambodians who had been killed by the Left, reflected a more important fact: We were no longer a part of the radical movement. But they were. The Left lived by its radical myths, which were crucial to its sense of moral superiority, of being chosen as humanity's moral vanguard. The Left could not do without them. Berman and Hertzberg may not have been "true believers," but they were believers nonetheless. It was all right, in their book, to recognize that Communists and Panthers had committed crimes, and that a fringe group of outlaw intellectuals like Collier and Horowitz were complicit in their commission. It was a point of honor to do so. But only so long as the Left to which they belonged was not implicated as well.

It was interesting to me that Berman, Hertzberg, and our other principal antagonists were self-styled "democratic socialists." This faction of the Left was reminiscent of the pacifists that Trotsky once described as people who were unwilling to step into the stream of politics because they were afraid to get their moral principles wet. They appropriated the Left's claim to champion social justice, while disavowing the practices that accompanied the claim. Establishing a distance from the crimes their fellow socialists committed, they imagined themselves to be members of a "third camp" in the Cold War—though in reality no such camp existed outside the offices of *Dissent.*

A theme of their attacks on us was that Peter and I had overlooked distinctions *within* the Left, and had lumped disparate factions together, in particular their faction. But if this was their real concern, why had they been roused to such a passion against us? Why had they not applauded our second thoughts—which, after all, were to embrace democracy and candor—and *then* insisted we should have specifically excluded them from our indictment? Their prosecutorial approach toward us betrayed the real meaning of their antagonism. What they shared with the Left, and what we had attacked—the hatred of America and American capitalism, and the fantasy of a redeemed future—were actually more important to them than any distinctions.

In May 1989, just after *Destructive Generation* appeared, Peter and I went to Poland, along with Radosh and several other "second-thoughters," to hold a conference calling for the end of Communist rule. We had been invited by dissident intellectuals in Cracow, grouped around the underground magazine *Arka,* which had translated a chapter of our book. The *Arka* editors were "Hayekians," followers of the free-market liberal, Friedrich Hayek (himself a second-thoughter), who had written *The Road To Serfdom, The Mirage of Social Justice,* and other works with which I was just becoming familiar. Along with fellow Austrian Ludwig von Mises, Hayek had argued, back in the Twenties, that socialist planning would not work because the information encapsulated in market prices was too complex for even the most sophisticated planner to know. It was an argument against all socially engineered utopias, and was about to be confirmed by the spectacular implosion of the experiment that the Bolsheviks had initiated.

All around us there was evidence of Hayek's wisdom. Socialism was dying a slow death from economic insanity. The city of Cracow had been an intellectual center since the Fourteenth Century and the founding of the Jagiellonian University, where our conference was to be held. When the Communists took power in 1947, they noted that Cracow had no proletariat—no "chosen people" in Marxist theology—and so decided to build a steelworks in adjacent Nova Huta, to create one. The steelworks was actually confiscated as war booty from Prussia, but in its new location had no easily accessible source of ore. The result was an industrial complex so uneconomic that every bar of finished steel lost money for the mill. Meanwhile, the soot from its blast furnaces blackened Cracow's historic buildings and ancient cathedrals, some of which dated to the Middle Ages. The air was so polluted that the U.S. State Department would not permit foreign-service employees with children under 10 to be assigned to the consulate.

The doctor with whom we stayed during our visit was earning $17 a month, a salary which had been deliberately set at less than the $20-a-month average assigned to Polish workers. She lacked even a telephone. It apparently had not occurred to the socialist planners that this effort at establishing "social justice" might actually disadvantage the workers who needed the doctor's services and might benefit if she had a phone. Or perhaps they just didn't care. On the other hand, everywhere we looked people were wearing imported blue-jeans which cost $20 apiece. How could they afford such a luxury, we asked our guide, since that price represented a full month's wages? "You have to understand," he answered, "that every Polish family has a member working in Western Europe. The most menial job in a capitalist enterprise pays more in a month than our people can earn in a year."

The more we learned about the lives of the people, the more apparent was the unimaginable constriction of human life and possibility imposed by the socialist economy and state. One night, I was invited to dinner by the editor of the largest Catholic weekly in Poland. He lived with his wife and child in a dilapidated government project. Although the building had been built in the Sixties, it lacked an elevator. We climbed the urine-drenched stairs of the gray slum to his sixth-floor apartment, which was no bigger than an American foyer, measuring about 8 by 10 feet. There was a closet space in which their child was asleep, and a one-person kitchen off the main room. A mattress, on which husband and wife slept, lay on the floor next to the table where we ate. My host informed me that the waiting list for an apartment like this was 20 years.

With a couple of hundred dollars in my pocket—a year's wages for the average Pole—I felt like a rich man. But when I went off looking for a store in which to spend it, I discovered there was nothing to buy. The only other place in which I had seen stores with such bare shelves was Managua. When I did manage to purchase a trinket in Cracow, the shopkeeper totaled the bill on an abacus—this at a time when purchases in ordinary American supermarkets were calculated by lasers and computers. We ate in Cracow's finest restaurant, but had to wait hours to be served a meal without vegetables, which we were told were "unavailable". For two hours of a minimum wage, I reflected, an American worker could enjoy an "all-you-can-eat" meal at a Sizzler restaurant that was more plentiful, nutritious, and gastronomically varied than even the socialist elite could buy at almost any price. Yet, before the Communists seized control of Poland and cannibalized its wealth, it was a country whose economy was on a level with those of Italy and Spain. Forty years of Marxist economics had reduced it to the abysmal poverty of a Third World state.

The Cracow square, with its Byzantine arches and Romanesque church, reminded me of the paintings of Chagall. I could imagine my ancestors hawking their wares in the open market. But all the Jews were gone. We visited Auschwitz, which was an hour's drive away. It was hard to believe that this was still the name of a city where people lived and worked. At the entrance to the death camp they had built a museum-like reception area, with a cafeteria where people ate and chatted as if they had come to view the bones of dinosaurs and other extinct life forms. From the official literature displayed in the shop, and the plaques explaining the exhibits, a visitor would hardly know that even one Jew had died there.

The speech I gave at our conference was called "Reality and Dream." Inspired by the fact that I was geographically close to my grandfather's starting-out point in the western Ukraine, I focused on his journey. I recalled how he had come to America to escape Czarist oppression, and how his son's modest success as a high-school teacher had brought him wealth and freedom beyond my grandfather's wildest dreams. The house my mother and father had purchased for $18,000 in 1949 was worth $200,000 at their death, and they had saved another $100,000 from the pensions that had been denied because of their politics but then returned with interest by a penitent state. America's abundance and tolerance, even for political revolutionaries and self-declared enemies, like my parents, was that great.

But my family's dream was not about the wealth and freedom they were actually able to achieve in America. The real bounties they had been given hardly impressed them. Success like theirs was so common that they took it for granted. What my family longed for was an impossible fantasy: that mankind would be released from history, which included individual success and failure; their ambition was that poverty and inequality would disappear from the earth. To realize this fantasy they dedicated themselves to the Communist cause.

In 1956, as a result of the Khrushchev Report, Communism was exposed—even to them—as a system that had produced human catastrophe beyond anyone's imagination. Yet they could not give up their socialist hope. Their own son then joined others in a move-ment to revive the dream that until then had produced only grief. We even said that the first revolution would take place in Russia, where the dream had failed. This was because Russia had a planned economy, and in our eyes lacked only political freedom to realize the socialist promise. What we did not appreciate was that without private property there was no freedom. The political revolution never came, and—just as Hayek and von Mises had predicted—the planned economy didn't work. In 1989, the Soviet superpower was an impoverished Third World nation, and the average Soviet citizen had a daily ration of meat that was smaller than the ration in 1913, under the czar. A nation the size of a continent had been left out of the Twentieth Century and the munificence available to the least of its capitalist neighbors. The lesson to me was clear: "Socialism makes men poor beyond their wildest dreams. The average Polish citizen is poorer today, in 1989, than my poor grandfather was in America, fifty years ago, when I was born."

And then I concluded:

> For myself, my family tradition of socialist dreams is over. Socialism is no longer a dream of the revolutionary future. It is only a nightmare of the past. But for you, the nightmare is not a dream. It is a reality that is still happening. My dream for the people of socialist Poland is that someday soon you will wake up from your nightmare and be free.

Just before our conference at the Jagiellonian, we marched over the cobble-stoned streets of Cracow in a May Day demonstration organized by Solidarity, the anti-Communist opposition. Watched by Polish police and Soviet troops, we chanted in unison: *"Communists get out! Soviets go home!"* Peter and I were happy. We were marching again, like Joshuas, as we had in the Sixties, and this time we felt that at last we had got it right. Months later, the Polish regime was toppled and the Berlin Wall came down; in Nicaragua, the Sandinistas were forced to hold elections, which the democratic opposition (and *La Prensa's* editor) won; and during the following August, the counter-revolution reached the Kremlin itself and brought the dictatorship to its knees. The long, unhappy experiment with socialist tyranny was over at last.

AFTER THE FALL

LIKE OTHERS BEFORE US WHO HAD SECOND THOUGHTS, WE HAD been labeled "conservatives" by our political adversaries. I was less uncomfortable with this identification than Peter, who continued to insist that we were *sui generis—anti* the left, rather than *for* anything else. But, however individual our views on specific issues, the large battles of politics and culture in which we were now engaged found us clearly on one side.

Who were these conservatives who were now so often our comrades? The question was posed for us in a piquant episode shortly after our *Washington Post* manifesto appeared. On the first leg of our book tour for *The Kennedys,* we had found ourselves in the "green room" of *The Today Show,* sitting awkwardly silent opposite William F. Buckley Jr. What should we say to this man we had regarded in our previous lives as a fascist? If he was indeed that, we didn't want him to think we were political comrades now, just because we shared his anti-Communist agendas. In this respect, our values had not really changed.

On the other hand, we had to admit that we really did not know who William F. Buckley was, or what he stood for. Like other Sixties radicals, we had an insular streak when it came to our right-wing opponents, having never really paid serious attention to their views. The focus of our political animus was the anti-Communist liberals, many of whom were eventually driven out of the Democratic Party under the pressure of our attacks. It was these liberals who, as "neoconservatives," had now become our most comfortable allies. Among them, Irving Kristol and Norman Podhoretz were prominent intellectual voices. Along with the rest of the Left, we had once despised them without really knowing who they were or what they said. Familiarizing ourselves with what they had actually written over the last few years was enough to detoxify them and make us belated admirers of their insight. At our first meeting with Podhoretz, he told us: "When you were on the left, you got away with everything. Now that you're on the right, you'd better be careful, because they won't let you get away with anything." We had already learned that this was sound advice.

Kristol and Podhoretz were easy conservatives to assimilate to, the difference between us being largely temperamental. They were more puritanical in their social attitudes, while Podhoretz had a dim view of the political horizon that made even Peter seem optimistic. But the name Buckley evoked images of Catholic reaction, and the dark end of the political spectrum where others lurked—like Franco and McCarthy—to whom we felt permanently averse.

While we pondered these issues, the silence deepened. Buckley was having a similar difficulty deciding how to approach *us*. It was not political consideration that caused his hesitation, however. His son Christopher had just written a scathing review of a book on the Kennedys, published at the same time as ours, and Buckley wasn't sure if we were its authors. The moment probably would have passed without contact except that Peter finally figured out a politic way to break the ice. "My mother is a great fan of yours," he said.

When our book tour was completed, I bought a copy of *Patron Saint of the Right,* the biography of Buckley written by John Judis. I had known John as an editor of *In These Times,* Jimmy Weinstein's socialist journal. He was in a transition less intense and extensive than Peter's and mine, but even his mild second thoughts had caused him to be attacked by readers of Jimmy's paper as "fascist vermin," and his days as a leftist were clearly numbered. His biography revealed that, far from being an authoritarian or reactionary, Buckley was a maverick conservative, mixing traditionalist ideas with a strong libertarian bent. He was the spiritual godfather of the "New Right," having purged Birchers, racists, and anti-Semites from the pages of his *National Review* and made their retrograde attitudes socially unacceptable in conservative circles. This was a more principled position,

I noted, than *The Nation* had been willing to take toward an anti-Semitic outburst by Gore Vidal, or the racist attitudes among radical blacks. A few years later, Buckley provided a comment on our work for a profile in *San Francisco Focus.* He praised us overgenerously in his usual gracious prose: "The brilliance of their writing and the tenacity of their thought make them dreadnoughts on the side of right reason. As a corpsman in the same army, I welcome the addition of a fighting division so talented and resourceful."

Another important introduction to the new company we were keeping was provided by a former helicopter gunner named Wally Nunn. We met Wally in 1989, when we gave a talk in Philadelphia about an article we had written for *Commentary,* and included later in *Destructive Generation.* The article was called "McCarthy's Ghost" and described how the Left used the specter of McCarthyism to close debate on its own indefensible agendas. You could not examine a leftist's commitment to totalitarian causes, for example, without being accused of witch-hunting. On being introduced to Wally, we apologized for having done our part to divide the home front at a time when he was putting his life on the line. "Oh, you guys don't need to apologize," he said, as though we were already buddies. "That's what I was in Vietnam fighting for: Your right to dissent." It was the beginning of a long and close friendship.

In 1992, Wally was elected councilman in his working-class Pennsylvania district, garnering 70 percent of the vote. The Philadelphia press quickly tagged him the "Rambo of responsibility" for the hard line he took with abusers of welfare. While espousing this position, Wally was no country-club Republican. The son of poor Appalachia whites, he had drifted for years after his release from the Army. It was not until almost mid-life that he pulled himself together and enrolled in night school, to learn accounting. In his forties, he worked his way up the corporate ladder from bond salesman to a vice presidency at Smith Barney, one of the largest brokerage houses in the country. When we met him, he was head of the Philadelphia Port Authority and the Convention Center, and sat on the boards of hospitals and charities with scions of Philadelphia's Main Line families. Yet Wally never lost the earthy simplicity of his roots, and still lived in the middle-class neighborhood of Drexel Hill, where he had started his ascent. To Wally, the welfare system was not so much a friend to the poor as an enemy—luring the vulnerable into dependence, draining them of self-reliance, and stranding them in a misery from which there would be no escape.

Wally turned out to be fairly representative of the conservative activists with whom we now became associated. They were generally of working- and middle-class origin and, if well off like Wally, self-made. They had not gone to elite schools, and in their attitudes did not betray the arrogance of a social aristocracy. Politically, their roots were in the other radical movement of the Sixties (which neither we nor anyone else paid much attention to), the Goldwater revolt. That movement was libertarian and supported by small-business and working-class ethnics, and eventually had led to the election of Ronald Reagan. Philosophically, they were antistatist and individualist—a far cry from the "fascist" image the Left had pinned on them—and they appeared to have been largely goaded into their political stances by the assaults of the Left on their communities and values.

We encountered authoritarians on the right, of course, and were as repelled by them as much as we were by their counterparts on the left. But I was struck by their isolation from the conservative mainstream, and by the expansive nature of the ideological space we seemed to have entered. It was immediately apparent that the conservative spectrum was much larger than the one we had left. Its outer limits were defined by libertarians who wanted people to be left alone, and "paleoconservatives" who wanted a return to the more-rigid strictures of the past. Even the journals of the intellectual Right—*Commentary, National Review, The American Spectator*—reflected this breadth, and tended to be idiosyncratic, mirroring in style and content the personalities that dominated them: Buckley, Podhoretz, and R. Emmett Tyrell, a black Irishman appropriately named for a revolutionary martyr.

Another facet of the Right that confounded our expectations was its tolerance for deviant tendencies within its ranks. Just as Buckley was not the McCarthyite we had anticipated, so the conservative forums were not policed by the kind of ideological *gauleiters* we had become accustomed to among "progressives." In our new intellectual circles a very different atmosphere prevailed. This was dramatized for me during the congressional hearings into the Iran-Contra affair when William Safire, the conservative columnist, wrote a piece in which he called for the jailing of its central figure, Oliver North. It was at a moment when North was at the height of his popularity on the right, their champion under attack on a critical battleground of the Cold War. It occurred to me that no one on the left could have assaulted a similar icon of the radical movement in the way Safire had, without being condemned as a renegade and then drummed out of its ranks. I waited for conservative attacks to follow Safire's column and tarnish his reputation, but they never came.

Another aspect of the hearings that piqued my interest was their ironic reprise of the McCarthy investigations. Like those who were accused of being Communists, the defendants in the dock had none of the legal protections of a court procedure, while the congressmen who accused them of disloyalty and even treason were immune to prosecution for libel. As in the McCarthy hearings, the investigating committee was ostensibly concerned with legislation, but in fact the televised proceedings made it judge, jury, and executioner as its inflammatory charges were aired before an entire nation. Because the targets of the investigation were conservatives, however, not a single editorial or public expression of concern was heard from the liberal side over this abuse of congressional power.

In the Sixties, we had scorned liberals *because* they believed in the "process"—the rule of law that created obstacles to our radical agendas. Now, these same principles appeared to me the essential premise of civil freedoms. It was the procedural orders that constrained human passions, protected minorities, and made liberty possible. Like Norman Podhoretz, I felt that the core politics Peter and I had embraced were classically liberal.

In December 1992, I was invited to give a lecture at the Heritage Foundation, the right's most important policy think tank. The subject was "Are We Conservatives?" The very posing of the question was interesting. It was difficult, for example, to imagine a parallel forum asking "Are We Progressives?" I explained this anomaly to my audience by pointing out that conservatism was an attitude about the lessons of an actual past. By contrast, the attention of progressives was directed toward an imagined future. Conservatism was an attitude of caution based on a sense of human limits and what politics could accomplish. To ask whether conservatives *were* conservative was to ask a practical question about whether particular institutions were worth preserving. In the last thirty years, the American political landscape had changed dramatically, so that conservatives found themselves opposing many aspects of a culture with which they could no longer identify. Thus, the answer to the question posed was "No." In some sense we were not conservatives, but rebels against the dominant liberal culture.

The reason why progressives were unable to ask a similar question went to the root of their intolerant attitudes. Because the outlook of progressives was based on the idea of a liberated future, there was no way to disagree with them without appearing to oppose what was decent and humane. To criticize the radical project placed one in opposition to a world in which social justice and harmony would prevail. That was why the question "Are We Progressives?" was impossible for progressives to ask, and why the question I had once asked my comrades about the practicality of socialism was viewed by them as a counter-revolutionary threat.

In my lecture, I tried to identify the core of my new beliefs by focusing on the issues of equality and freedom that once had inspired me as a radical. Surveying the recent past, I pointed out that socialists had contrived to demonstrate by bloody example what everyone else already knew: Equality and freedom are inherently in conflict. This was really all that socialist efforts had shown, over the dead bodies of millions of people. In talent, intelligence, and physical attributes, individuals were by nature different and unequal; consequently, the attempt to make them equal could only be achieved by restricting—ultimately eliminating—their individual freedom. For the same reason, economic redistribution could be carried out only by force. Socialism was theft.

Socialism could not even achieve the general welfare that its adherents promised. Socialist efforts to create economic equality invariably led, in practice, to the imposition of poverty on society as a whole, because socialism destroyed the incentives to produce. There were entire socialist libraries devoted to the confiscation and division of existing wealth, but not a single article on how people were motivated to create wealth. Socialists did not know how to make a society work. That was the lesson of the Communist debacle, which the Left had refused to learn.

In the final analysis, social injustice was rooted in humanity's flaws. There had been social institutions, like slavery and segregation, that were wicked and unjust, and needed to be abolished. But in America's democracy, social injustices—and other evils which leftists decried—were caused primarily by humanity itself. The problem of controlling humanity's dark side was what necessitated institutions of constraint—the economic market and the democratic state. There was no exit from the dilemmas of history.

It was this perspective—conservative in its essence—that had inspired the creators of the American republic. In the *Federalist Papers,* Madison had defended the American idea of liberty by means of legal checks and balances as a design to thwart the leveling agendas of the Left—"a rage for paper money, for an abolition of debts, for an equal division of property, or for any other improper or wicked project." The conservatism I had arrived at could be expressed in a single patriotic idea: The revolutionary failures of the Twentieth Century had demonstrated the wisdom of the American founding, and validated its tenets: private property, individual rights, and a limited state. Becoming a conservative turned out, ultimately, to be a way of coming home.

I attempted to sum up my political transformation in an "open letter" to my old mentor, Ralph Miliband, with whom I had not had any contact for ten years. It was a comprehensive balance sheet of my views of the radical project, which I called "The Road to Nowhere." In one passage, I took Ralph to task for an article he had written two years prior to the Communist collapse. The Soviet reforms under Gorbachev, he said, proved that our vision as New Leftists was right. Just as Isaac Deutscher had predicted, the Soviet Union was becoming politically free and moving toward a genuine socialist state. Miliband wrote: "[It was] a remarkable vindication of [Deutscher's] confidence that powerful forces for progressive change would eventually break through seemingly impenetrable barriers." (In America, the socialist writer Irving Howe had reached a similar conclusion.) I seized on this final embarrassment of Miliband's radical hope to try to free him from his radical illusions:

> *Nothing could more clearly reveal how blind your faith has made you. To describe the collapse of the Soviet Empire as a vindication of Deutscher's prophecies (and thus the Marxist tradition that underpins them) is to turn history on its head. We are indeed witnessing a form of "revolution from above" in the Soviet Union, but it is a revolution that refutes Deutscher and Marx. The events of the past year are not a triumph for socialism, but a tragedy. The rejection of planned economy by the leaders of actually existing socialist society, the pathetic search for the elements of a rule of law (following the relentless crusades against "bourgeois rights"), the humiliating admission that the military superpower is in all other respects a third world nation, the inability of the socialist mode of production to enter the technological future and the unseemly begging for the advanced technology that it has stolen for decades from the West—all this adds up to a declaration of socialism's utter bankruptcy and historic defeat.*

Before publishing an abbreviated version of the letter in *Commentary*, I sent it to Ralph with a personal note. Perhaps he would also publish it in *The Socialist Register*, the way he had Kolakowski's essay, years before. But my real purpose was to prevent him from mistaking the political argument between us for my personal feelings toward him, which were still affectionate.

October 12, 1990

Dear Ralph,

I've thought about you a lot over these years, many times I've wanted to pick up the phone and call you, but I always stopped. I knew you were angry at me over the political path I have taken, and I just didn't see any way around that. I still don't, but I'm hoping the huge events of these last years may have softened the edges of the issues that divide us. Still, I'm not too hopeful. I've tried to keep up on your recent writings, so I know pretty much where you stand. I do miss your friendship, though … I felt I had to write this political testament (which is really what it is) to go over all the issues that now lie between us, in order to approach you again. I wanted you to understand that I did not turn my back on the struggle we once shared for trivial or unreflected reasons. I felt I owed that to you.

There is sometimes a harshness in this public letter (which I have enclosed) which is the product of its nature as a political document. I do not feel harshly towards you, but only warmth for a friend who has remained on a path that I have left.... When you read this, I hope you will not feel more alienated from me, but less. Even more, I hope you will write me and that we can resume, in whatever fashion seems appropriate, the contact we lost a long time ago.

David

In the beginning of my open letter, I had mentioned the fact that I had heard from others that he regarded me as "one of the two tragedies of the New Left," and that my apostasy had wounded him personally. Two weeks after I mailed my letters, he replied:

30 October 1990

Dear David,

Thank you for your "Letter."

Yours,

Ralph

P.S.: I have never spoken of your "apostasy" as "one of the two tragedies of the New Left," or of its having inflicted an "emotional wound." The first notion grossly exaggerates its public importance, the second its personal importance to me.

I had lost another friend. Once again I was forced to confront the fact that the Movement I had left was about more than just politics. Ralph's bitter message merely confirmed that he *did* regard my second thoughts as a personal betrayal—as I knew he would. "I understand this," I had begun my open letter:

How could it be otherwise for people like us, for whom politics (despite our claim to be social realists) was less a matter of practical decisions than moral choices? We were partisans of a cause that confirmed our humanity, even as it denied humanity to those who opposed us. To leave such ranks was not a simple matter, like abandoning a misconception or admitting a mistake. It was more like accusing one's comrades. Like condemning a life.

My second thoughts had led me through a night of the soul that involved the condemnation of my own life. I knew the terrors of such self-confrontation, and I did not hold it against Ralph or others if they did not choose to do the same.

It had come to seem inevitable to me that my political testament would have no impact on the community I had left behind. It was—after all was said and done—a community of faith, hermetically sealed from knowledge that might wake it from its dream. The catastrophe of everything progressives had believed could not have been more complete, yet they refused to see it. From university lecterns, in their own political journals, and in the op-ed pages of the prestige press, they dismissed what had happened to the revolutionary future as irrelevant to everything they had said and done. It was only "actually existing socialism" that had failed; "real socialism" had not yet been tried. As though there was no connection between the thing they dreamed and the thing that dreams like theirs had produced. *Socialism:* It was still the name of their desire. As before the Fall, they were Platonists inhabiting a reality that was separate, and that could not be refuted by events. They had invested their lives in opposing the defenders of Western freedom and supporting the "progressive" revolutionary despotisms, and now they could not admit they were wrong. As they resumed their attack on the capitalist West, their imaginations were fixed so firmly on the idea of a redemptive future that no present event could cause them to have second thoughts. It was *because* they were revolutionaries—because they dreamed of the future that would be different from any past—that the present offered no indication to them of what that future might actually *be*.

From the very beginning, second-thoughters had escaped from the progressive utopias to bring back the bad news. But no one had listened. The names of the witnesses—Arthur Koestler, Walter Krivitsky, Jan Valtin, Benjamin Gitlow, Bella Dodd, Elizabeth Bentley, Whittaker Chambers, Aileen Kraditor, Carlos Franqui, and thousands of others vindicated by history—have been erased from memory, or are remembered by the Left merely to be reviled. Their truth is buried with the socialist dead. And so was mine. It had been just over a quarter of a century from my first May Day Parade in 1948 until Betty's murder in 1974. But the years I had dedicated to the progressive cause counted as nothing for Miliband and the others when I came to offer them the lessons that had been so costly for me to learn. I had nothing to teach them. As far as they were concerned, I was a renegade who had betrayed them—who announced today what he had denounced yesterday—and that was enough.

Two months after we left Poland, on August 22, 1989, Huey Newton was gunned down on an Oakland street, in the same neighborhood where he had murdered Officer Frey more than twenty years before. Justice was administered by a crack dealer named Tyrone Robinson, whom Newton had burned. For the last six years of his life, the former Minister of Defense for the Black Panther Party had been addicted to base cocaine, a pathetic shadow of his former self and an embarrassment to his supporters. But now, in death, he was being resurrected. A public funeral was held for him, attended by two thousand admirers. It was a front-page story in the Bay Area press. "Huey Newton lived just long enough to have been the unknown idealist, a popular and heroic champion of the oppressed," read the funeral program. He was "a world hero, our king in shining armor," said one of the eulogists. He was a "black Moses," said another, in a phrase that made the headlines. The same sentiments were echoed by Congressman Ron Dellums, and other black dignitaries and politicians who had learned to keep their distance from Newton when he was alive but came to pay tribute to him as a martyr when he could no longer threaten them.

Huey's death "is the culmination of twenty years of assassination attempts by the police," Elaine Brown intoned from the funeral pulpit, fanning the embers of the Panther cause. Newton's *consigliere*, Charles Garry, was more explicit: "The FBI destroyed him just as they destroyed the Black Panther Party," he said. The Panther torch was being passed to the next generation. The funeral was really a revival meeting, the beginning of a campaign to restore the faith and renew the war that Huey had begun.

Among the mourners was Marty Kenner, my initial guide into the Panther maze, who had remained faithful to Newton all those years. Kenner was now speculating in commodities and international currencies, and had made a handsome profit on an earthquake in Peru that killed several thousand people as it drove the price of coffee to new highs. Perhaps it was the cognitive dissonance of this career that caused him and others to embrace the charade.

With Newton dead, Peter and I could finally write the story of the Panthers that had not yet been told. "Baddest: The Life and Times of Huey P. Newton" provided the first history of the Party as a political street gang. Eventually our efforts would inspire others to reevaluate the Panther legend. For now, the cultural isolation imposed on us after the Second Thoughts conference insured that our story would have limited impact. It appeared in *Smart,* a startup glossy run by Terry McDonell, who had edited our Weatherman story at *Rolling Stone.* As a new magazine, *Smart's* circulation was not large, and the story caused no ripples of interest in the media nor did it alter much the public's awareness of the Panther reality. We also included "Baddest" in the newly released paperback edition of *Destructive Generation,* where it was destined to be read mainly by conservatives who already understood who the Panthers were.

Over the course of twenty years, the Panther myth had been firmly implanted in the literary culture by radical scholars and journalists. The silence of the witnesses—Hayden, Scheer, Kenner, and the others—left the mythmakers with no serious challenge, and made its construction relatively easy. Because of J. Edgar Hoover's racist obsessions with Martin Luther King, law enforcement views of the Panthers were effectively tainted. I urged historian David Garrow, who had written about King and the FBI, to examine the history and correct the misrepresentations about the Panther surveillance promoted by the Left, but he declined.

The Panther myth was propagated in the academy by tenured radicals who made them icons. Panther veterans had been hired to teach in African-American studies departments, and even Warren Kimbro, the convicted murderer of Alex Rackley, had been matriculated at Harvard as an affirmative-action student, and become a dean at a Connecticut college. The myth was also spread through campus speakers' programs, which were generally controlled by the Left and whose stars often were Panther enthusiasts like "Professor Griff," and Angela Davis—who commanded $10,000 fees and received official university honors (Davis even had a lounge named after her at the University of Michigan). And it was promoted under the auspices of public television, which produced five documentaries featuring the Panthers, including the widely distributed and award-winning *"Eyes on the Prize."* The PBS films glorified the Party, and perpetuated the image of its leaders as movement heroes who had been destroyed by the FBI because they were leaders of black liberation. The murders of Alex Rackley and Betty Van Patter, the assaults on the police, the bull-whippings and extortion and drugs, were never mentioned.

In the aftermath of Huey's death, the heroic myth of the Panthers began to establish itself in the popular culture, as well. In the black community, Martin Luther King's image had been eclipsed by Malcolm X, and the hope that King represented replaced by a racial paranoia resonant with the Panther message. Rap musicians like Public Enemy produced million-selling albums in which the Panthers figured as urban legends who showed the way to "fight the power," which was also the title score of Spike Lee's feature, *Do The Right Thing.* These messages reached into the inner cities and the gangs I had covered a decade before. They became an element in the witches' brew of racial hatred and criminal enterprise that erupted in 1992 in a gang-instigated Los Angeles riot. Two thousand Korean businesses were burned, and fifty-seven people killed—many of them targeted, like the businesses destroyed, simply because they were not black.

Shortly after the riot, I appeared on a radio talk show with Clark Kissinger, a former president of SDS. Kissinger had created a new organization in South Central, Refuse and Resist, to promote the idea that local Crip gangs were revolutionaries battling an oppressive state. On the air, Kissinger was adamant that the looters and burners were social rebels, and that anyone doubting this was a "racist." This was the ideologically required view of the academic left and its spokes-men, like Princeton professor Cornel West, who called the riots an "uprising" that expressed "justified social rage." In America's inner cities and on its campuses, the Black Panthers had been reborn as an emblem of the radical future.

The Panther myth was only one of the corrosive legacies of the Sixties left that had survived as a force into the present. In *Destructive Generation*, Peter and I seized on a medical analogy to describe their cumulative impact: "In the inchoate attack against authority, we had weakened our culture's immune system, making it vulnerable to opportunistic diseases. The origins of metaphorical epidemics of crime and drugs could be traced to the Sixties, as could literal ones such as AIDS." Peter was more skeptical than I about what anyone, let alone we, could do. His *métier*, he felt, was that of biographer, and he wanted to continue the series of books we had begun. But I was restless, and looked for a way in which we could counter the forces we had helped to unleash. I knew that if I found a vehicle for such efforts, Peter would join me. At the conclusion of his *own* autobiographical essay he had written:

> After my years as a New Leftist, I could never join another movement or subscribe to another orthodoxy. But I feel there is still a small role to play—keeping an eye on these deep swimmers [of the left] and, when I see one of them come near the surface, pointing out who he is, what he is doing, and what the consequences are likely to be.

Our experience with the Second Thoughts Conference had introduced us to the world of conservative activism, whose institutional base was a network of nonprofit "think tanks" like the Heritage Foundation. Our combative temperament was hardly suited to policy analysis, but our experience with Jim Denton's National Forum Foundation showed that the form could provide us with an appropriate vehicle. A room in my house served as office space for what I called the Center for the Study of Popular Culture, a name that identified its focus but also made it harder for the Left to attack. I put Peter, Wally Nunn, and Jim Denton on the board. The track record that Peter and I had established allowed me to raise modest sums from the three "foundations" who had funded our conference—Olin, Bradley, and Scaife.

My first project was to persuade public television to air a documentary about Castro's Cuba, where the last Communist gulag was still jammed with political dissidents. The film, aptly called *Nobody Listened*, was directed by Nestor Almendros, a Cuban refugee and Academy Award-winning cinematographer. Almendros had previously made a documentary titled *Improper Conduct*, which treated the Castro regime's abuse of homosexuals as a metaphor for its management of all deviance from the party orthodoxy. *Improper Conduct* was never shown on public TV. During the Eighties, however, PBS had run a series of propaganda documentaries promoting Castro and his disciples as the wave of the future in Latin America. These cinematic tracts were produced by radical filmmakers who in the Sixties had made promotional films for the Vietcong and the Black Panthers. Among these hucksters were the Newsreel radicals we had fired from the mailroom at *Ramparts*. After a year of effort by Almendros and others (in which I was pleased to play a modest role), PBS finally agreed to air *Nobody Listened*. But, in typical fashion, public broadcasters decided to "balance" Almendros' poignant portrayal of Castro's victims with a pro-Castro propaganda film. Its producer was my old friend Saul Landau, then in his thirtieth year of flacking for the dictatorship.

Small successes like this enabled me to increase the funding of the Center and to bring Peter into the fold. He had often talked about reviving *Ramparts,* and the capital we had raised seemed to provide the opportunity. Our target would be the tenured radicals who had turned university faculties into bastions of "political correctness" which was a Mao Tse-tung-inspired euphemism for the party line.

The situation in the universities was appalling. The Marxists and socialists who had been refuted by historical events were now the tenured establishment of the academic world. Marxism had produced the bloodiest and most oppressive regimes in human history—but after the fall, as one wit commented, more Marxists could be found on the faculties of American colleges than in the entire former Communist bloc. The American Historical Association was run by Marxists, as was the professional literature association, whose field had been transformed into a kind of pseudosociology of race-gender-class oppression. When Peter and I were undergraduates in the Fifties, the mission of the university had been described by its guardians as "the disinterested pursuit of knowledge." It was now officially recast in radical terms as that of "social transformation." Radical politics had become the intellectual currency of academic thought. With no trace of embarrassment, Richard Rorty, one of the most prominent figures in academic philosophy, even boasted that "the power base of the Left in America is in the universities," by which he meant not the students (who were generally apathetic if not conservative), but the faculties, administrations, and departments, who tried to recruit students to their political agendas.

As an undergraduate at Columbia in the McCarthy Fifties, I had written papers from a Marxist point of view, but had never been graded politically by my anti-Communist professors. Nor had I ever felt that the lectures I attended were veiled indoctrinations. As a student, I was invariably presented with both sides of an argument. When I visited university campuses now, however, the contrast was striking. Courses were often baldly ideological. Many left-wing professors gave one-sided presentations of subjects, expecting their views to be parroted on papers and exams. Students were graded politically, and frequently intimidated from expressing their own perspectives. The atmosphere of political terror was far greater and more pervasive than anything I had experienced, as a Marxist, in the McCarthy era. Although there was no statistical evidence to prove it, I would estimate that many more academic careers had been aborted for political reasons during these post-Sixties decades than during the entire Communist "witch-hunt" of the McCarthy period. The reason for the lack of statistics was the same as for the effectiveness of the purge: Unlike the McCarthy-ites, whose base was government, the left-wing witch-hunters were *inside* the academy, where they could operate in secrecy and to far greater effect.

Inevitably, the academic curriculum was also affected. A new theme of the academy was "multiculturalism," the Left's latest assault on the American identity and a direct appeal to alienated minorities not to assimilate into the American culture. In the multicultural perspective, the constitutional framework became the scheme of "dead white males" to shore up their privileged status. Conservative thinkers like

Hayek, von Mises, Kirk, Sowell, and Oakeshott were notable for their absence from college reading lists and courses (or their marginality, if present). The same was true of historical figures who had opposed the totalitarian left. Undergraduates I interviewed had never even heard of Whittaker Chambers, although the same students could identify the traitor Alger Hiss as a "victim of McCarthyism."

When Peter and I spoke at Carleton College, one of the leading liberal-arts schools in the country, we asked a seminar of fifty students if they had ever heard the names Hayek or von Mises, two seminal figures of Twentieth-Century thought who had predicted the socialist collapse. Only one student had. Yet thirty responded when we asked how many had *read* a book by Noam Chomsky, a leftist whose views were so extreme that his writings were no longer accepted even by liberal magazines like the *Atlantic* or the *New York Review of Books*. Conservatives who had been historically vindicated by the Twentieth Century's epic struggle against Marxist totalitarianism were generally consigned to obscurity, while radicals who had denigrated and betrayed Western freedom—political hacks like Angela Davis, intellectual commissars like Antonio Gramsci, and embittered nihilists like Michel Foucault—were given places of honor in the academic canon.

The wheel had come full circle. The first radical takeover of an American campus had occurred at Berkeley in 1964, when the "Free Speech Movement" occupied an administration building to protest a ban on political propagandizing and recruitment on campus property. At the time, such activity was deemed inappropriate to a university setting. But the university had long since lost the battle, and now the war. The radicals had moved onto the faculty and into the administration, and had changed the rules. Political propaganda and recruitment were now considered academic norms in an institution redefined as "an agency of social change". McCarthy and his allies had never been able to get inside the academy, but the radicals had. To consolidate their political control and stifle critics of their agendas, the radicals had instituted "speech codes"—the most stringent restrictions on intellectual discourse in the universities since their administration by religious sects. As a result of these changes, the liberal-arts faculties of American campuses were now at their lowest intellectual level since the creation of the modern university more than a hundred years before.

Peter thought our new anti-PC journal should be in tabloid format, like the old underground papers, and that its name should be *Heterodoxy*. This would emphasize the fact that *we* were the counterculture now, since the academic world and its intellectual canon were dominated by the Left. The lead feature in our first issue, which was published in April 1992, was titled "PC Cover-up" and addressed "the collection of pathologies known as 'political correctness'." Our agenda was to ridicule the faculty commissars (since intellectual argument with tenured ideologues was beside the point) and, by diligent reporting, to expose the pervasiveness of what Orwell had called "the smelly little orthodoxies" of the Left—a reality which was being strenuously denied.

As *Heterodoxy* became a presence on campuses across the country, our opponents' attacks typically focused on its foundation funding. This was not really surprising. No matter how sophisticated radical theory became, it never strayed far from its vulgar Marxist roots. For progressives it was always *cherchez l'argent*. Edward Said—Columbia professor, PLO spokesman, and friend of Christopher Hitchens— used the prestigious Reith Lectures to let out a typical whine about our financial support: "In a matter of months during the late 1980s, Second Thoughts aspired to become a movement, alarmingly well funded by right-wing Maecenases like the Bradley and Olin Foundations. The specific impresarios were David Horowitz and Peter Collier...."

I found these attacks annoying at first, but after awhile merely amusing—yet another confirmation of von Mises's insight that socialism was the cosmic aggrandizement of petty resentments. During the same 1980s, the Left had been funded and supported by the most opulent and elite institutions of American culture. Our adversaries were professors and deans at Harvard, Princeton, and Yale, institutions which would neither hire the likes of us nor extend the invitations and honors that were now being accorded less qualified representatives of our radical generation. Nor would they provide to intellectuals with our views the imprimaturs required for establishment funding. It was our adversaries' books and magazines that bore the imprint of the most prestigious university presses, now under the firm ideological control of the Left.

In November 1991, I attended a conference at the University of Michigan which called itself "The PC Frame-Up." This turned out to be a rally of leftists claiming that "political correctness" was something invented by right-wing witch-hunters. It featured a cast of radical academics like Houston Baker and Todd Gitlin, and nonacademic ideologues like columnist Julianne Malveaux. According to the organizers, funds for "The PC Frame-Up" conference were supplied by fourteen of the university's departments and programs. Even the audience was provided by a huge lecture class in communications, whose professor had made attendance virtually compulsory, counting it as a third of the grade. I regarded the whole spectacle as a violation of the students' academic freedom—the right *not* to be politically indoctrinated by their professors. But it proved to be a standard form of educational abuse in the new academic environment. Such resources, of course, were not available to us, had we been willing to draw on them, or to anyone else on our side of the political and cultural argument. Our exclusion from the academy, and from the commanding heights of the culture generally was as effective and complete as any blacklist.

Since the resources of the cultural establishment were denied to us, we had to rely on a surprisingly small group of conservative institutions for our core financial support. Their chief operating officers and principals reflected the broad spectrum of the conservative coalition, with a libertarian bent that made us comfortable. But I never really had a conversation about political philosophy with any of them. We undertook activities we thought appropriate, and they supported us because they liked what we did. An irony missed by our left-wing critics was that the "ruling class" foundations, such as Carnegie, Ford, and Rockefeller, were solidly behind the programs and ideas favored by Edward Said and his allies—multiculturalism, affirmative action, radical feminism, black separatist studies and the political redefinition of the university mission. Tens of millions of dollars had been invested by America's biggest capitalist fortunes in these anti-democratic and anti-capitalist agendas. The Maecenases who contributed "alarmingly" to us, by contrast, were far smaller, and marginal to the university itself.

One left-wing foundation, MacArthur, which was only half the size of Ford, was actually three times bigger than all the foundations that made up the right-wing core—Bradley, Scaife, and Olin—combined. MacArthur was a funder of *Harper's*, Lapham's left-wing journal, and the pro-Sandinista Christie Institute, a conspiracy-minded think tank whose wild-eyed theories had been thoroughly discredited in the courts. MacArthur's signature program was its prestigious "genius" awards, which took the form of fellowships to individuals identified as creative thinkers. In addition to funding scientists and other reasonable recipients, the five-year grants (roughly $250,000 each) provided an endowment program for the socialist left. Five editors of the tiny ideological journal *Dissent* had already received the grants (*Dissent's* presiding eminence, Irving Howe, was an adviser to the program), including Paul Berman. Berman's selection cast an unsparing light on the political character of the whole enterprise, since in mid-life his intellectual *oeuvre* amounted to little more than journalistic ephemera—columns and reviews for the *Village Voice* and the *New Republic*—and the assault on us.

Berman was not alone among our antagonists in reaping unearned benefits from the system they had made careers of attacking. The New Left's ubiquitous revolutionary, Tom Hayden, had remained in politics as a Democratic Party regular, receiving a White House Freedom Award from Jimmy Carter, and getting himself elected in 1982 as a California assemblyman by outspending his opponent. Hayden had devoted $1.7 million of his actress wife's fortune to the acquisition of the seat, a national record for money spent on a state office. When term limits were introduced in 1992, he set another spending record to gain a seat in the State Senate. He then ran for governor in 1994, building his campaign around the theme that money was a capitalist evil which should be eliminated from politics. The campaign was also financed by the Fonda fortune, this time in the form of Tom's divorce settlement.

The leader of the Seattle Liberation Front, Michael Lerner, had resurfaced as a social success in the post-Revolutionary era as well. Grandiose as ever, he had married a Safeway heiress just long enough to finance a magazine whose name, *Tikkun*, was a Hebrew word meaning "to heal and repair the world." He achieved his fifteen minutes of fame by writing an op-ed piece urging the Democratic Party to put "the meaning of life" at the center of its electoral agenda. President Clinton and his wife briefly thought this a good idea, until their public endorsement of "the politics of meaning" provoked enough derision and embarrassment for them to drop it and Lerner both.

Our old *Ramparts* boss, Bob Scheer, had also joined the liberal establishment while continuing his radical assault. In mid-life, the man who had once idolized Kim Il Sung assumed the posture of an urban squire, marrying again and acquiring an Orange County townhouse and, along with it, a Cadillac El Dorado, a boat with a marina slip, and an expense-account lifestyle. Following the path of his rival, he attached himself to the salon culture that Hayden had developed among the *glitterati* with the help of his movie-star wife. Scheer became a "political adviser" to celebrities like Jane Fonda and Barbra Streisand, helping them with their speeches to Harvard students and other "serious" audiences. Collecting handsome advances for prospective books on Fonda and Soviet ruler Mikhail Gorbachev, Scheer never managed to actually produce them. But he acquired a public platform as a columnist for *Playboy* and national correspondent for the *Los Angeles Times*, where his third wife was part of the management team.

Despite the passage of years, Scheer hadn't really changed. Still the talented cynic, he explored the good life on the money he made decrying the evils of wealth in his columns for the *Times*. As always, he reveled in the hypocrisy. Confronting an out-of-work journalist he had known in Berkeley who had political second thoughts, he mocked her mercilessly: "Look at you. You support the System, and you're struggling, while I attack it and have a six-figure salary and a yacht, and am surrounded by Hollywood stars."

Toward the end of the decade, I confronted the New Left's perennial juvenile delinquent, Abbie Hoffman, on a radio talk show in Los Angeles. I had met Abbie more than ten years before, when he was "underground" to escape prosecution for selling drugs, and performed some editing on the book he was writing, *Soon To Be A Major Motion Picture*. The talk show, which was on KABC Los Angeles, took place shortly before Abbie killed himself with an overdose of pills. Abbie was on a phone hookup from his home, slurring his words and sounding unusually depressed. "I don't like born-agains," he groused at one point, referring to my second thoughts. "The trouble with you, Abbie," I replied, "is that you never grew up."

The encounter with Abbie crystallized my thoughts about my former comrades. It occurred to me that F. Scott Fitzgerald's observation about the spoiled rich applied perfectly to the Left: *They break things and leave others to clean up after them.*

Milton Friedman once praised Friedrich Hayek as a man who "strengthened the moral and economic foundations of a free society." What would Abbie or Tom or Scheer make of that idea? They would not even understand what it meant. I thought of the people who had walked the ramparts of America's civil order to defend its institutions against us, and of the rank-and-file soldiers, like my friend Wally Nunn, who had risked their lives to protect our freedoms against the totalitarian threat. These heroes of the Cold War were the very people we had once scorned, and they did still.

If there was a symbolic figure to represent them, it was Ronald Reagan. There was a special satisfaction for me, therefore, when I went to his offices in Los Angeles to receive a Teach Freedom Award from him in 1990. Reagan was then eighty years old and retired, but he strode jauntily into the room to greet the little group organizing the ceremony. I had sent him a copy of the article Peter and I had written for the *Washington Post.* I was not sure if he had ever received it, or would remember if he had. But, when he shook my hand, he smiled and said: "I had second thoughts before you."

It had been nearly three years since I brought Shay into my household. Our life together was happy, and her high spirits had a salutary effect on my own disposition. I had recovered my health, and was enjoying myself to an extent I would not previously have thought possible. Depression no longer dogged me, nor was I fearful, even, of sliding back to that unenviable state. It seemed I was learning, in midlife, to take my pleasures as they came. I liked the warmth and solidity of the big house, and especially the fact that there was room for my children. I had torn down the old garage and built a new addition with high-beamed ceilings and hardwood floors, and a wooden deck that jutted into the lower branches of the redwood, giving it a treehouse effect. I took great pleasure in watching my vision realized, and imagined what it might have been like to be an architect. As a radical, I had focused on taking institutions apart and tearing them down. It was exhilarating to be part of a construction, however modest, that made a little piece of the earth better and more livable instead.

The addition was for my son Jonathan, who spent a year with me before going to New York with his band. Benjamin, who was the first of my children to be married, moved in with my new daughter-in-law, Felicia Wiley. Ben was completing a master's in computer science at UCLA, and Felicia, a USC graduate, had taken a job in junior management at Toyota. She was the first of her family of rural blacks from Louisiana to go to college. Her father, John Wiley, was a Korean War vet whose own father had been murdered by Klansmen when John was seven. After the war, John lost his job in Shreveport during a company lockout, and moved with his wife, Loretta, to San Pedro, California, where his military base had been. He found a job unloading banana boats, "because no one else wanted to do it," and settled in Carson, a city on the southern rim of the Los Angeles basin. Eventually he became an oil pipeline worker and accumulated enough money to buy his own house. When our extended family sat down for a joint dinner and plunged into political issues, I was interested to see that the Wileys and I shared socially conservative views, jointly confronting the more liberal attitudes of our children. On September 21, 1989, Felicia gave birth to my first grandchild, Julia. While her arrival caused a "metaphysical lurch," as Peter put it (was I *that old?*), her birth was almost as exciting to me as that of my own babies, and her presence the purest joy I could remember since they had come of age.

My older daughter, Sarah, was working as a journalist and poet, giving readings of her witty efforts at local clubs in the Bay Area. Three months before Julia's birth, she wrote a poem called "Ambivalence," which was published in the *Berkeley Poetry Review*. Its third stanza read:

> I'm on the phone to my father who is planning his third
> wedding. I'm arguing with him about government spending
> for the arts. He is an angry ex-Marxist and
> neo-Republican. As a result I can hold my own with
> both communists and right wingers.

I especially liked the phrase "hold my own." I took satisfaction in the fact that my children were independent and self-confident, and also attentive to the world around them. They seemed to have avoided the tunnel vision that had led me to so much trouble. The boys were more conservative in their views, but my daughters were shrewd observers of human nature in ways that I had failed to be. This was important to me, ensuring that none of them would follow my radical path.

None had made politics a vocation either, which caused me neither pleasure nor discomfort. Unlike many parents, I did not feel compelled to chart a course for my children, nor did I feel rejected if they failed to follow my choices. Life, as I had reason to know, was rich in surprises, not least in areas where you might consider yourself expert. Having lived almost a full span, I was impressed by how narrow one's perspectives remain, how small our grasp of human possibility. Living only once, as Kundera observed, we can never know what another life would be like. Despite my wealth of years, I had no surety of foresight when it came to deciding the paths my children should pursue. I would be pleased if they were just able to master the difficulties better than I had.

While my son Benjamin set up a household according to the pattern established in our family for generations, I was still grappling on the edge of the precipice I had climbed, unable to regain the sense of gravity that once guided my ascent. *How do you begin a life in mid-life?* It was a riddle I had not been able to solve. I would probably have asked Shay to marry me earlier, but I was trying to establish a discipline of caution after my previous mistake. My resolve was strengthened when I discovered the source of her overnight disappearances. The original episode had recurred, provoking other painful confrontations until I was able to pry out a piece of the truth. The problem was drugs, and specifically cocaine: She had been a user since she was seventeen. She had run away from home (after which her father had not spoken to her for a year), and then worked in a Monterey massage parlor called Foxy Lady. Yet, she had none of the surface hardness I would have expected from such a life. Her tearful resolves to do better now were cries for help to which every fiber in me resonated. I was not a puritan, nor blameless in my own life, and when I looked at the years we had already shared together, I felt I would be happy if I were able to spend the rest of my days with her. If only she could bring this desperate side of herself under control.

I should have been forewarned, but, having lost the stability of one life, I had entered a second of considerable risk. I took pride now in reaching for what I wanted, despite what others thought or the dangers courted. There was an existential pleasure in my life with Shay, a defiance that was not unlike the authenticity we had all felt once in being part of the "revolution."

Notwithstanding the relief her candor brought, it was difficult to understand how she could put someone she loved through the pain that these episodes involved. During one of our confrontations, I told her she would have to leave, but could not maintain my resolve when she begged for a reprieve, a chance to change. I could not divorce myself from the feelings I had for her. Nor could I face the prospect I imagined awaiting her if I turned her out. She had no money and no place to go, and I convinced myself that she would destroy herself with drugs, or on the street. This was self-flattery. Despite what I knew, I had become a rescuer again.

Shay enrolled herself in Alcoholics Anonymous, and attended meetings regularly for awhile before losing interest. I hoped that the problem was solved, but also realized that, because my speaking engagements took me out of town, I couldn't really know. After we visited a community of orthodox Jews in Venice that Michael Medved (one of our Second Thoughts participants) had founded, Shay expressed an interest in religion. We began attending the synagogue, a little building on the ocean boardwalk that was a junction of disparate worlds—Babylon and Jerusalem. After the service, bikini-clad roller-bladers would sail by, often with ghetto blasters in tow, to ogle the uncomfortable worshippers in their serious dark suits and ankle-length skirts worn to cover the flesh.

Shay's relationship to these religious people was ambivalent, as it was to most other things that attracted her. Underneath her surface enthusiasm was the conviction "They don't approve of me," and a resistance to becoming more deeply involved. My own attitude was ambivalent as well. Socialism was a secular faith: I had been a believer, and I had been burned. I did not feel an opening in my soul for renewed risk. I had affection for the Old Testament God, and was invariably moved during the service by the connection I felt, through the ancient prayers, to ancestors who lived millennia ago. But to God's actual existence, I remained stubbornly agnostic. If I believed in anything, it was in the mystery itself.

The prayers I read in the English translation often seemed to me like black humor. Every Sabbath morning, the congregation gave thanks to the God of Abraham, Isaac, and Jacob for looking after His chosen people, for always protecting them, and for vanquishing their enemies. Who, knowing the fate of the Jews in the two thousand years since they had entered the Promised Land, could not feel a grim irony in these gratitudes? If I found it impossible to conjure a traditional belief, I nonetheless thought of myself as religious. Even if no divinity watched over me, and despite the fact that my moorings had loosened, I felt the need to act morally. And guilty when I did not. I didn't know whether it all added up in the end—whether life had an intrinsic meaning, or my own any purpose. But I couldn't bring myself to act as though they did not.

The rabbi, Daniel Lapin, asked me to speak to the congregation as a "scholar in residence." My talk was called "The Fate of the Jews and the Radical Left." Since my early encounters with the writings of Buber, I had felt a powerful connection to religious texts. The entire unhappy story of Twentieth Century revolutions seemed to me encapsulated in the first chapters of Genesis, which provided as profound an insight into the human drama as I knew. The parable of the Garden seemed, finally, inescapable: Our primal parents had been given a paradise on earth, but proved themselves unfit for the privilege, by nature. By the very free will that defined us all as human. The serpent had only to promise human beings that they would be as gods, and that was enough. Created in His image, we aspired to *be* God. To eat forbidden fruit. To know good *and* evil. To *know* in the biblical sense: To get into bed with the evil along with the good. This was our downfall through time.

Our primal parents were expelled from paradise for their rebellious disobedience. This was the beginning of history. From that time on, an angel with a flaming sword has guarded the gates of Eden, barring our way back. The only way to paradise—if there is a way—is through a divine intervention. The idea that men can be as gods and re-create a paradise on earth is the serpentine promise of the Left. It is an idolatry that overshadows all others. When men put on the mantle of gods and attempt to remake the world in their own image, the results are hideous and destructive beyond conception.

One Sabbath in January 1990, Shay and I went to visit the rabbi. He took me into his study and offered me a shot glass of his favorite vodka and then, without warning, asked me when I was going to marry Shay. I was thrown off guard. I couldn't tell him about the drugs without betraying her. Instead, I told him I didn't think she was ready for such a commitment. Although she loved me, she seemed unhappy with me at some deep level of her being. She was overwhelmed by my circumstances and friends. A sense of inadequacy haunted her. Women are like that, the rabbi assured me. They need the security a man can give them. If you provide it, she will change.

When we left the rabbi's house and were standing in the street, I asked Shay to marry me. Inside, I was trembling. She wanted to know if I really meant it, then said yes, and then "It must be the vodka." For a moment her happiness overcame my doubts and allowed me to embrace my desire. Once again, I had acted on a powerful impulse. Everything I had learned through pain argued against what I was doing. *People don't change.* But I did not want to surrender to the fatalism of what I knew. I had experienced a moment of terror, and willed myself through it. Despite everything, the rebel was still in charge. I will *make this work.*

We were married on June 24, 1990 in the little synagogue by the ocean. Once again I made arrangements for a large wedding—in part, just because it was her first. I invited the entire congregation, hoping their presence would strengthen the bonds of a marriage whose risks I thought I knew and that I wanted to succeed. In keeping with the orthodox tradition, Shay went to stay with a family in the community for the prescribed three days prior to the ceremony, and we didn't see or speak to each other. She went to the ritual baths, while I "purified" myself, according to instructions, by swimming naked in the Santa

Monica ocean. On the day of the wedding, I led a procession of the male congregants to unveil my bride (another tradition), in order to avoid the mistake of Jacob, who was given Leah instead of Rachel after his seven-year labor. The procession returned to the synagogue, where we stood under the canopy as Shay circled seven times around me, and Rabbi Lapin said the ancient prayers. Then three rabbis signed the *ketubah*, the marriage contract that made me responsible for her well-being, and I placed the ring on her finger. Afterwards, we had a wedding party at which she and I sat on chairs like royalty while the congregants danced *kazatskies* and performed handstands and other feats to honor us. They then lifted our chairs over their heads while we held the ends of a handkerchief, and they danced with us in a circle.

For our honeymoon we went to Lake Louise in Canada, a teal mirror under a glacial ridge, the most romantic place I had ever been. Peter gave us the air tickets as a wedding present. His own marriage to Mary was nearing its twenty-fifth anniversary, and I could see in his eyes the hope that I had finally found an angle of repose for myself. I was fifty-one years old.

Despite a few false starts, our first married year was reassuring. Shay seemed to relish the household that was now officially hers, and announced to our single friends that they should all be married and share the joy she found in her new connubial state. But her restlessness persisted. She wanted me to sell the Fern Dell house, which she felt was too large and too associated with my previous marriage, even though that had ended six years before. She kept percolating new and impractical ambitions: On one occasion, she found a man in the town where her parents lived, who made a bread dough out of beans she wanted to sell to restaurants in Los Angeles, 200 miles away. I had a hard time discouraging her from wasting effort on this scheme. The pressure she felt to move on and to *do* was a restlessness I recalled from my own crisis. She never really felt in her life.

Even though I didn't want to leave the house, I knew it was necessary. In deciding to invest all my capital in the equity and improvements, I had outsmarted myself. I succeeded in avoiding depression, but was carried away by the desire to build, and by my innate optimism—which once again caused me to disregard the cautions that would have held others back. I borrowed money to create the addition, doubling my mortgage payments. With rising interest rates, property taxes, insurance, and other costs, I was soon paying far more than I could afford.

In December 1991, I sold the house, losing a substantial portion of the money I had invested, and we moved to a small cottage in Studio City. In one room I set up the offices of the Center for the Study of Popular Culture, and we began work on the first issue of *Heterodoxy*. After consulting with Peter, I hired Shay as art director, who seemed well-suited to the job. Her raw talent—which was dramatic, satiric, and eccentric—was perfect for the magazine Peter and I envisaged. The job seemed like it would be perfect for her as well. The skill she began to acquire on the computer was marketable, and would provide her with a security and independence that she had long wanted. Her salary was more than she had earned, legitimately, in her entire life, and I felt sure that the "fame" she also hankered after, which was more like a validation, would soon follow.

But Shay fought her success in this, as she had in everything else. *Heterodoxy's* second issue led with a story on "Queer Studies"—a new form of ideological discourse in the university. I suggested she do a caricature of Marx in drag, for the cover illustration. She rendered it outrageously, showing Marx in bra and garter belt, whip lasciviously in hand. It elicited letters from more than a dozen postmasters warning us to desist from sending obscene materials through the mail, or risk prosecution. The issue was a *coup* for us, defeating expectations about what a "conservative" magazine should be, and becoming a conversation piece across the country. But Shay refused to own the achievement: Because I had come up with the concept, she would not regard the work as hers.

I guessed she was in some phase of a mid-life crisis, and tried to convey to her what I had learned from mine: Don't confuse fantasy with reality; don't act on a feeling without considering the consequences; give yourself to the life you're in, and the work you do. But I could no more impress these modest insights on her than I was able to transmit the lessons in politics I had learned to my former comrades-in-arms.

As we entered our third year of marriage, Shay's unhappiness with herself became dominant, and I felt helpless to provide her relief. Alternately, she would turn to her chimeric business schemes, or refashion her physical being. "I want lips, cheekbones, and breasts," she would say, identifying what she perceived to be her deficits, and beginning her lobbying to have me finance the improvements. I was happy with the way she looked and knew this latest need was not the real source of her discontent. But on one cosmetic issue I acceded to her desires. She was self-conscious about her teeth, which had been neglected from childhood when her father denied his children dental care because he regarded it as too expensive. Sometimes I noticed her cover her mouth when she smiled, so her teeth wouldn't show. The problems that had lingered into adulthood were expensive, and would require surgery and caps. When she went for estimates, the bill was more than I had ever spent on myself—even on automobiles. But my fate was now inextricably entwined with hers, and I hoped she would feel that I cared for her in a way that no one in her life seemed to have before.

Shortly after we put out the second *Heterodoxy*, Shay's father had a heart attack, and a month later was dead. It was a selfish death, I thought. He was suffering from extreme hypertension, but had refused to take the medicine that would control it, complaining that the pills made him impotent. The attack followed a week of explosive confrontations with his unhappy sons, and struck when he was pulling up a huge stump on his property, a physical task he knew to avoid. In the hospital, he refused to be put on a respirator that would have saved him, preferring to die—as he told the nurses—rather than go through the ordeal of therapy to live in a partially diminished state. He had left his widow of forty years with no insurance, a large mortgage, and only a small Social Security check to pay for her expenses. His sons were too damaged to fill the vacuum he left. The youngest pulled up stakes and left for Wyoming before the month was out, and the homeless oldest—riven by guilt for the attacks that had preceded his father's collapse—tore into the mother for ruining his life, at one point threatening to bum down her house. Shay and I stepped into this breach, offering her mother comfort and support. I provided funds for her husband's cremation, and told her I would take care of her mortgage.

While these personal episodes unfolded, an autobiography by Elaine Brown appeared in the bookstores. Since her Panther days, she had moved to Paris and was living in a chateau with a wealthy Frenchman. She had spent eight years writing the book, which was called *A Taste of Power*. It came with blurbs from such famous writers as Alice Walker, who said that Elaine "[brought] us that amazing light of the black woman's magical resilience in the gloominess of our bitter despair," and that her book should be "put... on the shelf beside *The Autobiography of Malcolm X*." Claude Brown, the author of Manchild in the *Promised Land*, a famous text of the Sixties, wrote:

> *Finally I understand what the Black Panthers were all about. They were bold, daring and beautiful, and so is* A Taste of Power.

For a month, Elaine was the toast of national magazines and newspaper style pages. *Time* described her as discovering that "Love is the most demanding political act of all," while the *Los Angeles Times'* reviewer, Carolyn See, called her book "beautiful, touching ... astonishing.... Movie makers, where are you?" The *New York Times* displayed a full-page color photo of her in its Sunday magazine, with a text by one of its black editors that celebrated Elaine's emergence as a black feminist heroine, and followed with another feature profiling the college-age children of Panthers (Elaine's daughter among them), who were presented as voices of a new militancy among black youth that had emerged in the wake of the Los Angeles "uprising."

A Taste of Power turned out to be a self-serving account of Elaine's term as Panther leader and her mistreatment "as a woman" by the Party's male hierarchy, which was how she attempted to exculpate herself from the brutalities in which she had participated. There was a surprising amount of self-exposure, however, when she justified other brutalities—directed at males inside and outside the Party—as "revolutionary." In one incident, Huey pistol-whipped a middle-aged black tailor in his Oakland penthouse. Afterward, the tailor, Preston Callins, had to have brain surgery to repair the damage. Elaine went to see Huey in jail after his arrest for the assault:

I would take care of the blood, I told him. He shrugged. Callins, the tailor, had taken the brunt of his raging anguish. Callins's blood now stained the penthouse ceilings and carpets and walls and plants, and Gwen's clothes, even the fluffy blue-and-white towels in the bathroom. I assured Huey the blood would be washed away and his apartment renewed in time for his return.... [Huey] was pacing up and down the holding cell that occupied a corner of the police processing room. ... I caught a familiar look of arrogant satisfaction on his face. 'Fuck Callins,' his slight smile said....

While I noted Huey's irreverent attitude about the whole affair, it occurred to me how little I, too, actually cared about Callins. He was neither a man nor a victim to me. I had come to believe everything would balance out in the revolutionary end. I also knew that being concerned about Callins was too costly, particularly in terms of my position in the party. Yes, I thought, fuck Callins.

Elaine's book was the first time that the criminal side of the Panther activities—hitherto described only by an ignored handful that included Kate Coleman, Peter, and myself—were confirmed by an inside source. Given the candor with which Elaine reported some of these acts, and her obvious pleasure in doing so, the enthusiastic reception she received from the press was in some ways even more disturbing than the reflexive transmission of the Panther myth had been in the past.

In her text, Elaine devoted a passage to Betty's murder. It typified the way she coldly manipulated the facts in her book, and lied when it was necessary to cover her trail. To explain Betty's dismissal, and to hint at an explanation for her death, Elaine attempted to link the two of us to the Cleaver-Newton factional dispute, which had been the cause of several Panther murders:

I had fired Betty Van Patter shortly after hiring her. She had come to work for the Party at the behest of David Horowitz, who had been editor of Ramparts magazine and a onetime close friend of Eldridge Cleaver. He was also nominally on the board of our school.... She was having trouble finding work because of her arrest record....

Elaine further claimed that, after Betty's death, she "began reevaluating Horowitz and his old Eldridge alliance...." Her purpose in concocting these details was to lend credence to her conspiracy theory. But Betty had no arrest record, and I had met Cleaver only once, as a fledgling editor at *Ramparts* in 1968. My involvement with the Party in 1973 was premised on the removal of Cleaver's name from Ramparts' masthead, hardly the act of an ally.

Elaine's guilty conscience also caused her to reveal motives that—until then—only her accomplices and I had known, and only I had reported (to Kate Coleman):

> *Immediately Betty began asking Norma, and every other Panther with whom she had contact, about the sources of our cash, or the exact nature of this or that expenditure. Her job was to order and balance our books and records, not to investigate them. I ordered her to cease her interrogations. She continued. I knew that I had made a mistake in hiring her ...*

To discredit the dead woman, Elaine added this invention:

> *Moreover, I had learned after hiring her that Betty's arrest record was a prison record—on charges related to drug trafficking. Her prison record would weaken our position in any appearance we might have to make before a government body inquiring into our finances. Given her actions and her record, she was not, to say the least, an asset. I fired Betty without notice.*

Seeing one of her mother's killers lionized by the nation's press reopened Tamara's wounds. She and her brothers wrote a plaintive letter to the editors of the *New York Times*, informing them that Betty had never been charged with drug trafficking, and had no prison record. They asked that their letter be printed as a way of restoring their mother's good name. I also wrote to the editors, questioning their judgment in promoting a gangster like Elaine. The *New York Times* ignored our letters. However, an attorney's notice to Pantheon, the publisher of Elaine's original hardcover book, caused them to remove the offending lies about Betty from the paperback edition.

When I read *A Taste of Power* and saw how much of our own version of the Panther reality it confirmed, I decided to respond with an article. For the first time I would describe in detail my involvement, and identify Elaine and Huey as perpetrators of Betty's murder.

I knew that in naming Elaine I was taking a risk. She was now a rich woman, living with a wealthy Frenchman. When she appeared at her book promotions, she was flanked by Party thugs like Flores Forbes, who had been convicted and sentenced for his role in the witness-assassination attempt, and "Big Bob," who had been convicted of a murder committed after he left the Party. Both had been released after serving their time.

I tried to assess the situation coolly. If Elaine decided to retaliate, she would be taking a risk, too. I knew that she would not sue me for libel, because a court case would provide public opportunity to reopen the investigation of Betty's murder. Elaine would want to avoid this at all costs. On the other hand, if she resorted to violent measures and something happened to me, she would be a prime suspect. Moreover, the act itself would lend credibility to my charges. Elaine was now a respected figure with more success waiting on the horizon. Warners had already bought the rights to her book. A motion picture by the award-winning director John Singleton was in the works. Would she jeopardize all this to settle her score with me?

The odds seemed manageable, but I also went out and bought a 9-mm. Glock, and installed a sophisticated alarm system in my car. As I attended to these precautions, I felt my anger revive toward Gitlin, Hayden, Berman, and the others who knew the truth but continued their silence. If even one of them had stepped forward to write about these events, that would have taken some of the pressure off; I would not then appear to be quite so prominent and solitary a thorn in the Panther side. Nor would the risk have been as great for many of them (Hayden excepted), since they had never been directly involved. But they said nothing. It was as though Elaine's book had been published in another country and was about events of which they were ignorant.

My *Heterodoxy* feature was called "Black Murder Inc" and we ran it on the front page with a "Wanted" poster of Elaine. I wrote about my first meeting with her, my involvement with Huey, and the events leading up to Betty's death. I described the lunch after which he identified Elaine as the murderer, and how this had caused me to suspect his own role. I went over the passages that revealed Elaine's sociopathic personality, and rehearsed the criminal deeds the Panthers had committed. I concluded the article by quoting one unwitting self-revelation that was so powerful I could hardly believe Elaine had allowed it to be printed. Unlike the academic radicals who were destructive nihilists but seemed to have no inkling of the damage they had done, or the crimes in which they were complicit, Elaine *knew.* She had not committed brutalities through the agency of others, but with her own hands. It was only the noble ends, in which she still believed, that in her mind justified such criminal means:

> *Faith was all there was. If I did not believe in the ultimate rightness of our goals and our party, then what we did, what Huey was doing, what he was, what I was, was horrible.*

"Black Murder Inc" was published in the March 1993 issue of *Heterodoxy,* as we began our second year. The press run was 100,000 copies, and the story was reprinted in the *San Francisco Chronicle-Examiner's* Sunday edition as "The Unquiet Death of Betty Van Patter." The decision to print it was made by the editor of the Images & Ideas section, David Talbott, whom I had known at Media Alliance and who had defended Peter and me when we published the Fay Stender story.

Although my anxiety level was elevated because of the ongoing security problem, I felt a certain relief to have the full story out for the first time. There was a great unblocking of the passions inside me, the interminable internal argument, the memories that caused pain whenever they surfaced. As a result, the writing was swift—a matter of weeks instead of the long months it had taken me to produce the autobiographical passage of *Destructive Generation.*

Two years earlier, Adam Bellow, an editor at *The Free Press,* had approached me with the suggestion that I write my autobiography. I greatly respected his critical intelligence and judgment, but delayed responding to his request. It was not false modesty that caused this paralysis; I simply did not feel I could write such a book. I did not have a sense of my life as a whole—it seemed too fractured and inconclusive to add up to a story. I couldn't make it all cohere.

As a writer, too, I had no certain sense of my own talent. It was true that I had learned a lot from my partnership with Peter. But—except for the narrative about America, which had failed—all the books I had written on my own were abstract and analytic, their style unsuited to the autobiographical task. In the books we wrote together, it was Peter who had supplied both the authorial voice and the narrative plan. Without him, I was unsure of what I could achieve. I had always been disappointed by the memoirs of political figures on the left because of their inability to reflect on themselves— to even attempt to understand why they had seen the world the way they had, and how their visions had affected who they were. I did not think this omission accidental. If radicalism was a displacement of personal grievance, it wasn't surprising that radicals could not confront their interior lives. New Left radicals favored the slogan "the personal is political," but the intention behind it was not introspective. The phrase expressed, rather, their totalitarian agenda to *control* the personal in order to make utopian politics work. My understanding of the relationship between the two was different. When I looked into myself, I saw how integral my radical views were to my sense of myself and the world around me. The collapse of this faith had been inseparable from the collapse of the life I had lived. I could not conceive of an autobiographical work that would not attempt to plumb this connection.

In writing the memoir for *Heterodoxy,* the doubts I had about writing an autobiography were suddenly resolved. I had found a narrative voice that was capable of introspection, and realized that I had arrived at a point in my life where I felt a sense of completion in the themes that had shaped it. In the *Heterodoxy* article, I was finally able to describe my relationship to the Panthers and my feelings about Betty's death. In other writings, I had justified my rejection of the socialist vision and formulated a conservative outlook, expressing the continuities of my beliefs. I had also arrived at a sense of personal continuity that seemed satisfactory. Shay and I had been together for nearly seven years, long enough to be confident that we had passed the necessary trials to make a permanent household. I could look back now on the brief marriage to Sam as an aberration, an aftershock of the disruptions that had decentered my life.

I was myself again. A feeling of pure happiness came over me. Early in April, I called Adam and told him I was ready to begin.

Three weeks after I started to write, Shay left me. I discovered her absence after returning from a trip to San Francisco, where I had attended a weekend conference. Shay hadn't wanted to come, and I hadn't pressed her. Before departing, I had written a check to her dentist, for the last installment of Shay's bill for the caps; and a check to her mother, for the mortgage plus some extra cash to supplement her Social Security allowance. As Shay and I exchanged good-byes, she told me how much she loved me, and then burst suddenly into tears. In the moment, I recognized an ominous sign—but said nothing. I had other warnings I'd also discounted. Just a week earlier, she had put a question to me: "When people leave you, do you remain friends?" I turned to her and asked, "Are you leaving me?" But then I simply accepted her answer when she said "No."

There was a reason for my complacency. I thought the cataclysm had already occurred, and interpreted these signs as the wake of a storm that was subsiding. Two months earlier, I had been away on a trip, and called home late to find no answer. There was a message, however, from the agency that provided our security. The house alarm had gone off. They had a sent a guard over to check, who found a window open but no one to let him in. Changing my plans, I caught the midnight flight back to Los Angeles, knowing exactly what to expect.

Shay came in at 8 A.M., sullen at first and then, as usual, contrite. It was only the second time since our marriage that I had been forced to deal with an episode like this. But I was out of town frequently, and knew there had been other times as well—when I was unable to return quickly enough to be able to confront her. I confronted her now and reminded her that marriage was a commitment, and that she had violated a basic term of ours, which was her promise to give up drugs. The futility of what I was saying overwhelmed me as I spoke. She had revealed to me, earlier, that her drug was crack cocaine, and— as this episode showed—she was still out of control. Despite seven years of intimacies, we confronted each other like aliens from different planets. She promised tearfully to change. A week later, she went out in the evening "for an hour" to see a friend, and came back again the next morning.

I had already made an appointment with a lawyer, and told Shay to wait until I got back. The appointment was designed to scare her and sober her up. But when I returned, the high exploded inside her. She screamed and threw things, including an iron and her wedding ring, across the room. She tore her *ketubah* from the wall, smashing its frame—and then, piece by piece, shredded our marriage contract into tiny bits. She said she would divorce me, sue me, and blacken my name. When she came down the next day, remorse had overtaken her. I asked her if she would go to AA again, and this time take it seriously—try to kick her habit for good. "If I stay sober, will you marry me again?" she asked in a childlike plaint. I said I would.

Alcoholics Anonymous was a lifeline for many desperate souls, and had more than a few sound ideas. New members were warned not to make major decisions about their lives or relationships for the first year after entering the program. They were advised of the "pink cloud" effect, when the newly sober experienced a false sense of omnipotence, as though they were really in control. They were given a maxim to remind them of this: *Self will run riot.*

My trip to San Francisco took place just a little more than two months after Shay reentered the AA program. When I got off the return flight at the Bur-bank airport, there was a message for me at the airlines desk. It was from Shay, who had not come to meet me: *Take a taxi home.* When I got to the house, there was a note:

David,

This is very hard for me. While you were in San Francisco, I moved into my own apt. I took only my art desk, art drawers, my chest of drawers in bedroom, lamps in the living room, couch and I needed to have some music.

She also needed a television and other items:

You will notice charges on your Visa and Mastercard this month. Rather than inconvenience you I simply replaced the appliances for myself.

There was more than $10,000 worth of charges on the cards to pay for a refrigerator and other furnishings. It turned out she had secretly taken an apartment a month earlier. The deliberation with which she plotted her exit and the deception with which she concealed it took my breath away almost as much as the departure itself. She told a mutual acquaintance that she had timed her exit to coincide with the final payment for her dental caps.

The note provided the briefest of explanations as to why she had left without saying anything, and made as much sense as everything else:

> I have to face the fact I wasn't happy and instead of using, I did what made me happy. I'm going to miss *you* a lot.

It occurred to me that the reference to drugs was a perfect predicate to the user's credo: I did what made me happy.

She also said she would be in touch ("I'm happy to talk with you about it all"), but by this point I also knew not to believe her. She had left no address or phone number, and her mother, who appeared to be a witting accomplice, refused to give me either. Paging through a photo album she had left behind, I discovered a handwritten note saved from an old boyfriend whom she had lived with for several years and who, by odd coincidence, was named David, too. It began: "I can't believe you left me without saying goodbye. ..."

Within a week she had served me with divorce papers and a huge financial claim. The attitude of California's liberal "no-fault" divorce law was caveat emptor. The payment of attorney's fees, the interim support, and the final settlement were set by computer formula, without regard to the conduct of either of the parties during or after the marriage. Since Shay had left her job and had no income, the court required me to pay for her attorney. At the deposition hearing, her performance was so extreme that it caused my lawyer to shoot me a look of harrowing pity. During the proceedings she laughed, cried, and bared the teeth of her anger. She was the bereft wife too traumatized by the loss of her marriage to seek work, but also the irate spouse who would not be denied the "half of everything" she had "earned."

My attorney was a shrewd, avuncular man, who had been in psychotherapy. He tried to give me advice by using clinical terms, explaining that Shay was a "labile personality"—which meant that her character was fluid and lacked a moral center. At break time, while the two attorneys conferred at my expense, Shay and I stepped into the hall. Suddenly she threw her arms around my neck and began kissing my cheeks, as she said tearfully, "All I want is my husband back." I actually tested this proposition, just to see if I finally knew where I stood: "Call your attorney off," I said, "and we can talk." The tears stopped. "Oh," she replied "I can't do that."

I did what made me happy. More than once in the past she had disarmed me with what looked like heartfelt remorse over a cat she had put to sleep. The cat was named "Kanch," after her real family name, Kanchar. She was living alone with Kanch, and one day came home from a three-day drug binge to realize she had forgotten to feed her. Not wanting to see Kanch suffer, but also not willing to give up the drugs, she decided to put the cat to sleep. Years afterwards, Shay could still burst into tears and punish herself over the deed. I took her remorse as a sign of her resolve to change her life. I realized now the story was a parable of her self-absorption, and prefigured the end of our marriage.

When Shay finished her prosecution, the settlement and lawyer's fees, together with the money she had already taken, added up to about a year's income. The money provided a hard measure of loss, but was the lesser part of my pain. A perverse chemistry fueled the narcissism of users; no one else could put such attention on an object of desire. I had been such an object. Life with Shay was a continuous seduction. Our occasions together were ceremonies, celebrations, irresistible adventures. Now it was all gone, and I missed it badly When she left, she also took my confidence that there had been anything more to it than illusion. I felt like the socket of a limb that had been removed.

The legal proceedings also gave me an opportunity to confront Shay's mother, Ruth. I felt as though I needed someone on the other side of the wrong to recognize my grievance. As though that would give me relief When we sat down together, I thought of how I had come to the aid of this woman in her time of need, how I had cared for her daughter and provided for them both, and how they had taken from me what I would have given them gladly out of love, making the love itself feel soiled. I remembered the last check I had written for Ruth on the day Shay left, which she had cashed anyway. "How could you do it?" I asked when we were alone. The expression she returned was blank, as though we barely knew each other. "You're just a poor loser," she said.

The security problem created by my Panther article was becoming a serious concern. It was not only the threat posed by Elaine that prompted my attention. I had begun a public-radio show called "Second Thoughts," and my strongly expressed views about the black racism exhibited in the attacks on Koreans during the L.A. riots, provoked equally strong reactions, including two death threats from anonymous callers. *Heterodoxy* was inspiring hate mail, as well. My Studio City house, with the Center's offices in back, was situated on a little street easily accessible to passersby. In July, I moved both household and offices to security buildings in Los Angeles and Marina Del Rey.

The new offices in a glass tower on the west side marked other changes in the Center, as well. I realized that the institution was no longer merely a vehicle for Peter and myself, but had become significant in its own right. Over the next year and a half, its budget would grow to $2 million, and its staff to more than twenty employees. By then we were publishing four magazines, and books as well.

I had opened a Washington office, hiring Larry Jarvik from the Heritage Foundation to direct it. A noted documentary filmmaker and critic, Larry had received his Ph.D. from UCLA after writing a dissertation on PBS's *Masterpiece Theatre,* and knew more about public broadcasting than almost anyone in the field. He had been a liberal Democrat until the atmosphere of political correctness in the university prompted him to have second thoughts. Together we put out a magazine about public broadcasting and the National Endowments for the Humanities and the Arts, which was widely influential and helped to shape the debate on the future of those institutions.

I also had hired a corporate lawyer who had heard of our work and found *Heterodoxy* inspirational. Like many of those I encountered in my activities on the right, he had been a *Ramparts* reader in the Sixties and had become conservative after witnessing the results of radical efforts. I formed the "Individual Rights Foundation" as a program of the Center and, together with a third-year law student who was already on the staff, we began a legal campaign against the campus speech codes. Our most celebrated effort prevented the University of California at Riverside from banning a fraternity over a T-shirt the Left didn't like. We not only forced the university to rescind the ban, but, taking a leaf from the radical game book, compelled the vice chancellor to undergo five hours of "sensitivity training" in the First Amendment. The embarrassment served as a warning to other administrators, and speech codes were soon unenforceable throughout the state.

A political ally who now became a close friend was Lionel Chetwynd, writer-director of *Hanoi Hilton,* the only Hollywood feature to dramatize the abuse of American prisoners in Vietnam. Lionel was a vet himself and a second-thoughter, and his film was a reconstruction of the events based on interviews with virtually every American POW Lionel paid a heavy price for his loyalty to his comrades-in-arms, and for being right about the war. When it was released, *Hanoi Hilton* was savaged by the critics and hardly opened in cities like Philadelphia, where Wally Nunn rented a theater so that some of the vets who wanted to see it could do so. It was another sign of how outgunned in the culture we were.

With Lionel's advice and help, I began to try to change the Hollywood situation. The conservatives I encountered were afraid to identify themselves politically, and skittish about expressing their opinions. It was reminiscent of the early Cold War, when our radical community had been ghettoized and forced to the social margins. I began holding a series of forums on issues of interest to the entertainment industry, being careful to balance the panels with both sides of the argument. If there were two sides to a question in Hollywood, I calculated, conservatives were already one-up.

Another friend, Robert Carnegie, helped to make these forums a success by recruiting his students to provide the audiences. A former actor, Carnegie was the director of a North Hollywood acting school called Playhouse West. The most renowned acting teacher alive, Sandy Meisner, taught at the school—as did Jeff Goldblum, the star of *Jurassic Park.* One of the plays that Carnegie's students put on was *Welcome Home Soldier,* a seating evening about the mistreatment of Vietnam troops by the New Left. For two years running, the Playhouse West theater was packed every weekend with audiences whose core was always composed of veterans who felt for the first time that their voice was being heard.

Eventually our network became large enough to put on a performance of *Welcome Home Soldier* in a plush, 400-seat theater in Hollywood, and to host a "Conservative Summit" between political activists and entertainment industry professionals at the Century Plaza. The all-day conference was cohosted by William F. Buckley's *National Review* and was crowned by a banquet at which Rush Limbaugh presented an award to Charlton Heston, a man who for years had carried a lonely conservative torch in the industry. Heston was another second-thoughter, having been a Roosevelt Democrat and the chairman of the Hollywood committee to support Martin Luther King's civil-rights march on Washington in 1963. Like Ronald Reagan, he was fond of saying: "I didn't leave the Democratic Party. The Democratic Party left me."

Until these events, the absence of any institutions in Hollywood that were not politically to the left had been striking. When the Center was still a backroom operation in my house in Fern Dell, Heston's office received a call from a professor writing a book on political organizations in Hollywood. The professor told Heston's assistant, Mark McIntire, that he had already located over a hundred liberal and left-wing groups in his research. "Where are the *conservative* organizations?" he asked. "Go see David Horowitz," McIntire told him. "He's it."

I was more active than ever—speaking on campuses, making radio and television appearances, writing articles for *Heterodoxy,* and working on my autobiography. As a public spokesman for conservative causes, I often was the target of personal attacks. On one talk show, an anonymous left-wing caller barked over the airwaves: "Ask him why he couldn't keep his wife." On another, the liberal host asked me how I could support "traditional values" with a straight face when I had been divorced three times. Was there a contradiction between my personal life and my politics? Only the Left seemed to think so. Why would my life experiences cause me to think family was unimportant, especially for raising children? Should I be less hard on drugs because I had tried them, or because they had destroyed my marriage? I had often chosen to disregard conservative cautions in my personal affairs, but I had paid a price when I did so. It was my life experiences that had led to my appreciation of conservative values, even if my radical instincts often subverted their restraints. It was like the old joke about wisdom: What was its secret? Good judgment. And the secret of good judgment? Experience. And the secret of experience? Bad judgment.

What often impressed me was the tolerance of the conservatives I knew for human faults and failings, including my own. Some conservatives were like the flinty puritans of liberal caricature, but most of my new acquaintances and political associates were not. Over time, their tolerance became intelligible to me. What made one a conservative was recognition of the human capacity for evil, or for just plain screwing up. That was why the rules were important. Not because conservatives expected nobody to break them. But because having rules that were respected made it harder for people to do so. This was a more subtle—but in the long run more trustworthy—form of compassion than liberals' softness of heart.

The Friday after Shay left, I visited my mother at the Beverly Sinai Towers, the retirement home where I had placed her. It was evening when I arrived, and she was sitting in a little group in the musky day room. I noticed one of the women twirling the ends of paper napkins and putting them on the heads of the others, and an elderly gentleman standing in the center of the room, glancing at his watch. "What is going on?" I asked. "We're waiting for the sun to go down, which will be in three minutes, so the service can begin," he said. I looked at the women whose faces under their napkin hats were so old their expressions were like those of children again. When the minutes had passed, the old man looked at his watch once more and began reading the ancient prayers. *Boruh ato Adonoy, Elohaynu meleh ho-olom.*

When the old man finished the ritual prayers, he read from the service. I don't remember the exact words, but the passage he chose was something like *"Lord, when people treat us unkindly, when we are betrayed, don't let us make this a reason to lose our trust in others."* My mother had found a way to give me guidance again.

The move to my new quarters in Marina Del Rey made it harder for me to visit her. She was now in her eighty-fourth year, and had been leaving me for a long time. A series of small strokes had made her steps arduous and slow, and short-circuited her memory, which kept fading to black. There were days when I visited her and she seemed to have difficulty remembering me. Such occasions would leave me teary-eyed, mourning the loss of her even though she was still there. But when I came back the next time, just her presence was a comfort, and then she would recognize me again.

In the next month, I saw her less than usual. The press of work, which took me out of town, and managing a household alone, drained the energy I had for getting out. Then, toward the end of September, I received a call from Mrs. Klein, the woman who ran the Beverly Sinai Towers. "Mom's not well," she said; "I think she's just tired, but I took her out of her day class." It was in the midst of a busy week, and the doctor was across town. Almost reflexively, I asked, "Could you have someone take her to be examined?"—feeling guilty as I did so. Afterwards, I called to see how she was, and was told again that she was just tired. I resolved to look in on her, but wasn't able to manage it for several days. As I went about my affairs, I would visualize her face, so happy to see me when I came, and think of her alone in her room. I knew she was asking herself where I was. Finally, my conscience became so heavy that I set my alarm early, and went off to see her before work.

When I arrived, she was sitting asleep in her chair in the day room. An old woman next to her said with a smile, "She was dancing last night." I was relieved to hear this report. In the last year, her steps had become an effort, and though she made the gestures earnestly, the movement itself was hardly there. But if she was dancing, she was in good spirits and all right. "Hi, Mom," I said, waking her gently from her doze. She looked at me dreamily. "Oh, you've come," she said, "you're so lovely." I took her hand. "I'll always come, Mom. I'll be here for you." We sat for a long time, like two lovers holding hands, and then I kissed her goodbye and said, "I'll be back."

That night, I was roused from my sleep by the phone. It was Mrs. Klein. "Mom's had a heart attack," she said; "they took her to Cedars Sinai." I jumped out of bed and ran to my car, speeding through the dark, empty streets to the hospital, where I arrived twenty minutes later. But she was already gone. A doctor let me go in to see her. When I pulled back the curtain they had drawn, she was lying on a gurney, her face all yellow, the tubes they had tried to revive her with still jammed in her throat. I was not prepared for the violence of death. Her lifeless body was contorted and her head twisted, as though some unseen force had tried to rip it off. "Oh, mom," I blurted, putting my arms around her. Then I fled the room.

The hospital made me wait nearly an hour to fill out the required forms. Restless, I pushed open the glass doors and walked into the Los Angeles night. The air was balmy, and there were moonlit black clouds crossing the sky. I thought of this woman who had borne me in her womb, and looked after me so intensely and so faithfully all my life. I thought of how she had helped me with my first books, and set me up in my first house, and stood by me when I fell down. I was so utterly grateful that I had gone to see her that morning, that she had not had to leave this earth feeling abandoned; that we had been able to comfort each other one last time, and say goodbye. As I looked into the luminous heavens, for the first time in my life I felt a providence at work.

EPILOGUE

THE BEAUTY
OF RECOGNITION

FATHER AND SON

AFTER SHAY LEFT, I SAT DOWN WITH THE FILE OF PAPERS I HAD taken from my parents' house in Sunnyside when my father died, and began to read. It was the first time I had done so, even though they had been in my possession for seven years. When I had packed them for the move to California, I saw that they were love letters and some diary pages my father had written. At the time, they seemed too personal, almost incestuous, for a son to look at. But now I had begun to write my story, and the biographer insisted. How could I reconstruct my parents' lives and their influence on mine, and ignore the evidence that had been preserved for me? And so, in the evening hours after work, when I returned to my apartment alone, I began to sift through the little archive. What I found turned out to be my father's posthumous gift of healing to his prodigal son.

There was the exchange of letters with my mother that recorded their courtship during his trip west before they were married, and there was the journal of his visit to Russia in 1932, written in his fine hand and preserved in the little copybook he had taken for the purpose. The letters were mainly carbons of the originals he had typed. But at the back of the file drawer there was an even larger collection, preserved in their envelopes and tied up in little stacks with string. These were from Brunhilde Vasilio, a woman my father had lived with before he and my mother met. There was also a sheaf of notes he had written at the end of their affair.

I had long known about "Brunie"—which was how she was referred to, the few times her name was ever mentioned. Twenty-five years before, her daughter had even appeared at my door in Berkeley, with a mane of flaming-red hair like her mother's. Awkwardly, we introduced ourselves and exchanged the fragments of information our parents had transmitted to us about their doomed passion. She told me that Brunie was dead, and, when there was no more that either of us could think to say, she left. I wonder now why I was not more curious about this woman, why I did not try to make her stay longer, or why I let her vanish as mysteriously as she had come. I wish I could talk to her now. Now that I have read the letters, and lived long enough to have met my own Brunie, and discovered my father in myself.

The romance between Brunie and my father was a veiled episode rarely discussed in our family, and only in furtive asides. I knew by the way my mother referred to her, that she regarded Brunie rather than herself as the love of his life. Then, when my father was old and had relaxed his guard, he once described to me a few details of this long-ago engagement of his passionate self.

Brunie had lived with him in a companionate marriage, and was a heroin addict. (How had I failed to connect this piece of information before?) My father described to me how she would go out and use other men to get the drug she needed more than she needed him, and how he would wait at home, not knowing if she was safe or whom she was with. He would prepare the syringe he used for his allergy shots, and lay it on the table beside their bed. Then, when she returned, he would administer the drug she had brought back with her, in the same way he did his own medicine. Only her shot would be in the vein, directly to the heart.

My father would sit with her through it all, observing the solitary rush of illicit pleasure and the sweaty, harrowing withdrawal after it was gone. "It was terrible," he recalled to me, his only son. But he persevered. For seven years he stood by her through the terror: loved her, cared for her, and tried desperately to understand her, to fathom her bottomless need, and then to be what she needed. To fill the emptiness of her unhappy self. She took his love and his concern, and gave him adventure and passion back. She even tried to warn him, crying out one night: *I can't be what you want!* But he was no more able to heed her warning than she was to give up her need. Then, one day, she left him and went to stay with someone else. My father locked himself in a room for three days and nights afterwards. To smother his pain, he turned up the volume on his Victrola and played a vinyl recording of Beethoven's mordant variations in C-minor, over and over, until a friend came to rescue him from drowning in self-pity.

All that was left now of my father's romance with Brunie was the little sheaf of typewritten pages he had placed in the basement file of the house in Sunnyside, and the neatly bundled letters beside them. One note summarizes the beginning of the affair: "On her twenty-fourth birthday, she came. After a week, she left—to come back again after she had 'straightened' herself out. In the fall, to return to stay—to become my wife." It was the year after he graduated from college and began his indenture as a teacher in the city schools. A page dated Saturday, March 28, establishes the span of their marriage: "Finished, the seven years, this week. From the first week in March 1924, to the last week in March 1931." There is also a cryptic note, written six days earlier: "But Val is still a threat. I may not turn to him. There must be no 'we.'" She had betrayed him with his best friend, compounding the bitter pill of rejection she had fed him as regularly as she fed herself the drug.

Rummaging through Brunie's letters, I found one written four years earlier that gave a flavor of the love he had lost:

January 23, 1927

Philip Mine King:—

I'm all better today. Phil, I hope you never have a pain like the one I had yesterday—it was so torturous that I lost all control over myself—completely—and without a single effort to keep it. And your white face was a fresh pain in all this maze of agony.

Let's forget it, pliz. I'll always love you, Phil—I feel prophetic— may I spiel? This hard little core of self that I have in me will some day lead me away from you—why? I don't know except that maybe I'll be too selfish—one can't be selfish with you, sweetheart mine. Even when that time comes, Flip, I'll love you—and I'll love you as long as I live.

Even when I'm in love with someone else.

Send me the sonnet—I can't write more. I feel very tired—
I love you,

Flip, By

Brunie

As always, he refused to listen to her warning. When she made good on her promise, four years later, his despair seemed to have no bottom.

March 24, 1931

The ice melts. What is underneath I cannot see. I dare not. Very quickly now, I must take hold. There is no time to be lost. Silence. I must begin to think again. The silence is dreadful. It underlies my misery, surrounds it, fills all the crevices. I cannot bear it. And I must, I must. I have awakened to reality: She is gone forever, for all the days of your life. You must believe it. She is now someone else's mistress or wife. Or, she is alone somewhere, relieved to be so. She does not want you though she may be thinking of you now and then. She wished to be rid of you, deep in her heart, long ago. It was pity for you and not love that made her hesitate. These are the truths.

Truth for my father was something solid, a ground under him that he could stand on without falling into infinite space. But the truth that Brunie left him was a misery that was endless too. Reading my father's diary, I can feel his pain as if it had struck only yesterday, rather than more than sixty years ago. As though it was my pain.

Brunie why did you do it why...you should have known you should have cut out my heart first in mercy Brunie God please God when I was little there was no fire when I prayed every night Please God make me crazy for a while until this is over God it doesn't do any good God help me please what shall I do it is too early to sleep daylight god.

My father never recovered from this loss.

The pages my father left unlocked his secret and mine. We had loved women with an emptiness in their soul who left us for shadows. But it was an emptiness in us that hungered for these illusions and made us their passionate slaves.

I was sitting now in the spiritual place where my father had sat more than sixty years before, mourning his loss. Like him, I still loved my Brunie, and like his Brunie, she still claimed to love me—even though she had betrayed me and would betray me again, if I let her. What should I do with my feelings? I was afraid of the black hole in front of me. How should I avoid it? How could I begin to repair the fractured mirror of my own reality? How heal a soul that had been rent? I read my father's text:

So,

What fear is there? You are seeing it for the first time: That she is torn by many inconsistent motives, one of which is that she loves you and wishes to keep you. But there are others and the summation is she. Your error, the product of desire, is that these others are of little importance, and that they can be scrapped by living and living together: that in this way she will become you—yours. And the small success that has been yours has led to the more vicious mistake that you have been successful. But these have been accidents. You must realize that before all; and you must remember it. That you gave generously, that you effaced at times your self and neglected your own soul, that you did all this for a lost cause is unfortunate: But—IT IS SO.

It would be folly to stay on with her, for she is a fear to be met with every day of your staying. You will fear what you know; you will dread what you suspect.

Without her you will be alone to regard the world clearly in the light that has been given you—the vision that you have seen, and you will find quiet and content in the knowledge of WHAT IS—the beauty of recognition. And you will always be happy alone if you remember the past like a traveler who has long returned home. And the past will be yours, truly your possession, if you see it independently, a unit in a life. You must forever keep the present before you distinct and distant from it.

And may God bless you, as He will bless her according to ways that are not yours.

Amen.
February 3, 1931

These were the wisest words I ever received from my father. They addressed not only my life with Shay, I thought, but also my life with the Left—*your error, the product of desire*. This was the closest I ever felt to him. For the first time in my life he was talking directly to *me*, man to man.

And yet he was talking to himself. These were the words of a dead man whom I would never see again. Until I read his meditation, I had been alone with my pain. I had many friends to comfort me, and I was grateful for their support—but what could they *know*? How could they understand the love I had given, the coldness of the betrayal, and the unhappiness she left me? I thought of my father, lying alone in his room with his Beethoven and the terror of his loss, and the ice melting beneath. The testament he had left told me this: He *knew*. He had lived my pain. Suddenly, a calm enveloped me. I felt irrevocably, deliciously his son.

My father was teaching me again, as he had not since I was very young. He was instructing me in the limits of what I could do and understand. *Knew thy-*

I was my father's son. No longer a stranger. In my soul I felt the pulse of the genetic code, and I understood why it was almost as easy to move an Alp as to make a human being change. In my father I had found a "past life" through which to decipher my own.

Until the moment I opened his file, I had not noticed how seamless our destinies had been. This was a karma I could not escape. Yet, I *had* escaped. When I looked at the arc of my life, I saw how far I had traveled beyond the ghettos that had confined his. I had crossed boundaries that he did not even know existed, and survived to tell the tale. I was not a poor loser. I had paid my debts. I had taken the disappointments and the hits, and had not been defeated. I had freed myself from my father's fate.

But what about *mine*? The conservative in me, it was clear, was still incomplete. The rebel refused to surrender. As a teenager, I had read the plays of the Irish radical Sean O'Casey, whose books lined the shelves of the Sunnyside house. A phrase from them still strikes its chord in me. O'Casey wrote that a man should assault life with such energy that in dying he would "go out to greet the echo of his own shout." I know, now, the price one pays for this romance. Yet I cannot entirely give it up. Like any sensible person, I fear pain. But not all pain is the same. After the first death, there is no other.

Through pain I have learned stoicism and the secret of its restraint, which is to pay attention. If I knew at the beginning what I have learned, I would not have given my life to the socialist fantasy, or the Panther cause, or marriage to a woman addicted to an illusion. But I would not now give up the impulse to love or dream that brought me these travails, either. Or the passion for justice. Or the will to make myself better. If ever I were tempted to give up hope, I would only have to look at how far I have come.

A week after my mother's death, I buried her beside my father on Long Island, in the little plot reserved for the International Workers Order in Beth Moses cemetery. By an odd coincidence, Elissa's parents were buried there, too. I brought all four of my children, and my sister came from Canada with her son, Robin, creating a family reunion. My sister and I had been distant for years, separated partly by geography and partly by family. My mother *self,* he was telling me, *for this is the only wisdom we are granted.* had observed to me that, after their estrangement, she was drawn close to her brother by the death of their parents, and predicted that when she was gone we would heal our wounds, too. And she proved right.

I spoke at the graveside and tried to convey to my children and my sister's son what a powerful influence this woman had been on me, and on all of our lives; how various her interests; how she had maintained a spirit of enthusiasm throughout her life, embarking on a new career at the age of sixty. And yet how family had always been her bedrock—"more important than politics," she once told me. How she had been the force that made our family whole. How she had stood behind her children and each of her grandchildren, trying to help them along life's difficult paths. I read a poem that had been sent to me by the head of the day-care center in Los Angeles, where she had spent her last years. It was written by Betty Wilkerson, a black nurse assigned to her group:

> *The little things that we pass each day*
> *And don't seem to notice (Blanche did).*

The music, the dancing
The smile on her face when she heard the
Music and dancing to it. That's how we will
Remember (Blanche)
Rest Blanche, rest in peace.

The note accompanying the poem was signed by everyone in the group, in their aged and palsied scripts, and included the lyric of the song which the note said was my mother's favorite, Irving Berlin's "Always."

When my Panther story appeared, Tamara called to ask if I would come to Berkeley to see her. We had breakfast at the Buttercup Cafe, up the street from Norman's, where I had met Huey the last time. I knew that the purpose of the meeting was to thank me for what I had done, and the thought made me uncomfortable. I told her I had no choice, that I owed it to Betty and to her. But she said, "No, you didn't have to, and nobody else did." She told me that when Elaine's book came out, and before my article appeared, she had been overwhelmed with frustration and pain. She had gotten into her car and driven the streets of Oakland in tears, thinking there was no way for her to answer. No way to get justice for her mother, or herself. No one would ever know what had really happened. The appearance of my article allowed her to fight back. She felt her courage return, and she thanked me for that. I was grateful to her for these words. They made me feel as though the gesture was more than quixotic, and worth the risk.

Shortly afterwards, a young black journalist came to Los Angeles to interview me for a book he was writing about the events. He was Hugh Pearson, a columnist for the *San Francisco* Weekly, which was a left-wing paper. I knew the risks involved in such an interview, but Pearson had a reputation for independence. I agreed to it because I was not ready to give up the last vestige of my faith in the reasonableness of others. Elaine's book had lifted the political cover from the Panthers' criminality, which had the ironic effect of adding credibility to my story. During the interview, I learned that Pearson had talked to ex-Panthers who provided him with other glimpses of the Party's dark side. I hoped that his own political views, whatever they were, would not prevent him from recognizing how this confirmed what I had been maintaining with little support all these years. But during the interview Pearson's demeanor was formal and remote, and I worried about the result.

I could have spared myself the concern. When *The Shadow of the Panther* finally appeared, it was all I could have wanted—a definitive look at the Panthers' criminality from the point of view of a man who had once admired them, but whose admiration had been overwhelmed by the brutal facts. *The Shadow of the Panther* received a front-page review in the Sunday Book Review of the New *York Times.* For the first time since Betty's death, an institution of the cultural establishment had turned against the Panther myth and lent its weight to our claims. "Until Hugh Pearson's *The Shadow of the Panther,* there have been no serious book-length attempts to examine the Panthers' history and to evaluate their significance," the reviewer wrote, concluding that it was "an indispensable source" for future historians.

The writer of the review was Robert Blauner, who had been a member of the Marxist seminar I attended at Berkeley, making the occasion even more satisfying for me. As a leftist, Blauner was unwilling even now to confront the criminality of the Panthers head-on, preferring to call it "militarism," as though the problem was a tactical error committed by revolutionaries, instead of the pathology of gangsters. But he was candid enough: "In retrospect, I—and others—did not take the militarism of the party seriously enough, believing that the rifles, uniforms and drilling were largely symbolic.... The rationale that we didn't know what was happening is lame. That excuse has been heard before. The truth is that we didn't want to know." And that, at last, was the truth that I had labored twenty years to bring to light.

There were other vindications. In the nation's political life, the Sixties had run its course. A consensus was building across the nation that the reforms inspired by its radical passions had been tried and found wanting, that they were factors contributing to the social pathologies themselves. There was a newly tough attitude toward welfare and crime, a rejection of the radical attack on the American idea, and a revival of the principle of a single standard for all—the idea that the American founding had enshrined, that Martin Luther King had championed, and that the Left had betrayed.

Peter and I had remained somewhat skeptical of electoral politics, but we signed on to write a few speeches for Senator Robert Dole's 1988 presidential campaign. We found a consonant political voice in William Bennett, who had become a tribune of common sense in the culture wars, and we also responded to an invitation to dinner from Congressman Newt Gingrich, who told us *Destructive Generation* had been an important influence on his thinking. Gingrich was a product of the other radical movement of the Sixties, that had begun with the campaign of Barry Goldwater and had waged a thirty-year war with the Left. When the November 1994 elections overturned four decades of Democratic Party rule and Gingrich became Speaker of the House, his manifestos resonated with the second thoughts we had arrived at after leaving the radical cause:

> *It is impossible to take the Great Society structure of bureaucracy, the redistributionist model of how wealth is acquired, and the counter-culture value system that permeates the way we deal with the poor, and have any hope of fixing it. They are a disaster. They ruin the poor. They create a culture of poverty and a culture of violence which is destructive of this civilization, and they have to be replaced thoroughly from the ground up.*

We could have written this ourselves.

Days after I found myself alone again, my youngest daughter, Anne, flew down from the Bay Area to "see how Dad is doing." I was especially touched by her gesture because our bond had been the most strained in the family since the divorce. Her usually acerbic wit was tempered for the occasion by a filial care, and it was comforting to have her counsel. I enjoyed this reversal of roles, and the way she gave me reason to think better of myself than the circumstances might suggest. At one point our conversation turned to my other daughter, Sarah, the poet. I expressed my concern that I had not given her the proper fatherly direction. How would she be able to support herself as the years went on? Anne refused to be drawn into this circle of false self-pity: "You spent your life following your dreams," she said, "so let her." It was an endorsement that I could accept. I talked with Sarah, too, and with my sons who had grown to be more like comrades. As I did so, I felt the ground stabilize under me. My children: I had done this right.

I called Elissa. It was a moment when she could have exacted an acute sense of her own grievance. But there was no hint of recrimination in her voice. Instead, there was a bracing tenderness and concern. For a moment, I felt a terrific sense of relief, knowing I was forgiven, and then I unburdened myself. I told her I understood now what it was to be left, and how sorry I was for the grief I had caused her, which I could hardly imagine. I told her of my disintegrating sense of reality after Shay's departure, which made me wonder about the lost years and about myself. Just what was real? I let her know how important her own integrity was to me now, holding up a mirror to myself that I could trust. I said I was grateful for her dedication to our children over the years; the strength and love she had provided them through all their trials. I thanked her for the support she was giving me now. "This has been important to me, too," she said.

We spent a day at Disneyland together with two of our granddaughters (there were now three). The day was golden and filled with nostalgia for both of us. It recalled for me the endless hours we had spent there, and in other amusements with our own children, long ago. I remembered the two of us then, commiserating: How we were *always losing them.* They grew so fast it was as though they put on new personalities, and the toddlers we had yesterday were gone today. The moment seemed a metaphor for what had happened to us. Guiding the stroller beside her, I almost had the illusion that nothing had changed. That we were a couple again in Berkeley, pushing our kids. But it was only an illusion. We were not young any longer, or the parents of small children. At the end of the day, we would give our two little granddaughters back, and go our separate ways. Soon they would be parents themselves. Life was a chain of necessary losses.

Elissa and I were no longer husband and wife, and would never be again. But we were still family, bound through our children, and through the years of our friendship, as closely as flesh. "You will always be in my heart," I said to her. After I said it, she permitted me to glimpse the depth of feeling she still had for me, in the guarded way she allowed herself: "I can't imagine what Shay's life is without you. I had the children. They're so much like you."

The main task I sat down to every day now was writing my life. I had to order the events, and finally make sense of the whole. The discipline was so appropriate that it was almost religious in character. I was afraid, at first, that I would not be able to regain the fluency I had so recently found, but I did, and the writing proceeded. I felt myself confident in a way I had never been as a writer before. It had taken me a lifetime to find my voice, to come down from the heights my parents' ideas had started me off on and stand comfortably on ground that was mine.

My friendship with Peter had changed, too. Arthur Koestler once said that every coauthorship is a collaboration between two people, each of whom finds a father figure in the other. Peter and I had been together twenty-five years. In the political realm and the world of affairs, I had been the leader of our pack. But in writing and in life, it was Peter who was my counsel and guide. My father was a weak man, and Peter provided a model of strength. At times Peter's teaching had been harsh, but I was attracted by that, too—recognizing my own deficit, which was self-indulgence. In shaping the narrative of my life now, I found I no longer needed Peter as a guide. We had become equals. I had learned what I needed to know.

Even as I was gaining this independence, Peter was letting go. I felt a mellowing in his attitude toward me, a leveling from his side, too. When one of his sons fell seriously ill, he called to clear whatever between us remained to be resolved, and to reaffirm the bond we felt so strongly for each other. We had both had enough brushes with death to have changed our views of each other and the world around us. In one of our conversations, Peter expressed our conclusion. He said that the family histories we had written together on the Rockefellers and the Kennedys had affected his outlook. Our former comrades were always saying things like "smash monogamy," and putting the family under attack as an oppressive institution. But in our work he had come to appreciate two things. The first was the resilience and creativity of the family, which invents itself and heals its wounds and endures, and finally gets its members out of the messes they got themselves into. The second was that the family was a theater for lessons about the finite nature of the human enterprise. Its reality flew in the face of the radical utopians who felt they were going to live forever. They had failed to see the tragic dimension of human nature—that the pell-mell embrace of the ineffable and the infinite, the future without consequences, is dangerous.

I agreed. It *was* about mortality. What radicals wanted was to be midwives to a world that was different from the one in which they were going to die. To be present at the creation and, in that way, forever young. It was time to grow up. To put away childish things and to take up the burdens of parents. To tend to our children, and to the world we had inherited, as well. Time to take responsibility for who we are and what we do. And what is there to do, but live with passion, love wisely, and know oneself?

INDEX

ABOUT THE AUTHOR

David Horowitz is a conservative thinker and writer who has authored dozens of books over the course of his lifetime. He began his political career as one of the founders of the New Left in the 1960s and served as an editor of its largest magazine, *Ramparts*. As described in this best-selling autobiography, Horowitz was forced to confront some difficult truths about the political left after a close friend of his was murdered by the Black Panthers, and ultimately found a political and intellectual home as a conservative activist.